A HISTORY OF THE SPANISH HETERODOX

Book 1

A HISTORY OF THE SPANISH HETERODOX

Book 1

MARCELINO MENÉNDEZ PELAYO

Translated by

Eladia Gomez-Posthill, M.A., (Oxon)

The Saint Austin Press
2009

The translation and publication of this work has been made possible by the generous financial support of the Spanish Ministry of Culture.

ISBN 1 901157 98 9 (Paperback edition)

Books 2 and 3 are in preparation.

First published in 1880-1882.

This edition is a translation of the Second Edtion, 1910.

Cover photo: Martin Beek, under CC license:

http://creativecommons.org/licenses/by/2.0/

El Greco's 'The Martydom of St Maurice and the Theban' (detail),

el Escorial, Madrid. (A scene representing the third century martyrdom of a Roman legion that embraced Christianity.)

The Saint Austin Press

www.saintaustin.org

Contents

Chapter 4
The Magic Arts and Divination. Astrology.
Superstitious practices in the Roman and Visigoth worlds.

Introduction to the English edition

Poet, historian and literary critic, Marcelino Menéndez Pelayo (known also as Menéndez y Pelayo) was born at Santander, Spain, in 1856 and died there in 1912. After intial studies in his native town, he was admitted in 1871 at only fifteen years old to the University of Barcelona, where he spent two years and won the admiration of his fellow-students, his teachers and of the Government. At the unusually early age of twenty-two he was appointed to the chair of literature in the University of Madrid, and three years later was received into the Spanish Academy. In 1876 he published his *Estudios criticos sobre poetas Montañeses* and in 1880 his *Historia de los Heterodoxos Españoles*. This work, which is a proof of the writer's incomparable knowledge and skill, deals with the political and literary history of Spain in its relation to the Catholic Church from the time of Priscilian down to our age. A new phase of his genius was displayed in *Horacio en España*. Himself a lyric poet of no mean ability, as his "Oda a Horacio" and "La galerna del sábado de gloria" bear witness, he was fitted to undertake the task of collecting and criticizing the numerous Spanish translations and imitations of Horace.

His extensive *Historia de las ideas estéticas en España* includes not only a complete exposition of the æsthetic ideas of Spanish writers but also an elaborate and finished treatise on æsthetic ideas in Europe. Four volumes have been published on *Los orígines de la novela en España*, a treatise on the origin of the Spanish novel. This is one of the most learned and original of Menéndez y Pelayo's works. From a national as well as from a Catholic viewpoint the *Ciencia española* (1887) is one of the most valuable publications of this writer. The work is chiefly a collection of letters and essays which demonstrate that Spain is one of the richest nations in original and sound philosophy and is endowed with many scientists of remarkable genius. Here also he proves that the Inquisition did not hinder culture in Spain, but fostered it. Other works of Menéndez y Pelayo are: *Obras completas de Lope de Vega*, *Antología de poetas líricos castellanos*, *Crítica literaria* and *Poetas hispaño-americanos*. In the five volumes contained in the *Crítica literaria* are published his essays on the "Mystic poetry of Spain", "Saint Isidore", "History considered as an Art", "Tirsode Molina", etc. Menéndez y Pelayo was the president of the Academia Real de la Historia, director of the *Revista de archivos, Bibliotecas y museos*, editor of the *Nueva biblioteca de autores castellanos*, and member of countless literary and scientific societies both in Spain and in the other European countries.

With regard to his prose style Menéndez y Pelayo is regarded as the greatest of all writers who have flourished since the Golden Age of Spain. His first essays as well as his last works are composed with all his youthful enthusiasm and poetic taste. Every page of his writings reveals a wealth of strong common sense, clear perception, and a vein of wonderful and ever varying erudition. Thoroughly Catholic in spirit, he found his greatest delight, he declared, in devoting all his work to the glory of God and the exaltation of the name of Jesus.

Note: This Bibliographical information is taken from the *Catholic Encyclopedia,* 1917

In making his greatest work of scholarship available to the English-speaking public for the first time, the publishers earnestly hope that Menedez y Pelayo's work will serve as a beacon for the current renewal in the study of ancient, medieval and renaissance history. At a time when Europe is asking so many questions about its history and identity, perhaps some of the answers can be found within the pages of this book.

The present volume deals with early Christianity in Spain prior to the middle ages. Books 2 and 3 (in preparation) bring the history up to the eve of the Reformation. A subject index for all three volumes will be published at the end of Book 3. If there is sufficient interest in the work, it may be possible to organise the translation of the remaining material of *Historia de los heterodoxos españoles*, up to and including heterodoxy in nineteenth century Spain.

Published works

La novela entre los latinos (Santander, 1875). (His doctoral thesis)

Estudios críticos sobre escritores montañeses. I. Trueba y Cosío (Santander, 1876).

Polémicas, indicaciones y proyectos sobre la ciencia española (Madrid, 1876).

La ciencia española, 2ª edition (Madrid, 1887-1880).

Horacio en España (Madrid, 1877, 2ª ed. 1885).

Estudios poéticos (Madrid, 1878).

Odas, epístolas y tragedias (Madrid, 1906).

Traductores españoles de la Eneida (Madrid, 1879).

Traductores de las Églogas y Geórgicas de Virgilio (Madrid, 1879).

Historia de los heterodoxos españoles (Madrid, 1880-1882).

Calderón y su teatro (Madrid, 1881).

Dramas de Guillermo Shakespeare translation (Barcelona, 1881).

Obras completas de Marco Tulio Cicerón, translation (Madrid, 1881-1884).

Historia de las isdeas estéticas en España (Madrid, 1883-1889).

Estudios de crítica literaria (Madrid, 1884).

Obras de Lope de Vega, 1890-1902.

Antología de poetas líricos castellanos desde la formación del idioma hasta nuestros días, 1890-1908.

Ensayos de crítica filosófica (Madrid, 1892).

Antología de poetas hispano-americanos, 1893-1895.

Historia de la poesía hispano-americana (Madrid, 1911).

Bibliografía hispano-latina clásica (Madrid, 1902).

Orígenes de la novela (Madrid, 1905-1915).

El doctor D. Manuel Milá y Fontanals. Semblanza literaria (Barcelona, 1908).

Obras Completas, started in 1911.

"Biblioteca de traductores españoles", in *Obras Completas*, Madrid

Introduction to second edition

The first edition of *Historia de los Heterodoxos Españoles* comprised three volumes published between 1880 and 1882.[1] The original run was of four thousand issues, a figure seldom reached by books of learning in our country but it did not take long for that first edition to sell out. Indeed, the work has become something of a 'rare find' today, a fact which, I admit, does make me rather proud (though it procures little else), as a bibliophile of sorts. Booksellers are now wont to charge high prices for the few copies they manage to get their hands on, and since there seem to be aficionados for everything, even for being overcharged, these three volumes in ordinary paper have currently been known to fetch currently as much as twenty five *duros,*[2] and those in linen paper over fifty.

Since then I have often been asked in conversation and in writing to agree to a new edition because, I am told, this book is now the most popular of all the books I have written (though it is by no means the one I esteem the most). I should point out that had my interest rested purely on personal financial gain, the *Heterodox* would have been reprinted long ago. But I could not bring myself to consent to a new edition without first having submitted the book to a thorough and scrupulous revision, one that was to become ever more laborious as the years went by. Since new data of all types accumulated in my library day after day, a complete rewriting of some chapters became ever more urgent. My own two copies have now become inundated with annotations and amendments. Somehow I had to put a stop to this continuous note-gathering. Indeed, this was a duty my conscience as a researcher insisted upon, though something which one's mortal life span, such as it is, would not allow to continue forever.

Finally then, making good use of all the material I had hitherto gathered, I am glad to bring to light once more the *Historia de los Heterodoxos Españoles* in a form that for me this time has to be definitive. (Naturally, I will continue to document in footnotes and addenda such notices as may come to my attention during the course of this printing, or any other correction that might spring to mind).

There will be no shortage of those who will say that I am about to spoil the original. Well, be that as it may; this is a work of history, not a thriller or a romantic novel. History is not written for slack or frivolous readers. The first duty of an honest historian is to take his research, as far as he is able, to ever-greater depths, to spare no detail, and to correct himself whenever this is needed. Accuracy is a form of literary probity and must be extended to the most trivial piece of evidence, for one cannot have authority over the big picture if one shows oneself forgetful, or

---

[1]   A detailed plan with appropriate chapters had already appeared in *Revista Europea*, 1876, vol.8, pp.459, 485 and 522. The reader will find there also some paragraphs from the old Prologue I rewrote and enlarged upon again a year later. By then, I had already written the first few chapters. Do keep in mind this chronological indication if only to judge them with the indulgence due.

[2]   1 *duro* = 5 pesetas

negligent, in the detail. We might not be culpable of involuntary mistakes, but an historian who knowingly lets an error stand, however insignificant that error may be, does not deserve to be regarded as a reliable author.

I am aware that re-editing a scholarly book written more than thirty years ago, when we have witnessed an almost complete revival in the study of ecclesiastical history and very rapid progress in many other historical disciplines, is a task to intimidate the most intrepid. The first five centuries of the Church have now been studied in astonishing detail. Apostolic teaching, the history of dogma, the origins of Christian liturgy, Patristics, persecutions, councils, heresies, the constitution and discipline of the early church – as we read the works of contemporary historians all these are now beginning to look like new disciplines. The Middle Ages, viewed in times past with a romantic eye but in a serene and disinterested spirit today, offer by themselves a vast field where legions of researchers can rewrite the history of institutions in the light of *diplomatic criticism*. The tools of their trade have reached the finest precision. Vast collections of documents and collections of hagiographic texts, councils, decrees and pontifical letters, as well as every source for the study and analysis of canon law, have put into circulation an overwhelming mass of material, reproduced with palaeographic rigour and wisely annotated. There is hardly a nation now not in possession of a *corpus* on its medieval writers; a *monumenta historica*, a complete collection of its chronicles, laws and customs, and one or several publications on archaeological art to which progress in the area of graphic arts contributes on a daily basis to greater fidelity of reproduction.

With such magnificent resources, the landscape of social history widens and the mist with which the cradle of the modern world was once enveloped begins to clear. What was previously seen as arid, chronological data is now coming to terms with its true meaning, and a legitimate rehabilitation of the Middle Ages presumably compromised by earlier over-enthusiasm, has ceased to be a subject proper to orators and poets and has become instead the solid, reasoned and scientific work of eminent scholars, free from any suspicion of emotional outbursts.

This is not so easily eluded in Modern History. The problems that erupted during the Renaissance and the Reformation are, if the truth be told, the same that continue to unsettle consciences today, even if formulated in different terms or viewed from a wider horizon. However, historical research imparts to the historian who practises it honestly a certain uplifting and soothing strength that manages to silence passions even when these are of generous and noble stock, and restoring to the soul its once-perturbed harmony, leads him straight and clear along the path to the triumph of truth and of justice, the only goal for which a Catholic author should strive.

It is not necessary or advisable that this history be called a work of 'Apologetics' - the name would render it suspect. Human actions, when upright and in line with the law of God, need no apologia; when they are not, it would be rash or immoral to defend them. The subject matter of the historian lies outside the historian himself. Under no pretext is he licensed to deform it; nor is it a series of premises for scholastic disputation or artful and one-sided partisan subtleties, but a matter of individual and social psychology. Apologetics, or rather, the acknowledgement of the Church's lofty and divine mission in the destiny of the human race, comes from the bosom of history itself; the clearer this perception becomes, the sooner we will begin to discern the designs of Providence.

Those whose faith starts to waver when they see the many trials and tribulations with which God, throughout the ages, has tested and continues to test the Christian community in order to refine and purify it, must have a flimsy faith indeed. *Ut qui probati sunt manifesti fiant in vobis.* "[Indeed, there have to be factions among you], *so that it will become clear who among you are genuine*". 1 Cor. 11. v. 19.)

Guided by these principles, eminent Catholic writers of our time have written with admirable impartiality on the history of the Papacy during the fifteenth and sixteenth centuries and on the origins of the Reformation. And more than a few Protestant scholars when treating of these and more recent epochs have nobly rectified some of their sects' most entrenched preoccupations. Even rationalist criticism, with its implicit denial of the supernatural and its incompatibility with any positive theology, has been a factor of extraordinary importance in the study of ecclesiastical antiquities, due to the new questions it examines and perhaps because of the correct, if partial, answers it provides on external and documentantive history - the exclusive patrimony of no one.

Catholics, Protestants, and Rationalists have worked simultaneously on the great monument that ecclesiastical history undoubtedly is. An obedient subject of the Church myself, I am not wholly ignorant of the varying degrees of discretion their theological qualifications deserve, and of the prudent vigilance to be exercised when handling works written from an unorthodox viewpoint. But one cannot ignore them or fail to make good use of what their works contain in the realm of positive science, and this Catholic historians do practise and profess. Consider, for instance, the words of Cardinal Hergenroether in the Preface to his *History of the Church*, so well known and celebrated in religious schools: "We must take advantage and put to good use the work of Protestants who are friends of the truth, and familiarise ourselves with the study of their sources. Indeed, on a multitude of issues, and despite the different stand on which we place ourselves, it is not important in a given work whether the author is Protestant or Catholic. We have seen learned Protestants formulate on numerous points, sometimes of great importance, a more exact and better-founded judgement than that of certain Catholic writers who were in their time theologians of great renown." [3]

Thanks to this broad and generous judgement, Catholic erudition regains once more the pre-eminent place it once enjoyed in the sixteenth and seventeenth centuries, which it only in appearance lost at the end of the eighteenth and beginning of the nineteenth centuries. Today, as in ancient times, the work carried out by

---

[3]   *Histoire de l'Eglise par S.E. le Cardinal Hergenroether* (transl. by P. Belet), Paris, ed. 5. Palm, 1880, vol. 1, p.8.

dissidents serves as an effective stimulus to orthodox scholarship. Without the centurions of Magdeburg perhaps the *Annals* of Cardinal Baronius which buried them forever (despite Casaubon's *Exercitationes)* would never have existed. Since then, Catholic superiority in this field of study has been admirably sustained by the great works of the French School of the seventeenth century (Tillemont, Fleury, Natal Alexander, the Benedictines of St. Maury), and their worthy Italian emulators of the following century (Ughelli, Orsi, Mansi, Muratori, Zaccaria). But the decline of serious study, already beleaguered by superficial encyclopaedism and that spiritual languor with which a great part of the clergy and Christian people was afflicted in the days nearing the Revolution, brought with it an undeniable backward step in theology and canon law research. When it came back to life again the field of scholarship was not exactly the most avidly cultivated. The great majority of ecclesiastical histories published in southern Europe during the first half of the nineteenth century and even later were but compilations devoid of any creative merit, feeble works that contrast sadly with the solid and unmoveable pillars of ancient history. And this inability to discern what the true Christian spirit is - characteristic of French *philosophisme* and liberal doctrinarism in all its hues and shades, came to infect the faithful thus reducing religious polemic to a point of gratuitous vulgarism: a grave symptom from which the Latin nations are still recovering.

In Germany, where theological life has never ceased to be intense, this movement within the Protestant schools produced and was still producing works deserving of great merit as those of the Pietist Arnold (1705) and Mosheim's *Institutiones* (1755), the wide-ranging work of his disciple Schroeckh (1768), Walch's *History of Heresies* (1762), Neander's *General History of the Christian Religion* (1825-1845). It was influenced also by that sentimental or *pectoral* theology of Schleiermacher, Gieseler's *Manual* (1823-1855) - useful because of its annotations and sources - the publications of Bauer, spokesman for the critical-rationalist school of Tübingen and especially his *Ecclesiastical History* (1853-1863). It was not possible therefore for orthodox science to be lagging behind when Catholic peoples awoke to new intellectual life in the days of Stolberg and José de Goerres. The former's *History of the Church*, a work of fervent piety as well as of literary merit, announces since 1806 the advent of the new school of which the following were and are incontestable glories: Moehler, the illustrious author of *Simbolica* and biographer of St. Athanasius the Great; Hefele, the historian of the councils; Doellinger and the works he authored before his schismatic decline, such as *Paganism and Judaism, Church and Churches, Christianity and the Church at the time of her Foundation; The Reformation: its development and consequences,* not forgetting his excellent manuals; Jannsen, who with the title *History of the German peoples* has given us the most in-depth volume on the first one hundred years after the Reformation - his work ably continued by his famous disciple Ludwig von Pastor who threw such new and copious light on the history of the Renaissance popes.

But though Germany continues to be, in this as in all branches of scholarship, master of Europe, it would be an injustice not to mention the principal and glorious part played by Italy in the formation of Christian archaeology by the school of Rossi, or the proficient concurrence of French learning worthily represented today by Duchesne, author of *The Origins of Christian Worship* (1889) and of a concise and elegant history of the first centuries of the church, of which three volumes have so far been published.

The time is now for Spain to join this present course and to endow it with our honourable, solid, age-old tradition, one which we must never lose sight of if we are to continue to hold on to our culture. There is no shortage of nominally scholastic theologians who will have some misgivings about whatever possible danger this great historic movement that is invading even the teaching of dogmatic theology may bring. But the danger, if that is what it is, is not new; it goes back at least to the classic works of Dionysius Petavius and Thomassini[4], whose worthy precursor was our very own Diego Ruiz de Montoya.[5]

Melchor Cano qualified as ignorant and crude those 'theologians in whose *lucubration* the voice of history is not heard'.[6] Hergenroether said that without knowledge of ecclesiastical history, Christian knowledge or indeed knowledge of general history (for Christianity is at the heart of our history) cannot be complete. If the historian must be a theologian, the theologian, too, must be an historian to be able to render account of the past of the Church to whoever may question it or seek to falsify it. Ecclesiastical history is a great apologia for the Church and her dogma, a

---

[4]   Dion. Petavii, S.J. *Opus de theologicis dogmatibus* (Paris, 1644 and ss.), 6 vols., folio. There are several later editions expanded and annotated by Catholics and Protestants. The best regarded is that of Venice, 1757, in which the *Opus* appears *in meliorem ordinem redactum et locupletatum*, by Father Zaccaria. Ludovici Thomassini (of the Congragation of the Oratory), *Dogmata theologica*, Paris, 1684 and ss., 3 vols., folio.

[5]   See, especially, the treatises *De Scientia, Ideis, veritate ac vita Dei* (1629); *De voluntate Dei et propriis actibus ejus* (1630); *De Providential Dei* (1631); *De Praedestinatione et preprobatione hominum et angelorum* (1629); *De Trinitate* (1625), and several others of this illustrious Jesuit, who tried to bring together positive and scholastic theology more than any one of his contemporaries. Of Montoya said Kleutgen, *Theologie der Vorseit*, vol. ult., number 44: "Ganz besonders aber zeichnete sich durch Verbindung der positiven Theologie mit deer Scholastik im Anfange des 17 Jahhunderts der Spanier D. Ruiz von Montoya aus". (Apur Hurter, *Nomemclatur Literarius recentioris Theologiae Catholicae Theologos exhibems qui inde a Concilio Tridentino Floruerunt...*Innsbruck (Oeniponti), 1871, vol. 1, p.520).

Half-way through the eighteenth century, another Father of the Society, the Catalan Juan Bautista Gener, envisaged and to a large extent put into effect a plan for a vast and detailed theological-scholastic, dogmatic, positive and moral encyclopaedia, including in it councils, heresies, writers, memorials sacred and profane, epigraphs and numismatics, etc. In addition to the proposal, or *Prodromus*, there are six printed volumes that today lay forgotten, as so very many laudable endeavours from that century.

[6]   "Etemin viri omnes consentiunt, rudes omnino Theologos illos esse, in quorum lucubrationibus historia muta est. Mihi quidem non Theologi solum, sed nulli satis eruditi videntur, quibus res olim gestae ignotae sint. Multa enim nobis e thesauris suis historia suppeditat, quibus si careamus, et in Theologia, et in quacumque ferme alia etiam in scholastica disputatione opus esse ex annalium monumentis testes excitare clarissimos veritatis? (De Locis Theologicis, liber undecimus, cap. II)

magnificent proof of her divine institution, of the beauty, ever ancient and ever new, of the Bride of Christ. Its study carried out thoughtfully and with love, graciously transcends knowledge and life itself with its brilliance illuminating both. [7]

Our own theological flourishing in the sixteenth century was unequalled by any other Catholic nation. One illustrious gentleman applied the methodology used by Classical philologists to ecclesiastical antiquities and with his dialogues *De Emendatione Gratiani* opened up the critical-analytical age in knowledge of canon law. And from this school that Antonio Agustín created or inspired came the first scholars of our own church councils whose work was compiled in the Loaysa collection (1593), those who under the auspices of Felipe II prepared the St. Isidore's edition (1599) and those who began the work of enlightening us on the annals of our church.[8] Neither was there any lack of methodology, critical rigour or firm and solid erudition in the annotations and corrections made by the bishop of Segorbe, Juan Bautista Pérez, nor in the famous treatise of Fernando de Mendoza *De Confirmando concilio Illiberitano* (1594). Though somewhat encyclopaedic because to a large degree he was dealing with a new-born discipline, he nevertheless showed the stage of maturity these studies had reached at the time as he made use of every beam of light, sacred and profane, that scholarship could then impart. The comprehensive work on the lives of the Popes written by the Dominican Alfonso Chacón (1601-1602) who was also one of the first explorers of subterranean Rome, appeared simultaneously with Baronius' *Annales* and though its pages are infrequently opened today it represents a notable contribution to Spanish scholarship and ecclesiastical history in general, as were also *Crónica de la Orden de San Benito* by Father Yepes (1609-1621); *Annales Cistercienses* by Father Angel Manrique (1642-1659), *Historia General de la Orden de Santo Domingo* by Fray Hernando del Castillo (1584-1592) and Fray Juan López (1613-1621) and *Crónica de la Orden de San Francisco* by Fray Damián Cornejo, published in the last years of the seventeenth century (1682-1698) and continued on by Fray Eusebio González de Torres in the eighteenth.[9]

But speaking in general terms, our scholars' efforts, continuing on the path set by Morales and Sandoval, were nevertheless put to use primarily in the area of our national history – undoubtedly the first we should endeavour to cultivate.

---

[7]   Hergenroether, *Hist. Ecl.*, 1, p. 60

[8]   In addition to the names cited in this text, it is difficult to omit (though this may not be the time to assess their merit) the names of Juan de Grial and Alvar Gómez de Castro; the illustrious Pedro Chacón, of Toledo; the two brothers Diego and Antonio de Covarrubias, Pedro de Fuentidueñas, Miguel Tomás Taxaquet, Juan Bautista Cardona, Father Cipriano Suárez, and Mariana himself, less known for his other erudite works than for his great and popular *Historia*.

[9]   There was an essay, *Historia Eclesiástica de España* by Francisco de Padilla (Málaga, 1605), in two vols. that goes as far as the eighth century but it is so weak that it is hardly useful today. However, this is not the case with *Historia Pontifical y Católica*, by Gonzalo de Illescas (1574), successively continued by Luís de Bavia, Juan Baños de Velasco and Fray Marcos de Guadalajara. Though the Popes' biographies are nothing more than a compilation, elegantly written, of Platina and others, and ecclesiastical and civil history mixed together, it is nevertheless of interest because of specific details on events of that time.

Unfortunately, throughout the first half of the seventeenth century, it was chaff that was sown in that particular field by a legion of brazen falsifiers who combined their credulity with a lack of consideration of regional and village historians. A gigantic but factual and clearly noticeable backward step took place (even disregarding the monstrosities of Tamayo de Salazar's *Martirologio* and Argáiz's *Población eclesiástica* and *Soledad laureada*) when we compare what was produced in the previous century with the weak albeit well-intentioned minor attempts by Gil González Dávila's *Teatros eclesiásticos* on several dioceses in Spain and the Indies which hardly go beyond the modest category of *episcopologies*.

But though lethargic, the critical spirit of the sixteenth century was not dead. Nor did it wait, as some would have it, for the storming of eighteenth century ideas to bring it back to life. [10] In fact, in strict chronological rigour, it is during the ill-starred days of Carlos II that some of the most notable works on national scholarship belong, for example, the *Dissertationes ecclesiasticae*, by the Benedictine Pérez (1688), the innumerable works of the Marquis of Mondéjar, the Councils collection by Aguirre (1688) still awaiting someone who will worthily re-edit and complete it, and the two *Bibliothecas* by Nicolás Antonio as well as his *Censura de historias fabulosas*.

Accordingly, the reign of Felipe IV brings with it not the real rebirth of historical studies but a continuation of a school formed during the previous reign which was fully cognisant of what was happening in Italy and in France. Nicolás Antonio and Cardinal Aguirre spent a great part of their life in Rome, and the Marquis of Mondéjar corresponded with Baluze and other erudite Frenchmen of the period.

And to the seventeenth century belong also, by reason of birth and education, Berganza, Salazar y Castro, and Ferreras, principal fomenters during the reign of the first Bourbon, of the monastic, genealogical, and universal history of Spain which from the time of Mariana had not been compiled all in one book. The Academies of Madrid, Barcelona, Seville and Valencia were open, following an impetus that was shaping analogous institutions all over Europe, seasoned here with a little of our own Spanish *salt*, so to speak, as well as sound foreign scholarship, and wisely assimilated here at home neither with bigotry nor obsequiousness but with good common sense and a calm that could well set an example for us today.

The vast majority of all the old legends that had entered our chronicles or penetrated our ecclesiastical prayers were now being quietly relegated to the unrefined writings of 'belfry scholars'.[11] Destructive and sceptical criticism gave way

---

[10]   Some of this preoccupation can still be detected in the speech given by José Caveda, *Sobre el desarrollo de los estudios históricos en España desde el reinado de Felipe V hasta el de Fernando VII*, read before the Academy of History on 18th April 1854.

[11]   *Eruditos de campanario:* The phrase is one of many coined by Menéndez y Pelayo. Another was *Poetas de vacuna* when challenging the *afrancesados* (secularist, anti-clerical intellectuals) and their

instead to a criticism that was wise and prudent, as shown by the treatises on historical methodology by the Dominican Fray Jacinto Segura (*Norte Crítico,* 1736) and the Marquis of Llió and his colleagues at the Barcelona Academy (*Observaciones sobre los principios de la Historia,* 1756); in the articles published in *Diario de los Literatos* (1737), and in *Bibliographia Critica Sacra et Prophana,* by the Trinitarian Fray Miguel de San José (1740), a great man of Letters, unjustly forgotten. Father Feijoo, though he did not specifically pursue history as a subject of study, did spread in a popular and entertaining manner to the general public some very useful reflections which must have been *fermenta cognitionis* to a people whose scientific curiosity was being awakened, and challenged them in his candid and light-hearted way on a good number of popular customs and reputed miracles.

Scholarship: that was the characteristic note of our eighteenth century historians. That is where our cultural nerve laid, not on the sundry literary genres that came to such prostration later. No other period shows so great a number of unselfish hands at work. Of course some would succumb under the weight of their own scholarship but they do nonetheless bequeath to their forgetful nation huge collections of documents and whole libraries of dissertations and papers which others with much less fatigue will explore and gain credit for as renowned historians. Their names deserve a mention: Sarmiento, Burriel, Velázquez, Floránez, Muñoz, Abad y la Sierra, Vargas Ponce and so many others who sacrificed their names to anonymity, a fact that did not in the least dampen their vocation to scholarship. Historical documentation that penetrated secluded but authentic archives was gathered in the field; travels of scientific exploration succeeded one another from the reign of Fernando VI to that of Carlos IV; the Academy of History brought this movement together compiling and building with the consensus of all a great part of Spain's diplomatic and epigraphic wealth.

Thanks to this modest but noble school which shined neither in style or artistic sophistication but had a quality that in history may well be worth more, i.e. scrupulous veracity of testimony, solid organisation of prior knowledge, certain and practical methodology in research, good sense and prudence in judgement, we began to sieve through our narrative sources. Some of our chronicles were republished with great care; the first collections of *Fueros* (Royal Charters or Parliamentary Privileges) came to light; the *cartas pueblas and cuadernos de Cortes* (albeit at that time in manuscript form only); the study of institutions advanced to that point of maturity as is shown in books by Martinez Marina, Capmany, Asso, Sempere, Larruga and Fray Liciniano Sáez who initiated our studies on industrial and economic history; Ponz y Lagunó, Jove-Llanos, Ceán and Bosarte covered the field of archaeological art; numismatics was scientifically instituted in the works of Velázquez, Pérez Bayer and Maestro Flórez; the ancient geography of Spain was studied under the double light of classical texts and Roman epigraphy honourably represented by the Count of

---

writings. 'Why don't you stick to what you can understand?' he charged. 'Write odes to the vaccine, or the printing press' (Translator's note).

Lumiares; Hervás anticipated the study of comparative philology well ahead of Humboldt. Bastero did the same on Provençal studies one century before Raynouard. Tomás Antonio Sánchez laid the foundation for our literary history when he published a *cantar de gesta* for the first time in Europe. [12]

Ecclesiastical history, as may be expected, benefited from this great historical movement. This is because throughout the centuries our national life had always revolved around the Church. Were we to pin down one work and one sole author that represented scholarly activity in Spain during the eighteenth century, the representative work would be *España Sagrada* and its author Fray Enrique Flórez, followed at a great distance by his disciples including his own pupils who received his tradition more directly. Spanish historiography has not produced another work of history that bears comparison to this one save perhaps Zurita's *Annales* which, had they been brought to light in another century and under different conditions, would also be admirable proof of earnest and in-depth research. The vast and encyclopaedic character of *España Sagrada* however places it outside any possible comparison, whatever imperfection of detail or need for a more precise methodology it may be guilty of. The book is not an ecclesiastical history of Spain as such, but without it the ecclesiastical history of Spain could not have been written. Nor is it a mere collection of documents, although nowhere has such an immense wealth of documentation been compiled on the Spanish Middle Ages: chronicles, lives of saints, councils' Acta, diplomas, privileges, certificates, epitaphs, and all manner of antiquities. It is also a series of enlightening dissertations that touch the most capital and obscure points of our liturgy, solve arduous geographical questions, fix the date of important events, and discuss the authenticity of many sources while condemning others to the discredit and opprobrium owed to works of falsifiers. The merit of these discourses is such that within our peninsular scholarship they have no rival save for *Dissertations* by the Portuguese author Juan Pedro Ribeiro, and even these more often than not shrink before the diplomatic science of which Florez was master. [13]

---

[12]   To avoid going through an interminable list here, I shall omit other aspects of our cultural history worthy of being considered separately such as studies on America (Barcia, Ulloa, Muñoz, etc), those on physical geography, travels, and nautical history (Tofiño, Vargas Ponce, Navarrete, Antillón, etc); descriptions and particular histories of some regions, cities and towns, as the great book by the botanist Cavanilles on Valencia, Lopáez's on the diocese of Osma, Viera y Clavijo's book on the Canary Islands, Ignacio Pérez Ayala's on Gibraltar; the development of general bibliography (Pérez Bayer, Rodríquez de Castro) and provincial (Ximeno, Latassa), and the undertaking, bold to be sure, of the Mohedanos who, among many other works, expertly illustrated the literature of Roman Spain.

[13]   *Disertações Chronologicas e Criticas sobre a Historia e Jurisprudencia Ecclesiastica e Civil de Portugal por orden da Academia R. das Sciencias de Lisboa...*, Lisboa, 1810-1836, 5 vols. Portuguese scholarship in the eighteenth century contributed honourably to the illustration of Hispanic Annals, first with the voluminous publications by *Academia Real de Historia*, founded in 1720 (Antonio Caetano de Sousa, José Soáres de Silva, the great bibliographer Diego Barbosa Machado, the Templarians' historian Alejandro Ferreira, etc.); later with the more critical and elaborated works of the *Academia Real das Sciencias*, begun in 1780. The *Memorias de Litteratura* of this Academy, in great part historical, the *Inéditos de Historia Portuguesa*, and several other academic publications, will forever honour the illustrious names of Ribeiro,

Father Flórez was a humble Religious who had spent his youth teaching and studying scholastic theology until he finally discovered his true and definitive vocation. To carry out the Herculean task of writing this book he had to educate himself in all the historical disciplines, improvising as geographer, chronologist, epigraphist, coin expert, palaeographer, bibliographer, archaeologist, and even nature scientist – not all with equal perfection but with outstanding eminence in some. His style is prosaic and plain, as that of Muratori and most of the great scholars of that century. But deficiencies in literary style are more than compensated for by sound and serene judgement, a sharp and discerning eye, and the rectitude of a simple and devout heart that overflows with love for truth and for learning. *España Sagrada* was not only a great book: it was a great example. Virtually a School of Criticism in itself, bold and respectful at the same time. Father Flórez was ahead of all others in carrying out the toil of shifting through our *Annales eclesiásticos* within the bounds of the strictest orthodoxy, not once giving in to either pious fraud or hasty credulity. Had he not written it, it would have undoubtedly been written later by someone else but then it would have been done with a spirit already tainted with the negativity about to surface in the eighteenth century.

This negativity did not influence Spain much though one can get a glimpse of it in some of the writings of the great palaeographer from Valencia, Gregorio Mayans, the Nestorius of Spanish Letters of that century, and in the last volumes of *Historia Crítica de España* by the Jesuit Masdeu who went as far as viciously attacking the censuring of some documents which had been proved to be indisputably

---

Correia da Serra, and Antonio Caetano do Amaral, who shares with Martínez Marina the glory of having studied for the first time the social institutions of the middle centuries; José Anastasio de Figueiredo, the notable Santa Rosa de Viterbo, author of the most useful *Elucidario*. These men of learning lived in frequent communication with our own. The Academy of Valencia, the heart of which was Gregorio Mayans, sometimes sought help from the Portuguese Academy of Count da Ericeira, especially in its struggle against the false chronicles. Mayans dedicated the *Censura de historias fabulosas* by Nicolás Antonio to King Juan V in 1742, and in 1747 he printed in Lisbon through the learned master Francisco de Almeida Mascareñas, the *Disertaciones Eclesiásticas* of the Marquis of Mondéjar. Pérez Bayer, Cornide and Father Sánchez Sobrino extended their literary and archaeological journeys to Portugal, and the Portuguese Ferreira Gordo worked in the libraries and archives of Madrid.

In Portugal there were published during the eighteenth century, especially during Pombal's time, a great number of books on canonical questions, but almost all have a somewhat polemic, *ultraregalista* and Jansenist tone (Antonio Pereira, Seabra da Silva). The works on ecclesiastical history are not many and none can compete with *España Sagrada*, not even *Teatro de las iglesias de Aragón*, by Father Huesca. The most extensive and useful for us are *Memorias para a historia ecclesiastica do Arcebispado de Braga*, by Jerónimo Contador de Argote (1732-1744); *Historia da Sancta Inquisiçaõ do Reyno de Portugal* by Father Pedro Monteiro (1749) which covers only as far as the sixteenth century and contains many things immaterial to the issue at hand; the printed works and those in manuscript of the learned bishop of Beja, Manuel do Cenaculo, by himself a whole academy; *Memorias* of Antonio Ribeiro dos Sanctos on the sacred literature of the Portuguese Jews, and on Bible translations; the work of Juan Pedro Ribeiro on the period of the introduction of Decrees Law in Portugal; the attentively edited work on canons and opuscules by St. Martin of Braga, the *Bracarense*, published under the auspices of archbishop Brandão by A.C. Amaral with extensive and learned commentary (1803); the *Catálogo de los Códices de Alcobaza*, by the Cistercian Fray Fortunato de San Buenaventura (1827), and the three volumes *of Inéditos Portugueses* of the fourteenth and fifteenth centuries that serve as supplement to it (1829).

authentic, and of events for which we have irrefutable evidence and cannot therefore be ignored.

But this rather Pyrrhic approach to history was of no great consequence. Much more dangerous was the *cismontane* spirit that took hold of our canonists blended as it was with political ideas not yet tried hence nebulous and deep-down exceedingly ill-matched to the traditional constitution of our monarchy. The wind of revolution propagated these seeds, and men of letters of indisputable merit were swept along in this whirlpool shattering the objectivity with which they had until then proceeded. The Martínez Marina of *Teoría de las Cortes* no longer seems the same person as the author of *Ensayo crítico-histórico* about ancient Castilian legislation. The impartiality he lacked was found even more wanting in others. Canon Villanueva placed his erudition at the service of Gallicism almost to the point of schism, and the apostate Llorente, turning history into calumny, strived to flatter the worst passions of his time.

But before history was turned into an arm of political controversy, the school of the eighteenth century continued to labour on, giving excellent fruits amidst the frigid air one breathed at the time, favourable (and this cannot be denied) to dedication to earnest scientific inquiry and devotion to a life of study that demands tranquillity of spirit and discipline of mind. From one religious order, we could say from one sole monastery, emerged the disciples of Father Flórez, who truly formed an Augustinian School of history. We owe much also to the Dominicans of Valencia, especially to Father Teixidor, whose works remain for the most part unpublished, [14] as well as to Fray Jaime Villanueva, whose *Viaje Literario a las Iglesias de España*, of which twenty two volumes have been published (the first in 1803) is a mine of startling news and an indispensable supplement to *España Sagrada*. Another valuable contribution is *Teatro de las Iglesias de Aragón,* in nine volumes (1770-1807), the work of two Capuchins (though the work of Fray Ramón de Juesca, disciple of Fray Lamberto of Saragossa, has greater advantage over that of his master).

With the same mindfulness and dedication worked the three Catalan Premonstratensians Caresmar, Pasqual and Martí, the great Romanist and archaeologist Finestres, glory of the University of Cervera, his brother the historian of Poblet, the Canon Dorca, author of an excellent critique on the saints of Gerona. [15] In Mallorca, the Cistercian Pascual dedicated his entire life to illustrating the life of Raimundo Lull and his doctrine, and so many others worthy of remembrance (but this is not the time or place to catalogue their works).

Official protection, at times crucial and less dangerous to science than it is to the literary arts, was for the most part never wanting to the scholars of the eighteenth

---

14   See the two volumes of dissertations (many concerning ecclesiastical history) which with the title *Antigüedades de Valencia* by Fray Josef Teixidor, figure in the collection, unfortunately interrupted, of *Monumentos históricos de Valencia y su Reino*, directed by Roque Chabás (Valencia, 1895 and 1896).

15   See his respective articles in the *Diccionario de escritores catalanes* by Torres Amat (1836), excellent if we take into account the author is from the eighteenth century.

century. They found patrons, at times magnificent: the good king Fernando VI and his confessor Father Rábago; Carlos III and his ministers Roda and Floridablanca; Infante don Gabriel; Campomanes, the most zealous director of the Academy of History, [16] diplomat Azara, *fino estimador* of Letters and Art; Cardinal Lorenzana, under whose auspices were printed with regal magnificence the works of the Toledo Fathers, the Gothic Missal and Breviary, and the first collection of the Councils in America; and even the Prince of Peace, who despite his poor Letters and the tortuous origin of his *privanza*, had the good instinct to support many initiatives that might perhaps serve to attenuate the severe judgement history passed upon his conduct. [17]

There is a cloud in this beautiful and sunny landscape. The expulsion of the Jesuits took away from Spain a great number of scholars formed in the School of Father Andrés Maracos Burriel, Flórez's emulator in diligence, superior to him in breath of vision, formidable collector and shrewd critic, who applied himself principally to the study of our canonical sources and municipal legislation. This great but unfortunate gentleman did not experience the same estrangement his own did, for he had succumbed victim a little earlier to an official arbitrary action that stripped him off the treasure of his papers. But to Italy they all went, and in Italy shone his brother, the master biographer of Catalina de Sforza; Father Aymerich, elegant author of the Barcelona *episcologio*; Fathers Maceda, Tolrá, and Menchaca, authors of notable monographs; Father Juan Andrés, the only Spanish historian who included ecclesiastical sciences in the vast frame of his literary encyclopaedia (*Dell'origine, progressi ed stato attuale d'ogni letteratura*). Others are better known: Father Faustino Arévalo, who made truly classical editions of the works of St. Isidore, the early Christian poets (Juvencus, Sedulius, Dracontius), and *Himnodia Hispanica*, illustrating them both with learned Prologues at the level of the best critique of his time and worthy or ours. Thanks to these exiles and other Spaniards resident in Rome, the plan for an Ecclesiastical History outlined in 1747 in an elegant Latin oration by

---

[16] Illustrious scholar of historical sciences in varied and diverse themes, as shown by *Periplo de Hannon, Disertaciones sobre los Templarios, Apendix of the Educación Popular* which teaches us so much about our economic history, and the *Regalía de Amortización*, brilliantly documented. Save for his canonical opinions, of which we shall speak in due course, he was one the most illustrious and notable Spaniards of the eighteenth century.

[17] One of the first tasks in which the activity of our scholars was employed in the eighteenth century was the critical edition of our old canonical collection. It is true that the gigantic works of Father Burriel never came to be in the public domain, which we know by the letter he sent from Toledo to Father Rábago, on 30th December 1754 *(Cartas Eruditas y Críticas*, by Father Andrés Marcos Burriel, published by Balladares, no year shown, pp. 229-278), and by the writing by La Serna Santander, *Praefatio histórico-crítica in veam et genuinam collectionem veterum Canonum Ecclesiae Hispaniae* (Brussels, 1800). But to the Royal Academy, today the *Academia Nacional*, and to his director, Francisco Antonio Gonzálex, we owe the very appreciable edition of 1808, which did not enter into circulation until 1821. Of the learning and fine critique of our eighteenth century canonists the three volumes of Vicente González Arnao in the *Colecciones de Cánones Griegos y Latinos* (1793) are an excellent example.

Alfonso Clemente de Aróstegui, exhorting his compatriots to explore the archives of the Eternal City, began to take shape.[18]

The books of eighteenth century Spanish scholarship enjoy not only care and application but also a trait of persevering effort, an impetus that is communal and unselfish, an impartiality (or *objectivity* as it is now called) which gives solidity to their results and contrasts markedly with the anarchic individualism in which we fell later. All of our intellectual activity in the nineteenth century suffers from this confusion and this disorder. The inattention, the frivolous disdain with which we look at our scholarship of old, is not just ingratitude and injustice; it is a sad sign to the fact that the thread of tradition has been broken and that Spaniards have lost consciousness of themselves. I will not extend this pessimistic outlook to suggest that this occurred in all historical disciplines, but it did extend to the ones I am addressing here. Actually, some do not see degeneration in this at all; they see it instead as revival and progress. Literary history, especially that of the middle ages, archaeological and history of art, history of legislation and institutions, ancient geography of Spain, Roman epigraphy, Iberian numismatics, the promotion of the study of the Arabic language, the political history of some reigns and particular histories of towns and villages, bibliography and palaeography - all these have had, and have now, illustrious representatives, and in greater quality than number. Let us emphasise that the best of our contemporary learning is based on monographs we owe to them and not in *General Histories of Spain* - undertaken with varying degrees of success.

Other branches of history that flourished much in times past appear in the greater part of the nineteenth century to have withered and died and none more than ecclesiastical history: the utter prostration and dejection it has succumbed to being an indication, if further proof were needed, of the sad predicament in which the religious conscience of our people finds itself today. One is hard pressed to find any book of this kind written in the last fifty years that manages to see something beyond our borders and enters into current Catholic learning, save perhaps Balmes' apologetical work *El Protestantismo* which is not quite a work of history but of the philosophy of history.

The War of Independence, two or three civil wars, revolutions and counter-revolutions, a few mutinies here and there and small-town *pronunciamientos*, in short, an utter political mess and an economic chaos that has turned us into buffoons in the eyes of strangers, while we, foolishly and recklessly, like scatter-brained hooligans,

---

[18]   *Ildephonsi Clementis de Arostegui de Historia Ecclesiae Hispaniensis excolenda exhortatio ad Hispanos, habita in palatio C.M. Reg. Hisp. Rom. XII Kal. Sept. MDCCXLVII*, printed in the Appendix to vol. of *Historia Eclesiástica de España* by Vicente de la Fuente, second ed. pp. 285-292.

It was as if these Spaniards resident in Rome had formed the origin of a small Academy of Ecclesiastical History to which we owe some of the very good dissertations we shall be mentioning throughout this book. It is a pity that this institution had such short life and could not bring out a work to counteract the grave errors of Cayetano Cenni's *De Antiquitatibus Ecclesiae Hispaniae Dissertationes* (1741). Its affected rhetorical style was a poor attempt to mask his cynical partiality for the traditions of our church.

were busy divesting and squandering the clergy's possessions. The result was the ruin of many charitable and teaching foundations, the extinction of Regular Orders to the sinister majesty of flames devouring renowned artistic monuments, the destruction or dispersion of whole libraries and archives, in short, the suicidal and godless furore with which Spanish Liberalism has always persevered in its insistence to make a *tabula rasa* of Catholic Spain. All this should be enough, more than enough, to explain the phenomenon we are here lamenting, although in no way will I neglect to exempt traditionalists from their share of the blame.

There is little hope for our public education system. Its rancorous organization is enough to dishearten the most zealous vocations. To the university body belong – had belonged (it is *their* own glory not the state's) – the greater part of any researchers of merit that Spain has had recently, but almost all of them were autodidacts and none managed to form a School. Our system of education, from 1845 onwards, has been a servile copy of French legislation, abandoned even by the French themselves.

Let me make this point very clear: this centralising and bureaucratic bent the French have runs totally counter to our nature. It never works with us. It never will. Attempts such as these are futile and useless. The problem is getting worse by the day but never mind, here we go oblivious again, patching here, patching there, patching everywhere. In the meantime, cultivation of the classical languages of wisdom without which there can be no solid learning has been shamelessly abandoned with very few, hence more laudable, exceptions.

I will limit myself to the issue at hand and mention briefly only two examples: The only existing chair of Ecclesiastical History has now been closed down. It had been doing its best to survive for a while, nominally, as an annex to the Faculty of Jurisprudence, God only knows how, so perhaps we haven't lost much. One has to ask: what could our university canonists possibly have learnt during their *Licenciatura* with only one year of Institutions, and start and finish their degrees not knowing Latin and not being able to read the simplest text of the Church's decrees? Another example is the Faculty of Theology. It too has vanished from our universities. It had not been taken seriously for some time: looked at with suspicion by some, with contempt by others, with indifference by most. No one missed it and no one has seriously attempted to bring it back though one could do so legally now, at the very least to save ourselves the ignominy that Spain, the homeland of Suárez and Melchor Cano is currently the only European country that has expelled theology from its universities. All others, Catholic and Protestant alike, Germany, England, most nations, preserve it without it being looked upon as a sign of backwardness.

Thus, the only shelter and refuge theology and canon law have on our soil is to be found in our Episcopal seminaries which, by the way, according to the mind of the Council of Trent, were established rather for the moral formation of aspirants to the priesthood [19] than for the cultivation of *Letras Sacras*, the true place for which were our university classrooms and the flourishing colleges of some religious Orders. It could be said that the scientific life of Spanish seminaries did not start until the reign of Carlos III: some great learned and zealous prelates organised them as true houses of study in Barcelona, Vich, Murcia, Córdoba, Cuenca, Osma, Salamanca, and other dioceses. Their method and pedagogic discipline could be said to have been superior to those of declining universities. Unfortunately, a little of that 'modern theology', as it is called today, filtered through and made them suspicious of Gaullicist and Jansenist tendencies, perhaps of a little more than that at times. But all of it was very short lived and had little impact. Barely any sign of it remained by the time of Fernando VII's reign, and the 1824 Plan of Studies re-organised theological teaching on solely a Thomist model.

When the horrible convulsion of the Seven Year Civil War was over and the finally modified 1851 Concordat was agreed to after lengthy negotiations, our seminaries began to re-organise again. It is truly remarkable what the zeal of a few prelates, struggling for the most part in abject economic penury, managed to accomplish. Obviously, the study of Dogmatic and Moral Theology had to prevail above all else and in our Charterhouses men of solid and profound doctrine are witness to the fact that there are still theologians and canonists in Spain. Biblicists, experts on Scripture, are rarer because biblical exegesis demands an encyclopaedia of specialized knowledge that is almost impossible to acquire in our country where contemporary bibliographic materials are so poor. Nonetheless chairs in Greek and Hebrew are on the increase and, please God, will yield some fruit in the not too distant future. Chairs in Natural Sciences, earnestly upheld, have also been established in other seminaries as well as in Archaeology of Art for the practical and theoretical teaching of which there exist already important Diocesan museums and good manuals.

The restoration of religious Orders, painfully and laboriously completed in the third quarter of the nineteenth century and at all times embattled by sectarian intolerance, has given Spain excellent educators and writers on various branches of human learning. Some of the best journals we now have are written exclusively by Religious, and their contribution to more recent scientific conferences should not be deemed insignificant. In general we could say without any attempt to exaggerate, that the knowledge of our secular and regular clergy is in no way inferior to that of laymen most advanced in their own disciplines within their respective professions.

But we still have a long way to go, and ecclesiastical erudition cannot but feel the effects of that languor proper of our dispirited country. Translations and compilations are much more numerous than original works. We still lack a general history of the church written by a Spaniard. [20] The book by the archbishop of

---

[19]   Session XXIII, cap. XXIII: *'cum adolescentium aetas, nisi recte instituator, prona sit ad mundi voluptates sequendas…'*

[20]   Spanish erudition during the eighteenth century produced nothing important in matters of ecclesiastical history in general save for the monographs of the Jesuits exiled to Italy. The content of

Palmira, Felix Amat, of remote date now (2nd ed. 1807) hardly goes beyond being a summary of Natal and Alexander Fleury, whose Gallicist ideas he shared. At about the same time *Siglos Cristianos* by Ducreux, the Canon of Auxerre (1790, 2nd. Ed., 1805-1808) was translated and expanded, and later *Historia de la Iglesia* by Receveur (1842-1848) as well as Béraul-Bercastel's with additions by the Baron de Henrion (1852-1855), extensive, but mediocre. Much more useful have been the excellent German manuals by Alzog, Hergenroether, and Funk, translated successively by Puig and Esteve (1852), García Ayuso (1855), and Father Ruíz Amado (1908); and Berti's Latin compendium, kept up to date by a venerable and modest monk, Father Tirso López, of the Order of St. Augustine (1889). Also translated, at least in part, was the encyclopaedist work by Rohrbacher, not exempt of traditionalism and which according to the plan adopted by the author brings all universal history to the centre of ecclesiastical history. Finally, as I am writing this, the first volume of an attractive work by Monsignor Duchesne on the first early Christian centuries is about to appear, most conscientiously rendered into our tongue by the Augustinian Father Pedro Rodríguez.

Nor has the particular history of our church been written to the extent and analysis that present times require. And God forbid that I should start haggling here with the merits of the one sole work in this genre published in our language![21] Its author, whose name lives in the hearts and minds of all Spanish Catholics and especially in those of us who had the privilege to be his pupils and colleagues, was a Catholic whose sincere piety did not interfere with the frank expression of his vigorous and unaffected speech. He was a carefree spirit who went about opining on just about everything licitly opinable, but a scholar of solid canonical learning proven in his university chair for more than half a century. A clear and fun-loving expositor, a sharp and feared polemicist, a bit roguish at times and a touch extreme, his language somewhat biting for lack of literary delicacy and journalistic habits not corrected in time, but in all a salt-of-the-earth type, a joyful and amusing writer amidst all his impolitic precipitation; a diligent and well-oriented researcher just a tad lacking in precision and elegance; a first-rate artisan on a host of historical issues which he illustrated with important findings; at times quick to judge but swift always to rectify his mistakes; a trifle prone to scepticism on things old and excessive credulity on things new: such was don Vicente de La Fuente, an original, an amiable archetype of the Spanish student of days gone by who saw the end of our old universities, continued to behave as if they were still there, and collected their traditions in a book as curious as it was chaotic.

Still scholarship owes him much and for many reasons. He collaborated in the continuation of *España Sagrada*. He was practically the only Spaniard of our time

---

Historia de la Iglesia y del Mundo by the librarian Gabriel Alvarez de Toledo doesn't even come near its ambitious title. The only volume published (1713) got as far as the Deluge! As a philosophical and theological book it is not without interest but its composition is as extravagant as is its style.

21   Hardly to be taken into account.

---

who brought to light an unpublished work from the Middle Ages and pertaining to things Spanish, namely the important poem by Rangerio *Vita Anselmi Lucensis* which contains so much history about St. Gregory VII and about the countess Mathilde; he elucidated with very original criticism several points on the history of Jurisprudence in Aragon and of the obscure and controversial origins of the Pyrenean monarchy; he devoted a great part of his life to shifting through the texts of the works of St. Teresa, producing editions superior to all known until then and illustrating them with invaluable documents. His work, despite all other failings due mostly to imperfect or negligent palaeography and to having attached too much importance to eighteenth century copies, mark epoch in Teresian studies, so flourishing today outside Spain.

Had La Fuente mastered a stricter inner discipline, had he managed a larger bibliographical arsenal and possessed the knowledge he lacked on current scholarship, and had he a little more stylistic gravity and serenity, he could have easily become our ecclesiastical historian. He possessed notable qualities to be so, above all a pure and sincere love for truth and great bravery to proclaim it, even when it run into deep-rooted concerns or won him enemies in his own camp. Like those ancient men of Letters, he was the hammer and terror of makers of fables and fakes, charging at them without qualms or misgivings. That overwhelming critical spirit that had started with Mondéjar and Nicolás Antonio, had continued with *España Sagrada* and ended in a certain Volterian tone with the delightful *Historia de los falsos cronicones* by Godoy Alcantara, had in don Vicente a brilliant collaborator who nonetheless knew how to keep himself well within the ample limits the Church allows in this type of contentions. Turning a blind eye to his style, which is often mundane and inadequate for the subject at hand, there are excellent articles in the *Historia eclesiástica de España*, especially those devoted to the Middle Ages. The author goes to the original sources almost every time, he shows himself familiarised with archives and manages to bring out new documents, a rare quality in authors of textbooks. In all other respects *España Sagrada* was his principal guide as it is to all future work on the subject, but to have organised and arranged the multitude of general annotations scattered throughout this book and to have made good use of the voluminous documentation found there without losing himself in that forest is of no small merit. The two volumes on the modern era however are weak and seem to have been improvised, in form and content. The main failing of La Fuente's work consists on it being too basic. When it appeared for the first time in 1855, it had the modest character of being an addition to the Alzog's *Manual*, and though in the new edition of 1873 to 1875 our professor's work stands on its own and fills six volumes instead of three, it remains insufficient as history though it does have good scope as a compendium.

Something similar has to be said of the work by the wise German Benedictine Father Boniface Gams *Die Kirchengeschichte von Spanien* (Ratisbona, 1876-1879), an excellent historian from the best school, Moehller's biographer and disciple. We Spaniards are especially indebted to Father Gams for this book, as well as for his *Series episcoporum* (1873); for his work is better than La Fuentes's in all points of our history relating to the general history of the Church and to the universal sources of Canon Law and Patristic literature. Of course, what pertains specifically to Spain is richer in our compatriot's since the understanding of issues relating to our national character is clearer with him. A foreigner, however learned and well informed, will attain this with greater difficulty. In other words, both histories have their own particular merits and one cannot be a substitute for the other. Gams' great merit lies in having taken advantage of the vast wealth of German theological literature and having put it at the service of the Annals of our Church.

It pains me to have to mention, albeit as an afterthought, *L'Espagne Chrétienne* by the French Benedictine Dom Leclerq (1906), which covers the time up to Visigoth period. But since in Spain at the present time any book written in French is seen as the fifth gospel (by modernists and pious alike), I believe it to be my duty to warn unsuspecting readers of the flippancy and superficiality of Dom Leclercq's little manual, for it lacks not only scientific merit but is also inspired on a profound disdain for the tradition of the Spanish Church as well as for the temperament and character of our people. There are pages that are so atrocious, so brutal and so vicious, that only in Buckle, Draper and other positivists, consistent denigrators of Spain, can there be found pages that surpass them. But perhaps it was heedlessness and not malevolence that played a part here. It seems incredible to me that a Catholic priest, and a Benedictine Catholic priest, can so deferentially plagiarise entire paragraphs from one of those pedantic and pompous so-called sociologies or peoples' psychologies published by Alcan.[22] We expected a very different book from

---

[22]   The charge is a serious one, so allow me to illustrate my stand with two or three examples:

A. Fouillée, *Esquisse psychologique des peuples européens*, Paris, 1903, pp.167-168: "Suivant la tradition populaire, à l'origine du monde l'Espagne demanda au Créateur un beau ciel, elle l'obtint; une belle mer, de beaux fruits, de belles femmes, elle l'obtint encore; - un bon gouvernement? Non, ce serait trop, et l'Espagne serait alors un paradis terrestre. Mais ce ne fut pas seulement de bons gouvernants qui furent refusés à l'Espagne; ce furent aussi, trop souvent, des hommes gouvernables. Ferdinand le Catholique s'en plaignait à Guichardin, ambassadeur àupres de lui: "Nation très propre aux armes, disait-il, mais desordonnée, où les soldats sont meilleurs que les capitaines et où l'on s'entend mieux à combattre qu'à commander et à gouverner". Et Guichardin ajoute, dans sa Relazione di Spagna. "C'est peut-être par ce la discorde est dans le sang des Espagnols, nation d'ésprits inquiets, pauvres et tournés aux violences" Ce protrait, de nos jours, n' pas encore perdu toute sa vérité…"

Dom Leclercq, *L'Espagne Chrétienne*, pp. XXIII: "A l'origine du monde, raconte une legende, l'Espagne demanda au Créateur un beau ciel…. etc., and he goes on to copy Fouillée for sixteen lines, with only two variants, the first of which is rather funny. Instead of *belles femmes,* the prudish Benedictine writes *belles épouses:* apparently, non-married Spanish ladies can be ugly with impunity.

Fouillée, p. 145: "Durs pour les animaux domestiques, durs pour les hommes, durs pour eux-mêmes, c'est par l'absence de nobté sympathique et sociable qu'ils contrasten avec d'autres peuples. Cette dureté est un des signes caractéristique de la race ibère et berbère, comme de la race sémitique, telle que nous la monstrent sur tout les Phéniciens. Les Espagnols se croyaint bien differents des Maures; au point de vue ethnique, ils en étaient déjà très voisins. Ils n'ont pas reçu assez d'élements celtiques et germaniques pour avoir le douceur dans le sang; ils sont demeurés Africains, et ces Occidentaux sont aussi des Orientaux. Leur insensibilité, don't les Indes conquis firent l'épreuve, alla

a learned liturgist who knows the meaning of correct methodology and who has authored important works on Christian Africa and other matters. This is not to say that we do not find some interesting chapters in his book, the one on Priscillian, for example, although, true enough, it is written without much originality. Dom Leclercq shows himself to be in touch with main research carried out in the last few years and when not blinded by passion he does not reason badly. But a person cannot write well about something that deep down he despises, which is the case with Dom Leclercq on the subject of Spain, as much the old Spain as the new.

When in 1887 I started publishing the modest essay I am now submitting, Dr. La Fuente who as ecclesiastical censor had to examine it was carrying on his shoulders almost entirely the full weight of Catholic controversy on the subject of history, and this he did with an energy that the weight of his years would not diminish; nor would the reigning spirit of contradiction that his genial and easygoing temperament always seemed to bump into when least it should. But a new generation of writers was beginning to form who with a more strict methodology in research and a more immediate contact with learning flourishing elsewhere were providing in monographic form praiseworthy contributions and rectifications to our ecclesiastical history. At the top of the list and leading them all we must place, and not only in chronological order, Father Fidel Fita, a name by itself a legion, known as

---

souvent jusqu'à la cruauté froide et à la férocité. Les peintres eux-mêmes se plaisent à représenter des supplices".

Dom Leclercq, p. XXVII: "Durs pours les animaux domestiques, durs pour les hommes, durs pour eux-mêmes... etc. etc." Fourteen lines plagiarised without changing a word. The only thing Dom Leclercq does is to re-inforce more and more the misohispanism of Fouillée, adding phrases such as this one, and I am not sure if it is of his own invention or of someone else's: "*il* (l'Espagnol) *met en toutes choses une passion de bête déchaînée, furieuse, dépourvue de vastes horizons intellectuels et de reflexion... n'a plus qu'une sensibilité de tête qui est l'egoisme farouche*".

And he who writes these atrocities is a Benedictine, and a Benedictine from Farnborough Abbey at that, where he and his brethren are at that moment receiving asylum and splendid protection at the hands of a great Andalusian lady of tragic and memorable fate to the memory of the world!

But it is not right that we become indignant with an historian whose reliability can be judged by this penstroke of his on our poet Prudentius: " Prudence ne tarit plus dès qu'il parle gril, tenailles, pinces et chaudières; dix siècles plus tard il partagerait son temps entre les courses de taureaux et les auto-da-fe. Il faut plaindre ceux qui ont à gouverner de pareilles gens."

Those who have to be pitied are the public who read these stupidities written in French.

Fouillée's chapter into which Dom Leclercq barges is a jumbled and incoherent rhapsody, as is almost everything that has been written on Spanish *sociology*. Fouillée is a metaphysician of great talent but his works on ethnic psychology cannot be taken seriously because they have been improvised without due historical preparation, and with regards to Spain he ignores all: he doesn't know her language, her literature, or her customs. He cites but one Castilian phrase consisting of six words, and two of them, grossly altered (p. 164). Such is Dom Leclercq's oracle in matters of Spanish psychology.

It is a proverbial and overly-used phrase to call those labours that have been patiently and painstakingly carried out *obras de benedictino*. Dom Leclercq's book is by a Benedictine, but a Benedictine who seems to me to be leagues away from Dom Mabillon and Dom Montfaucon, let alone one of their brethren. *Corruptio optimi pessima.*

an illustrious epigraphist since 1866 when he illustrated Diana's *ara* inscriptions in León, and since 1872 as researcher of *Memorias* of the Middle Ages when his wonderful book *Los Reys d'Aragó y la Seu de Girona* appeared. From that date and especially since he joined the Academy of History (1879) the activity of this learned Jesuit has reached peaks almost too high to be believed. The Association's bulletin owes a great part of its content to him, and dispensing now with his notorious merit as an archaeologist, he is, without question, the one Spaniard who in our days has published the greatest number of documents pertaining to the Middle Ages linked to our canonical and liturgical history and the life (both internal and external) of our churches. On this, his efforts have seen no equal after *España Sagrada*. And not only with this eminent gentleman who still *in senectute bona* continues tirelessly his work but also with others wholeheartedly worthy of praise has the Society of Jesus contributed to the furthering of historical studies in our country as evidenced by the edition of *Cartas de San Ignacio, Monumenta Societatis Jesu, Historia del primer siglo de la Compañia*, by Father Astrain, and the bibliographical monument of Father Uriarte which, when comprehensively studied, will eclipse the Backer brothers, Sommervogel, and all others versed in the same discipline.

Other religious institutes also have honourably revived their history and cultural tradition: the Augustinians above all, of whom much is expected because of the example set by Father Flórez. The healthy upsurge manifested on all intellectual disciplines in the journals *Revista Agustiniana* and *La Ciudad de Dios* where many good critical and learned articles have appeared will find deserving application in the *Biblioteca Escurialense* now trusted to their custody, an assurance of which we already see in the first volume of the Latin codex Catalogue of that remarkable foundation, fresh from the printers today thanks to the diligence of its librarian Father Guillermo Antolín, thus a genre of wise publications seemingly interrupted since the days of Pérez Bayer, Casiri, and Juan de Iriarte to the honour and glory of Spain.

Our gratitude to the French Benedictines of the Solesmes School who have contributed to this our historical progress not only with their own excellent works such as the history and *cartulario* of the Silos monastery by Dom Férotin but also by educating several Spanish monks in diplomatic science who have now begun publication of *Fuentes de la Historia de Castilla*, an assignment characteristic of those who wear the same habit as Father Berganza.

Naturally, in the glorious Order of St. Dominic the study of theology and scholastic philosophy predominate over historical studies but even these enjoy outstanding representation with Father Justo Cuervo who has given us the best edition of the works of Fray Luis de Granada and is preparing a book, perhaps a definitive one, on the Melchor Cano vs. Archbishop Carranza affair and the latter's trial ordeal. Other names of Franciscans and Carmelites and of other regular congregations could be cited here but I shall not try to improvise a catalogue that would by necessity be incomplete. I am sure that in the course of this work there will be ample opportunity for mentioning them all, or the vast majority of them.

Honourable too has been the contribution made by the secular clergy to the revival we are here saluting. The Canon of Santiago de Compostela, Antonio López Ferreiro, for example (whose recent loss our nation is presently mourning), who entirely rebuilt the ecclesiastical and civil history of Galicia during the Middle Ages in a series of books that to date have not yet been studied in depth nor yielded the fruit they should have done (*Historia de la Iglesia Compostelana, Fueros Municipales de Santiago y su tierra, Galicia en el último tercio del siglo XV*, among others). López Ferreiro was a model researcher, his only flaw being an excessive apologetic tendency with regard to the tradition of his Church. His first monograph, *Estudios críticos sobre el Priscilianismo* (1879) is now outdated, as are all writings done on the famous dissenter before Schepss's discoveries. But even in that essay, written in his youth, one can see the luminous and sharp discernment of this most eminent gentleman who forthrightly tackled the religious and social history of his land. Honour is due also to our Roque Chabás who has admirably organised the archive of the Cathedral of Valencia and does not cease to illustrate the annals of that ancient kingdom with learned publications relating not only to ecclesiastical history but to juridical and literary history as well; Mariano Arigita, the Canon of Pamplona, who has written with utmost diligence the biographies of the great canonist Martín de Azpilcueta and other notable figures of Navarre. But I shall stop here with this enumeration so as not to incur omissions that I myself would be the first to deplore.

The few names I have so far cited suffice to prove that the picture of Spanish ecclesiastical learning is today very different from what it was in 1880 when I first wrote this book, albeit nowhere near what our patriotic desire would wish for.

An so my book now reappears in conditions more favourable than they were then because it finds a better prepared readership more attentive to matters of history and because its author has learnt and improved a little during the course of a life of study now close to old age.

Let me therefore use these my twilight years to correct a work written in the bright days of my youth; correct, I say, with the love of a father, not with the indulgence that tends to make some parents blind. Let it not be said of me *bis patriae cecidere manus*.

Nothing ages more than a book of history. It is a sad truth but one must admit it. He who dreams of giving indefinite permanence to his work and is fond of stereotyped reports and verdicts for now and evermore shall do well to dedicate himself to other literary genres and not to this prolonged and toilsome activity, where each day calls for new corrections and brings fresh documents to light. Historical subject matter is fleeting and mobile. The historian must resign himself to being a perpetual student and dedicate himself to the pursuit of truth wherever he may find but a speck of it, fear of being judged inconsistent notwithstanding. He shall not be inconsistent on general principles of history if these be well implanted in him, nor on the philosophical criteria with which he judges systems and ideas, or the moral judgement he passes on human actions. But on the point of sorting through facts he is obliged to be so, and even more rigorously in ecclesiastical history, because its subject matter is lofty, there being nothing in it that is small or insignificant. Ecclesiastical history is written for edification, not for scandal, and scandal is not caused by stating the truth, however harsh, when this truth is stated respectfully and with Christian intent, not out of concealment and dissimulation, which are a hair's breadth away from being a lie. Fortunately, all great Catholic historians have given us admirable examples that can appease the conscience of the most scrupulous, and our literature is not exactly lacking in masters of manly integrity and rectitude.

I tried modestly to follow in their footsteps in the first edition of this history, the success of which, well beyond my aspirations and hopes, I must attribute only to my determination to go back to the original sources and due consideration to heterodox and very especially Protestant literature, barely touched upon by our scholars.

Today I see many faults in this work of my youth. They are due mainly to insufficient knowledge and the youthful impetuosity with which I threw myself at it with an effort far superior to my ability. But I do not regret having written it. It was done with the best of intentions and was thought out with sincere conviction. I gathered information that was new at the time and, as far as I was able within my modest faculties, I widened the boundaries of the subject. An entire chapter of our ecclesiastical history was written here for the first time, undoubtedly not one of the most important chapters, but one that relates to almost all of them, and one of the most arduous and difficult to carry out.

I am not displeased with the general layout and shall keep it with little alteration. It has been said, in a censuring tone, that the *Historia de los Heteredoxos Españoles* is a series of monographs. That would not be a bad thing if they were any good. Tillemont's *Mémoires* are written in monographic form, and they do not for that reason cease to be one of the most solid and permanent works that ancient learning has produced. But without the need to evoke so eminent a work, the reader will see that in my layout each heresiarch's monograph is ordered in a way such that they are all harmonious, one leading to the next. Also, they form an historical body of work, subject to a fundamental thought on which I shall not insist now because it is stated with some clarity in the Prologue to the first edition that follows. This thought is at the root of the work and is imbedded in the words of the Apostle which serve as an epigraph. Understood in this way, *Historia de los Heterodoxos Españoles* is bound to constitute a peculiar and contradictory history within the history of Spain. It is, one could say, the history of Spain upside down. Its content is fragmentary and heterogeneous but it is not lacking in a certain summarising and synthetic unity seen more clearly as the narrative advances and culminating at the high point of the sixteenth century, the heart of this specific history as of any other written from a Spanish viewpoint.

If I have not changed anything substantially in the layout of the work, I cannot say the same for its content. There is hardly a page that has not undergone a few changes, and those that have been entirely re-written or edited are countless. I introduce totally new chapters and in almost all those left from the old edition I insert paragraphs and new sections that were not there before or were little developed, and add footnotes and appendices without compassion. To this and more I am compelled by the prodigious historical progress of our days difficult to sustain in Spain so I have resigned myself in advance to the fact that the outcome of this work of mine, the toil of a self taught recluse after all, will look in many areas as if it was left limping, defective despite all my efforts to the contrary.

Since Schepss discovered eleven treatises on Priscillian in the Würzburg library, published in 1889, there has emerged from German theological schools as well as other countries a vast Priscillianist literature in the form of theses, journal articles, polemical books and textual publications.

Thanks to Künstle and others, our knowledge of Patristic literature from the fourth and fifth centuries, so meagre before, has begun to be filled with books: some unpublished, others anonymous which had been dispersed in church collections and no one suspected their Spanish origin. Not only the Priscillian heresy but other more relevant points relating to the dogma, discipline and liturgy of our early church have received new light with the unexpected support these findings brought with them.

With regards to the history of the Swabian and Visigoth kingdoms, and the critical revival that Félix Dahn began, it suffices to recall that in the *Monumenta Germaniae historica*, Mommsen worked on edition of the chronicles and Zeumer on the area of legal sources, with all the prestige and authority that accompanies those names. On this, fortunately, the collaboration of our indigenous learning was not small, as proven by the excellent works of Pérez Pujol, Fernández-Guerra, Hinojosa and Ureña.

The same could be said of our Arabists who form one of the most active groups in Spanish scholarship though not as numerous as one would like. Their works, especially Simonet's wise and compassionate *Historia de los Mozárabes* whose publication had been delayed for so long are indispensable to an understanding of the religious interrelationship between the invading race and the conquered peoples.

The School of Translators of Toledo, main crossroads between oriental knowledge and the Christian schools, has been most aptly illustrated not only by the classical works of Wüstenfeld and Leclerc but also by Steinschneider's leading work on the Hebrew translations of the Middle Ages and on the Jewish people seen as interpreters (1898) by Guttmann on Scholastics of the thirteenth century and its relationship with Jewish literature (1902) as well as the new monographs that Hauréau, Alberto Loewenthal (1890), J.A. Endres (1890), Pablo Correns (1891), Jorge Bulow (1897), C. Baeumker (1898), and Louis Baur (1903) have written on the philosophical works of archdeacon Gundisalvo or Gundisalino (1879) and other collaborators of the learned publication that appears in Münster with the title *Beiträge zur Geschichte der Philosophie des Mittelalters* to which we owe, among other great services, the complete text of *Fons Viatae* by Avicebrón.

When in 1880 I published *Liber de procesione*, the name Gundisalvo had hardly been heard in the history of philosophy but today he is recognised to be the author of the famous *Liber de unitate*, one of the most influential to play a part in the scholastic crisis of the twelfth century.

The extensive and erudite monographs by Hauréau and Littré on Arnaldo de Vilanova and Raimundo Lull, published respectively in volumes 28 and 29 of the *Histoire Littéraire de la France* (1881 and 1885) once again called scholars' attention on these two great figures who personify the intellectual life of Catalonia during the Middle Ages. With regards to the life of Vilanova, renowned doctor to the kings of Aragon and Sicily about whom I had the great fortune to elucidate with important and new documentation in 1879, now the Freiburg's professor Henry Finke has added much more, first with his book on Boniface VIII (1902) and later in his *Acta Aragonensia*. Other very important documents have been discovered by Roque Chabás and my good friend Antonio Rubió y Lluch, honourable professor at the University of Barcelona. And as I am writing this, a *cartulario* started appearing on many documents printed or unpublished as are presently known concerning Arnaldo in the *Journal Estudis universitaris catalans*. In these last few years there have been several theses in which he is studied not only as a doctor (i.e. in those of E. Allende and Marcos Haven, 1896) but also on the influence he exerted in the area of politics and as a lay theologian (Pablo Diepgen, 1909).

This vigorous rebirth of Catalan historiography has helped much to the filtering through of Arnaldo's biography and to the growth in Lullian studies, practically interrupted since the eighteenth century, with the only important exception being Jerónimo Roselló's work. They have now started flourishing in Mallorca with a spirit truly critical as manifested by the wonderful collection of the *Doctor Iluminado*'s original texts in whose study and compilation my ill-fated colleague Mateo Obrador y Bennasar played a great part.

To summarise: hardly a theme can be found in volume 1 of my early *Heterodoxos* that has not been completely updated by work carried out in these last years be it on the Albigensian heresy of Provence and its Catalans adherents or the 'mystic' sects of Italian or German origin which also had proselytes in our land.

The history of the Inquisition, so closely linked with that of heresy, has been written with vast and solid material, and with what at least appears to be objectivity, by the North American Henry Charles Lea in several books that must be regarded as fundamental on this subject until others come that may refute or improve them. As far as documentation is concerned, they represent a great advance on the subject, but to penetrate the spirit and proceedings of that institution, the publication of as many original Acta trials as possible is of utmost importance since those already published are relatively few. That is how Father Fita understood it, giving us to know in the *Boletín de la Real Academia de la Historia* the most important documents pertaining to the Castilian Inquisition at the time of the Catholic monarchs. Dr. Ernest Schaeffer of the University of Rostock agrees, and to him we owe not only an ample extract of the trials against the Lutherans of Valladolid at the time of Felipe II, but also a truly scientific and impartial commentary in which the author, though a Protestant, reaches conclusions that no Catholic author should reject.

I could refer to the Index of my book step by step and point to all that we have now learned since it was first published about Eramists and Protestants, Illuminados and sorcerers, Judaizers and Moriscos, Jansenists, Encyclopaedists, even on the religious troubles of our day. But as well as being highly tiresome this recapitulation would be useless, because the relevant bibliographical indications have been inserted in the text, something which I have tried to do as exactly and completely as possible, endeavouring to redress here as in the rest of the book the flaws of the first edition.

Faced with this cluster of new material that obliged me to make so many additions and corrections, perhaps it would have been easier for me to write a second *Historia* than to edit the old one. But no one, least of all one who has long ago bidden farewell to youth, can make large calculations on his life span, and that which God has condescended to give me I would rather devote to other thankless literary projects. I have therefore adopted a happy medium. I am not unaware of its drawbacks, but it is perhaps the only feasible way now.

I have retained from the old text as much as could be retained, making corrections and updating the text without in this instance calling the reader's attention to footnotes, and all the factual errors I have noticed of dates, names and historical details of any kind.

I have scrupulously revised all quotations and verified them against the originals, endeavouring to cite them all from the same edition of a work, hopefully from the best one, or at least one that can be quoted that is free from erroneous lessons. The bibliographical description of each book will be made, as a general rule, the first time it is mentioned. On works widely known by everyone which are general sources of canon law and ecclesiastical history, the indication will be succinct but exact and to the point.

Addenda will be inserted in the text itself as long as it does not break the flow or give rise to confusion. But when these are numerous and of a nature such that will alter or vary the facts previously stated, as happened with the Priscillian heresy, they will be shown in sequence to the old chapter (cleared up and corrected of the errors already there in 1880) in a way that the reader can check and compare what historical investigation knew up to that time against what has been discovered since then.

Rectification of serious matters, by which the author corrects or moderates judgements passed on persons and events by virtue of new discoveries, will be stated in special annotations. I neither seek to conceal my previous beliefs nor assume the present ones to be infallible. I am certainly not intimidated by the puerile fear, unworthy of an historian, of appearing to have contradicted myself.

I have brushed up the style a little, doing away with some peculiarities that today I consider gratuitous and belonging to youthful naiveté; also, many grammatical errors and other failings patently obvious to the most benevolent reader and which could only be excused on account of the young age of the author. This approach, though extensive, was not excessively intense. I did not want to deprive the book of one of the few merits it may have, namely the spontaneity and freshness that, other qualities lacking, is found only in the very first fruits of a young person´s creative output. One does not write in the same way at twenty than at fifty, and to correct one's early style later, to me is to falsify it; I see it as the futile task of academic purists, simply not worth the effort and something that puts into evidence an excessive satisfaction with oneself. To my mind, the best style is that which is least evident. I now try to write more and more simply every time but in my youth I couldn't help paying tribute to the rhetorical and emphatic prose predominant at the time. There are many pages in this book that make me smile but I am not going to prim them up. I leave them intact because the book has its date and I was very far then from the literary form I now prefer, although I can see I was heading towards it already. That is why the prose of the *Heterodoxos* is so unequal and fluctuates between two opposing hurdles: utter barrenness and extreme excess.

There is another fault, especially in the last volume. It is the excessive acrimony and intemperance of expression with which I qualified certain tendencies and the judgements I passed on some men. I need not protest this charge for at no time was I moved by personal hostility towards these persons. The majority of them I did not know personally. I knew of them only through their actions and the doctrines stated in their books and their teaching. My thoughts on almost all of them are now what they were before but if I were to write today about the same issues I would do it with more temperance and calm, aspiring to that tranquil uplifting that history, even contemporary history, graciously bestows on us, but a calm that could hardly be expected of a lad of twenty-three, passionate, inexperienced, infected by the polemical air he breathed and still not quite master of his own words or thoughts. Even for aesthetic reasons alone I would like to have given another tone to the last chapters of my work, but I felt I had no right to do so. What I did, and I believe I fulfilled my obligation of conscience in this and the other sections of my *History*, was to amend all mistaken information, for the same justice is owed to the contemporary as to the ancient, to the living as to the dead. When I rectify or attenuate a judgement, I add it as a footnote. In the text itself, I erased only expressions that today seem to me to be rather impertinent, harsh or cruel, because they would be a bad example, and because it would be in bad taste to keep them. The licit, inoffensive and slight little mockeries I did keep because even by literary standards they do not seem to me to be the worst part of the book.

This second edition ends where the first ended, in 1876, date of the Constitution that passed the current government decree that forces us to Religious Tolerance. Only in some note or other do I refer to later events but merely in order to complete some narrative or the bibliography of a specific person. What comes after that date will be for others to write. I do not envy them such a sorry and thankless task.

Reprinted with these corrections, *Historia de los Heterodoxos españoles* will cease to be a rare find. Hopefully it will be a useful one.

Santander, July 1910.

Preface to the First Edition [23]

The history of heterodox thought in our country was practically unknown at the beginning of the nineteenth century. We had knowledge of some old heresies thanks to the incomparable *España Sagrada*. Also, a Catalan by the name of Girves had collected in a curious dissertation of all data known up until that time about Priscillianism. Father Meceda had written an Apologia on Hosius, and Walch, a German, had written the history of Adoptionism. But these monographs printed either in Italy or Germany did not circulate widely enough in our Peninsula.

Some diligent writer had come across one or two reports about Claudio of Turin, Arnaldo de Vilanova, Pedro de Osma, and the Alumbrados of Toledo, Extremadura and Seville but the majority of our learned scholars depended for their sources on what they found in Nicolás Antonio's *Bibliotheca*, Eymerich's *Directorium*, the great *De haeresibus* by Father Alfonso de Castro, *Historia Literaria de Francia*, Carranza's *Summa Conciliorum*, Rezábal's *Biblioteca de los colegios mayores*, Fray Alonso Fernández's *Anales de Plasencia*, and one or two other books that briefly and only incidentally made reference to some of our heretics. The scandal caused by Miguel de Molinos' *Guía Espiritual* in the seventeenth and eighteenth centuries was still in the air and Jansenism was still far too close for its history to have been forgotten though no one had thought of writing it with reference to our country. [A]

With regard to Spanish Protestants of the sixteenth century, a few scarce and scattered pieces of evidence had been preserved. The librarian Pellicer had written a work for his literary history which he published in several articles with the heading *Francisco de Enzinas, Casiodoro de Reina, Cyprian de Valera*, and a couple of others in *Ensayo de una biblioteca de traductores*, the first issue of which appeared in 1778, but the work was never completed.

Speaking generally, no books on Spanish heterodoxy, most of them rare anyway, made it into the hands of scholars thanks to the concern, discrimination and rigour exercised by the Holy Office at the time they appeared. Nor was the history of, let us say, these aborted attempts by their authors well known. One heard the name of Juan de Valdés as something from a rather shadowy tradition, and when Mayans printed *Diálogo de la lengua* (entitling it *de las lenguas*) he could not, or did not want to, reveal the name of the author. The scholar Cerdá y Rico, one of the most distinguished and respected in the eighteenth century, when treating of Constantino de la Fuente was content to repeat (mostly in quotations) the brief article that Nicolás Antonio had devoted to him in his works. Latassa spoke of Servetus in his *Biblioteca Aragonesa* acknowledging that he had been unable to examine his books personally. The *Expurgatory Indices* had managed to accomplish, if not their complete

---

[23]   Notes added in this second edition are marked by a number, those of the first edition by letters.

[A]   All books which in this Prologue and on the previous one are summarily mentioned are described in the course of the work with the necessary bibliographical indications.

extinction, at least a somewhat sudden disappearance of most of these volumes from our soil, which in any case neither in Spain nor abroad were arousing much interest as the eighteenth century drew to a close. This was not because some fervent German and Dutch Protestants had desisted from urging us towards the benefit of studying these books and the need to write a history of their doctrines in Spain but because their exhortations were met with general indifference - the ardour with which theological issues were addressed in the sixteenth century having subsided considerably by then. As a result, all they knew abroad about our Lutherans, Calvinists and Unitarians was not much more than what one finds in Bayle's *Dictionnaire historique*, J.Christ Sand's *Bibliotheca Anti-trinitariorum*, Geddes' *Martyrologio*, Büsching's dissertation *De vestigiis Lutheranism in Hispania* (Göttingen, 1755) and in one or two other books by some distant authors.

Nonetheless, Mosheim and Allwoerden had written in German and in Latin notable biographies of Servetus. Strobel and Prosperus Marchand had written also on Enzinas (Dryander). Though actual documentation was rare, they nevertheless sparked in some (be it with good or ill intentions depending on whether their motive was zeal for truth, scholarly curiosity, sectarian spirit, or rather an appetite for perverse innovations) the desire to go into such bizarre and unfamiliar news in greater depth, since the facts and figures provided by Gonzalo de Illescas in *Historia Pontifical Católica* were hardly enough to satisfy one's curiosity, and those by Cabrera's *Felipe II* even less.

All of a sudden it seemed as if a publication due to come out shortly on the history of the Holy Office with compilations of documents from its archives and written by a secretary to this famous tribunal (a figure truly worthy of a good chapter in the future history of Spanish heterodox) was going to shed copious light on this and other issues as entangled as they were obscure. And so it was. Juan Antonio Llorente, in *Historia crítica de la Inquisición*, published in the French language in 1818 and translated for the first time into Spanish in 1822, did give us these sources, unfortunately however in a somewhat arid and undigested form, devoid of artistic style, critically inapt, and hardly ever citing or quoting anyone; and the little he did cite he did it in a partial and incomplete manner, far too often writing odd reports from memory about the trials and imprisonment of several of the heterodox punished by the Tribunal.

To these must be added one or two others made public in Cádiz in 1811 by the Catalan philologist Antonio Puig y Blanch (Puigblanch) in his book *La Inquisición sin máscara*, printed under the pseudonym Natael Jomtomb and translated into English in 1816 by William Walton. But neither Llorente nor Puig y Blanch (and leaving aside their religious errors and political radicalism which in many cases deprived them of objectivity) wrote with sufficient preparedness nor did they adequately respect the rules and norms of historical writing. Nor in fact did they choose our heterodox as the principal theme for their work or touched upon if only incidentally on bibliographical and scholarly criticism, something not entirely insignificant in this subject area.

Protestant enthusiasm finally found an echo in the first history of the Reformation in Spain, unquestionably not written with as much detail and care as the Lessing father would have wished in the previous century [B] but useful nonetheless and worthy of remembrance as a first essay. I am referring to the work of the Scottish Presbyterian M'Crae, published in 1829 with the title *History of the progress and suppression of the Reformation in Spain in the sixteenth century* [C] which goes together with his *History of the Reformation in Italy*, twice published. M'Crae's book is a compilation, not inelegantly written, of information scattered in the works of Reinaldo González de Montes, Geddes, Pellicer, Llorente and others, the author's own contribution not amounting to much. It has little in it worthy of praise save the novelty of the enterprise and its clear and lucid exposition. It was from this book, impregnated with sectarian spirit (as one was to expect) that the English learnt the history of our Reformists, almost totally unknown to them until that time.[D] Several years passed with no new research coming forth to smooth out such uneven ground. At last, a scholar from Cádiz, fortunately still alive [E] and fortunately still enlightening our country with his extraordinary talent and exemplary labour, and given from his early years to all manner of historical inquiry particularly when novel and rare, conceived the idea of writing a history of our Protestants which proved to be a more complete and more carefully thought-out and well crafted work than M'Crae's. Adolfo de Castro, understandably the person I am alluding to here, had by 1847 finished a *Historia del Protestantismo en España* which he subsequently re-edited and expanded to become a new work, one which with the heading *Historia de los Protestantes españoles y de su persecución por Felipe II* was brought to light in Cádiz in the year 1851. [F] His own beliefs, if not altogether heterodox, were cutting-edge enough, to say the least, as far as religious liberty will allow and his historical perceptiveness imprecise, sometimes extreme, particularly on anything concerning the Inquisition and Felipe II. But who am I to speak of flaws in a book written in the fiery years of one's youth! The author himself has publicly and sincerely acknowledged them in several occasions, by so doing raising himself to the eyes of his own conscience and that of men of clean and healthy heart and mind; doubtlessly also before the eyes of God to whom he has offered in expiation his last remarkable works. I will say only that in my respected

---

[B]   "Historia Reformationis non paucis defectibus laborat. Insigni igitur utilitate, quamvis multi labore, historiam Hispanorum Protestantium conscribi posse, mihi certe persuadeo. Quamvis enim libri jukus commatis rarissime esse loleant, ex rivulis tamen, si non fontibus, hinc et inde latentibus, nonnulli meo quidem judicio deduci possent quae non contemnendam lucem historiae reformationis universali affundere posse in propatulo est." (J. Gottfried Lessing, De fidei confessione quam Protestantes Hispania ejecti Londini 1559 ediderunt. Lipsiae, 1730, p. 17).

[C]   Translated into German by Gustav Plieninger (Stutgart, 1835), with some addenda.

[D]   It should also be added in eulogy of M'Crae's work that it is a better written book than that of Adolfo de Castro and contains notes omitted by him.

[E]   Died in 1898

[F]   Translated into English by Thomas Parker, and published simultaneously with the original (London, 1851), and into German by Enrique Hertz (Frankfurt, 1866).

friend's book one will find outstanding erudition and extremely interesting historical research, as the great Belgian archivist M. Marchand, so admirable a scholar of our history, acknowledged when treating of works written on the life of the ill-fated youth Prince Carlos in his excellent monograph. G Of course one can find gaps in an otherwise remarkable book, recurrent whimsical remarks, and a scarcity, perhaps even absence, of new information in some chapters. Books on our heterodox have always been rare in Spain. It is natural therefore that some should have escaped Castro's diligence.

In a later work written in the same spirit of *Historia de los protestantes*, I am referring to *Exámen filosófico de las principales causas de la decadencia en España* (Cádiz, 1852), translated into English by Thomas Parker with the title *History of religious intolerance in Spain* (London, 1853), the learned Andalusian did add curious and appreciable information to the history of heresy in the Peninsula.

By now, two tireless and enthusiastic men were already working on issues of religious agitation in Spain during the sixteenth century: two men whose birth seems to have obeyed some ultimate and mysterious synchronism - such was the intimate friendship they always enjoyed and the mutual help and support they gave each other during their long and much too gruelling research.

This is what actually happened: There was once an erudite Englishman, a Quaker, by the name of Benjamin Barron Wiffen who was given to the study of the literatures of Southern Europe on which he had been initiated by a brother of his, himself a translator of Tasso and Garcilaso de la Vega. In time Mr. Wiffen was to find, for his good fortune and doubtlessly that of Spanish Letters, someone who would second him in his projects and plans. This man was Luis Usoz y Río who began a relationship with Wiffen during his trip to England in 1839. And now, heartening each other in love for a cause mixed with reasons more innocent, i.e. bibliographic mania, they began publication of *Reformistas antiguos españoles*. Between 1837 and 1865 they published twenty volumes. Wiffen's niece wrote that they contained "the history of the early Spanish Protestants: their churches, their martyrdom, their exile". The volumes circulated little. They were printed with great care but the issues were in short supply. European scholars knew them well however and to their publication is due the bountiful material that came to dissipate the darkness hovering over the history of our early Protestants until that time.

Usoz y Rio opened the series with *Carrascón,* by Fernando de Texeda, almost at the same time that Wiffen was reprinting *Epístola consolatoria* by Dr. Juan Pérez. To these first volumes soon followed *Imagen del Anticristo* and *Carta a Felipe II*, both works by Juan de Valdés together with most works by Cipriano de Valera and Juan Pérez. Also, *Dos Informaciones*, whose translation is attributed to Francisco de Enzinas; the treatise on the Inquisition by Reinaldo G. Montano, the autobiography

---

G   "Enfin, j'ai fait quelques emprunts à l'Histoire des protestants espagnols, de M. de Castro, où l'on regrette que des recherches infiniment curieuses soient mêlées à des assertions hasardées et à des jugements inspirés par l'esprit de système."

of Nicolas Sacharles, Constantino's *Opusculos* and *Historia de la muerte de Juan Díaz*, accompanied by a brief *Summa Christianae religionis*. With few exceptions such as *Epístola consolatoria* and *Alfabeto christiano*, all the other editions came out of Madrid *ex aedibus Laetitiae* (Press of Martín Alegría). Some of these works were translated by Usoz from the Italian or Latin, the languages in which their authors had written or published them first. Of Valdes' *Consideraciones divinas* as many as three editions were made, the text being refined more each time.

In a word, as far as material execution was concerned, *Reformistas Españoles* left nothing to be desired. If out of the copious explanatory notes that precede and accompany this great number of volumes were we to remove the constant and insipid Quaker declamations of the editors (which sometimes verge on the absurd and makes one smile out of compassion for these two honest men who with their books, quite innocent today, hoped in good faith to *evangelise* Spain), we shall find in them a rich arsenal of information and documents. Our appreciation for Wiffen's and Usoz's intelligence and hard work will grow even when we disapprove of the pathetic rather than dangerous motives that induced them to this enterprise. Sound and loyal scholarship and sincere, though misplaced, enthusiasm, are always worthy of respect. And truly, one cannot read the narrative Wiffen makes of his and his friend's labours, of the difficulties they encountered trying to get hold of sample copies, the diligence with which they transcribed manuscripts and rare editions from private and public libraries, in fine, all of the incidents that go with the reprinting and circulation of books of this kind, without feeling a certain degree of sympathy and affection for these two men.

Accordingly, and due to the care and consciousness with which Usoz and Wiffen proceeded, the work *Reformistas* became a precedent for *Bibliografía protestante española*. Both friends had agreed to work together on it, but Usoz's death in 1865 brought the course of their work to a halt leaving the Englishman to work for himself when he was barely starting to organise and put his records together. Deprived now of his partner and friend, the author of *Vida de Juan Valdes* sought the collaboration and assistance in his last years of another young and enthusiastic scholar, Dr. Eduard Boehmer, presently Professor of Romance Languages at the University of Strasbourg. [H]

When Wiffen died it was to Boehmer that the executors of his will and friends came pleading with him to take charge of Wiffen's papers, books and notes. Among them were found several lists with the names of the authors he had proposed to include in the *Bibliotheca*, a considerable number of bibliographical notes, and

---

[H]   This eminent philologist died in 1905 soon after having published the third volume of *Bibliotheca Wiffeniana*. The second had appeared in 1883. Boehmer added to Usoz's collection three more volumes of Juan de Valdes' works and one by Constantino (1880-1881) discovered by him in the libraries of Vienna and Munich, and published several other documents to which I will draw attention at the appropriate time. In his *Romanische Studien* (1881 and 1895) he published critical editions of *Diálogo de Mercurio* and *Dialogo de la lengua*, which improved those of Usoz. There has been no other more eminent scholar on the literary history of Spanish Protestantism.

expanded articles on Texeda (author of *Carrascón*), Juan Pérez, and Nicolás Sacharles, all three brief and the second incomplete. At Mr. John Betts's request, himself the translator of the *Confesión del pecador* by Constantino, and Wiffen's executor, Boehmer began the arduous task of a *Biblioteca de reformistas españoles*, accommodating himself with slight variations to the plan envisaged by the learned Quaker and making use of his material. He added also a magnitude of news, fruits of his own research in the libraries of Germany, England, France and the Low Countries, and on this broad and sound foundation he erected his *Bibliotheca Wiffeniana-Spanish reformers*, the first volume of which he offered to the printers in the year 1874. (The second hasn't come to light yet, at least it hasn't reached our hands).

The Strasbourgian professor was no stranger to this kind of work. Back in 1860, in Halle of Saxony he had published a very good reprinting of the Italian translation of the Valdesian *Consideraciones*, including a *Memoria* in the Appendix modestly entitled *Cenni biographici sui fratelli Giovanni ed Alphonso di Valdesso*. In 1865 he had republished in Spanish a section of *Dialogo de la lengua*, and to him we owe also the publication of *Lac Spirituale* and *Cinco tratadillos evangelicos* attributed to Valdés, the famous reformer from Cuenca and doctrinaire of Naples. By then he had also become known as a specialist of this branch of literary history with his book on *Francisca Hernández* and several articles and essays distributed in English and German journals.

One must humbly concede that this new book by the Saxon professor exceeds what the Republic of Letters expected from his widely acknowledged and acclaimed scholarship. The published volume begins (fairly enough) with Wiffen's biography written by his niece and with incidents relating to the reprinting of the *Reformistas* written by Wiffen himself, something he saw as a preamble to his planned library. The remainder of the volume is filled with bibliographical information on Juan and Alfonso de Valdés, Francisco and Jaime de Enzinas, and Juan Díaz.

The work on the Valdés brothers can be regarded as prototype of how the rest are to follow. Few times have I seen brought together in one work such wealth of material, such exactitude and care, such delicate attention to minor detail. Dr. Boehmer calls attention to and details the slightest of differences, practically imperceptible to a less scrutinising and experienced eye, I am sure. He knows how to tell apart the early printings of the Valdesian *Dialogues* with remarkable precision, some being so alike they all appear to be from the same edition. The bibliography of the brothers from Cuenca is made up of a hundred and eleven articles classified by the professor, comprising in it detailed information of diplomatic papers drawn out by Alfonso about Juan's writings and their printings in several languages. Fifty-seven, if I have not miscounted, are the number of editions described or cited in this catalogue. The bibliographical notes are considerable too, but on this Dr. Boehmer's book has now been surpassed, as we are about to see, by Fermín Caballero.

Concerning Francisco de Enzinas, much light had already been shed on him with the publication of his *Memorias* by the History Society of Belgium in 1862, but his biography is better illustrated with the documents collected by Dr. Boehmer who has examined the voluminous correspondence addressed to Enzinas, the manuscript of which is entrusted to the Archives of the Protestant Seminary of Strasbourg. We are clear, then, about the full and eventful life of the humanist from Burgos, Professor of Greek at Cambridge, friend of Melanchton's, Crammer, and Calvin. The bibliographical section also is not in want of additional supplements or amendments. However, I regret that the German professor forgot to mention that two of the Plutarch *Lives* were not translated by Enzinas but by Diego Gracián de Alderete, published in Cologne Argentina in 1551: namely, the *Lives* of Themistocles and Camillus, something evident at least to me and also suspected by the Galician bibliographer Manuel Acosta in his letter to Bartolomé Jose Gallardo. This was probably because he had no occasion to examine personally Lucian's *Dialogues*, printed in Lyon in 1550, and Lucian's *Historia verdadera* in Argentina (Strasbourg) in 1551, he chanced not to confirm them as being Enzina's versions, nor did he notice that the former includes a translation in Castilian verse of one of Mosco's idylls. But his critical sagacity makes him guess the truth about *Historia verdadera* and we can and should believe the same about *Dialogos*, easily proven when we examine typographic particulars and especially the style of both books.

On the subject of the death of Juan Díaz, Boehmer collates his contemporaries' reports with great care, and though he does not refine he does at least elucidate considerably on the history of that sad and disastrous event. Worked also into Enzinas' biography is the little we know of his brother Jaime and Francisco de San Román.

What singles out *Bibliotheca Wiffeniana*, apart from its copious and faithful scholarship, is to find the professor effectively distancing himself from the fervent sectarian spirit that had so often stained Usoz and Wiffen's books. With a slight varying of some words and withdrawing of some precepts, they could easily be translated from English into Spanish. The Strasbourg professor wants and knows how to be a philologist and a bibliographer: that is why his work will always be consulted with benefit and neither friends nor foes will view it as a suspect source. We await, then, the publication of the second volume and his study on Michael Servetus whom Boehmer did not cover in his *Bibliotheca* because it was his consideration, and rightly so, that of the general group of heterodox of that period, he, Servetus, stands out as the one and separate personality, the most vigorous Anti-Trinitarian spokesman Aragon had produced and who was ultimately to fall victim to Calvin's hatred.

Thankfully however works on Servetus abound. Soon they will satisfy the most demanding. In 1839, Trechsel published the first book on the history of Unitarian Protestants, all of it devoted to Servetus. In 1844, the Society of History and Archaeology of Geneva inserted in volume III of its *Memorias* an extensive extract from his trial. In 1848, Emile Saisset analyzed, with due French brilliance, our heretic's character, works, and his theological and philosophical system. In 1855, an anonymous biography was published in Madrid, and the following year a series of studies in *Revista de Instrucción Pública*, signed by the librarian from Oviedo Aquilino

Suárez Bárcena. Lastly, and leaving other minor studies aside, Magdeburg's theologian Dr. Tollin has shown and continues to show with very laudable German meticulosity though with serious errors on dogma, the life and doctrine of Michael Servetus. Tollin's principal work, *Das Lehrsystem Michael Servet,* occupies no less than three volumes and be it in pamphlets or journals he has so far published the following *Memorias* and a few others besides: *Luther and Servetus, Melanchton and Servetus, Childhood and Youth of Servetus, Servetus and the Bible, Servetus and the Diet of Ausburg, Servetus and Bucer, Michael Servetus as Geographer, Michael Servetus as Doctor, the Pantheism of Servetus.* He has announced he intends to follow with *Servetus: Discoverer of the Circulation of the Blood.* One could not ask for more: we have here a true *Bibliotheca Servitiana.*

No less could be said of the works about Juan de Valdés. Of them all, the first prize goes to volume 4 of *Conquenses ilustres* – Fermín Caballero´s last book, noble gentleman of an era long gone whom I was fortunate to meet and know in his last years as pupil and friend. We all saw him consecrate his robust and laborious old age to the exaltation of the glories of the province of Cuenca, his birthplace, and one after another from his pen came the biographies of Hervás y Panduro, our best philologist; of Melchor Cano, one of our better theologians; of Alfonso Díaz de Montalvo, one of the Fathers of our Jurisprudence, and finally of the brothers Juan and Alfonso Valdés which is what interests us here. Volume 4 of the *Hijos Ilustres de Cuenca,* in addition to collating and summing up results from former studies includes many new data and settles questions relative to the birthplace, parentage and kinship of the Valdés brothers and expels all doubts until then expressed by some scholars. All of Alfonso's life, as far as it is possible to do so, is accounted for; his theological stand is stated beyond any doubt, his relationship with Erasmus made clear - an important point not deeply looked into until then; he expands also the catalogue of diplomatic documents he had subscribed to, and in regards to Juan, ample elucidation of his doctrine, his teaching, his disciples... Surely this work, in accuracy and certitude, exceeds all that former biographers (Usoz, Wiffen, Boehmer, Stern included) had written.

Written with the elegant simplicity characteristic of the author of *Población rural,* most fitting to this line of study, this book is accompanied by an appendix of eighty-five documents, among them more than thirty unpublished letters either by or addressed to Alfonso Valdés, kept in the fine collection of *Cartas de Erasmo y otros* in the library of the *Real Academia de la Historia.* This section is much enriched by some hereto-unknown papers taken from the archives of Simancas and the city of Cuenca which perhaps naturally enough escaped many otherwise diligent foreign writers.

It has been Juan de Valdés' good fortune to have had such eminent biographers and commentators, one after another. And a well deserved prize too (his errors notwithstanding) to such a dazzling writer, for his prose is a model of Castilian prose of whom David Rogers said: *Valdesio hispanus scriptore superbiat orbis!*

Shortly before his death, Fermín Caballero was working on the biography of an old heterodox - Gonzalo de Cuenca, and those of Juan Díaz and Constantino de la Fuente. They were left virtually completed and ready for press, something that will soon be done, one hopes, to make up in some measure for the irreparable loss that Spanish scholarship suffered since the death of this eminent author.

If we add to the books and *Memorias* above cited four more articles on *España protestante* written in the French language by Guardia in *Revistas de ambos mundos* and *Germanica* on occasion of the publications of M'Crae, Castro and Usoz, we would have now mentioned almost all that has been published during the course of the last few years about the Reformation in Spain. The material has for the most part been gathered and its history can now be written. If only Pedro José Pidal who first thought of this idea were here to carry it out we would all be reading a history written with clarity and wisdom and not this arid and feeble chronicle I am here submitting. It was Pidal who first among us initiated this genre of studies (only McCrae's work was available) when he published in 1848 his article *De Juan de Valdés y si es autor del Diálogo de las lenguas*, had in his mind the project of *Historia de la reforma en España*. He even left three or four notes to this purpose among his papers; but other tasks diverted his attention and the work was never carried through.

Of other heterodox manifestations before or after the Reformation little has been written, at least in explicit monographs. Vicente de la Fuente, with his characteristic mastery as a canonist and expositor included some in chapters on *Historia eclesiástica*. [24] To him we owe also *Historia de las sociedades secretas en España*, and several other useful opuscules. The biographies of each heterodox and other dispersed writings will be found in their respective places as also essays regarding the history of the magic arts, where the work of José Amador de los Rios is prominent.

So whether I have a calling to write this history or not (for I am not too sure myself), I am convinced of the magnitude of the task and aware of its significance. I have observed with anguish of heart that with few exceptions only dissenting foreign writers had exploited this issue and so a while back I conceived the idea of writing *Historia de los Heterodoxos españoles* myself. Please note that, for a change, this is a history written from a Spanish and a Catholic perspective.

In addition to what is already out there, I plan to bring my own research and my own judgements about events and people, in my opinion little or ill studied. This is because the history of our Protestants would have no meaning and be virtually futile were we to judge it in isolation and as separate from the general picture and whole context of Iberian heterodoxy. It should not be a work apart but a chapter, the longest though perhaps not even the most important, of a book in which the origin, growth, and vicissitudes of all doctrines in Spain opposed to Catholicism, though born of it, are presented.

Every person who strayed in this or that direction from orthodoxy will have their due page in this book: Priscillian, Elipando and Félix, Hostegesis, Claudius, Spanish Mauritius, Arnaldo de Vilanova, Fray Tomas Scotus, Pedro de Osma…all of

---

[24]   Second edition (1873-1875)

these have the same right to appear as do Valdés, Enzinas, Servetus, Constantino, Cazalla, Casiodoro de Reina, or Cipriano de Valera.

Honest and sincere Protestants will shout and scream to see themselves sitting next to Alumbrados and Quietists, Jansenists and Encyclopaedists. Devotees of modern *nouvelles philosophies* will complain they are being mixed up with the witches of Logroño! It cannot be helped. They will all appear here, each and every one of them as if on a *tabula de excommunio*. Rest assured that we will deal honourably and fairly with all, according to each one's merits.

I thought that a title like *History of our heterodox* would be broader and more comprehensive than *History of our heretics*. They all have something in common in that they were all Catholics first and went their separate ways later, wholly or in part, from the teachings of the church be this under protests of submission or not, to take another religion, or to take none.

This history then comprises:

a) What properly and more generally is called heresy, that is to say, error in some element of dogma or in several, but as a minimum not denying Revelation.

b) Impiety, in all the varied names and forms it takes: deism, naturalism, pantheism, atheism, etc.

c) Occult sects and *iluminados*. Devil cults and witchcraft. Idolatrous residues. Fatalist superstitions, etc.

d) Apostasy (Judaizers, Moriscos, etc.) though strictly speaking all heretics are apostates. [1]

---

[1]   One ought to be careful not to confuse schism and heresy with scholastic disagreements which verse only on the form of theological knowledge without altering its content, or with opinions and controversies that have not been expressly and doctrinally resolved by the Church. But as in ecclesiastical history all is linked, and heresies cannot be presented in isolation, we will have to treat also of the general movement of religious ideas in each epoch, which does not mean that we will have the temerity to brand anyone as a heretic if the Infallible Cathedra of Truth has not condemned their doctrine. This warning is particularly necessary when it comes to certain persons in the eighteenth and nineteenth centuries who did not evidently separate themselves from Catholic communion, but whose actions, ideas, and writings I consider censurable within the historical criteria that I shall apply with all liberty and frankness. No one particular individual, least of all I, layman and unqualified, is here to grant or withdraw orthodoxy patents to or from anyone. The qualifications of this book have not, therefore, any more worth than that of my own personal judgement and of the documents that back me up.

I do not hold the vain presumption that I have achieved certainty, but I have endeavoured to apply to the subject matter of which I am writing those *sapientisimas* rules of criticism that Benedict XIV gave to the censors of books in his illustrious constitution *Sollicita et Provida*.

"III: De variis opinionibus, atque sententiis in unoquoque libro contentis, animo a praejudiciis omnibus vacuo, iudicandum sibi esse sciant. Itaque nationis, familiae, scholae, instituti affectum excutiant; studia partium seponant; Ecclesiae sanctae dogmata, et communem catholicorum doctrinam, quae conciliorum generalium decretis, romanorum Pontificum constitutionibus, et orthodoxorum patrum, atque doctorum consensu continetur, unice prae oculis habeant; hoc de caetero cogitantes, *non paucas esse opiniones, quae uni scholae, instituto, aut nationi certo certioris videntur, et nihilominus, sine ullo fidei, aut religionis detrimento, ab aliis*

We shall also treat in passing of issues other than the above in order to defend persons defamed or accused of heterodoxy, and to make explicitly clear the relationship between heterodoxy and social, political and literary history, etc. I will try to do this as clearly and clearly as I can.

But this history, as all history, has its limits of time and place. It begins with the origins of our Church and will finish with the last system or heretical propaganda divulgated in Spain up to the point and time I shall close the last volume. J

For a long time I hesitated as to whether to include persons still alive for I judge it a literary courtesy to respect them and more so in a sensitive matter easily given to complications since it does touch the tabernacle of one's conscience. Certainly, had there reigned Catholic unity in Spain, I would not have included them because I do not want this work to denounce or defame anyone, something totally opposed to my intention here and contrary to my character. But since against the will of the majority of Spanish people our legislators decreed what they like to call *Religious Tolerance*, which in effect means freedom to worship whomsoever and in whichever way one sees fit, I ask you: who am I hurting by writing about a person's religious leaning and pointing to elements that are considerably harmful to the prevailing atmosphere of moral confusion Spaniards are now going through? Am I perchance unveiling any secret when I treat of opinions that their own authors, far from hiding them, divulge from rooftops in books and magazines, in lectures and speeches? Yet to banish all suspicion, I shall disregard (with very rare exceptions) in this last part of my history private papers, correspondence, etc. What I write shall be based solely on published material, public appearances and official documents. What to some will prove to be disagreeable will be to see recounted and exposed here their progression from good to bad and bad to worse, their false assertions of Catholicism and other lapses that have no doubt been forgotten. But *littera scripta manet*. I am not the one to blame for things having happened in this way and not in some other.

---

catholicis viris rejiciuntur, atque impugnatur, oppositaeque defenduntur, sciente ac permittente Apostolica Sede, quae unamquamque opinionem huiusmodi in suo probabilitatis gradu relinquit.

"IV. Hoc quoque diligenter animadvertendum monemus haud rectum iudicium de vero auctoris sensu fieri posse, nisi omni ex parte illius liber legatur, quaeque diversa in locis posita, et collocata sunt, inter se comparentur; universum praeterea auctoris consilium, et institutum attente dispiciatur, neque vero ex una, vel altera propositione a suo contextu divulsa, vel seorsim ab aliis, quae eodem libro continentur, considerata et expensa, de ea pronunciandum esse; saepe enim accidit, ut quod ab auctore in aliquo operis loco perfunctorie, aut suboscure traditum est, ita alio in loco distincte, copiose ac dilucide explicatur, ut offusae priori sententiaw tenebrae quibus involuta pravi sensus speciem exhibetat, penitus dispellatur, omnisque labis expers propositio dignoscatur.

"V. Quod si ambigua quaedam exciderint auctori; qui alioquin catholicus sit, et integra religionis, doctrinaeque fama, aequitas ipsa postulare videtur, ut eius dicta benigne, quantum licuerit, explicata, in bonam partem accipiantur."

J   Afterwards I thought better of it and so that the work might not be interminable and without interest, I preferred to take the Constitution of 1876 as the place to end. This is the date after all when government established *religious tolerance* by decree, and this same date I preserve in the present edition.

As far as geographical places, this book embraces all of Spain, that is, the whole of the Hispanic Peninsula, ill-called Iberian because the unity of history, and of this one more than any other, prevents us from paying heed to artificial political divisions. At the same time and with the same characteristics did heterodoxy develop in Portugal as in Castile. To study it in one of the kingdoms and not the other means leaving many issues incomplete and unexplained. This is why next to Francisco de Enzinas we will see Damián de Goes and next Cipriano de Valera, Juan Ferreira de Almeida; Oliveira will head the list of the scarce number of Protestants in the last century, and the famous author of *Tentativa teológica* along with the canonists at the court of Carlos III will be for us the exemplar of Spanish Jansenism.

History has to show unity of thought lest it degenerate into a mere anthology of facts more or less curious or exotic. It is therefore proper that we establish clearly the one underlying criterion common to all these pages.

The history of Spanish heterodoxy could be written in three ways:

a) from the perspective of absolute indifference, i.e. not assessing the merit of differing doctrines, or by weighing these against some indecisive and dithering judgement camouflaging itself under the cloak of fairness or impartiality or objectivity.

b) from a heterodox, Protestant, or rationalist perspective, or

c) from an orthodox Catholic standpoint.

I do not think it should be written with indifference that passes for impartiality. One could only take this approach (and with great difficulty I would submit) when narrating facts about external acts, battles, diplomatic negotiations, conquests (and these only as to their outcomes not their causes) but never on a history of doctrines or books where inevitably critical judgement has to decide between good and bad, light or shadow, truth or error. Criticism has to submit itself to a standing principle and judge each and every particular case with reference to that principle. And of necessity from the moment the author begins to do this, he does lose that strict impartiality which, by the way, many publicize and very few keep, and he ends up having to face the crux of the dilemma: either he views it from the standpoint that I judge heterodox, that is, Protestant or Rationalist depending on whether he does or does not accept Revelation, or bows his head to Catholic truth (blessed humility) from which he will be given light and guidance in analysis and judgment. If the goal of an historian is to use criticism merely to state actions and collect news, I believe he is forfeiting the title of being such: he will be putting together excellent bibliographies such as Dr. Boehmer's but he will not be writing history.

I am no fatalist. I have never doubted and will never doubt human free will nor do I believe, as Hegelians do, on the identity of contrary propositions, both of them true, as manifestations of the *Idea* or diverse developments of the *Absolute*. Nor do I judge history merely as observable and experiential material, as Positivists do. No, I am a Catholic. And as a Catholic I affirm Providence, I affirm Revelation, I affirm free will, and I affirm the moral law – the basis of all history. And if the history I am to write is a history of religious ideas and these ideas contest with mine and with the doctrine of the church, what am I to do but denounce them? By the laws of logic and by the rule of an honest man and sincere believer, I have an obligation to do so.

So the reader will ask: Have you forgotten you are supposed to be objective? When are you keeping impartiality for? Is not impartiality the first quality of a narrator as all textbooks of *conscribenda historia* have maintained from Lucian to the present day?

The answer is easy: my history will be *partial* (and please forgive the inexact use of the word, for history is not part but whole). Partial on principles; impartial, that is to say, unreservedly true, on facts. I shall do my best not to allow my love for the holy cause to draw me towards injustice against its utmost adversaries. I shall respect all that is noble and worthy of respect, never seeking to find sordid or mean motives in actions that human precepts know are laudable. In short, I shall proceed with charity towards persons, with no indulgence whatever towards error. I will tell the truth plain and whole to Thyrians and Trojans alike, not retreating from any find and hiding nothing because Catholicism, which is light, hates the shadows, and no truth can be hostile to ultimate truth, for all are reflections of it and all are enkindled and purified in its radiance.

> For truth is word of God, severe
>
> And the word of God is never silent.[25]

Rest assured, reader, that when true, no facts brought to the open by non-Catholic writers will be missing from my history - I will even add new ones worthy of being known. No sectarian will outdo me on the scrupulosity with which I shall try to clarify and verify associations (as far as my weak strength will allow) and do justice to all. In fact I might well be branded as one who holds more than due regard and affection, perhaps excessive, for some of our heretics, those whose moral or literary qualities seem to me worthy of praise. But on this I am following the example of the great Christian controversialists though in other matters I am a hundred leagues apart. No one has manifested more affection for the character of Melanchton than Bossuet did in *Historia de las Variaciones*, and if theologians sense some excess on my part, I ask their forgiveness on account of my profane learning which perhaps makes me appreciate more than it is fair certain ethical and aesthetical conditions that, being in the nature of natural gifts, God has equally granted to Gentiles with abundance and does not cease to bestow on those who with deliberate and stubborn blindness depart from His law.

And what is one to say to a person who tries to write a history such as this from a heterodox perspective? I would say that whatever he writes is bound, even before he begins, to find no rationale for anything whatever. He will not be able to

---

25   Francisco de Quevedo y Villegas (1580-1645).

find his way out of such a tangled labyrinth. He will give us fragments of history but he will not give us a body of history. And the reason for this is clear: how is a writer biased against Catholicism to speak of anything Spanish if, by being so, he starts by not getting to the core of the Spanish psyche? How will he understand the historical reasons for the birth and death of all the heretical, impious and superstitious doctrines that grew on our soil, precisely when these heresies, impieties and superstitions are, for us, isolated phenomena, loose links in our cultural chain, plants that when deprived of their nutritive sap simply wither and die, veritable intellectual aberrations that can only be explained precisely by relating them to the keystone they are running away from? How can a writer writing from an anti-Catholic perspective even begin to explain why Protestantism in sixteenth century Spain did not take root, a Protestantism sustained by eminent writers such as Juan de Valdés, learned Hellenists like Francisco de Enzinas and Pedro Nuñez Vela, distinguished Judaizers like Antonio del Corro and Casiodoro de Reina, intellectuals full of vivacity and talent such as the forgotten author of *El Crotalón,* [L] and tireless propagandists in the manner of Julián Fernández and Cipriano de Valera? How is it that a doctrine that found echo in the palaces of magnates, in army quarters, university classrooms and monasteries, a doctrine not lacking in both social and religious precedents; a doctrine that managed to establish secret associations in Valladolid and Seville, how was it that this doctrine totally disappears in the course of a short number of years leaving no more trace behind than a few fugitives who publish their books in foreign lands, unread and scoffed at in Spain?

To say it was fanaticism, religious intolerance, the rigours of the Spanish Inquisition and good old Philip II, forgive me, but that is to confuse the effect with the cause. That is to resort to common havens that not by a long shot serve to resolve the difficulty. Could the Inquisition have existed if the underlying principle that gave life to this tribunal, a tribunal popular with the majority of the population by the way, had not from ancient times been incarnate in the thoughts and in the conscientiousness of the Spanish people? If the Protestantism of Germany or Geneva had not been repugnant to the religious sentiment of our fathers, could the Inquisition, Philip II or any other power on earth been enough to alter the fact that these new doctrines did not take hold, not a bit, in our land? That, in time, different churches and congregations would not settle in each town? That the Bible without explanatory notes not be printed in Romance publicly or secretly? That Prayer Books, *Dialogues* and reformed confessions not set triumphal foot in our soil despite a most strict vigilance by the Holy Office, as indeed tried Julianillo Hernández who brought these books in wineskins and barrels via Jaca and the Aragon Pyrenees? Why did Spanish Lutherans succumb without protest and without a fight? Why didn't the religious wars that covered Germany and neighbourly France in blood implant themselves here among us? Were the few drops of blood shed in the *autos*

[L]   Today I think it proven that the author of this book and of others no less curious was Cristóbal de Villalón. But I do not consider him to have been Protestant but an Eramist, as I shall try to prove when I write on his life and work.

of Valladolid and Seville enough to drown them all at birth? Indeed, by the same token, the horrendous events of Saint-Barthélemy, the furores of the League, and the frightful laws of the Duke of Alba in Flanders should have been sufficient in those countries too! Do we not see, instead, that almost the whole of the Pensinsula stayed free of that contagion and that except for two or three cities we hardly find any vestiges of Protestant organization anywhere?

Let us not deceive ourselves. There is nothing more unpopular in Spain than heresy, and of all heresies, Protestantism. The same happened in Italy. Here as there (even when we leave the religious element aside), the Latin spirit, vivified by the Renaissance, protested with startling outrage against the Reformation - the legitimate offspring of Teutonic individualism. The communal spirit of the Roman character rejected the anarchic variety of Free Interpretation, and Spain, her hands still stained with Moorish blood and having just expelled the Jews, showed in the struggle for the preservation of unity, gained at such high prize, an incredible determination. You may call it harsh, you may call it intolerant if you like, but a noble intolerance. Yes, noble. We, Spaniards, who freed Europe from Muslim fatalism, were we now to open our doors now to the doctrine of *servo arbitrio* (enslavement of the will) and a faith that disconnected faith from conduct? And that is not all we held against the Reformation: even our artistic inner sense clamoured against iconoclast barbarism.

That the danger was great we shall not deny, and among those swept along the whirlwind were some of no little intelligence and others sufficiently formidable on account of their influence and prestige. But what were they, what could they do, all of them together, against a unanimous national sentiment? Even today, in spite of so many attempts to bringing them back, none of these names is popular or even known in Spain. Even our free thinkers disregard and ridicule them. Doesn't this absolute indifference, an entire peoples' disdain prove anything? Does it not show clearly that these men were the interpreters, not of our race, but of their own solitary imaginations? And if more proof were needed even their own writing style would give them away: generally very good, I grant you, but not very Spanish when they start speaking on matters theological. There is something foreign in the best of them (whether they wrote in Latin or Castillian) an aridity, a lack of life and abundance that contrasts very markedly with the general way our authors write on matters theological or in other matters. Compare the style of Juan de Valdés in his *Comentarios a las epistolas de San Pablo* with the Valdés of the *Dialogues* and you will see the difference. Juan Peréz's prose as that of Cipriano de Valera's are more Genevan than Castillian. The Spanish language was not forged to voice heresies. Your knowledge of things Spanish will be scant indeed if all you know of theologians, mystics, and Spanish men of letters is no more than the ten or twelve reformers whose books Usoz printed, or if you believe you can find in them the soul of sixteenth century Spain - something, it seems to me, of what actually happened to Wiffen and other learned foreigners.

To me, the Reformation in Spain is a curious episode and not one of considerable significance. Our Iberian thinking is indeed prone to very serious derailing but in other directions. This is because each time we depart from Catholicism, we cannot just simply rest content with *viae mediae,* in fact we are openly hostile to them. Luther and Calvin are not enough, you see. When we err we don't beat about the bush with reticent excuses - we take error to its final consequences and fling ourselves onto anti-Trinitarism, Rationalism, and more often than not onto a plain and crude Pantheism. This pantheistic germ is easy to see in practically all Spanish heterodox writings of any originality worth noting, but even this is not indigenous: Gnosticism comes from Egypt, Avicebronism and Averroism from Jews and Arabs. The theories of Michael Servetus are but an alteration of neo-Platonism; the Alumbrados and Quietist sects passed through Italy and Germany before coming to our land. Molinonism, which at first sight could be seen (and some have seen) as a home-grown heresy born of our general character, an exaggeration of mysticism run amok, has nothing at all in common with the sublime mysticism of our classics. We know where it came from: the error of the *Illuminati* came from Italy. It was in Italy that Molinos got himself infected with this disease, one that was staunchly fought by us. It did give occasion to a few trials of *beatas* (overly pious women) and old nuns up to the end of the last century, but it never made such noise or produced such scandal and debacle as it did in the France of Louis XIV, nor did it count among us with sectarians as venerated as Francis Le Combe and Joanne Guyon, or found a Fenelon who in good faith came to its defence. Because in Spain the healthy mysticism of our classics proved to be an insuperable wall against aberration, as was also the scarce affection our forefathers held for fine and dainty novelties, though they come dressed in the attire of devotion.

The same can be said for satanic cults and witchcraft - vulgar expressions of Manichaeism, or remnants of pagan worship to infernal divinities. The following are witnesses to the fact that it lives on and keeps itself occult in the Peninsula as in other parts of Europe: the heretics of Ambotto, the narratives of the *El Crotalón*'s author, the *auto-de-fe* of the city of Logroño, the demonological books of Benito Pereiro and Martín del Río, Pedro de Valencia's *Discurso* about witches and things magical, Cervantes' *Coloquio de los perros* …and a thousand more authorities that could be cited. But with us it never reaches the extremes it does in other lands, nor is it ever stopped with the same horrendous cruelty with which it was punished in Germany, or taken as seriously as their challengers proclaim, because unlike us they view it as much more than just superstitious practices. For us it is simply a cloak under which the stupidity or malice of lowlifes and shady characters who attend these secret meetings comes to hide itself, and that is the reason why in our literature our novelists always depict witchcraft and sorcery as something inseparable from and worthy only of those who engage in, let us say, a certain *darning of wills* or businesses affairs proper only to *celestinas*. These general leanings apart, what does Spanish heterodoxy offer us? Obscure names of anti-Trinitarians like Alfonso Lincurio; of Deists, like Uriel da Costa y Prado; one or two Emanatists, like Martinez Pascual; some teophilantropes, like Santa Cruz; a couple of liberal Protestants, like Juan de Calderón; one Quaker, Usoz, … in other words, extravagances. Personal error. And then the inevitable foreign influences: French Jansenism, encouraged and sustained by the civil authorities; Encyclopedism; nouveau German systems; Positivism. But none of these doctrines have managed, and those that are still alive and in vogue with proselytes today will never manage, to avoid the inevitable death that in Spain threatens all doctrines repugnant to our culture, repugnant, that is, to that *mica salis* entrenched in the heart of hearts of all our institutions and beliefs. Let all flamboyant apostles, evangelizers and dogmatizers of fortune be convinced of the fate that awaits them in this unappreciative land. Their names will fall into oblivion until a bibliographer comes to raise them from their ashes, as we today raise the name of Miguel de Monserrate or Sir Oliveira. Their books will go to that honourable library section called *Oddities* keeping company to treasures like *Exemplar humanae vitae, Tratado de la reintegración de los seres, Culto de la humanidad, Unidad simbólica,* and *Armonía del mundo racional.* They'll be placed next to *Analytica*, with its harmonious rationalism, its hypocritical pantheism, its labyrinthic definitions of substance and the concept of man, defined there as *'in, under, through God divine and the union of nature and spirit which, in the scheme of being, is the shape of a lentil'.*

Pray tell, is it even within the realm of possibility that a heterodox writer will leave behind all his preoccupations and fancy reasonings and come to acknowledge and confess the reason why all heresies, superstitions and impieties end up crashing down on our soil and get to live such short, obscure and laborious little lives here? I think not. I think the history of our heterodox can only be written from within a Catholic understanding, and only in Catholicism will it find the unifying principle shining through in all human endeavours, precisely because Catholic dogma is the axis of our culture; our philosophy, our art are and, in a word, all other manifestations upon which the basis of our culture depend, are Catholic, and doctrines contrary to it will never survive. Not one heresy was born in our country, but all came and went, that the words of the Apostle might be fulfilled: *Oportet haereses esse.* [26]

And if it is good that they exist, it is also beneficial for us to study them so that knowledge of what they are and where they come from, when well known and understood, will not allow them to go about dazzling the gullible when after a face-lift these old ladies make their grand entrance again dressed up to the nines in glittering and youthful attire.

The study of heterodoxy's history is beneficial in three ways:

---

[26]   On the benefit of the study of heresies, we should reflect on these two passages from Tertullian and Origenes.

Tertulian (De Praescript. Chapter 1): "Ad hoc enim sunt (haereses) ut fides habendo tentationem, haberet etiam probationem. Vane ergo et inconsiderate plerique hoc ipso scandalizantur, quod tantum haereses valeant quantum si non fuissent".

Origen: (Homilia IX in Num.): "Nan si doctrina ecclesiastica simplex esset, et nullis intrinsecus haereticorum dogmatum assertionibus cingeretur, non poterat tam clara et tam examinata videri fides nostra. Sed idcirco doctrinan catholicam contradicentium obsidet oppugnatio, ut fides nostra non otio porpescat, sed exercitiis elimetur".

a) as a recapitulation of intriguing and forgotten facts - more important that combats and diplomatic treaties;

b) as incidental recollection of literary and even scientific glories, lost or forgotten due to our laxity and neglect;

c) because as all history of human aberration it contains great and very useful lessons. It serves to knock down the arrogance of Masters of Intellect and Reason and show them that the high and lofty cedar can fall just as well as the humble shrub, and if Priscillian, Arnaldo de Vilanova, Pedro de Osma, Valdés, Enzina and Blanco went down, what head can believe itself not subject to fainting or collapse?

I will summarise briefly what the capital and underlying thought running through this book is, and it is this: The Spanish character is eminently Catholic: Heterodoxy is for us an accident, a passing storm. It is for the reader to judge whether this conclusion can be reached from the large number of facts I shall relate here as an honest and faithful narrator.

I should now explain the order and interrelationship of the issues dealt with in these volumes, their outline as it were, and on this I shall be succinct for I dislike leaving the reader standing on the doorway for long though it seems to be in the best tradition of history writing to begin a book with prolix and tedious introductions.

Our church was born in the bosom of the Apostle's sacred word and that of the apostolic men St. Peter sent to our country. It was distilled and purified in the fires of persecution and martyrdom and from her very inception she shows herself resolute in battle and wise and rigorous in discipline. The only disturbance at this otherwise glorious time is the apostasy of the *libeláticos* Basilides and Martial, of some remaining vestiges of superstition condemned at the Council of Elvira, and the support given by Spanish Lucilla to the Donatists of Carthage. In the fifth century, the Priscillian heresy provides us with ample material for discussion on all questions pertaining to its origins, diffusion, literature and its theological-philosophical system. We shall not forget the Ithacian and Originist reactions represented by the two Aviti from Braga.

Among the heresies during the Visigoth era, Arianism stands out (though it was not accepted by even a minimal part of the Spanish population) but against which the Hispano-Latin episcopate, defender of the faith and of western civilisation, had to fight hard-fought battles. It is gratifying to watch its defeat, first in Galicia under the Swabian domination and later at the Third Council of Toledo during Recared's reign. But these were not the only dangers closing in on the Spanish peoples: Nestorianism, denounced in 431 by the presbyters Vitalisand Constantius to St. Capreolo; Manichaeism, preached in the lands of León and Extremadura by Pacentius; one bishop's materialism, whose name was silenced by his energetic adversary Licinianus; the heresy of the Acefalli, spread by a Syrian bishop throughout Andalucia, and so forth.

We are not surprised to find during the miserable century that followed (the eighth, first in the Spanish Reconquest) again some bright know-it-alls clouding up the purity of the faith of some troubled spirits, though thankfully its defence was not in want of zealous champions either. A controversy which bears witness to both is that between Beatus and Heterius against the heresy of Elipando of Toledo and Félix of Urgel which was enough to send the whole Christian world into commotion, with Alcuin, Paulinus of Aquilia and Abogard picking up their valiant pens to refute it.

Following an analysis of this heresy with its origins and consequences, there will follow a study of heterodoxy among the *mozarabes* of Córdoba i.e. the apostasy of Bodo Eleazaro, spiritedly challenged by Alvarus of Córdoba; new errors like those of the *Casians* or *Acefalli* condemned by the Council of Córdoba in 839; the weakness of Recafred, [27] and the last and perhaps most hideous, the Anthropomorphism of bishop Hostegesis against whose vulgar and materialistic teaching rose the abbot Sansom with his eloquent *Apologia*.

More troubles and tribulations in the ninth century, not in Spain this time but in Italy by *Spanish Claudius*, bishop of Turin and disciple of Felix which once again brought back the fanaticism of Byzantium's iconoclasts trying to defend it in his curious *Apologeticon* convincingly repudiated by Jonas Aurelianensis and Dungalo. We shall not forget another Spanish sage, Prudentius Galindus, bishop of Troyes, one of the many who flourished in Gaul during the Carolingian domination. The reason he belongs in this history is twofold: as one falsely accused of heresy, and as one who brilliantly discredited the opinions of John Scotus Eurigena, teacher to Charles the Bold.

In the tenth and eleventh centuries Spain managed to stay free of error (save from puerile points found by grammarians). I end this second book of my history in 1085, date of the memorable reconquest of Toledo. This armed conflict was to bring significant changes to our culture. Two influences began to hold sway at the same time. One of them was the ultra-Pyrenean or Gaullicist influence, supported by our own kings and encouraged by the general spirit of the times which forced us to the changing of our Rite with heartbreaking anguish to the Spanish soul (perhaps in the end beneficial in as much as it tightened our bond to all other Christian peoples). In so doing, Spain sacrificed her glorious tradition at the altar of Unity. The national sentiment wept, and to this day we feel the grief of the consequences of that change. We conceded because what we were giving up was not after all something absolutely indispensable and it brought us closer to Rome. Spain has always throughout the whole of our history been faithful to the see of Peter.

The ways and means by which the Semitic influence implanted itself in Spanish learning is not as well known as it ought to be though it is extremely important for the history of ideas in Western Europe. In the twelfth century, the

---

[27]   I do not mean to say here that Recafred was heterodox, only that his weakness as leader was cause for apostasies.

learning of Arabs and Jews gave way to grave errors of doctrine when, through the college of interpreters that archbishop Raimundo instituted in Toledo and thanks to the assiduous labour of Hebrews and *mozarabes*, the philosophical writings of Avicena, Algazel, Alfarabi, Avicebron and others were successively translated. The most illustrious of these translators, Domingo Gundisalvo, archdeacon of Segovia, taught openly the principal ideas of the Alexandrine school in his treatise *De Processione mundi*, drinking at *Fuente de la Vida* (*Fons Vitae*) written by the great Jewish poet Aben Gabirol. When these doctrines spread throughout the classrooms of Paris on account of the books and translations of Gundisalvo, Juan Hispalensis and other foreigners who desirous of oriental knowledge visited Toledo, a new and formidable heresy cropped up, the leaders of which, twice anathematised, were Amaury de Chartres, David de Dinant, and *Spanish Mauritius*. Hispano-Semitic pantheism continued to contaminate Scholastics during the thirteenth century, but no longer as *avicebronism* but as *averroism*, and the *theory of intelecto uno*. That was how Albert the Great and St. Thomas Aquinas combated it. But notwithstanding its defeat, and having been turned into banner, flag and pretext for all impieties then fermenting, it touched the very limits of scandal during the turbulent and obscure fourteenth century and as far as Spain was concerned embodied in the singular figure of Fray Tomas Scotus and in the mythical blasphemy (not a book) '*De tribus impostoribus*'.

The duplicitous Averroist distinction between theological and philosophical truth provoked the vigorous Lullian reaction which, by going beyond its due limits, blurred the boundaries of both camps, tilting towards the theory of *propedeutic faith* (quite against the authors' intention). We find gleams of this in several of the master's books and in the Prologue to the treatise *Las Criaturas* by Raimundo Sabunde: hence the Dominicans' opposition and the impassioned controversy between Thomists and Lullians - Eymerich being the one sticking his neck out here and breaking the first lances.

But along with study of controversies in the Schools, we must also study those in the public square, simply because abstract ideas have a way of trickling down into action. We shall therefore have to enter into the labyrinth of heresies among the common people during the Middle Ages and direct our inquiry to the scarce vestiges they left in Spain along the way. The Albigensians, with one such Arnaldo as their leader in the land of León; the Valdenses, *Insabattatos* and *Poor of Lugduno*, chased in Catalonia by the edicts of Pedro the Catholic, later himself defender of the heretics of Provençe; the Bergards or Beguines, sectarians all who (under diverse names) resembled each other in their aspiration for social renewal. No more than a few names and dates are recorded in this period. Durán de Huesca, Pedro Oler, Fray Bonanato, Durán de Baldach, Jacobo Yusti, Bartolomé Janoessio and other activists have barely left more than their own names in Eymerich's invaluable pages.

We know much more about those who dreamed of the near coming of the Kingdom of the Millenium or *Milenarios* who fixed the exact date of the coming of the Antichrist, at the same time clamouring (untimely and with no true vocation for it) for reforms in the church. They saw themselves as *iluminados* and prophets, in their outbursts showing a marked propensity to secularism. An eminent doctor, Arnaldo de Vilanova, made himself apostle of such views, followed by Juan de Peratallada (*Ruperscissa*) and one or two other visionaries. With them joined the mystics in favour of the prophecies of Abbot Joaquin and of the *Eternal Gospel.*

The personal extravagances of Gonzalo de Cuenca, Nicolás de Calabria, Raimundo de Tárrega, Pedro Riera, etc., contributed to the confusion. The *Fraticelli* sect, known to us as the *Heretics of Durango*, served as a bridge between the old Beguines and the Alumbrados of the sixteenth century.

Pedro de Osma, a Spanish Jan Huss, or Wycliffe, true precursor of the pseudo-Reformation, closes the Middle Ages. Henceforth heterodoxy will be characterised by free interpretation and the abandonment of the principle of authority.

But before moving on to studying the great crisis, we will do well to say farewell to Averroism which by the sixteenth century was in its last legs in the school of Padua. There taught Juan Montes de Oca, from Seville, in whom we notice (in addition to defending the supposed opposition between theological and philosophical truth) a leaning towards the disastrous audacities that by then his co-professor Pedro Pomponazzi was already propagating.

The capital event of the sixteenth century, the so-called Reformation, reached Spain at its very start. Its way had been smoothed out by the published reprinting and translations of the scathing writings of Erasmus. The arguments instigated by these books aroused a sordid agitation of passions, both prelude and warning of an impending storm. Among his defenders were many orthodox that did so in good faith. His adversaries did not lack authority or credibility either. If on the one side we find archbishop Fonseca, Fray Alonso de Virués, Juan de Vergara (who without approving everything Erasmus said tended to excuse him moved by their mutual friendship and the prestige of Erasmus learning), fighting on the other side was Diego López de Stúñiga, Sancho Carranza de Miranda, and later, Carvajal y Sepúlveda. The strength of the camps was about equal; the dispute, however, was not to last long, overtaken by events, and after Erasmus came Luther which made it rather risky to call oneself an Eramist. Of those in Spain who followed his voice very few went as far as the ultimate consequences - perhaps Pedro de Lerma and Mateo Pascual; Alfonso de Valdés and Damián de Goes did so for sure: both are two steps away from Lutheranism despite their timidity and vacillations. Carlos V's secretary showed very clearly his religious leanings in *Dialogo de Lactancio,* and in much of his political acts. Concerning the Portuguese reporter, documents of his trial make it rather clear what his real tendencies were.

But the first who resolutely threw himself in the thwarted path of free interpretation was Juan de Valdés, the most noble, affable, and the most elegant writer of all Spanish heretics. He started, as they all start, with mockeries and contemptuous jokes against Rome in *Dialogo de Mercurio y Caron* but he soon grew tired of the first reformers' ideas and started professing a new genre of asceticism. Since he was willing to apply the principle of individual interpretation of Scripture in all its rigour, he was branded a Unitarian, though orthodox Protestants vehemently denied this. In Valdés' hands, the crude and academic Protestantism of the Germans was transformed, one may say latinised, as far as this is possible. Its style became tender, poetic, flattering, fine tuned I suppose to the ears of the lovely and demure Julia Gonzaga, Diotima to this new Socrates. Poetic too, I am sure, was the way he taught her at his side by the banks of the river Chiaja, looking out onto the magnificent gulf of Naples, where nature brought and reflected all its harmonies into one.

To this first generation of Spanish Protestants belong the Hellenist Francisco de Enzinas, disciple of Melanchton and man of pilgrim adventures described in part by himself; also, Juan Díaz, Jaime de Enzinas and Francisco de San Román, first victims of these early transmutations.

But Michael Servetus obscures them all. He is the most original, the most profound thinker coming out of that windstorm, the very incarnation of that spirit of rebelliousness and adventure that others followed with more timidity and less logic. He would later be sacrificed at the altar of Protestant intolerance: a case of free interpretation now being frightened by what it had itself wrought but lacking the courage to face its consequences. We shall have the opportunity when we come to write of Servetus to investigate the origin of his theological doctrine, the points that separate and distinguish it from Socinianism and other anti-Trinitarian heresies, and we shall also appreciate the neo-platonic element evident in his theory of the *Logos* and the similarities and differences between this pantheism and others present in the history of philosophy, especially our own. As to his anti-Trinitarianism, Servetus had only one disciple in the sixteenth century: the Catalan Alfonso Lincurio of whom we know little more than his name.

All Protestants cited here who form this first group (Servetus and Lincurio in a group by themselves) dogmatised, wrote, and ended their lives outside of Spain. But the Reformation came to Spain soon after and formed two principal focuses, two churches (profaning the word is not my intention - I am using it only in its etymological sense) in Valladolid and Seville. The former led by Dr. Cazalla branching out in Toro, Zamora, and other parts of Old Castile, and *licenciado* Herrezuelo who distinguished himself from among all other spokesmen.

In Seville, the first heretic was a extremist, Rodrigo de Valer, with whom the Inquisition was proving to be a little too tolerant. There was great turmoil at the time due to the frustrated ambitions of master Egidio, the active propaganda of Juan Pérez and his emissary Julián Hernández and the sermons of Master Constantino. Two *autos de fe* in Seville and another two in Valladolid were enough to dissipate that summer cloud but I point out that the magnitude of the blood shed was nevertheless far less than any liberal tolerant government today is prepared to shed to repress a military uprising or some small town mutiny.

The fugitives from Seville sought asylum in Holland, Germany and England from where Casiodoro de Reina, Antonio del Corro, Cipriano de Valera and Reinaldo González de Montes dispatched their biblical renderings and their spiteful and libellous books. But the cause they were defending had been totally defeated in Spain now, and their efforts and protests were to no effect.

Along with the Reformation and sometimes favoured by it, the mysterious sects of the Alumbrados began to raise their heads with their false and grating mysticism and their scorn for hierarchy and liturgical ritual. The successive trials in Toledo, Extremadura, Seville and elsewhere denounced the existence of several heretical centres used also for immoral practices. The moment they were destroyed they would immediately shoot up again like the heads of Hydra. No effort by the Holy Office was enough to eradicate them.

The whole of the seventeenth century is but a sequel to the previous one. The only thing to be noted, apart from some Protestants like Nicolás Sacharles, Tejeda, Juan de Luna and Salgado (voices without sound or consequence) is something like a renaissance of the doctrines of the *Iluminados* reduced to a system of doctrine by Miguel de Molinos. Quietism came to introduce in the midst of Christian Europe the devastating theories of annihilation and oriental *nirvana*. Protestants clapped their hands seeing an ally in Molinonism: we have enough documentation to testify to this. Rome condemned the error and punished its founders. Their train of admirers was less in Spain than elsewhere.

Judaizers and Moriscos, the *plomos of Sacro-Monte*, freethinkers and deists who had taken refuge in Amsterdam (Prado, Uriel de Costa, etc.) complete the picture of this epoch of degeneration and residue. [1] The magic arts, which seemed to have come to their high point in the *Auto of Logroño* began to decline then and throughout the course of that century.

In the eighteenth century, Protestants are rare and of little account (Alvarado, Enzina, Sandóval); Alumbrados and Molinonists are rarer by the day.

---

[1]   It is worth noting the propensity of the Judaizers of this time towards pantheism and deism. With these precedents, one can understand the appearance of Benito Espinosa (Spinoza) and David Nieto, though the later was shielded under orthodox Judaism. However, neither of them will form part of this history; not because they had been born outside Spain, since they were Spanish by family and Spanish was their language, but because they had never been Christians, therefore never heretics. Benito Espinosa wrote in Spanish the *Apología* of his renouncing the synagogue, later re-written in *Tractatus theologico-politicus*.

Every now and then we hear of some trial of some naïve nun or other, or some old *beatas,* which bring back old memories.

But then French influence caused by the change of dynasty came to regale us with the following:

a)   Regal-Jansenism - not without precedent at the time of the Hapsburg dynasty.

b)   Encyclopedism, revealing itself in various forms and to a greater or lesser extent wrapped in literature, financial companies and executive empires.

c)   Secret societies – the powerful instruments of the above. Pereira, Campomanes, Aranda, Olavide, Cabarrús, Urquijo, Marchena, Llorente… number and summarise these various leanings. All of them had lent each other a helping hand in the expulsion of the Jesuits.

The first thirty-three years of this present nineteenth century are but a mere sequence and extension of the previous one. Jansenism and Encyclopedism running wild once more in the *Cortes* (Parliament) of Cádiz and throughout the constitutional phase from the year 20 to 23. Protestantism can hardly account for more than two supporters, both out of spite: Blanco (White) and Juan Calderón. One and the other departed later from reformed orthodoxy to fall respectively into Unitarianism and liberal Protestantism.

Of the reign of Isabel II, of the revolutionary era and successive events, I shall say nothing here and leave it until the appropriate and opportune time. The main manifestation, in a philosophical context, is the propagation of Germanic pantheism. But this aside, practically all opinions and tendencies, some dangerous, some risible, born in Europe at this time of intellectual chaos, came to our soil (usually late and ailing) in a most curious array of leaps and bounces. May God give us life and patience to deal with this last part of our history. May He grant me enough serenity not to turn it into satire or be tempted to portray it as gross caricature.

To sum up, the sources for this History are many and varied but can be summarized in the following categories:

1.   The works of the heterodox themselves that have reached us, as is the case with the writings of Elipando, Claudio of Turin, Gundisalvo, Arnaldo de Vilanova and Pedro de Osma, and with practically all heretics after the invention of the printing press. [LL]
2.   The works of their challengers, to wit, Beatus and Heterius writings against Elipando or Abbot Sansón's *Apologia* against Hostegesis.
3.   Previous works written on these issues, such as McCrae's, A. de Castro, Usoz, Wiffen, Boehmer, etc., the biographies of each heterodox and the main dictionaries and bibliographic catalogues, old and new, Spanish and foreign.

[L]   For the first centuries of the Church, *Corpus Haereseologicum* is essential reading.

4. The *Indices Expurgatorios* of the Holy Office
5. Almost all works and papers relating to the history of the Inquisition, from Eymerich *Directorium* onwards.
6. Trials previous and subsequent to the Inquisition, with other analogous documents, i.e. the *Acta* of the Congregation that condemned Pedro de Osma.
7. General treatises against heresies and on the church itself, for example, *Collyrium fidei* and *De planctu Ecclesiae* by Alvaro Pelagio, the work *De haeresibus* by Fray Alfonso de Castro, etc.
8. Treatises on demonology and sorcery.
9. The ecclesiastical histories of Spain and Councils collections.
10. Some general histories and certain works that not many would consult to find anything relating to these matters. I include in this section virtually all books and papers not covered in any of the previous ones. [M]

No need to go into further details now. Each chapter has an indication in the footnotes of the printed sources and manuscripts I made use of.

So here is the book. It will answer for me. I do not want to put it display as a museum curiosity but I do think it has a great deal of information that is new, and I hope that it will arouse (because satisfy it will not) some interest on points obscure up to now. If in other areas is not as complete as I would have wanted, blame my poor fortune not my lack of diligence. From good Catholics especially, from good Spaniards (a fruit more rare each day), and from bibliophiles (another rare species), not *bibliofools,* I ask their advice and feedback. None will go amiss.

Convinced of the seriousness of the issues here covered and of the munificence in the cause I maintain, I have not spared, nor shall I spare, any effort or fatigue towards which the fulfilment of my desire may lead. I have explored, and continue to explore now, the principal libraries and archives of Spain and of the countries that have been a stage to the events I am about to describe. I do not refuse but seek the opinion and advice of those who know better. Pray give it in good faith – my open hand is sincere.

May God give me the light of understanding and a humble firmness of will; may He steer and guide my pen to narrate *sine ira et studio* the sad history of error

---

[M]   Only as a last resort should one depend on dictionaries and anthologies although there are some of merit, as the old one by Abate Pluquet *Mémoires pour servir à l'histoire des égaremens de l'esprit humain, par rapport à la religion chrétienne, ou dictionaire des héresies,* (Paris, 1762-1764; second edition 1817-1818), and the well-known *Diccionaire de Migne,* of which there is *re-making* of it in Spanish in seven volumes (*Diccionario de las herejías, errores y cismas...,* Madrid, 1850-1851). It forms part of *Biblioteca Religiosa.*

among our peninsular people!   May He grant that this history may foster enlightenment and benefit, not scandal, to Christians everywhere.

Book 1

Chapter 1

General framework of religious life in the Peninsula before Priscillianism.

Preliminaries.

Propagation of Christianity.

First Spanish heterodox: The *Libellus* apostates - Basilides and Martial.

Errors regarding the Incarnation of the Word.

The Council of Iliberis (Council of Elvira – Granada)

Vindication of Hosius. Potamius and Florentius.

The Donatist schism: Lucilla.

The Luciferian schism: Vincent.

Preliminaries

Begin at the beginning: a wise maxim accepted by all and followed by few – perhaps because of its apparent triviality. Of course, a good methodology for the writing of history consists in not mutilating the facts narrated or the issues discussed; but also, and to a large extent, in not introducing events or additional elements alien to those that demand the writer's attention at any given time. Much time and space would be saved if superfluous introductions were to be well ordered, trimmed down, who knows perhaps done away with altogether!

Anxious myself not to stumble at this hurdle, I shall take things from their beginning and no earlier: I shall open this *History of the Spanish Heterodox* precisely at the point and time when Christianity enters Spain.

The Propagation of Christianity in Spain

Who was the first to evangelise this wise, prosperous and wealthy Roman Spain, fertile mother of Seneca and Lucan, Martial and Columella? Ancient and pious tradition tells us that it was the apostle St. James the Great who spread the sacred word throughout the four corners of the land: he built the first church by the banks of the Ebro River where the Most Holy Virgin appeared on the Pilar, and took his preaching to the lands of Galicia and Lusitania. Back in Judea, he was the first of the apostles to suffer martyrdom. His disciples transported his holy body back on a small boat from Joppa to the Galician coast.

In reality, the tradition of the coming of James to Compostela goes back to the seventh century. St. Isidore confirms it in the small tract *De ortu et obitu Patrum*, and though some doubts have been expressed as to whether this book came from his pen, it does undoubtedly belong to the Visigothic epoch. Also the testimony of the Missal known as Gothic or Mozarabic, in these verses of one hymn:

> Regens Joannes dextram solus Asiam
>
> Ejusque frater potitus Spaniam (sic)…
>
> Caput refulgens aureum Spaniae…[28]

If to this we add a commentary on the prophet Nahum attributed to St. Julian and found among the works of the Toledo Fathers, we will then have almost all the authorities that affirm, plainly and straightforwardly to be sure, the coming of the apostle to our Peninsula. More ancient, there are none. Didymus the Alexandrine in *De Trinitate* (Book 2, chapter 4) and St. Jerome on Isaiah (chapter 34) do not mention the son of Zebedee by name, saying only that "an apostle had been to Spain". [29]

It would be temerarious to deny the preaching of James in Spain but we cannot affirm it with total confidence either. The issue has been in debate since the sixteenth century. Cardinal Baronius accepted it as a tradition of the Spanish Church in volume 1 of his *Annales,* questioned it in volume 9, and managed to have Clement VIII modify the Breviary accordingly. Many Spaniards challenged Baronius on the matter, especially Juan de Mariana in *De adventu B. Jacobi apostoli in Hispaniam,* a treatise written with elegance, method, and serenity of judgement, [30] and Urban VIII reinstated this ancient Lesson to the Breviary. But the polemics continued with the old (and not yet cooled-down dispute) between the primacies of Toledo and Santiago. The dispute over the patronage of Saint Teresa did not help matters much and resolution of the principal issue advanced little. [31]

---

[28]   I cannot place this quote before St. Isidore's time, although many learned authors hold this hymn to be from the fourth century. Fr. Flórez demonstrated that the hymn was prior to the Arabic invasion, but not that it preceded the Fourth Council of Toledo, when the liturgy was standardised.

[29]   At the end of the last century, Fr. Daniel Farlatti published the life of St. Clement, written by Hesychius, bishop of Salona (fourth century), who says emphatically that James was sent to Spain by St. Peter (Maceda, *Actas de San Saturnino*).

[30]   *Joannis Marianae e Societate Jesu Tractatus VII.* 1. *De adventu B. Jacobi Apostoli in Hispaniam… Coloniae Agrippinae. Sumptibus Antonii Hierati… Anno 1609*, fol. 1 to 31.

[31]   Fr. Flórez summarised all debate on the matter up to his time and advanced all arguments in favour of the coming of James (*España Sagrada*, vol. 3, 1748): Didymus work, *De Trinitate,* was not included, for it was published for the first time by Fr. Mingarelli in 1769 (Bologne). Vid. in addition, Fr. Torá's *Venida de Santiago a España*, Madrid, 1797, accepted as a classic on the matter.

As for the tradition linked to the coming of James, there is even more uncertainty. That of the *Pilar*, as far as its written documentation is concerned, is relatively modern. In 1155, the bishop of Saragossa, Pedro Librana, speaks of an ancient temple to the Virgin in that city but gives no further details. [32]

But if the coming of James to Spain is based on no historical data that of St. Paul's is based on a most sure foundation, acknowledged even by those who hesitate on the former. The Apostle of the Gentiles, in chapter 15 v. 28 of his *Epistle to the Romans*, promises to visit them "on his way to Spain". The text is explicit: δι ' δμών είς Σπανίν (*by you*, that is, *when passing through your land*). And note that he says Σπανίν and not *Iberia*, lest any one get the strange notion that he was talking about the Iberians of the Caucasus! Besides, the apostle was writing from Corinth, and Rome is not exactly on the way to Georgia but it is on the way to Spain. There is no doubt, then, that St. Paul was thinking about coming to Spain. But since the *Acts of the Apostles* cover only the period up to the first imprisonment in Rome of the man from Tarsus and no further, we do not read there any notice of this journey ever having taken place or indeed of any other during the last eight years of his life. St. Clement (a disciple of Paul), shows that his preaching in Spain wsa something certain and proven, when he asserts that his master took the faith "to the very end and limits of the West" (Ep. *Ad Corinthios)*, St. Hippolytus, St. Epiphanius (*De haeresibus*, chapter 27), St. John Chrysostom (*Homily* 27, *in Matthaeum*), St. Jerome in two or three places, the Muratori Canon (generally held to be a document from the second century), St. Gregory the Great, St. Isidore, and many others, all in direct, explicit and specific terms, and referring to the Peninsula by its less ambiguous name. We are not dealing here with a tradition of the Spanish Church alone but with an ancient and widespread belief of both the Greek and Roman Churches that marvellously corresponds to the plan and words of the Apostle himself, as well as with the chronology of the first Christian century. [33]

This silence of history on things that interest us most is regrettable: of St. Paul's preaching to Spaniards we know nothing. It is tradition that he landed in Tarragona and both Simon Metaphrastes (an author of little credibility) and the Greek *Menologion*, attribute to him the conversion of Xanthipa, wife of the Prefect Probus, and of his sister Polyxena.

But surely Saul's holy word must have yielded some fruit, perhaps even a little more than some: it cleared the way for the Seven Apostolic Fathers sent by St. Peter to the Betis region around the years 64 and 65.

---

[32]   Per Antón Beuter says he found the history of the *Pilar* in "a book written in old language" in the Library of Minerva, in Rome. '*A book in old language'* is no way to reference anything. A great scholarly authority, Beuter is! I think he is probably referring to some thirteenth or fourteenth-century codex, much like the document Risco published in volume 30 of *España Sagrada*.

[33]   *España Sagrada*, vol. 3, pp. 5 to 39.

Let their names be heard: Torquatus, Ctesiphon, Indalecius, Euphrasius, Cecilius, Hesychyus and Secundus. History, which with such overwhelming abundance remembers the most insipid of genealogies and lamentable events of wars, barely has a page for these heroes that gave life to the most holy and prodigious metamorphosis ever to have taken place on Spanish soil.

Let us imagine for a brief moment the Betis region at the time of Nero: a region with villages and town halls, agricultural, industrious, passionate, a lover of novelties, lulled by the songs of her poets, admonished with grave words by her philosophers. Keep your eye on those two brilliant and bustling towns, Corduba and Hispalis (Seville) with the sons of the Turdetan soil duly observing the laws of pleasure and busy mimicking imperial Rome's glossy lifestyle. One thinks of Athens where St. Paul preached. We see the *agora* (here *forum*) where the *populus*, eager for fresh news, gather and listen in awe to the voice of the sophist or the Greek rhetorician, watch the hoax and quackery of Assyrian or Chaldean charlatans and sorcerers and the dazzle and 'snake-oil' dealings of importers of oriental cults. And out of this concourse of sounds, we shall hear the new voice of one or two generous spirits whom Simon Bar-Jonah entrusted with the high and noble undertaking of announcing the New Law to Horace's *peritus Iber*, to the countrymen of Portius Latron, Balbo and Seneca. Conceivably well disposed to hear it because of the light that knowledge always imparts, but also hard and obstinate because of the arrogance that same knowledge instils in man, and because of the vices and overall moral weakness that prosperity and opulence inevitably bring along.

What battles did these men sent by the Lord endure? How did they build our ancient Church? Did they attain the palm of martyrdom? How did the primitive church cope with it all? We know little except for that prompt conversion en masse of the people of Acci (Guadix, Cádiz) confirmed in the Mozarabic rite:

Plebs hic continuo pervolat ad fidem,

Et fit catholico dogmate multiplex…[34]

The founding of the *Accitana* (Guadix, Cádiz) church is attributed to Torquatus; that of *Urci* to Indalecius; *Bergium's* (Verja) to Ctesiphon; *Iliturgi* (Andujar) to Euphrasius; *Iliberis* (Granada) to Cecilius; *Carteya* to Hesychius; *Avila*, the only city outside the Betis region, to Secundus. As for the rest of Spain, there is nothing but silence. *Braga* has St. Peter de Rates (supposed disciple of James) as its first bishop. *Astigis* (Ecija) prides itself, on very thin grounds I must say, on having been visited by St. Paul. *Italica* calls up Gerontius as "her own prelate and martyr". The light of the Gospel comes to Pamplona from the other side of the Pyrenees with Honestus, the presbyter, and Saturninus, the bishop of Tolosa. The first bishop of Toledo is St. Eugenius,

---

[34]   Dr. Agustín de Tejeda dedicated a beautiful hymn to this first *Landing of the apostolic men on our soil*. Vid. *Flores De poetas ilustres,* by P. de Espinosa, Valladolid, 1605.

martyred in Gaul during the Decian's persecution. This tradition and that of Pamplona were unrecognised, unknown to Spaniards for more than eight centuries. Of other churches, like those of Saragossa and Tortosa, we can affirm their antiquity but not how or when they came to being. It matters little: they themselves will give in time ample testimony of their existence when the gales of persecution strike.

An inscription said to have been found near the Pisuerga River and first included in the suspect *Aldina* collection of 1571, has preserved memory of the rigours exercised against the first Spanish Christians during Nero's time: "his qui novam generi humano superstitionem inculcabant", but it is probably apocryphal and few defend it. [35] It was only in the third century that Navarre's Saint Firminus, or Fermín, suffered martyrdom in Toulouse of Aquitaine. The death of St. Mancius, bishop of Evora, the second Lusitanian city to be named in ecclesiastical history, is placed during the reign of Spaniard emperor Trajan. The martyrdom of Sts. Fecundus and Primitivus in Galicia is referred to with some hesitation by Ambrosio de Morales as having taken place during the epoch of the Antonines, but others (on stronger ground) date it much closer, to the era of Heliogabulos or Gordian II. Pérez Bayer made clear that St. Laurentius, or Lorenzo (Lawrence), deacon and treasurer of the church in Rome, was from Huesca (Aragón) and earned the palm of martyrdom during the eighth persecution, in Valerian's reign. The memory of the frightful punishment inflicted on the Huesca Confessor was immortalised by Prudentius in his stirring hymn:

> mors illa sancti martyris
>
> mors vera templorum fuit…[36]

In fact, the best chronicle of Spanish Christianity in its very early days is to be found in the verses of this outstanding poet. Hymn VI of the *Peristephanon* describes in vivid colour the death of St. Fructuosus, bishop of Tarragona, and that of the deacons Augurius and Eulogius, witnesses to the Faith both, at about the year 259.

> Felix Tarraco, Fructuose, vestris
>
> attollit caput ignibus coruscum,
>
> levitis geminis procul relucens,

---

[35] It can be seen, together with number 172, in Masdeu's collection, *Historia Crítica de España,* vol. 5. Ambrosio de Morales included it, too, although hesitantly because he had not seen it himself (lib. IX). Muratori also regards it as suspect.

[36] *M. Aurelii Clementis Prudentii Carmina, Romae, 1789,* ed. Arévalo, vol. 2, p. 928. Pérez Bayer, *Damasus et Laurentius Hispanis asserti et vindicati…Romae,* 1756. As late as the beginning of eighteenth century, the historian and poet Gabriel Alvarez de Toledo put noble words on the lips of the deacon from Huesca (Vid. *Líricos del siglo XVIII,* by D.L.A. de Cueto).

Hispanos Deus aspicit benignus.

arcem quandoquidem potens Iberam

trino martyre Trinitas coronat.

(Happy Tarraco, Fructuosus, lifts a head that flashes in the fires of
your pyre. She shines afar in virtue of her two deacons. God surely
looks with kindness on Spaniards, since the mighty Trinity crowns
an Iberian city with three martyrs).

And the poet remembers them again in that brilliant enumeration of
Caesaraugustian (Saragossan) confessors:

bis nouem noster populus sub uno

martyrum seruat cineres sepulchro,

Caesaraugustam uocitamus urbem,

res cui tanta est.

plena magnorum domus angelorum

non timet mundi fragilis ruinam

tot sinu gestans simul offerenda

numera Christo

cum Deus dextram quatiens coruscam

nube subnixus ueniet rubente

gentibus iustam positorus aequo

pondere libram,

orbe de magno caput excitata

obuiam Christo properanter ibit

ciuitas quaeque pretisa portans

dona canistris.

Afra Carthago tua promet ossa,

ore facundo Cypriane doctor,

Corduba Acisclum dabit et Zoëllum

tresque coronas.

tu tribus gemmis diadema pulchrum

offeres Christo, genitrix piorum

Tarraco, intexit cui Fructuosus

sutile uinclum.

nomen hoc gemmae strofio inligatae est,

emicant iuxta lapides gemelli

ardet splendor parilis duorum

igne corusco.

(Eighteen martyrs' ashes our people keep in a single grave, and Caesaraugusta is the name we call the city which has this great possession. A house that is filled with great saints fears not the downfall of this mortal world, since it bears in its bosom so many gifts to be offered together to Christ. When God, seated on a fiery cloud and shaking his flashing hand, shall come to set up his true balance for the nations, and weigh them justly, then from out the great world every city will raise its head and quickly to meet Christ, carrying its costly gifts in baskets. African Carthage will bring forth thy bones, Cyprian, teacher of the eloquent lips. Corduba will give Acisclus and Zoellus and her three crowns. Thou, Tarraco, mother of godly children, wilt offer to Christ e jewel fastened on the band, and beside it shine twin stona beatous diadem with three jewels for Fructuosus works there a band in which they are set. This name belongs to ones, both blazing in equal lustre with a flash of fire).

Prudentius said it well: new martyrs blossomed with each hailstone that fell. This truth was made clear during the last and most terrible of persecutions directed against the Gospel, that of Diocletian and Maximilian (year 301). One such persecutor, Dacian, came to Spain as governor (*praeses*) and of him Prudentius' *martyrologios* and hymns give us a long and sad (though for our Church, glorious) remembrance. No corner in the whole of the Peninsula, however isolated, from Laletania to Celtiberia, from Celtiberia to Lusitania, was spared from the cruel implementation of his imperial decrees. In Gerunda (Gerona), "small though rich due to such treasures", said Prudentius, was torn in pieces "the holy body of glorious Felix".

Eight days later his brother Cucufates was martyred in Barcelona - fervently venerated to this day in Catalonia as Saint Cugat; and soon after, in the same city, the virgin Eulalia (not to be confused with Eulalia of Mérida whom Prudentius also celebrates). But no other city "neither Carthage nor Rome" says the poet, exceeded Saragossa in the number and distinction of these glorious trophies. One has to read the poet's hymn from beginning to end to get a true picture of that last and desperate clash between a now moribund paganism and the New Law that advances, radiant and serene, held high by the indomitable determination and heroic spirit of the Celtiberian character. The Aragonese of the third and early fourth centuries succumbed to Dacian's executioners with valour as stoic and impassive as that of their descendants in the nineteenth century before the legions of Corso. And Prudentius, a worthy poet of such times and of such men sang:

> singulis paucae, tribus aut duobus,
>
> forsan et quinis aliquae placebunt
>
> testibus Christi prius hostiarum
>
> pignere functae:
>
> tu decem sanctos revehes et octo,
>
> Caesaraugusta studiosa Christo,
>
> verticem flavis oleis revincta,
>
> pacis honore.
>
> sola in occursum numerosiores
>
> martyrum turbas Domino parasti,
>
> sola praedives pietate multa
>
> luce frueris.
>
> vix parens orbis populosa Poeni,
>
> ipsa vix Roma in solio locata
>
> te, decus nostrum, superare in isto
>
> munere digna est.
>
> omnibus portis sacer immolatus
>
> anguis exclusit genus inuidorum
>
> daemonum et nigras pepulit tenebras
>
> urbe piata.
>
> nullus umbrarum latet intus horror;
>
> pulsa nam pestis populum refugit,
>
> Christus in totis habitat plateis,
>
> Christus ubique est.
>
> martyrum credas patriam coronis
>
> debitam sacris, chorus unde surgens
>
> tendit in caelum niueus togatae
>
> nobilitatis.
>
> inde, Vicenti, tua palma nata est,
>
> clerus hic tantum peperit triumfum,

hic sacerdotum domus infulata

Valeriorum.

(A few cities will find favour because of only one, some because of two or three, perhaps of five witnesses to Christ, the sacrifices they gave in pledge before. But thou, Caesaraugusta, that art zealous for Christ, wilt bring again thy holy eighteen, thy head wreathed with olden olives, the ornament of peace. In number greater than any other city thou hast companies of martyrs ready to meet the Lord; thou wilt enjoy great light because thou dost surpass all in the riches of thy devotion. Scarce is the populous mother of the Punic world, scarce Rome herself, set on her throne, worthy to outstrip thee, our glory, in this offering. The sacrifice of holy blood has shut out the race of malign devils from all thy gates and driven black darkness from thy cleansed city. No shuddering fear of spirits lurks within, for the plague has been driven away in flight from thy people, and Christ dwells in all thy streets, Christ is everywhere. It is as if this homeland of martyrs had been destined for the sacred crowns, there rises from it towards heaven such a company of its highborn citizens clad in snow-white robes. It was here, Vincent, thy victory began, here the clergy won their great triumph and here the vested family of the priestly Valerii).

The poet himself was Aragonese, and it was in Saragossa itself that Vincent was anointed with the oil of faith and virtue; he to whose glory Prudentius dedicates his fifth hymn, and of whom, in the triumphal song just cited, he continues:

hoc colunt ciues, uelut ipsa membra

caespes includat suus et paterno

seruet amplectens tumulo beati

martyris ossa.

noster est, quamuis procul hine in urbe

passus ignota dederit sepulchri

gloriam uictor prope litus altae

forte Sagunti.

(This thy fellow citizens reverence just as if its native ground covered the very body, keeping the blessed martyr's bones in its embrace within his family tomb. Ours he is, though as it befell it was in a strange city far from here that he suffered and in victory gave it the honour of having his burial place, near the shore of lofty Saguntus).

The poet, in another passage, weaves again a crown of evergreen flowers to the virgin Encrates or Engracia:

viuis ac poenas seriem retexis

carnis et caesae spolium retentans,

Ttaetra quam sulcos habeant amaros

uulnera, narras.

barbarus tortor latus omne carpsit,

sanguis impensus, lacerata membra,

pectus abscisa patuit papilla

corde sub ipso.

iam minus mortis pretium peractae est,

quae uenenatos abolens dolores

concitam membris tribuit quietem

fine soporo.

cruda te longum tenuit cicatrix

et diu uenis dolor haesit ardens,

dum putrescentes tenuat medullas

tabidus umor.

inuidos quamuis obitum supremum

persecutoris gladius negarit,

plena te, martyr, tamen ut peremptam

poena coronat.

vidimus partem iecoris reuulsam

ungulis longe iacuisse pressis,

mors habet pallens aliquid tuorum

te quoque uiua.

hunc nouum nostrae titulum fruendum

Caesaraugustae dedit ipse Christus,

iuge uiuentis domus ut dicata

martyris esset.

(Here too, Encratis, lies the body that lodged thy virtues with which, a forceful maiden, thou didst put to shame the spirit of the savage world. To none of the martyrs was it given to live on and dwell in our land; thou art the only one to survive thy death and live in the world. Thou didst live and recount the story of thy sufferings one after another; thou didst not quit hold of thy flesh though they cut it and would have robbed thee of it, and thou didst tell how grievous were the gases of thy hideous wounds. The barbarous tormentor tore all thy side, thy blood was shed, thy limbs mangled, thy breast cut off and thy bosom laid open down to the very heart. Death surely when it is carried through is a lesser price to pay, for it puts an end to the envenomed pains and quickly gives the body rest in the final sleep. But the bleeding wound long held thee back, the burning pain clung long to thy flesh, till corrupt discharge wasted thy vitals in decay. Though the sword of the persecutor grudged and denied thee death to end all, yet the full measure of suffering gives thee the crown as much as if thou hadst been slain. We salute thee as martyr).

Never mind the Horatian wrapping: this is poetry made of iron. It is in these stanzas as we feel the shrillness of chains and of torture, it is in these verses, I say, that we are to seek the most radiant expression of Spanish Catholicism, a Catholicism armed for combat always: solid, tenacious, firm, strong and unequivocal, be it battling pagans in the plazas of Saragossa, or sixteenth-century Protestants in the fields of Germany and Flanders. Our poetry was forged in these hymns – our poetry was Catholic from Day One! How can the Catholic Faith ever be wiped away from Spain when she engendered such martyrs to be her witnesses and produced such poets to sing of her!

Eighteen others shed their blood for Christ with St. Engracia: Prudentius tells us their names (not without some difficulties and rhythmical hurdles!) in the last stanzas of his hymn. To all must be added the Confessors Caius and Clement

> ...quibus incruentum
>
> ferre prouenit decus ex secundo
>
> laudis agone
>
> (For you twain are not to be passed over; it was your fortune to win bloodless honour out of a victorious contest for glory).

And finally, the Innumerable, whose names we could say with the poet: "Christ knows them, written in the Book celestial".

Not one single city in Spain failed to yield this fruit for heaven – all of them victims of Dacian's unbridled brutality. Prudentius preserved their many names for us in his hymns. Let no sceptic of our time, I mean any one of those 'moderns' incapable of understanding the greatness and sublimity of sacrifice, dare doubt indubitable facts confirmed by an authority almost their contemporary and in all points irrefutable.

From Calahorra he names "the two warriors" Emeterius and Caledonius to whom he dedicates a special hymn, the first of the *Peristephanon*; from Mérida, "noble Eulalia" who has also her own hymn, listed number three; from Compluto, the children Justus and Pastor; from Córdoba, Acisclos, Zoylos and Victoria "the three crowns".

He does not mention other martyrs and confessors who have nonetheless their own Office in the Missal and Breviary of St. Isidore, or are mentioned in ancient Martyrologies and Sanctorals, such as Leucadia or Leocadia (Blanca) of Toledo; Justa and Rufina of Seville; Vincent, Sabina, and Cristeta, of Avila; Servandus and Germán, of Mérida; centurion Marcelo and his twelve children, from León. We may read of these and of many others in the books of Ambrosio de Morales, Flórez, and Dr. de la Fuente who gathered the facts pertaining to this issue and laboured to distinguish and separate what is certain and historical fact from what is dubious and fanciful legend.

The emperors judged they had triumphed over the "folly of the Cross" (*insania crucis*) and defiantly dared place on their inscriptions "Nomine Christianorum deleto qui rempublicam evertebant", "Superstitione Christianorum ubique deleta et cultu Deorum propagato"- [37] epigraphs that show the double character of that persecution, as much political as it was religious. But at last the ancient storm cleared, and the ship that until then looked like foundering moved assuredly on its course, as had Peter's boat in lake Tiberias. Constantine brought peace to the Church, granted her free exercise of worship, a certain degree of protection even, thanks to which the era of persecution and martyrdom came to an end, albeit not forever.

But then we see controversies and heresies erupting, and Catholicism through the Councils and Doctors of the Church attending to the definition of dogma, to the establishment of discipline, and to defending herself from enemies of all kinds, those from outside as well as those from within.

The *insania crucis*, the religion of the "crucified sophist" as that impious Lucian or whoever the author of *Philopatris* and *Pilgrim* was, had now triumphed over its first adversaries in Spain as it had triumphed in the entire Roman world. The official Roman cult, defended at all costs with the emperors' sword, had fought against it, but it was defeated in the combat. It was defeated because pagan cult was absurd and insufficient and had long run its course, and because it had been dead for a long time already in the minds of the learned and

---

[37]   Many doubt the authenticity of these inscriptions.

disparaged in the heart of the populace who had held on to polytheism's superstitions but not to its beliefs.

But Rome fought in defence of her gods. It fought because gods and *patria* were one, because it brought to mind ancient heroic battles and because it was to the gods that the everlastingness of the empire was linked. Rome fought, and so adamantly, that one is at a loss to explain or understand, save for an miracle perhaps, how the new religion could have spread so easily and rapidly, even when we grant the power of a new idea its due and take into consideration the vast multitude of Christians that embraced it (*ingens multitudo*).

In the Peninsula, by the time of Tertullian, Catholicism had already reached the farthest corners of our land (*omnes termini*). [38] It had even penetrated the Asturian and Cantabrian mountains, inaccessible as they had been, to the Roman legions (*loca inaccessa*). "Innumerable" is how Arnobious described the Christians in Spain. [39]

It has been said that since ancient cults had already become obsolete, destroying them with a final blow could not have been very difficult: philosophers and poets had discredited them by then in their disputations and with their mockery. Indeed. But those who say that do not take account of the fact that Christianity had not come simply to set altar against altar. It came to wound an old society in its heart: to preach a new philosophical doctrine never before taught at Athens or Alexandria. And because of this, it was going to arouse, it did arouse against itself, the entire range of fanaticisms from the Schools. Because what the New Law was preaching was a new morality, and in order to undermine this New Law, all the base passions running wild during Nero and Domitian's time were stirred up and unleashed. This is why the battle was long, resolute, and horrendous. It was not a war between an old, decadent and decaying religion against a new, vigorous and generous one: it was a struggle between the lower instincts of the flesh and the law of the spirit, between the vices and calamities built into the body politic and the law of justice; between all the philosophical sects and the one, true wisdom.

Cunning and visionary priests, *flamines* and vestal virgins were not the only ones keeping vigil around the fire of Vesta, the temple of Janus Bifrons or the altar to Victory. If that were the case, how could we explain the fact that classical polytheism, all-inclusive and lenient in dogma as all weak and vague religions are, persecuted Christians with such acerbity, unceasingly and without rest? A new sect that lacked the divine, universal, and infallible seal of Christianity would have eventually been brought into the common fold of disbelieved beliefs. Putting up a new god in their Pantheon would not have bothered the Romans much!

---

38   Lib. *Contra Judaeos*, ch. 7

39   *Contra gentes,* lib. I

But enough of general ruminations. It is not my intention to write about the fall of paganism here, a subject much studied already, though perhaps never enough. Let us come back to the Spanish Church, which in the fourth century is already reaping a plentiful harvest of wisdom and virtue.

A few seeds of heresy began to appear though they were promptly stifled at birth by the vigilance of those holy and glorious men the Western world produced in that epoch. Let us, then, commence this History.

Libellus heretics: Basílides and Martial

It was to be the sad fortune of bishops Basílides of Astorga and Martial of Mérida to head the list of Spanish apostates. Their fall occurred before the year 254, during Decian's persecution: it was a turbulent fall because of the circumstances surrounding the case.

These two bishops, faint-hearted Christians afraid of persecution, did not hesitate to ask pagan magistrates for what was then called a *libellus*, that is, a certificate of protection, a document that would prevent them from being punished in case of idolatry, for instance. The faithful regarded this kind of apostasy with horror even when extracted by force and called offenders of such sin *the libellatici* to distinguish them from those who actually turned to the worshipping of idols and who received the dishonourable appellation of *sacrificados* - or *sacrificulos*. The two bishops retracted but their retraction was feigned. They had obtained the *libellus* through exchange of monies to avoid running the risk of being seen as idolaters or, alternatively, to be exposed to martyrdom, but Martial and Basilides did not stop there. The former made public acts of paganism, burying his children in profane places, attending Gentile gatherings and sullying himself with their abominations, until finally he denied the faith altogether before his province's *ducenarius**. He also blasphemed against Christ during a grave illness. Both having finally acknowledged their offences, the churches of Astorga and Mérida agreed to their deposition. The regional bishops convened *cum assensu plebis*, as was the norm and custom of the time, and elected Sabinus as Basílides' successor and Felix as bishop of Mérida. Basílides feigned submission, was re-admitted to lay communion, and showed great repentance for his sins and willingness to dedicate the rest of his life to penance. But his good intentions did not last long. Determined to be reinstated to his see, he headed for Rome. There, with artifice and false signs of fellowship, he deceived pope Stephen I who asked that he be reinstated to his diocese because his deposition, the pontiff judged, had been non-canonical.

This is the first appeal to Rome we find in our ecclesiastical history. Martial gained his nerve with the success of Basilides' pretensions and tried for

---

*   In the original volume, Menéndez Pelayo had erased the words "or collector of tributes" after *ducenario*. (Editor, 1912).

a second time to return to the see of Mérida. In the thick of such conflict, the Spanish churches consulted Saint Cyprian, bishop of Carthage, Christianity's shining light in the third century. Relations were friendly and frequent between Spain and what was later called Mauritania Tingitana. Being in possession of the letters from Mérida that Sabinus and Felix had brought with them, St. Cyprian proceeded to consult with thirty-six African bishops. The verdict was unanimous: the apostates' deposition had been a legitimate one and the pontifical *rescriptum* to the contrary was not binding since pope St. Cornelius' constitution which admitted *libellaci* to public penance but not the sacerdotal ministry, was still in force. And in conformity to this decision, St. Cyprian responded "to presbyter Felix and to the faithful of León and Astorga, and to deacon Laelius and the people of Mérida" in a celebrated epistle, numbered sixty-eight in his Works. There he censures in sorrowful and piercing terms the bishops who had taken up Basilides' and Martial's cause, emphasises categorically that the *rescript* had been extracted "surreptitiously" and exhorts Christians not to communicate with the prevaricators. This letter was written in 254, during Valerian's reign, and it is the only document we have on the matter. It is to be supposed that the pontiff, subsequently better informed, annulled his previous order, and that Felix and Sabinus continued in their prelacies.

Somewhat connected with this case, and of more gravity, was the issue of the *re-baptised,* where we see St. Cyprian in open opposition to the pontiff. After writing several letters, some of them a little irreverent to be sure, he convened a council of eighty African bishops in Carthage in the year 258 who judged that apostates and heretics should be *re-baptised.* Foes of papal authority like to turn St. Cyprian's words into their own battle cry: "Neque enim quisquam nostrûm Episcopum se esse Episcoporum constituit, aut tyrannico terrore ad obsequendam neccessitatem collegas suos adigit, quando habeat omnis Episcopus pro licentia libertatis arbitrium proprium judicare". But this harsh and fiery sentence has to be seen in the context of the passion and acrimony the conflict excited at the time and is no argument against the Holy See. St. Cyprian himself, in his treatise *De unitate Ecclesiae,* wrote: "Qui cathedram Petri super quam fundata est Ecclessia, deserit, in Ecclessia non est: qui vero Ecclessiae unitatem not tenet, nec fidem habet". Nor should the holy African bishop be accused of rebellion: he did not show himself to be particularly obstinate on the matter of the *re-baptised,* nor did the pontiff ever sever him from the communion of the faithful, as indeed he did in the case of Firmilianus of Cesarea for the same error, but one he stubbornly held to after being censured.

As for the *libellatici,* an issue more to the point here, there was no real dissension between the bishops of Africa and Spain and the pontiff because the issue was not one of dogma or based on an *ex cathedra* ruling but a point of *fact*: Stephen had been wrongly and sinisterly informed, as St. Cyprian pointed out. And note that neither he nor the other bishops ever denied or questioned the authority of Rome; on the contrary, they based their decision on a pontifical Constitution, that of St. Cornelius which, because of its *universal* character, could not be annulled simply by means of a *rescriptum* or a few personal letters that had been obtained by artful deceit. [40]

Errors regarding the Incarnation of the Word

We can reasonably infer from a *false decretal* attributed to pope St. Eutychianus (275-283) and addressed to bishop John and other Andalusian prelates, that some heretics had been propagating error with regard to the Incarnation of the Son of God, in the Betis region. The Decretal is dated at the time of the Consulate of Aurelianus and Titus Annonius Mercelinus which corresponds to the year 276 of the Christian era; but it is apocryphal and acknowledged as such, and is therefore invalid. The heresy itself, however, could be factual. Later we shall see more than one heterodoxy regarding this same article of faith.

The Iliberis (Elvira) Council

The Council of Elvira, the first of many councils held in Spain of which the Acta have been preserved, merits a detailed, thoughtful study, respect and a special tribute from us all.

In the early years of the fourth century, at the beginning of Constantine's reign and some twenty-four years before the Nicene Synod was called, a council was convened at Iliberis (Granada). It was attended by nineteen bishops from several Spanish provinces, thus listed in the final *subscription*: Accitano, Hispalense, Evagrense, Mentesano, Urcitano, Cesaraugustano, Toledano, Ossonobense, Eliocrocense, Malaccitano, Cordubense (the eminent Hosius), Castulonense, Tuccitano, Iliberitano, Emeritense, Legionense or Asturicense, Salariense, Elboronense and Bastetano. Aside from Hosius, only one of these bishops' names is known, that of Valerius, from Saragossa, who belonged to the "casa mitrada", the *domus infulata* referred to by Prudentius.

In eighty-one canons, the Iliberis Fathers gave the Christian peoples of Spain their first Constitution. They focused, not on points of dogma for there was no noted opposition here, but on conduct and discipline. They did condemn nonetheless some heretical and superstitious practices, and one or two remnants of paganism - all of which are worth mentioning now (though I shall deal with a couple of specific points in more detail when we come to speak of the magic arts).

---

[40]   Sources for the Basilides and Martial case*: S. Caecilii Cypriani Opera omnia illustrata studio ac labore Stephani Baluzii...* Ep. 68, *Ad clerum et plebes in Hispania consistentes*, col. 281 and following, and in volume 4 of *España Sagrada*, p. 271. See our Appendix.

España Sagrada, vol. 13 (*Iglesia de Mérida*), article on *Marcial y Felix*, pp. 133 to 139.

What our bishops at this Council were principally trying to do in order to do away with new apostasies, scandalous relapses and fake conversions, was to draw a clear dividing line between what was Christian and what was pagan. At a time when the fires of old persecutions had not yet been thoroughly extinguished, a clear and strict discipline that would define what was licit and what was not could not be have been a futile enterprise.

Canon I was written to condemn apostasy. It excludes from communion, even at the time of death, the adult Christian who frequents pagan temples, "in order to worship idols"[41]. Equal punishment is imposed on *flámines*, that is, pagan priests, who having been baptised return to "sacrificing" or soil themselves with homicide or fornication; [42] those who do not go as far as sacrificing with flesh or blood but are nonetheless involved in gift propitiation, they grant final pardon incumbent upon having done due penance. These canons show the very large number of pagan priests (*flamines*) that had embraced the Christian faith but would frequently lapse. Canon IV also asks the *flamen* catechumen to be admitted to baptism as long as he has abstained from profane sacrifices for a period of three years. A baptised person who goes up to Jupiter Capitolinus' temple to worship can return to the bosom of the Church only after ten years (canon LIX). Two years penance is imposed on a *flamen* carrying the sacrificial crowns (canon LV);[43] one year to the player, or gambler, probably because to *play* in this sense was tantamount to invoking pagan divinities engraved on the dice (canon LXXIX). So that contact with paganism be avoided, canon XL bans the faithful from receiving any item that has previously been used as an offering to the gods, severing the offender from communion for a period of five years, and admonishing slave owners in canon XLI not to consent to the worshipping of idols in their houses. [44]

Another article [45] prohibits marriage of Christians to pagans, heretics and Jews "for there can be no society between believer and non-believer" and with yet more severity condemns him who marries off his daughter to a pagan priest, because that would exclude her from the communion of the faithful *in articulo*

---

[41]   'Placuit ut quicumque post fidem baptismi salutaris, adulta aetate ad templum idoli idlolatraturus accessit, et fecerit quod est crimen capitale, nec in fine eum in communionen suscipere'.

[42]   'Flamines qui post fidem lavacri et regenerationis sacrificaverint, eo quod geminaverint scelera, accedente homicidio, vel triplicarint facinus cohaerente moechia, placuit eos nec in fine accipere communionen'.

[43]   Can. LV. 'Sacerdotes qui tantum sacrificantium coronas portent'

[44]   'Admonere placuit fideles, ut quantum possint, prohibeant ne idola in domibus suis habeant. Si vero vim metuunt servorum, vel seipsos puros conservent. Si non fecerint, alieni ab Ecclesia habeantur'.

[45]   'Gentilibus minime in matrimonium dandae sunt virgines christianae...' (can. XV). 'Haereticis qui errant ab Ecclesia catholica, nec ipsis catholicas danda puellas, sed neque Judaeis... eo quod nulla possit esse societas fidelis cum infideli'. (can. XVI)

mortis, whereas in analogous situations, the penance imposed would be of five years only. [46]

Canon XXII was written with converts from heresy in mind. They were to be welcomed back into the bosom of the Church after a ten-year penance for their error. [47] The Christian apostate who leaves the Church for an indefinite period but who does not go as far as to worship idols, will be received back to penance under the same conditions (canon XLVI).

An apostate or a convert heretic will not be elevated to the priesthood, and should he previously had been a cleric, he will be deposed (canon LI). With this ruling, the council of Eliberis confirmed the decision of St Cyprian's and the other African bishops at the Carthage Synod concerning the case of Basilides and Martial.

Eager to rein in overly rash and reckless zealousness, the council of Elvira excludes in canon LX those who have engaged in pulling down idols (and were killed because of it) from being counted among the number of martyrs "for neither is it written in the Gospel nor can we anywhere read that the Apostles did so".

We find only one heterodox doctrine expressly condemned by the Fathers. It refers to the celebration of Pentecost, then a matter of discord between the eastern and western Churches. "Let us all celebrate the Pasch" they say, "in accordance with the authority of Holy Scripture, and he who so refuses will be considered a supporter of a new heresy". [48] It also ordains fasting on Saturdays, condemning the error of those who would not, judging it, one imagines, to be a Jewish custom. [49]

Witchcraft and the evil arts are banned in canon VI, separating from communion, even at the time of death, him who with spells causes the death of another, for such crime can only be committed through idolatrous invocations.
[50]

---

[46]   'Si quis sacerdotibus idolorum filias suas junxerint, placuit nec in fine eis dandam communionen...' (can. XVII).

[47]   'Si quis de catholica Ecclesia ad haeresim transitum fecerit... placuit huic poenitentiam non esse denegandam, eo quod cognoverit peccatum suum, qui etiam decem annis agat poenitentiam'. (can. XXII).

[48]   'Pravam institutionem emendari placuit juxta auctoritatem Scripturarum, ut cuncti diem Pentecostes celebremus. Quod qui non fecerit, quasi novam haeresim induxisse notetur". (can. XLIII).

[49]   'Errorem placuit corrigi ut omni sabbati die jejunium super portionem celebremus" (can. XXVI).

[50]   'Si quis vero maleficio interficiat alterum, eo quod sine idolatria perficere scelus non potuit, nec in fine impartiendam esse illi communionen'.

Not the *augural arts*, as some have interpreted, but the arts practised by the *aurigae*, that is, the circus' charioteers as well as *pantomimes*, incur in the Council's reprobation. Canon LXII [51] establishes that all those involved in the said arts must renounce them before converting to Christianity, and should they lapse be expelled from the Church. The banning of pantomimes is linked to that of scenic plays, at the time a focus of idolatry and incitement to lustful conduct. We can infer this from the Holy Fathers' rebukes against the *comedia libertina*, most interesting, to be sure, for the history of art now but of which we barely have any notices at all. "No Christian or catechumen maiden (we read in canon LXVII) is to marry actors or those engaged in play-acting on pain of being separated from the communion of the faithful". [52]

Old superstitions persisted, and the council saw its role as doing away with them altogether. Canon XXXIV prohibits lighting candles in cemeteries during the day "not to disturb the souls of Saints", and canon XXXV opposes women's vigils in cemeteries under the pretext of prayer due to the consequent problems and sins resulting from this practice. [53] Both were pagan customs, especially the custom of the *vigil*. Let us remember, as an aside, the amusing and pointed tale in Petronius' *Satyricon* about the Matron of Ephesus: he shows, if other proofs were needed, that the dangers and evils censured by the council were not figments of the Fathers' imaginations. [54]

---

[51]   'Si Augur aut Pantomini credere voluerit, placuit ut prius artibus suis renuntient, et tunc demum suscipiantur ut ulterius non revertantur.   Quod si facere contra interdictum tentaverint, projiciantur ab Ecclesia'.

[52]   "Prohibendum ne qua fidelis vel catechumena aut comicos aut viros scenicos habeat: quaecumque hoc fecerit, a communione fidelium arceatur"

Some have translated *habere viros* as "*to have in their company*": I think mistakenly.

[53]   'Caereos per diem placuit in coemeterio non incendi: inquietandi enim sanctorum spiritus non sunt.   Qui hoc non observaverint, arceantur ab Ecclesiae communione. – Placuit prohiberi ne foeminae in coemeterio pervigilent, eo quod saepe sub obtentu orationis, scelera latenter committant". "Prohibendum etiam ne lucernas publice accendant.   Si facere contra interdictum voluerit, abstineant a communione'.

[54]   [Vigils, not in cemeteries, but in churches, persisted still and gave occasion to more than just minor scandals during the mid-sixteenth century, as can be deduced from the Constitutions of the Synod celebrated by Archbishop of Valencia, St. Tomás de Villanueva, on 12th June 1548, chapter 16. "Cum domum Domini sanctitudo deceat, et laicis in ecclesia vigilantibus multa passim in ecclesia fiant profana, atque decori domus Domini indecentia: proinde ecclesiarium rectoribus (at que sicariis) nostrae dioccesis S.S.A. sub poenis excommunicationis et decem librarum districte mandamus, ne illos ad dictas vigilias admittant, et ne in festis SS. Nicolai et MM. Innocentium seu aliis prophani ad populum sermones seu actus in ecclesiis fieri permittant.   Quamobrem si qui de vigiliano in aliqua ecclesia votum emiserint aut emittent in posterum, votum hujusmodi in alia pietatis opera commutandi propriis eorum sacerdotibus hoc nostro statuto facimus facultatem". (Villanueva, *Viaje Literario*, vol. 1 p. 198).

In Segorbe, these vigils lasted at least until 1592, as can be inferred from chapter LIV of the Synod which D. Juan Bautista Pérez on that date celebrated . (*Viaje Literario*, vol. 3, p. 127). [Editor, 1912].

The number of Jews in that epoch must have been extensive and quite mixed with the Christian population, given that our bishops sought to avoid its expansion by prohibiting clerics and all faithful to eat with Jews under punishment of excommunication (canon II), asking that under no circumstances should proprietors (canon I) permit Jews to bless their wheat lest the blessing of Christians be "sterilised" (canon XXI), and again excommunicating (canon LXXVIII) any faithful who sinned with a Jewess (or pagan), a crime expurgated only after five years' penance.

Having so established the Church's relations with pagans, Jews, and heretics, the council then moved on to the reform of cleric and lay customs, proceeding with inexorable severity on this point.

In fourteen canons relating to marriage, it ordered the customary and dire penalty of denying communion even *in hora mortis* to those engaged in bigamy (canon VIII), incest (LXVI), recurrent adultery (XLVII and LXIV), a woman guilty of infanticide (LXIII) (if she had been baptised, for the catechumen was admitted to communion *in fine*) (LXVIII), and a husband consenting to his wife's adultery (LXX). It imposed very rigorous penalties, though not as severe, on the widow fallen in sin (LXXII), the woman who abandoned her consort (IX), parents who sever the pledge of the betrothed (LIV), and even to married women who address in their own name amorous or indifferent letters to the secular clergy (LXXXI). The council excludes from communion in perpetuity those guilty of heinous sin (LXXI), prostitutes and *lenas* or third-parties (XII), clerics involved in fornication (XIX), the virgin offered to God who loses her virginity and does not make penance for the remainder of her life (XIII); it denies the subdiaconate to those fallen into impurity (XXX): commands bishops, presbyters, deacons, etc., *in ministerio positi,* to abstain from their wives (XXXIII), and prohibits them from having their own or those of others in their houses unless they are sisters or daughters offered to God (XXVII). It imposes seven years' penance on the woman who causes a slave's death due to mistreatment (V): notable proof of how the Church endeavoured from the very beginning to diminish and mitigate the plague of slavery, one of the most shameful of ancient society.

Singular and characteristic of the epoch are the two canons numbered XVIII and XX which prohibit clerics from exercising usury, although commerce *"ad victum conquirendum"* is allowed provided they do not abandon their churches to do business. Canon XXIV curtailed other type of abuses, banning the conferring of Orders on those baptised in foreign lands when not enough corroboration has been obtained as to their being Christian; and number XXV regulates the use of "confessorial" letters given by martyrs and confessors to those subject to public penance, letters that had to be examined by the bishop *primae cathedrae,* in conformity with canon LVIII.

Canons LXXIII, LXXIV, LXXV, and LXXX, censure informers and false witnesses, those who accuse a cleric without proof, and those who display defamatory libels in church. Five years' penance is imposed on the deacon found to have committed homicide before being ordained, and three years on those who lend their priestly vestments for profane ceremonies [55] and accept offerings from those separated from the communion of the faithful (canon XXVIII). Such *"energumenoi"* can have no ministry in the Church (canon XIX).

With regard to excommunication, canon XXXII reserves to bishops the faculty of imposing it or absolve from it provided appropriate penance has been done, and number LIII precludes a bishop from receiving someone excommunicated by another.

On the administering of Sacraments: canon XXXVIII grants to any faithful, the bigamous excepted, the authority to administer baptism in case of urgent need, as long as the baptised receives the imposition of hands by the bishop if he recovers; number XLVIII prohibits the practice of washing the feet of the baptised, as was the custom in other churches, and of receiving alms from those who have done so; number XXXIX is on the Sacrament of Confirmation. Those canons that directly or indirectly refer to the Sacraments of Penance and the Eucharist we have already mentioned above in their opportune place.

Finally, I must mention number XXXVI which prohibits pictures in churches as conducive to idolatry - a natural prohibition from the Church at that time since they were dealing with peoples raised in paganism and little capable, moreover, of discerning the meaning pictures and images were to have in the new and true religion.[56]

I am aware that many of this council's canons are not directly connected to the purpose of this History. I have cited them in detail however because these canons are the most ancient and complete of all the disciplinary codices of our Church, and show, better than any long dissertation, the state of Christian society in the Peninsula before the Priscillian heresy. What we see here is unity in dogma, save for a few glimpses of pagan remnants, more superstitious than heretical; and we see order and severity strictly applied to discipline.

Many have criticised what they see as the "draconian harshness" of the Elvira canons; but how else was one to proceed so as to preserve the vigour and purity of the New Law among a people so various and mixed as those inhabiting the Peninsula, Christian for the most part, but not immune from backsliding into old pagan ways, and exposed continually to error and sin because of their living side by side with peoples of foreign or antagonistic cults? The rigour with which the *lapsus* is punished is not so much categorical proof of

---

[55]   See canons LXXVI and LVII.

[56]   'Placuit picturas in Ecclesia esse non debere, ne quod colitur aut adoratur, in parietibus depingatur'. (This canon has given rise to the most contradictory interpretations).

---

an underlying, entrenched or widespread corruption as many have thought (for offences of that kind exist now and have always existed, and they are not the exclusive heritage or the reproach to one specific epoch); on the contrary, it is a manifest indication of the vigour and sturdy mettle of men who demanded such high standards and were thus willing to chastise all cowardly feebleness. The Hosius and Valerius of that time, those true confessors of Christ who still bore on their own bodies the physical marks of torture when they attended the Iliberis Synod, those men, I say, had every right to be uncompromising with apostates and sacrilegious.

As to the refusal of the Eucharist to the dying, this did not include the refusal of sacramental Penance, however much Fr. Villanuño and others have adhered to that opinion, which seems harsh and opposed to Christian charity something that, unquestionably, the Fathers convened at Elvira had in abundance. Please, let us be allowed to admire the wisdom and prudence of their decisions - notwithstanding the many difficulties caused in correctly interpreting that precious and enviable monument of our primitive Church. [57]

Hosius and Arianism. Potamius and Florentius.

Not necessarily in order to vindicate him (he does not need my vindication; many others, principally Fathers Flórez and Miguel José de Maceda [58] have done so already), but because this man's history is so intertwined with Arianism, and because it is my intention not to omit in this work any person who, rightly or wrongly, has been branded a heterodox, that I would like to say a few words here about our great Hosius and take full advantage of this favourable occasion to refresh our memory about that

[57]   See the Ilibitarian *Acta* in vol. 1 of *Collectio Maxima Conciliorum Hispaniae et Novi Orbis...* Rome, 1693, and dissertations on it in vol. 2.

Gabriel Albaspineo: *Notae in Concilium Illiberitanum...* In vol. 2 of the *Collectio Maxima Conciliorum Omnium Hispaniae... Curante Josepho Catalano, Romae, 1753.*

Binio: *Notae in Concilium Illiberitanum.* In vol. 2 of the same collection.

Loaisa: *Annotationes in Concil. Illiberit.* Idem id.

Mendoza, Fernando: *De concilio Illiberitano confirmando libri tres.* In vol. 2 of the same collection.

Arjona, Manuel M: *Defensa e ilustración latina del Concilio Iliberitano* (Manuscript).

Villanuño, Fr. Matías de: *Summa Conciliorum Hispaniae, notis novisque disertationibus adornata.* Madrid, 1785, 4 vols.

Masdeu: *Historia crítica de España*, vol. 8, ilustración XIII: *Eucaristía negada a los moribundos.*

La Fuente, Vicente: *Historia eclesiástica de España*, 2nd ed. vol. 1

[58]   In his thesis *Hosius vere Hosius* ("Hosius truly a Saint"), printed in Bologne, 1790, 4°, XVI-492 pgs. It comprises three dissertations: 1. *De commentitio... Hosii lapsu*; 2. *De sanctitate et cultu legitimo Hosii*; the third vindicates Potamius.

ornament and pillar of our Church, the most notable man that Spain produced from Seneca to St. Isidore.

The name *Hosius* (Saint) is Greek, but he who was so named belonged to our Hispano-Latin race. The Acta of the Nicean Council say that he had to make himself understood via interpreters. [59] Hosius was born in Córdoba (if we accept the irrefutable testimony of St. Athanasius [60] and Simeon Mataphrastes) [61] towards the year 256, for we know for sure that he died in 357 at the age of one hundred and one years. He must have been elected bishop of Córdoba around 294 because, according to St. Athanasius, in 355 he had been a bishop for sixty years. [62] Confessor of the Faith during Diocletian's persecution, he suffered torture - its physical signs still evident at Nicea - [63] as well as exile, as the holy bishop of Alexandria tell us (*Apolog. De fuga sua*).

Of his Confession, Hosius himself will speak in his letter to Constantium: "Ego confessionis munus explevi, primum cum persecutio moveretur ab avo tuo Maximiano". He attended the Iliberis Council, his signature appearing among the many others in the eleventh place, for he had been a bishop for only nine or ten years at the time. He left Spain, perhaps summoned by Constantine whom we find accompanied by him in Milan in the year 313. [64] The emperor held Hosius' counsel in high esteem especially in matters ecclesiastical, and it seems incontestable that it was Hosius who converted him to Christianity or at least who finally made him decide in favour of the one true religion. Zosimus, a pagan,[65] attributes the Caesar's conversion to an "Egyptian" from Spain, the word Egyptian to be understood in the sense of "magus", "priest", or "sage" as practically all historians have interpreted it, as they agree also on identifying Hosius as that "Egyptian", since no other Spanish catechist is known in Constantine's court at that time.

At about this time the Donatist heresy began to raise its head in Africa sustained by a Spanish woman called Lucilla (of whom more below). These sectarians deposed Caecilianus, bishop of Carthage, accusing him of being a "*traditor*"(surrendered), that is, of having given the sacred books to the pagans during the last persecution, and un-canonically proceeded to elect Maiorinus in his place. When pope Melchiades (311-314) heard of this, he called Caecilianus

---

59   Lib. II: *De eo quod oportet tres personas intelligi*, etc.

60   'Reversus in patriam suam' (Ep. *Ad Solitarios*)

61   'Corduba…urbe Hispaniae de eo se jactabat.' (*Narratio eorum quae gesta sunt Niceae a Synodo*.)

62   All these dates were checked, agreed, and explained by Flórez, (*España Sagrada*, vol. X, pp. 200 and following).

63   Niceph. Lib. VIII, ch. XIV.

64   Vid. Letter from Constantine to Cecilianus, bishop of Carthage, in Euseb. lib. X, ch. 6.

65   Lib. II, *Hist.*

to Rome. Caecilianus came with twelve of his own supporters and about the same number of Donatists. The pope pronounced in favour of the legitimate bishop after due consultation with three prelates from Gaul and fifteen Italians (in 313). The Donatists appealed, were found guilty again the following year, and turned to Constantine who, far from hearing them, threatened them with the utmost severity. They took revenge by accusing Hosius, counsel to the Emperor, and pope Melchiades of being *traditores*, supporters and accomplices of Caecilianus. But as St. Augustine said in the Psalm *Contra Donatistas:*

> Sed hoc libenter finxerunt quod se noverunt fecisse,
>
> Quia fama jam loquebatur de librorum traditione,
>
> Sed qui fecerunt latebant in illa perditione:
>
> Inde alios infamaverunt ut se ipsos possint celare.

The crime, then, appears to be on the side of the Donatists. They said of Hosius that he had been convicted of *traditio* by the Spanish bishops and absolved by those of Gaul, and that he had stirred up Constantine against the Donatist faction. St. Augustine (*Contra Parmenianum*, lib.1) calls both accusations slanderous and, in truth, they are at odds with all we know of the persecution Hosius endured. Also worth noting is that the Arians never repeated the Donatists' charge. In regard to his handling of these sectarians, St. Augustine notes that Hosius influenced *"in leniorem partem"* the spirit of the emperor, irritated as the latter with the leaders and proselytes of this schism. Of Hosius' wholesome and vigorous influence on Constantine's disposition, the law *Manumissionibus in Ecclesia* addressed to him is testimony. It can be read in the Theodosian Codex (lib. IV, tit. VII).

A graver danger for the Church than the Donatist schism was the heresy of Arius, an Alexandrian presbyter, of whose history and proclivities I shall speak when we come to the Arians and Visigoths in our peninsula.. Suffice it to remember here what everybody knows, that Arius denied the divinity of the Word and his consubstantiality with the Father. Hosius was sent to Alexandria to calm the waters of dissension between Arius and St. Athanasius, but he judged the silencing of the former as nigh impossible and chose instead to convene a council. The council he called met at Nicea in Bithynia in the year 325, with three hundred and eighteen bishops attending and Hosius presiding. His signature appears first after the pope's delegates in this way: "Hosius episcopus civitatis Cordubensis, provinciae Hispaniae, dixit: Ita credo, sicut superius dictum est. Victor et Vicentius presbyteri urbis Romae pro venerabili viro Papa et Episcopo nostro Sylvestro subscripsimus," etc. This council, the first of the Ecumenicals, must be considered as the most important event to take place in the first Christian centuries, a time of so many glorious wonders. We see the Church rescuing unscathed the treasure of her faith represented here by one of its capital dogmas - the divinity of the *Logos* - from Arius' sharp and sophistical dialectics, and placing it upon a firm foundation. They formulated it in terms so clear that all doors to possible double-meanings and misinterpretations were now closed. The Church, who never introduces new doctrine, defined here the principle of consubstantiality such as one reads it in the first chapter of St. John's Gospel. The world *homousios* (consubstantial) used for the first time by the Nicean Council is no more than a paraphrases of *"Verbum erat apud Deum et Deus erat Verbum"*. Christianity has never changed and will never change its doctrine.

Glorious, indeed, that it was our own Hosius who wrote the Nicene Profession of Faith which the whole of Christendom repeats today as an article of faith and a rule of belief! "We believe in one God, the Father Almighty, maker of all things visible and invisible, and in Jesus Christ, Son of God, Only-begotten of the Father, that is, of one substance (Being) with the Father, God from God, light from light, true God from True God, begotten, not made, *homosius*, that is, *consubstantial* with the Father, through Him all things of heaven and earth were made...". The fact that it was Hosius who drew up this admirable Symbol, a model of precision of style and theological vigour, is expressly confirmed by St. Athana*sius* (Ep. *Ad Solitarios*): "Hic formulam fidei in Nicaena Synodo concepit". Three hundred and eighteen bishops signed it, only five Arians abstained. In some of the Nicean council canons on discipline, numbers III and XVIII especially, one can detect of the Iliberis council's and Hosius' own influence.

In the year 324 he attended the Gagrensis council celebrated in Paphlagonia. He signed the *Acta*, not in first place. Practically all its canons refer to discipline.

We are told that Hosius returned to Spain on Constantine's death in 327. In the last years of his life the emperor seems to have leaned towards the Arian party, even sending St. Athanasius, the great champion of the Nicean faith, to exile in Treveris. We know, however (following Sozomenus), that in his last will he revoked this order and ordered Athanasius' return. Back in his dioceses in Alexandria, the Arians rose once more against this passionate and unyielding athlete of a man, and at a meeting in Antioch in 314 deposed Athanasius and in his place elected Gregory who entered Alexandria with armed soldiers at his side. St. Athanasius had to retire to Rome where he secured the revocation of these anti-canonical acts from pope St. Julius. Emperor Constantius, however, so persecuted this holy bishop that he continuously found himself having to change his place of refuge, though he never gave up fighting the Arians on every point, both in speech and in writing. Finally, a council was called at Sardis, a city of Illyria, in the year 347. Three hundred Greek bishops and seventy-six Latin bishops attended, Hosius presiding and his signature appearing first. He proposed and wrote the majority of the canons, headed with *"Osious Episcopus dixit"*; the synod responded to all: *"Placet"*. St. Athanasius was restored to his see and the Arians were again condemned. Back in Spain, Hosius called for a provincial council to take place in Córdoba to enforce the

Sardis council's' resolutions pronouncing new anathemas against Arius' followers. [66] The *Acta* of this Synod have not been preserved.

By this time, Constantius had firmly placed himself on the side of the Arians. He consented in 355 to the exile of pope Liberius (352-366) for refusing to sign Athanasius' condemnation. Not satisfied with this, the emperor and those close to him insisted on breaking Hosius' determination, of whom they said, according to St. Athanasius, that "his authority alone can rise the world against us: he is the Prince of Councils; whatsoever he says, is heard and complied with everywhere. He wrote the Profession of Faith at the Nicean Synod; he calls the Arians heretics." [67]

To Constantius' insistent threats and demands, this great prelate responded with an admirable letter, the most honourable, valiant, and severe address a priest has ever written to a monarch: [68]

"I was already confessing the Faith" - he wrote to him – "during your grandfather Maximian's persecutions. If you reinstate them, I am ready and willing to suffer it all again, but never to shed innocent blood or betray the truth. You do wrong in writing to me in such manner... in threatening me... Do remember that you are mortal, fear the day of judgement, keep yourself clean for that day, and do not mix in ecclesiastical matters or aspire to teach us. It is you, Sir, who need to be instructed by us. God entrusted the empire to you, the things of the Church He entrusted to us. He who usurps your power contradicts divine ordinance; do not make yourself guilty of a bigger crime by usurping the treasures of the temple. It is written: "Render on to Ceasar what is Ceasar's and to God what is of God". Neither is it licit for us to have command on earth, nor is it for you, emperor, to lord it over what is sacred. I write this to you out of concern for your salvation. I do not agree with the Arians, I do not support them; on the contrary, I anathematise their heresy with all my heart. Nor can I subscribe to your condemnation of Athanasius, whom we, the Roman Church, and one council have declared and pronounced innocent".

A marvellous delineation of each authority's boundaries; an anticipated anathema to the ramblings of all prince-cum-theologians, be they Constantius, Leo the Isaurian, Henry VIII, or James I; an unusual firmness of tone – the sure indication of an iron will; a profound sentiment for truth and justice. We admire it all in the transcribed passage above - the whole epistle was preserved for us

---

[66]   'Quapropter Cordubae Episcopus Santissimus πανόσιος, Osius, Synodum Divinam et Sanctam Episcoporum sua in Civitate convocans, divinitus expositam illustravit doctrinam, condemnans eosdem quos Sardicensis abdicaverat Synodus, et quos ea absolverat recipiens". (*Libell. Synod. in Fabricii Bibliotheca Graeca*, vol. XI, p. 183). This is a ninth-century document but based on older originals.

[67]   Ep. *Ad Solitarios*

[68]   Vid. Appendix, number 2.

by St. Athanasius. Hosius was one hundred years old when he wrote this letter. It made the pedantic and haughty emperor roar with rage before commanding him to present himself at Sirmio, a city of Pannonia.

At the council convened there, preternatural efforts were made to break the bishop of Córdoba's resolve; but he absolutely refused to sign against Athanasius, condescending only to "communicate" with the Arians Ursacius and Valens, a weakness of which he repented much later, as St. Athanasius confirms. "Verum ne ita quidem eam rem pro levi habuit: moriturus enim quasi in testamento suo vim protestatus est, et Arianam haeresim condemnavit, vetuitque eam a quoquam probari aut recipi". And in fact Hosius died that same year 357, at the age of one hundred and one years after being whipped and tortured by Constantius' henchmen, as Socrates Scholasticus tells us (Lib. II, chp. XXXI). [69]

Inconceivable that a man such as this could later be accused of heterodoxy! The man who wrote the Nicene Creed, the man who cleared St. Athanasius' name at the council of Sardis, the man who at the age of one hundred and one wrote to Constantine's son in the terms we have just seen! Nonetheless, it is common to read in many histories that Hosius gave in at the end of his life, and that, not content with signing a profession of faith to the Arian doctrine, he came back to Andalucía to persecute St. Gregory of Elvira and tried to depose him for not wanting to "communicate" with him! And this fable is rounded off with that absurd notorious tale about Hosius' sudden death when, we are told, his mouth "started writhing into a hideous look" [70] at the moment he was about to pronounce sentence against the prelate of Elvira.

A tale so pitifully concocted has been torn down and excluded from history by a large number of critics, above all by Fr. Flórez in his *Disertación Apologética*, and Maceda's *Hosius vere Hosius*, cited above. Let us not dwell unnecessarily on his exoneration.

The accusations against Hosius can be summed up in the following three charges:

1) He communicated with the Arians Ursacius and Valens. So says a text that passes as being written by St. Athanasius: "Ut afflictus, attritusque malis, tandem aegreque cum Ursacio et Valente communicavit, non tamen ut contra Athanasium scriberet". [71] Accepting these words as authentic, all of Hosius' apologists, Flórez included, reason in the following way: when communicating with excommunicated heretics, an action severely prohibited by ancient canons, Hosius succumbed to the inescapable violence inflicted upon

---

69   In all these biographical notes I am following, for the most part, Flórez and Maceda.

70   Mariana's words.

71   Μή ξπογάψαι δε χατα Αθανασιοο (Ep. *Ad Solitarios*)

him, a deed for which he truly repented later with sincere anguish of heart; he never sinned against the faith, however, nor did he ever subscribe to Arian doctrine. He did, in sum, what St. Martin of Tours also ended up doing (as we shall see in the next chapter), when he consented to communicate with the Ithacian bishops in trying to save the Priscillianists from the emperors' wrath, also suffering bitter remorse for his earlier weakness, and *"moestus ingemuit"*, says Sulpicius Severus. St. Athanasius mentions Hosius' action, in every way similar, but without a hint of scandal. It was obviously not sufficient reason for St. Anathasius to cease calling the bishop of Córdoba a saint, as he does repeatedly!

Fr. Maceda goes further. He maintains that the passage from the Epistle *Ad Solitarios* had to be interpolated in the text (already pointed out by pope Liberius' apologists). If not, he contends, we are faced here with more than one irresolvable chronological contradiction, i.e. presuming the bishop of Antioch Leontius alive in the year 358; [72] it would have to have been interpolated also because it does not hold with what precedes and follows in the text. Furthermore, since there are three passages in St. Athanasius (in the two *Apologias* and the Letter *Ad Solitarios*) where one reads that Hosius weakened for a moment (*"cessit ad horam"*), Fr Maceda declares the three of them apocryphal, for the first *Apologia* seems to have been written towards the year 350 and the second in 356.

But could not St. Athanasius have included them later in the text? The truth is that they are present in all the codices and it seems to me that it is always risky to reject a text on the basis of mere conjecture, albeit developed with much ingenuity. Nor does Hosius' defence require going to such extremes. The apologist, steadfast in his plan, dedicates a large number of pages to invalidating the testimonies of St. Hilary as apocryphal, when all that was needed was to point out (as he does at the beginning) that this Father was in exile in Phrygia, and knowing little of Hosius' matters, he let himself be deceived by the slanders propagated by Ursacius and Valens, and thus held Sirmio's second formula to be authentic.

2) The second charge is that in Sirmio he signed a profession to the Arian faith. Nowhere does St. Athanasius mention this, and he must have been better informed than most on a matter so closely concerning him. St. Epiphanius' testimony is cited here (*Adversus haereses*, lib. III, *haer.* LXXIII, number 14): but these are not his words; they were inserted by a copyist who took them from the *Hypomnematismo* of Basilius Ancyranus and George of Laodicea. [73] There one reads about the letters that the Arians "chased" or seized

---

[72]   Maceda's argument is this: either the Epistle *Ad Solitarios* was written before the year 357 and in this case St. Athanasius could not have spoken of Hosius' fall, or it was written later, and then he could not have mentioned Leontius as a person still alive. Maceda inclines, with good reason, towards the first opinion.

[73]   Vid. Maceda, pp. 176 and following; also D. Petavius, *Animadversiones in Epiphanium.*

by fraud from venerable bishop Hosius: "Quo nomine Ecclesiam condemnare se posse putarunt in litteris quas a Venerabili viro Episcopo Hosio per fraudem abstulerunt". St. Athanasius' silence on this matter is sure proof that no such letter signed by Hosius existed, however much the Arians propagated this rumour, which came to the ears of the *Hypomnetatismo*'s authors. Moreover, if such a signature was obtained deceitfully, it is as if it never existed.

True, when St. Hilary in his book *De Synodis* transcribes the formula of the Sirmio heresy, he heads it with these words: "Exemplar blasphemiae apud Syrmium per Hosium et Potamium conscriptae"; but this heading is at odds with the content that follows, where the heresy is attributed to Ursacius, Valens and Germinius, never to Hosius or to Potamius, the bishop of Lisbon. [74] It seems evident that St. Hilary (or his interpolator, if we follow Fr. Meceda's rather awkward method) yielded to popular rumour disseminated by the Arians in the East, to the detriment of Hosiuss and Potamius's good name. That it was no more than a rumour is confirmed by Sulpicius Severus: "Opinio fuit". Could we accept, trusting Sozomen's testimony, [75] that Hosius considered it prudent to dispense with the words '*Homousio*' and '*Homoiousio*' for the love of peace in order to reconcile the heretics and help clear the storm? Fr. Maceda is not far from this view and defends Hosius' supposed stand with examples about St. Hilary and St. Basil the Great who, in similar circumstances, inclined towards a prudent "*economy*", sacrificing words to realities. If this be accepted, all else can be explained. Hosius' condescension was misinterpreted, whether by ignorance or malice, and gave rise to the consequent fables made up by Arians and Luciferians.

3) St. Isidore, in chapters 5 and 14 of *De viris illustribus* relates, based solely on Marcellinus' account, the portentous death of the sacrilegious Hosius as he was about to pass sentence of deposition against St. Gregory. Bishop Gregory had refused to communicate with him judging him an Arian, and Hosius was apparently by now working hand in glove with the Vicar Imperial to have Gregory exiled because of it. But this account falls to pieces the moment we know that Hosius did not die in Spain, as St. Isidore supposes, but in exile at Sirmio. We know this from the Greek *Menologion*: εν ἐξορία τόν δίον χατέλυσε (his life ended while in exile), and all other dates confirm it. Constantius left Rome for Sirmio on the fourth day of the Kalends of June 357. Hosius was

---

[74] 'Quoniam de fide placuerat disceptationem fieri, omnia cum sedulitate inquisita et examinata fuere Syrmii, in praesentia Valentis, Ursacii, Germanii, caeterorumque omnium. Constitit ergo unum esse Deum Omnipotentem, sicuti in universo orbe praedicatur, et unum ejus unigenitum filium, Dominum nostrum Jesum Christum, ex eo ante saecula genitum... Caeterum quae multos conmovet vox, latine quidem dicta *substantia*, graece autem *ousia*, hoc est (ut diligentius cognoscatur) illud quod *omousion* aut *omoiousion* dicitur, nullam eorum vocum mutationem debere fieri, neque de iis sermocinandum in Ecclesia censemus, quod de iis nihil sit scriptum in sacris litteris, et quod illa hominum intellectum et mentem transcendunt...", etc.

[75] Lib. IV, chpts. XII and XV

tortured there to consent to communion with Ursacius and Valens. He died that same year of 357 according to St. Athanasius, on 27th August, and this is confirmed by the Greek *Menologion*. It would have been very difficult in the fourth century to make the journey from Sirmio to Spain in scarcely one and a half months, even accounting for the time it took Constantius to make his way to Pannonia for the celebration of the council. And Hosius, at the grand old age of one hundred and one years and having been lashed, whipped, and tortured at Constantius' command, was not, one might say, in the best of form for a speedy journey.

St. Isidore's authority does not carry the argument here because his narration is based on references exclusive to Marcellinus' writings. And this Marcellinus, who was a Luciferian presbyter, in union with another of the same sect called Faustinus, submitted a *libellus precum*, or more correctly, a *defamatory libel*, to emperors Valentinan and Theodosius in order to justify the offence that they themselves had committed, namely of not admitting to communion or having dealings with any bishop or presbyter who had fallen into any error, even after he had repented and came back to the fold of the Church. This writing by these two Luciferians has been the source of much historical deception; I am thinking particularly of the story about pope St. Marcelinus' *traditio*. The piece that specifically concerns Hosius, Potamius and Florentius, Spaniards all, is worth translating here if only as a historical curiosity, because it is pertinent to the purpose of this book. It reads (and I am transcribing literally): [76]

---

[76] 'Potamius Odissiponae civitatis episcopus, primum quidem fidem Catholicam vindicans, postea vero praemio fundi fiscalis quem habere concupiverat, fidem praevaricatus est. Hunc Osius de Corduba apud Ecclesias Hispaniarum et detexit et repulit ut impium haereticum. Sed et ipse Osius, Potamii querela accersitus ad Constantium Regem minisque perterritus, et metuens, ne senex et dives exilium proscriptionemve pateretur, dat manus impietati et post tot annos praevaricatur in fidem, et regreditur in Hispanias majore cum auctoritate, habens regis terribilem jussionem, ut si quis eidem Episcopus jam facto praevaricatori minique velit communicare, in exilium mitteretur. Sed ad Sanctum Gregorium, Eliberitanae Civitatis Episcopum constantissimum, fidelis nuntius detulit impiam Osii praevaricationem. Unde non acquievit, memor sacrae fidei ac divini judicii, in ejus nefariam communionem... Erat autem tunc temporis Clementinus Vicarius qui ex conventione Osii, et generali praecepto Regis, Sanctum Gregorium per officium Cordubam jussit exhiberi. Interea fama in cognitionem rei cunctos inquietat, et frequens sermo populorum est: quinan est ille Gregorius qui audet Osio resistere? Plurimi eorum et Osii praevaricationem adhuc ignorabant, et quinan esset Sanctus Gregorius nondum bene compertum habetant. Erat etiam apud eos qui illum forte noverant, rudis adhuc Episcopus... Sed ecce ventum est ad Vicarium... et Osius sedet judex...et Sanctus Gregorius... ut reus adsistit...Magna expectatio singulorum ad quam partem victoria declinaret. Et Osius quidem auctoritate nititur suae aetatis, Gregorius vero nititur auctoritate veritatis. Ille quidem fiducia regis terreni, iste autem fiducia regis sempiterni. Et Osius scripto imperatoris nititur, sed Gregorius scripta divinae vocis obtinet. Et cum per omnia Osius confutatur, ita ut suis vocibus quas...scripserat, vindicaretur, commotus ad Clementinum Vicarium: "Non, inquit, cognitio tibi mandata est, sed executio: vides ut resistit praeceptis regabilus; exequere ergo quod mandatum est, mitte eum in exilium". Sed Clementinus, licet non esset Christianus, tamen exhibens reverentiam nomini Episcopatus, respondit Osio: "Non audeo (inquiens) Episcopum in exilium mittere, quandiu in Episcopi nomine perseverat. Sed da tu prior sententiam, eum de Episcopatus honore

"Potamius, bishop of Lisbon, a former defender of the Catholic Faith, prevaricated later for love of a fiscal *fundus* which he wanted to acquire. Hosius, bishop of Córdoba, discovered his wickedness and made all churches of Spain declare him impious and heretic. Oh but this same Hosius, summoned and threatened by emperor Constantius, and fearful, since he was old and rich, of exile and of losing his wealth, surrendered to impiety, prevaricated of the faith after so many years, and came back to Spain with terrible regal authority to exile all bishops that would not consent to communion with prevaricators. And to the ear of holy Gregory, bishop of Iliberis, comes the news of Hosius' impious prevarication and faithfully and steadfastly refuses any nefarious communion with him... The Vicar Clementinus, at Hosius' request, and in obedience to imperial command, called Gregory to Córdoba... and the people asked: "Who is this Gregory that dares defy Hosius?" because many did not know of Hosius' weakness but knew much about holy Gregory's virtue whom they judged a fledgling and novice prelate... So they both come to the Vicar's presence, Hosius as judge, Gregory as accused... great anxiety all around in expectation of the outcome of this event. Hosius, with the authority of his white hair; Gregory with the authority of virtue. Hosius, his faith placed on an earthly king; Gregory's faith on the King Eternal. Hosius, with his trust on an imperial prescript; Gregory, on the divine Word... And Hosius, seeing that he had the worst in the affair because Gregory refuted him with arguments taken from his own writings, cried out at the Vicar: "You see how he is resisting the legal mandates: carry out what has been commanded of you. Send him into exile". The Vicar was not a Christian but had respect for Episcopal dignity and answered Hosius, saying: "I dare not send a bishop into exile. You pass the

---

dejiciens, et tunc demum exequar in eum quasi privatum quod ex praecepto Imperatoris fieri desideras". Ut autem vidit Sanctus Gregorius quod Osius vellet dare sententiam, appellat ad verum et potentem judicem Christum, totis fidei suae viribus exclamans: "Christe Deus, qui venturus es judicare vivos et mortuos, ne patiaris hodie humanam proferri sententiam adversum me, minimum servum tuum, qui pro fide tui nominis ut reus assistens spectaculum praebeo. Sed tu ipse, quaeso, in causa tua hodie judica: ipsa sententiam proferre dignaveris per ultionem. Non hoc quasi metuens exilium fieri cupio, cum mihi pro tuo nomine nullum supplicium non suave sit: sed ut multi praevaricationis errore liberentur, cum praesentem et momentaneam videant ultionem". Et cum multo invidiosius et sanctius Deum verbis fidelibus interpellat, ecce repente Osius, cum sententiam conatur exponere, os vertit, distorquens pariter et cervicem, defessus in terram eliditur, atque illic expirat, aut, ut quidam dicunt, obmutuit. Inde tamen effertur ut mortuus. Sed et Potamio non fuit inulta sacrae fidei praevaricatio. Denique cum ad fundum properat, quem pro impia fidei subscriptione ab Imperatore meruerat impetrare, dans novas poenas linguae per quam blasphemaverat, in via moritur, nullus fructus fundi vel visione percipiens. Sed et Florentius, qui Osio et Potamio jam praevaricatoribus in loco quodam communicavit, dedit et ipse nova supplicia. Nan cum in conventu plebis sedet in throno, repente eliditur et palpitat, atque foras sublatus vires resumpsit. Et iterum et alia vice eum ingressus sedisset, similitet patitur...Nihilominus postea cum intrare perseverasset, ita tertia vice de throno excutitur, ut quasi indignus throno repelli videatur, atque elisus in terram, ita palpitans torquebatur, ut cum quadam duritie et magnis cruciatibus eidem spiritus extorquerentur. Et inde jam tollitur, non ex more resumendus, sed sepeliendus"., etc. (*Libellus Precum*, in Flórez, *España Sagrada*, vol. X, Appendix).

sentence of deposition". And St. Gregory, seeing that Hosius was about to pronounce sentence, appealed to the true and omnipotent judge, Christ, with all the ardour of his faith, crying: "O Christ, my Lord, thee who are to come to judge the living and the dead, do not permit this day that sentence be passed against me, your unworthy servant, persecuted for confessing your name. Not because I fear exile, for all torture is sweet to me for your love, but so that many may stay free from prevarication upon seeing your swift and prompt revenge". And then, suddenly, as he was about to pass sentence, Hosius' mouth and neck started wriggling all about and, contorted, he fell to the ground and there expired, or *as others say*, was left unconscious. They say that afterwards the Vicar threw himself at the feet of the saint and pleaded forgiveness".

And they go on…

"Potamius' prevarication did not go unpunished. He died on his way to acquire that *fundus* he had obtained from the emperor in compensation for his impious endorsement, and did not live to see (nor even come close to seeing!) the fruit of his vineyard. He died of cancer of that same tongue he had so blasphemed with".

…and on:

"Florentinus (the bishop of Mérida) who had communicated with the prevaricators Hosius and Potamius was punished with a different kind of torture. When he went to occupy his see before the people, he was thrown off it by a mysterious power, and started shaking. He tried again and again, but was always thrown off as unworthy, and flat on the ground, he wriggled and twisted as if, with great violence, he was being tormented from inside. From there he went to his grave".

Well now, what are we to make of all these melodramas? Actually, they show considerable imagination on the part of their authors. What are we to make indeed of that Hosius robed with such "terrible authority", of St. Gregory Beticus who asks for - and gets - such swift and terrible revenge, a prayer so alien to charity and meekness of heart, to justice even, when we are here speaking of the great Hosius, pillar of the Church, even if he showed a moment of weakness when he was one hundred years old; of that Vicar, pagan yet so respectful of Episcopal authority (when during Constantius' reign sending bishops into exile was an everyday affair), but who then asks Hosius to be the one to exile Gregory as if, for him, the issue was changed by changing the procedure; and finally, the doubt by which the authors of the *libellus* show themselves, not quite knowing if Hosius fell down dead or merely fainted. What is all this but the unequivocal sign of a clumsy work of fiction? Note also that the death or punishment Florentius gets is similar to that of Hosius. But of course! They all come from the same workshop. They even finish with the same cry: "All of Spain knows we are not telling tales" *("scit melius omnis Hispania, quod ista non fingimus")*; "This, all of Mérida knows: its citizens saw it with their very own eyes".

Let us not insist on the contradictions and anachronisms of a fairy tale that so easily betrays itself.

Of Florentius and Potamius we know little, so I will not dedicate a separate chapter to them. They were probably good bishops, free from the obstinacy and barbarous intolerance of the schismatic Luciferians. St. Febadius mentions an epistle, *De possibilitate Dei*, that the Fotinian heretics publicised with Potamius' name on it. [77]

Against this absurd tale that calls Hosius - the man who wrote that letter to Constantius - timid and greedy (this said of a man twice confessor of the Faith!) - against this, I say, we submit St. Athanasius' lucid testimony of the man who so bravely fought the Arians with him side by side:

"Hosius died protesting against violence, condemning the Arian heresy and forbidding everyone to follow or protect it..." "But why go on praising this holy old man" (continues St. Athanasius), "this outstanding confessor of Christ! The whole world knows Hosius was exiled and persecuted because of the Faith. What council did he not preside over? When did he speak before bishops that even one was not of one mind with him? What church was left undefended or unprotected by him? What sinner came to him that did not regain hope and encouragement? What sick, ailing or needy person who came to him did not receive favour and succour in all things?" [78]

The Greek Church venerates Hosius as a saint on the 27th of August. The Latin Church has not as yet canonised him. It is probably this *libellus* by the Luciferians that stands in the way. [79]

Writings by Hosius that have come down to us are brief and few in number - true jewels nonetheless. They are Nicea's Profession of Faith, the letter to Constantius, and fifteen canons of the Sardis Council. St. Isidore also attributes to him a letter to his sister, *De laude virginitatis*, written, he says, in a beautiful and even-tempered style, and a treatise on the interpretation of priestly vestments in the Old Law. [80] St. Athanasius appears to allude to some polemic writings by Hosius against the Arians. Hosius also considered translating Plato's

---

[77]   Could this Potamius be a different person from the bishop of Lisbon? Father Maceda maintains they are the same.

[78]   Ποιας γαρ ού χαθηγήσατο συνόδου χαί λέγων όρθως ού παντας έπειδε ποια τις προσήλθην αύτώ χαί ού χαρίων άπήλθε παρ αύτού τις ήτησε δεόμενος χαί ούχ ανεχω ρησε τυχών ών ήθέλησε…(Apologia *De fuga sua*).

[79]   On the sanctity and age-old veneration of Hosius, see Maceda's second dissertation.

[80]   'Hosius Episcopus Cordubensis Ecclesiae civitatis Hispaniarum, eloquentiae viribus exercitatus, scripsit ad sororem suam *De Laude virginitatis*, epistolam pulchro ac disserto comptam eloquio. Composuitque aliud opus *De interpretatione vestium sacerdotalium*, quae sunt in Veteri Testamento, egregio quidem sensu et ingenio elaboratum." *De viris illustribus*.

Fr. Macesa (as is his custom), doubts that these chapters are St. Isidore's.

Timeo from the Latin but never managed to get to it and bid Caldicius with this task. This Caldicius did and dedicated the book to him - known in the history of Philosophy as being practically the only writing by Plato known in the Middle Ages.

The beneficent influence of Hosius has even been felt in philosophical studies, representing for us the Catholic Platonism of the Early Fathers! [81]

The Donatists: Lucilla

I incidentally touched above on the issue of the Donatists. Allow me to add a few more words on the schism they advocated. I will put it in these terms: Once upon a time there was once a wealthy Spanish lady [82] called Lucilla who lived in Carthage. She was devout and very arrogant, and not too scrupulous in her devotions. She loathed Caecilianus, bishop of Carthage, because he had reprimanded her on the quasi-idolatrous cult she offered to the relics of a non-canonised martyr. Incensed, Lucilla, a *"potens et factiosa femina"*, Optatus Milevitanus calls her, joined Donatus of the *Casae Nigrae* party and other discontents from Caecilianus' election, lavishly started throwing money around to buy a good number of recruits to her cause, and created a schism that was to divide the African Church for many years.

There were about seventy of these schismatics when they all gathered together and celebrated a *conciliabulum* in Carthage. They proceeded to depose Caecilianus and in his place named Maiorinus, Lucila's servant. To validate her impertinence, they accused Caecilianus of being a *traditor* ('surrenderer'). To this schism they added some errors on dogma saying, for example, that theirs was the one and true church, hence anyone who wanted to join them had to be re-baptised because "baptism is not valid outside of the church". On this issue of the re-baptised, they were putting into practice the ancient decision of African bishops who had tenaciously sustained the same opinion on apostates and heretics. The Donatist church, risen against Rome, was but one of those

---

[81]   When treating of Hosius, I did not merit Eusebius Vercelli's letter to Gregory Iliberitanus or Beticus, where these words are written: 'Transgressori te Hosio didici restitisse et pluribus cedentibus Arimino in communicatione Valentis et Ursatii', because this letter is considered apocryphal. If proof were needed, it would suffice to mention that it supposes Hosius alive at the time of the council of Rimini, when in fact he had been in his grave since the year 357.

Others, in addition to Flórez and Meceda, have taken up Hosius' vindication: Cardinal Baronius, Dr. Aldrete, Don Francisco de Mendoza, Cardinal Aguirre, Gómez Bravo, Sánchez de Feria, and other Spaniards as well as foreigners, among the latter Josafat Massaro.

[See also the book by Vicente Sancho del Castillo (Pedro Roca): *Osius, Evêque de Cordoue (256-357)*; Namur, 1898, and A. Bonilla, *Historia de la Filosofía Española*, I, Madrid, 1908, p. 182 and following (Editor, 1912].

[82]   Concerning Lucilla, see St. Augustine's epistles, especially those numbered 43, 47, 57, 58, 60, 61, 70, 108-112, 120, etc. in the *Maurina* edition.

innumerable forms which the spirit of rebellion takes and will take till the end of time. But on questions of dogma it had little influence. We have already mentioned the first councils that condemned it and of the many voices the schismatics raised against Hosius. Among challengers to their insolence stands Olympius, bishop of Barcelona, who in the company of Eunomius crossed over to Africa commissioned by the emperor to allay those scandals. In the forty days they were in Carthage they held audience with both sides and passed sentence against the Donatists. But the conflict did not stop. A second Donatus, a man of sharp mind who propagated Arian doctrines, succeeded Maiorinus. St. Augustine had his hands full in finishing off all remnants of this heresy. Let us remember his most curious psalm *Contra Donatistas.*

> Omnes qui gaudetis pace, modo verum judicate:
>
> Homines multum superbi, qui justos se dicunt esse
>
> Sic fecerunt scissuram et altare contra altare:
>
> Diabolo se tradiderunt, cum pugnant de traditione
>
> Et crimen quod commisserunt in alios volunt transferre,
>
> Ipsi tradiderunt libros et nos audent accusare,
>
> Ut pejus committant scelus quam commiserunt ante.

This type of Psalmody, which is very long and should be recited in the tone of the Church's chants, contributed much to ruining the credit of the last Donatists among the people of Hippo, Tagaste and Carthage.

Donatism continued to exist in Africa (in leaps and bounds) for about one and a half centuries longer. The history of this theological polemic is rather curious, sometimes degenerating into armed conflict in open fields and in public squares. It was fought with all the ardour of the African character, but it is not incumbent upon me to proceed with its history now; I content myself with pointing out in passing Lucilla's role in such disturbances. As a footnote below, I quote passages from Optatus of Milevis that refer to her. [83]

---

[83]   'Hoc apud Carthaginem post ordinationem Caeciliani factum esse, nemo est qui nesciat: per *Lucillam* scilicet, nescio quam, feminam factiosam, quae ante concussam persecutionis turbinibus pacem, dum adhuc in tranquillo esset Ecclesia, cum correctionem Archidiaconi Caeciliani ferre non posset, quae ante spiritualem cibum et potum, os nescio cujus Martyris, si tamen Martyris, libare dicebatur, et cum praeponeret calici salutari os nescio cujus hominis mortui, etsi Martyris sed necdum vindicati, correpta, cum confusione, irata discessit. Irascenti et dolenti, ne disciplinae succumberet, occurrit subito persecutionis irata tempestas...'

He continues relating Caecilianus' election, and adds: "Convocantur supra memorati seniores qui faucibus avaritiae commendatam ebiberant praedam. Cum reddere cogerentur, subduxerunt communioni plebem. Non minus et ambitores quibus et ordinari non contigi, necnon et *Lucilla*...cum omnibus suis, potens et factiosa femina, communioni miscere noluit... Schisma igitur illo tempore confusae mulieris iracundia peperit, ambitus nutrivit, avaritia roboravit... Sic exitum est foras et altare contra altare erectum est, et ordinatio illicite celebrata, et

The Luciferians: Vincent

At the council of Rimini celebrated in 359 some prelates subscribed to the Arian profession of faith. A notable scandal arose subsequently in the whole of the Christian world, and many bishops proceeded to excommunicate the prevaricators. Luciferus, bishop of Caller, in Sardegna, went further. He refused unconditionally to have any dealings with the Arians, which refusal included not receiving them to penance even when they repented. Out of this conviction, unwaveringly maintained - one truly opposed to the spirit of the Gospel which does not wish for the sinner to die but to be converted and live - arose a sect, more schismatic than heretical, refuted by St. Jerome in the Dialogue *Adversus Luciferianos*. Some have chosen to believe that St. Gregory of Betis belonged to this sect based on the Marcellinus' *libellus* we saw above when discussing Hosius; on Eusebius Vercelli's letter, which is surely apocryphal, in whichever light one cares to look at it; and finally (and this is the only testimony that carries weight) on the words of St. Jerome: "Lucifer Calaritanus Episcopus moritur, qui cum Gregorio Episcopo Hispaniarum et Philone Lybiae, numquam se Arianae miscuit pravitati". My own conclusion from this is that Gregory and Philo did not mix with the Arians or succumbed to their impiety, not that they agreed with Luciferus in denying them penance. Of Luciferus alone, not of the others, St. Jerome goes on to say: "Ipse a suorum communione descivit".

I am simply at a loss regarding what to make of presbyter Vincent. His story is told in that same *libellus* by the Luciferians. Told, again literally, in this way:

"Oh how Vincent suffered in Spain! And only because he did not consent to the malice of prevaricators and did not want to follow them, and because he belonged to the confession of holy Gregory! First, they accused him to the consular Governor of Betis. Then, one Sunday, they all came to church... a great multitude following, but they did not find Vincent. Alas, he had suspected their coming and told the people what was going to happen... But they, who had come ready to feed their revenge, not wanting to let their rage go idle, started hitting with clubs several ministers of the Lord who soon after expired". [84]

Then the authors of this book tell us how these Arians (the ones who were attacking them, the Luciferians) had some of the leading citizens arrested, and by means of hunger and cold killed one of them who had remained

---

Maiorinus qui Lector in Diacono Caeciliani fuerat, domesticus Lucillae, ipsa suffragante, Episcopus ordinatus est a traditoribus qui in Concilio Numidiae...' etc. (St. Optati Afri, *De Schismate Donatistarum*, lib. I, in volume IV, p. 344, second column of the *Max. Coll. Vet. Pat.* Lugd., 1677).

[84]   *Libellus Precum*, in Flórez, vol. X, Appendices.

steadfast in the faith. The prime movers in this whole commotion and in the profanation of the church were, apparently, two bishops, Luciosus and Higinius. But the masses had taken themselves off with Vincent and built a separate church on an open field next to the city. And so these two evil bishops, they say, irritated once more, called the *decuriones* and the people for help, went to the recently founded chapel, broke open its doors, stole the sacred vessels, and placed the Christian altar at the feet of an idol.

I think all of this is a tale re-arranged by the Luciferians to the measure of their desire! Nowhere do we find news of any such riots, nor is the city mentioned where this is supposed to have occurred. There was one Higinius, for sure, bishop of Córdoba, whose name will resound more loudly on the chapter on the Priscillianists. Presbyter Vincent or Vincentius is so obscure that we need not dwell on his vindication – there is insufficient data for this - so we can neither affirm nor deny that he was a Luciferian. It matters little.

From some of these previous stories I think we can infer that there were already Arians in Spain about this time, but we have no more notices than those mentioned, and so I shall not give them a separate chapter.

In sum: At a time like this, when discord was mounting among our bishops and the tight knot of unity between the churches was beginning to loosen; with the great Hosius dead and his successors engaged in bloody battles amongst themselves, and (if indeed we can believe Marcellinus' *libellus*) when the Arians and the Luciferians were busy turning temples into battlefields; when, from Africa, the Donatist spirit was beginning to make itself felt, at this precise moment Priscillianism raised its ugly head: the first of the great calamities the Spanish Church has had to endure and conquer in the long and glorious course of her history. This we shall see in the next chapter.[85]

---

[85]   On St. Gregory Béticus, see Nicolás Antonio, *Bibliotheca Hispana Vetus*, vol. I, p. 138.
Flórez, *España Sagrada*, vol. XII, tract XXXVII, chpt. 3.

Chapter 2

Roman Spain (continued)

The Fourth and Fifth centuries

Gnosticism. Origin and evolution of the Gnostic schools.

The Agapeae (Marcus, Elpidius, Agape).

Priscillian and his followers.

Priscillianism after Priscillian.

Priscillian Literature.

Exposition of Priscillianism: its importance in the history of heresy and in Spanish Letters.

Anti-Priscillianist reaction: the *Ithacians*.

Origenism (The two Aviti).

On the theological polemics in Roman Spain: Prudentius, Orosius and others refute several heretics of their time.

Origin and Evolution of the Gnostic Schools

A number of heterodox sects appeared at this time in Roman Spain. They all went by the general name of *Agapetes* or *Priscillianists*. They were, in fact, but the last coils of that large Gnostic serpent that since the first Christian century had been snarling itself perfidiously around the robust trunk of the Faith, seeking to choke it.

Gnosticism is not one sole or individual heresy. It is a collection, or *pandemonium,* of diverse theosophical speculations – all concurring on principles that link up with beliefs and philosophies dating back to pre-Christian times. But before we give a general indication of each particular School, especially of those that in one way or another influenced Priscillian most, let us first look at what all of these doctrines had in common.

They all answered to the general label, for them complimentary, of "Gnostics". Gnostic heresiarchs aspired to *Gnosis* – to them, the "perfect" science or knowledge - and looked upon all other Christians as unknowing or unenlightened. "They call themselves Gnostics", says St. John Chrysostom plainly, "because they like to think they know more than everybody else". But this portentous knowledge of theirs was not based on scholarship, rational analysis, logic, or any other systematic intellectual labour. Gnostics do not dispute, they affirm. They maintained that their esoteric science - banned to the profane, of course – had come to them through the apostolic tradition or, even, via supernatural communications. Both the Gnostics and Pneumatics made a point of distancing themselves from the Psychics, that is to say, from all those still subject to the darkness of error and the stimuli of the flesh. The Gnostic was the one person in possession of knowledge that was unique – knowledge reserved for the initiated.

Was this presumption to a hidden and mysterious science something new? Of course not! Oriental priests, the Brahmin, Magi, Chaldeans and Egyptians, they all had, as a sacred deposit, a doctrine that was not to be revealed to the mob. In Greece, this was the case with the Eleusinian mysteries in religion and the Pythagorean initiations in philosophy. This separation, this distinction that all masters, including Plato, including Aristotle, made among their disciples between *exoterics* and *esoterics* (outward and inward) is indicative also, to a lesser degree, of a tendency born of human conceit: to turn what is a point of view, a philosophy, an opinion, into something obscure and full of incomprehensible symbolism, with the aim of making it more alluring, rarer, thus more valuable. At other times, it arose simply out of the desire or necessity to avoid wounding directly official thinking or Government rule.

Gnosticism in the East arose out of pride of caste or political interest, and in Greece out of any of the above reasons or perhaps simply from the aesthetic aim of making learning more attractive by bathing it in that twilight that often dazzles more than full brilliance. Within Christianity, this approach was no longer plausible or tenable. Christian teaching is universal and eternal: it speaks the same words to Jew and Gentile, to the ignorant and the wise. Christianity does not have – cannot have – arcane cults or secret doctrines. If during the times of persecution it took its books and doctrine underground, this was to protect them from pagans, but never from those who had already been baptised. And when that storm cleared, it showed and displayed itself before the whole world as something that neither minds nor fears however many scrutinising eyes care to investigate or inspect it. Gnosis, then, was regression, a step backwards that contradicted the popular nature of Christianity in every way. After Christianity, the motive for Gnostic doctrines was unbridled pride; a desire for knowledge denied to all others, a fondness for putting up class and initiation barriers to a doctrine that admits none.

A second characteristic common to all these sects was "mysticism", a false, heterodox mysticism, because a rotten tree can never yield wholesome fruit. Gnostics commence with reason and then slaughter common sense: the route could not be more direct. They do not demonstrate, they do not prove, and they do not debate. Like those German idealists of the first third of this century [86] they build their systems *a priori*; and when they come up against some logical barrier or sensible axiom, or any other essential element of consciousness

---

[86]   Nineteenth century (Editor, 1912).

that conflicts with their system, they look away, ignore it, twist it, alter it, or simply disregard it as the offspring of some vulgar intelligence - something from someone not yet capable of Gnosis - of that vision of God "in the true light". They accepted Scripture in whole or in part, but with the liberty to apply their own exegesis, which of course meant rejecting any book, chapter or paragraph that contradicted their imaginations. And what they did keep and not throw out, they brutally interpreted; Marcion is the prototype of these *exegetes*.

Gnosticism, in aim and method, is theosophy. The questions it principally seeks to resolve are three: the origin of being, the source or cause of evil in the world, and redemption.

On the first - the origin of being - all Gnostics are *emanatists:* they substitute for Creation an on-going or eternal progression of the divine essence. We will have occasion to see the many ingenious combinations they came up with to demonstrate this. As for the cause of evil, all Gnostics are dualists, with this difference: some suppose the sources of good and evil to be eternal, whereas others attach an inferior or subordinate existence to the root of disorder and sin, as if dependent upon temporal causes. As to redemption, practically all Gnostics understood this to include the intellectual or celestial world. In all else, they were Docetists: they denied the hypostatic union and the humanity of Christ whose body they understood as something close to that of a phantom. Their Christology shows a most diverse range of tonality (not to say peculiar extravagances). On morality, they differ greatly among themselves, but they never really set out to speculate on it. Some sects called for asceticism and self-flagellation as a means to conquer the *hylic*, or material side, so as to liberate oneself from it, while others taught and practised the principle that once perfect Gnosis is reached, the straying of the flesh does not matter because *everything is pure for the pure*. In this, they were the precursors of Molinonism and the Illuminati and Alumbrados sects of the sixteenth century.

In its teaching, as in its symbolism, Gnosticism's doctrine was novel enough. Not original, however, but syncretist, for syncretism was the law of the philosophical world when these heresies appeared. In Greece (and under this name I include all Greek-speaking peoples), creative activity had been exhausted. Instead of founding new systems they gathered and assembled old ones and strove to reconcile them. It was a time of erudition, of scholarship, of philosophical old age; of a movement that was vast but barely fruitful. The old Schools were dying out or transforming themselves. Some taught morals only, the Stoics for example, who had come to set up camp in Rome; the Epicureans, also, who battled with them in the field of ethics, having by now quite forgotten their physical and cosmological theories to which, not long before, Lucretius had built such an everlasting monument. These aside, the tendency was to blend and fuse with Platonism, alive and thriving even after the two *Academic* metamorphoses. But syncretism did not stop there. It became broader and richer (if accumulation of theories can be called wealth) when in Alexandria it happened to stumble upon the dogmas of Egypt, Judea, Persia, even India, second-hand in this case. And this is how Neo-Platonism and Gnosis proper began - two systems parallel and in many ways identical however fiercely they may have fought one another - the Gnostics shielding themselves under the umbrella of Christianity (which they understood badly and explicated worse), and the last of the Neo-Platonists ending up as the champions of paganism, symbolically interpreted.

The first *synchretic school* of Alexandria before Gnosticism was that of the Hellenist Jews Aristobulus and Philo. Equally in love with Mosaic Law and Greek philosophy, they tried to reconcile both by giving the former an allegorical interpretation of which the latter was to be copy and reflection. Aristobulus attempted this conciliation with *Peripatetism*, which was by then losing supporters by the day. Philo, more fortunate or wiser, created Neo-Platonism. He does violence to the texts, he contorts Biblical passages, and there he finds the Platonic *logos*, the *archetypal ideas*, the intellectual world, κόσμος νοητός, eternal *Sophia*, and the δαίμονες. Philo says there is an irrational principle in the soul, ἄλογον, which does not come from God but from the inferior spirits; he teaches purification by means of a series of successive transformations once the spirit has been freed from the prison chains of matter. He sees a combat between light and darkness, good and evil, a combat that began with sin - the offspring of the inferior part of the soul - and which will end with the reestablishment of order thanks to the succour of divine *Sophia* and the good δαίμονες, which he equates to the angels of Scripture. Philo's Judeo-Platonic syncretism eulogises the ascetic life, and it is here that the Hebrew sect of the Therapeutae joins in. Philo is the progenitor of Gnosis, not only because of his emanatist and dualist visions but also, and principally, because of the arcane science he sees in Scripture, and the illuminations and ecstasies he imagines necessary in order to know something of the divine essence.

Many (including Jacques Matter himself in the first edition of his excellent book) see the Kabbalah as one of the precedents of Gnosis. Its beginnings are similar to those we are soon going to study: the king of light, *Ensoph*, from whom all emanates; the *Sephirot*, or successive emanations; the *Adam Kadmon*, type and model of universal existence, creator and preserver of the world; a malefic primal principle represented by the *Klippoth* and their leader Belial, a principle that will be absorbed by the good, which will then result in universal *palingenesis*; the distinction of four principles in the soul of man (*Nephes*, appetitive; Ruah, affective; Neshamah, rational; and *Jaiah*, spiritual); the concept of matter as the prison cell of the spirit... all this resembles the πατήρ ἄγνωστος of the Gnostics, their *aeons* and *pleroma*, *Sophia* and the *demiurge*, the two roots of Manichaeism, and the separation of the πνευμα, the ψυχη, and the ὕλη within *hyle*, the vital human principle. But today, since it has been proven *usque ad evidentiam* that the Kabbalah was not systematised and classified until the Middle Ages, and that the Zohar, the most famous of the books in which it is contained was written by Moises de León, a Spanish Jew from the thirteenth century [87] (even if Kabbalah doctrines go back to the most remote times of Judaism), we have to accept that the Kabbalah is a residuum, a blend, not only of Zoroastrianism and Talmud traditions, but of Gnosticism and neo-Platonism as well, in the transmission of which our own Avicebron's emanatist book, *Fuente de la Vida (Fons Vitae)* must have exercised more than a little influence.

Syrian Gnosticism was influenced in no small measure by doctrines from Persia, above all by the Mazdaist reform, by then already modified by Parsism. *Zrwan Akarana* (eternity) is equivalent to πατήρ άγνωστος. The dualism of its emanations - Ohrmuzd (Ahura Mazda) and Ahriman (Angra Mainyu) – is copied almost point by point by practically all heresies of the first four centuries: the good spirits *Amhaspands*, *Izeds* and *Feruers*, and the malefic ones or *devas* figure, under different names, in the Kabbalah and in Gnosis. The same resemblance exists in the part attributed to an evil or ignorant spirit, always of an inferior class (called *demiurge* by the Gnostics), in the creation of the world and of man; in restoration of order or the final *palingenesis*, which will end the dominion of evil in the world.

Egyptian Gnosis, richer than the Syriac, also adorned itself with the remains of the ancient cults of that land. There, too, was a hidden god called *Ammon* or *Ammon Ra*. But Egypt's celestial hierarchy was much more complex that that of the Persians. The Gnostics imitated point by point the popular distribution of Egyptian deities in *triads* and *tetrads* and called them *syzygias*. *Neith* became *Ennoia*. They kept *Horus,* varying his attributes slightly. They adopted the symbols of *Knuphis* and *Phta* as well as some of the legends of Hermes whom they identified with their *Christos*. This was before the Neoplatonists took over the *hermetic* myth attributing books to Hermes, or the Alchemists came to believe him the inventor of the Philosopher's Stone. To summarise: Egypt's Gnostics made a bold attempt to Christianise the ancient and confused religion of their nation. Christianity, however, rejected this syncretic doctrine because its pantheist and dualist elements disturbed and tarnished the purity of its faith.

In truth, Gnostics were Christian in name only. Nothing can be more contrary to the sober and severe teaching of St. Paul's epistles, to that "non magis sapere quam oportet sapere" than those theosophies and oriental visions that sought to reveal the indecipherable. It was Christianity's destiny to wrestle with each of its many diverse enemies in both great regions of the ancient world. In the West, the struggle was to overcome official paganism and the tyranny of the Caesars; in the East, this war was always about origins and primal principles. But recalcitrant Jews, Persian and Syrian priests and Alexandrian philosophers were not the ones to be most feared in this struggle: it was that

---

[87]   See *La Kabbale ou philosophie religieuse des Hébreux*, by Franck, and *Diálogos sobre la Cábala y el Zohar* (1852), written by the learned Jew Luzzato. [Also, S. Karppe: *Etude sur les origines et la nature du Zohar*, Paris, 1901 (Editor, 1912)].

subtle, guarded and underhand war upon which the Gnostics embarked against Christianity by mixing with the faithful in appearance only, sharing deceitfully in their language and teaching.

We see the first traces of this struggle in the New Testament. St. Paul described the Gnostics of his time in vivid colours. He said to Timothy: "Depositam custodi, devitans profanas verborum novitates et oppositiones falsi nominis scientiae" (καινοφονίας, says the Greek text). In another passage of the same epistle, he condemns those "myths and interminable genealogies" which must have been the *aeons-sephirot* of the Gnostics, as ancient interpreters see it. In his Letter to the Colossians, he more specifically refutes opinions which, if they did not belong to the Gnostics, must be attributed to their immediate forefathers and masters. St. John's Gospel, the first chapter especially, goes directly against the Nicolaites and the Cerinthians, two branches of primitive Gnosticism.

But it is not my intention to write the history of Gnosticism here. This has already been done well, with good method and ample wealth of data by Mr. Matter though, in my view, with an overly excessive enthusiasm on his part towards these sects. [88] Should the reader wish to go to the sources, he would do well to consult the following: *Pistis Sophia*, erroneously attributed to the heresiarch Valentinus; some of the apocryphal gospels, where one finds remnants of the errors I refer to here; St. Irenaeus' five books against heresies; the *Stromata* of Clement of Alexandria; Origen's works against Celsus and Marcion, and the *Philosophoumena*, also with scant foundation attributed to him; St. Ephrem of Syria's anti-Gnostic hymns; the treatise on *Heresies* by St. Epiphanius, and Theodoret's *Heretical Fables*. As for the Latins (who are of little help here), the books by Tertullian against Valentinus and Marcion, the *Register of Heresies* compiled by Philastrius, bishop of Brescia, and St. Augustine. If to these we add the refutation of Gnostic doctrines done by Plotinus the Neoplatonist, and the collection of stones and amulets used by partisans of Egyptian Gnosis, [89] we shall have accounted for all the contributory material submitted to date by the historians of these heresies.

I will try to give a very brief summary of each of these principal sects as a preliminary requisite to our study.

Let us agree in naming Simon of Samaria, also known as Simon Magus, as the first leader of the Gnostics. Of him we read in the Acts of the Apostles that he tried to buy from St. Peter the gift of conferring the *pneuma* by imposition of hands. This Simon, archetypal representative of the theosophical

---

[88]   *Histoire critique du Gnosticisme et de son influence sur les sectes religieuses et philosophiques des six premiers siècles de l'ère chrétienne*, par Jacques Matter, Paris, 1828, 3 vols in octavo. The second edition with much addenda. [Vid. also E. H. Schmitt, *Gnosis der Altertums*, 1903 (Editor, 1912)].

[89]   Matter shows a good number of them in the third volume of his work.

and magic speculations of his time, was above all a theurgist, much like Apollonius of Tyana. In Samaria they called him 'the great power of God' (ή δῦναμίς τοῦ θεού ή μεγάλη). After his separation from the Apostles, he gave himself the names of Virtue of God, Word of God, Paraclitus, Omnipotent, and even on some occasion managed to say "ego omnia Dei", as the most close-minded Germanic pantheist could have done in our century. In Simon Magus' mind, the immutable and permanent being had numerous ways of manifesting itself in things temporal and transitory - much like Hegel's *Idea*, in fact, around which all is movement, variety and change; much like Spinoza's *substance*, too, whose attributes are infinite matter and infinite thought. Because, for the Samarian soothsayer, the root of the universe is *determined* (to use today's word) by two classes of emanations or progressions: the *material* and the *intellectual*, the visible and the invisible. On other issues, Simon ends up concocting a mixture of Christianity and Neoplatonism. For example, he attributes Creation to the ἔννοια, *logos*, or divine thought. From this ἔννοια he creates another myth, similar to *Sophia*, which he believes had been exiled in the human body, subjected to transmigration and a whole range of other calamities until, finally, it is to go back to the celestial sphere which he symbolised, or rather, he maintained it had been incarnated in a slave of his by the beautiful name of *Helena*, whom he had bought in the Troad and quickly turned into his concubine. It seems certain that Simon's disciples confused the ἔννοια with the *Pneuma* and with *Sophia*. On the whole, this magus of Samaria appears (to all manner of understanding) a suave, cunning, and rather creative trickster. He even divined the principal tenet of the sixteenth-century pseudo-Reformation! Theodoret tells us that Simon went about exhorting his disciples not to fear the rule of law but freely to do as they saw fit, for *justification* (he said) comes from grace, not good works (ου δια πραξεων αγαθων αλλα δια χαριτος). Good conduct, obviously, had nothing to do with it. We shall have an opportunity to see how faithfully many Gnostics followed this tenet.

The Simonic sect spread to Syria, Phrygia, Rome and other regions. From it, with other less known branches, sprang the Docetists or Phantastics, who denied that the Word had truly taken our human flesh as his own and participated in our nature, and the Menandrians, so named after their leader who, like Simon, took on airs of pseudo-prophet and said he had been sent by the supreme power of God, in whose name he baptised. To his devotees he promised immortality and eternal youth.

More Gnostic than all of these was the Christian Judaizer Cerinthus, nurtured in the Egyptian schools. He considered Moseism and Christianity to be imperfect revelations and maintained that both Testaments were the work and inspiration of inferior spirits. Unlike most Gnostics, for him the χριστος was not of divine essence but a just, prudent, wise man, gifted with of a great miracle-working power. Cerinthus was, in addition, χιλιαστος, that is, a Millenarist, as practically all Jews of that time were, and wrote an apocalypse to defend this view.

By the second century of our era the Gnostic schools appear to be well organised and firmly established. They can be divided into three main focuses: a) Syrian Gnosis; b) Gnosis from Asia Minor and Italy (as Mr. Matter labels them, though others prefer to call it *sporadic* because of its widespread appeal in diverse regions); c) Egyptian Gnosis.

a) Syrian Gnosticism, as taught by Simon, Menander and Cerinthus shows less variety and richness of doctrine than that of Egypt. The Syrian Gnostics placed greater emphasis on the dualist principle, proper to Zoroastrianism, than on emanation in pairs (*syzygias*), which is closer to the triad of the ancient worshippers of Memphis. The primal principle of evil is not a negation or a limitation as it is in Egypt, but an intellectual and vigorous principle, active, and fecund. It created the inferior world: from it emanates all that is matter (commonly called the demiurge). [90] This Syrian School aims at asceticism in all of its branches. Saturninus, the first of its masters, seems to have even been a mystic. In his doctrine, dualism is vigorously intensified. The influence of Zend-Avesta is evident: the seven creating and preserving angels of the visible world, partakers of one thin ray of the divine light, created man, nay, created a kind of a *homunculus*, something close to a worm, subject and tied to the soil, incapable of rising to contemplation of the divine. But God took pity on the sad state he saw him in and sent him a breath of life, a soul, called in Saturninus' system, not ψυχη but *pneuma*. The Satan of this doctrine is different from the demiurge and the seven angels: here it is the source of all evil, as spirit and as matter. Saturninus teaches redemption with a Docetist slant, and an ultimate *palingenesis* whereby all being returns finally to its source. His rigid morality, blown out of all proportion, bans even marriage because it contributes to the continuance of an imperfect world.

Bar-Daisan, or Bardaisanes, a native of Edessa, a man learned in Greek philosophy and in the arts of the Chaldeans, started off by challenging Gentiles and Gnostics alike. Later, however, he embraced Saturninus' doctrines and to diffuse them he composed one hundred and fifty hymns: hymns of great artistic beauty, in fact, which were sung in Syria well into the fourth century when St. Ephrem replaced them with orthodox poems written in rhythms equal to the heretical. Bar-Daisan modified Saturninus' Gnosis with ideas taken from the Valentinians of Egypt. Like them, he believed matter to be the mother of Satan and begetter of all evil. He also took from Valentinus's teaching the *aeons* and the *syzeygias* - seven in his system - which together with the πατήρ άγνωστος complete the *ogdoad* or *pleroma* (plenitude of essence). He asserted the decisive influence of sidereal spirits on human acts (vestiges of Sabianism), and made futile attempts to reconcile this influence with free will. [91] In his hymns, he

---

[90]   Matter points to a relationship between Syrian Gnosis and the theology and cosmology of the Phoenicians, such as we know them through fragments, but I cannot pause now on these details.

[91]   By distinguishing between the *hylic* and the *pneumatic* man.

attributes creation to the demiurge under the guidance of *Sophia Axamoth*, an imperfect emanation and degenerate spirit from the *pleroma,* the one in touch with matter. Its own redemption first and later that of the Pneumatics was to be accomplished by the χριστος, which was not made flesh, as this particular heretic saw it, but appeared in the form of a celestial body (σῶμα οὐράνιον). He was not born of Mary, εκ Μαρίας but through Mary διά Μαρίας: a miserable sophism promoted later by Marinus, Bar-Daisan's disciple. As if saying that a human body of celestial origin (even the terminology is absurd) is somehow easier to understand than the hypostatic union of the Word! Of the history of the Bardaisanists we know little. Harmonius, the founder's son, expanded this system to include new principles, among them metempsychosis, and wrote a great number of hymns. Later, Bar-Daisan's and Saturninus' disciples started coming into the orthodox fold, and Syrian Gnosis was no more.

b) *Sporadic* Gnosis, that is to say, Gnosis from Asia Minor and Italy, a School known for its practical approach, critical spirit, and sparing affection for theosophical nebulosities, did not last long either. Its moral code was pure, even ascetic, like that of the Syrians; in fact it was from Syria that Cerdo, its founder, came. Cerdo taught (and was condemned) in Rome. There he met Marcion, a native of Pontus Euxine, a man pious enough though fanatical in his hostility towards the Jews and the Chiliastaes, or Millenarists, who awaited the temporal kingdom of the Messiah. Possessed with catechumen fervour over and above all rule and measure, he was resolute on proving that the Christian revelation shared no kinship whatever with the Old Law. He denied that Christ was the Emmanuel awaited by the Jews, and rejected the Old Testament as something inspired by the demiurge, an ignorant, incompetent, and thoroughly stupid being incapable of comprehending what he had done; precisely the reason, he felt, why this world, which could have been created by no else but him, turned out to be such a disaster. He equated this demiurge with the God of the Jews but did not identify it with the principle of evil. He wrote a book called *Antithesis* where he tried to spell out the most profound and radical differences between the Jehovah of the Prophets and the Father revealed by the Christ. But his audacity went further: convinced that the new faith had been contaminated with memories of Judaism, he proceeded to announce that he was going to take it back to its original purity. But since the books of the Old Testament proved rather an impediment for this, he rejected the whole Bible, save for the Gospel of St. Luke and ten of St. Paul's epistles. Then he went ahead and mutilated these too, at his own whim and caprice, to the point where the Apostle of the Gentiles and his disciple would be hard pressed to recognise them as their own were they to come back from the grave. Suffice it to say, as one instance of such mutations, that the first two chapters of St. Luke were simply thrown out and discarded by this Marcion who, like all Gnostics, was a Docetist and had a problem with the dogma of the Incarnation and a greater problem still with Christ being born of a Hebrew virgin. So his gospel starts with Jesus at the synagogue in Capharneum.

Marcion's disciples continued their master's exuberant *exegetic* work (if that is the word). Marcus, Lucian and Apelles brought into the system a few other alterations of little importance, exaggerating antithesis and dualism more and more. His doctrine lasted until the fourth century and had followers (bishops included) throughout Christendom - probably because it was the most furious backlash yet against the judaizing sects.

c) Others went even further: these were the advocates of Egyptian Gnosis, the least Christian, least Jewish, and most pantheist of them all - as one born and nurtured at the bosom of the Alexandrian school. But let it be noted that the founder of this sect, as that of the *Italic*, was a Syrian; Syria is the cradle of all Gnostic teaching. Basilides, who was Saturninus' companion and probably Simon and Menander's disciple, took this arcane tradition to Egypt under the pretension that he had learnt it from Glaucias, St. Peter's disciple. He combined it and fused it with that country's beliefs, already altered by Greek influence, and gave new form to the Pythagoreanism and Platonism of Aristobulus and Philo. A doctrine mixed with these ingredients and kept alive with the false prophetic revelations of Cham and Barchor was displayed in the twenty-four books of the *Exegetica* or *Interpretations*, lost today save for some left-over debris. Basilides, naturally, appears more dualist than the Egyptian heresiarchs that came after him. He believes the two primal principles to be eternal, contradicting the Zend-Avesta on this. He establishes the *ogdoad*, which together with the *pater ignotus* form his seven hypostatic attributes: *Nous* (understanding), *Logos* (Word), *Phronesis* (prudence or good judgment), *Sophia* (knowledge/wisdom), *Dynamis* (power), *and Dikaiosune* (justice). To this first circle, or *crown*, he adds a second – a reflection of the first – and then another reflection of this reflection, and on and on he goes, adding reflections to reflections until he reaches the grand figure of 365 intelligences expressed by the word *Abrakas*, later to become an amulet to be engraved on all *Basilidic* stones and talismans.

These intelligences began their degeneration according to their rank on the hierarchical scale. However, harmony was not broken until the Empire of Evil and Darkness invaded the Empire of Light. To re-establish order and draw a dividing line (ά διάκρισις) between these two forces, an inferior intelligence, άρχων, the equivalent to the other sects' demiurge (inspired and created by the Most High) the visible world, a place of expiation and strife. And here *Pneuma*, an emanation of divine light, wandered about the varying degrees of *hylic* existence guided always by celestial intelligences until it was thoroughly purified and could then return to the nucleus it came from. Yet, chained to the fetters of matter and blinded by the darkness of the senses as it was, it would have never fulfilled its desire had not the Father condescended to reveal his first emanation (*Nous*) to the world; this he did by joining it to the man Jesus when he was baptised by the Precursor (who for Basilides was *"the last Prophet* of the

Archon" or Demiurge) on the banks of the Jordan. His Christology is Docetist, and offers nothing of particular interest.

Basilides instituted Pythagorical silence in his school. He would divide his fellow sectarians into classes according to the stage of initiation they were at, and reserved his most sublime doctrine only for the ἐκλεκοι, or elect. But the system soon went through diverse alterations and by the time the founder's son, Isidorus, took over, Cerinthian and especially Valentinian doctrines had already permeated the fraternity's system of beliefs. The latter, with its freshness and riches, drowned out Basilides' modest theories and all others born alongside them. Basilidianism continued to subsist, but obscurely and only as a secret society, until at least the fifth century.

The Valentinus' school of 136 AD is, truly, Gnosis' most brilliant and poetic expression. In dogma and in myth, his Gnosis encapsulates the best of former heterodox philosophical systems. It took syncretism to its utmost limits gaining in size what it had lost in depth, thus influencing a greater number of recruits. A true Gnostic, Valentinus had esoteric teachings of which we know little today. The symbolic and *external* part of his doctrine was defined in *Pistis Sophia* ("faithful wisdom"), a book unquestionably lost today although its discovery has been announced twice; there are two Gnostic books in print, one of them quite important, that carry the same title. [92]

A summary of how Valentinus understood the source of evil and the generation of *aeons* follows below (I shall do my level best to present it as succinctly and as clearly as I can, which is not easy). It goes something like this:

Up in the invisible and ineffable heights, from all eternity, there inhabited the Father (Βυθος or *Abyss*), accompanied by his faithful consort, a certain power or intelligence, which later emanated from him and goes by two names: *Ennoia* χαρις (happiness) and σιγή (silence). These two aeons begot, in the plenitude of time, *Nous* and ´Αλήθεια (knowledge and truth). To these first *syzygias* (these two pairs or these two couples), there followed *Logos* and *Zoe* (word and life) and *Anthropos* and *Ecclesia* (man and church), thus constituting the *Ogdoad* which is the first and highest manifestation of *Bythos*. The second generation of the *Pleroma* is the *decade*, the third the *dodecade*, and from the rest of these particulars I shall gracefully spare the reader, fatigued, I am sure, with lengthy mystical genealogies, only to say that the last emanation of the *dodecade* is *Sophia*. And it is here that disorder in the universe begins. Because *Sophia*, devoured by the desire to know *Bythos* (whose sight was blocked by other intelligences standing in the way because they were higher on the hierarchical scale than she was), went about wandering in space, her pristine excellence waning, until the Father, taking pity on her, sent the *aeon Horus* to her aid and

---

[92]   *Dictionnaire des Apocryphes*, by Abbot Migne, vol. II.

brought her back to the *Pleroma*. [93] For harmony to be re-established, however, an emanation of two new *aeons* was necessary, Χριστος and *Pneuma,* which proceeded from *Nous* and *Aletheia*. Thanks to them, the intellectual world was restored and *Sophia's* sin redeemed. During her peregrination she produced (we are not told how) an *aeon* of inferior quality called *Sophia Axamoth,* mirror and replica of her mother's attributes, though diminished. And this *Axamoth,* excluded from the *Pleroma* and consumed always by a yearning to be in it, roamed about in space wailing and uttering sad groans. She said to her mother: 'O why hast thou created me!' This daughter of adultery gave life to many *aeons,* all inferior to their mother, such as the *Soul of the world,* the *Creator* or *demiurge,* and others, until finally she was taken to the *Pleroma* by *Horus* and redeemed by *Christos* who made her his *syzygia,* and with her celebrates eternal betrothals and mystical feasts.

Now the demiurge born of *Sophia Axamoth* was the creator of the world. He separated the *psychic* from the *hylic* principle previously fused in the Chaos, and established six spheres, or regions, governed by both spirits. Then he created man to whom *Sophia* communicated a ray of divine light, making him superior to the demiurge itself. Jealous, the demiurge forbade man to touch of the tree of knowledge, but man violated this mandate and was therefore sent to an inferior world where he remains tied to the *hylic* principle and all the impurities of the flesh.

Valentinus divided mortals into *Pneumatics, Psychics* and *Hylics.* Redemption of Pneumatics is realised by means of union with *Christos* (no need to insist here on the Docetism Valentinus applies to the Gospel passage, or the way he explained the union of his three principles in Jesus Christ. On essentials, he does not differ from other Gnostics).

For the Hylics, there is no possible redemption. The Psychics, however, are saved by the merits of the crucifixion suffered by the man Jesus after the *Pneuma,* or *Christos,* parted from him. The system ends with the usual *palingenesis* and return of the spirits to the πληρωμα from where they came, directly or indirectly.

The little we see in this theory about the source of evil is purely negative. It is reduced to the *darkness,* to the *void,* to that inert and confused matter of which the demiurge is the architect. Contempt for matter reached its limits with these Gnostic sects. Hence we have this interminable series of *aeons,* or secondary intelligences, until we come to the one that degenerates and participates in the hylic element and can therefore begin the wretched work of creation, unworthy of the *pater ignotus* or any of his first emanations to soil their hands with. Creation, the Valentinians said with poetic but absurd voice "is a stain in God's dress". And they seemed totally unaware of the futility of all

---

[93]   A beautiful allegory, I think, of knowledge and man: forfeited, because he wanted to know more than he should!

those *aeons:* if they were attributes of God or, as they said, *God himself,* it would be as difficult for *Sophia* and *Pneuma* to be in touch with matter as it was for *Bythos* or *Logos.*

These absurdities and contradictions are due to the notion of the eternity and independence of matter, and the rejection of creation *ex nihilo!*

Valentinism had innumerable disciples throughout the Roman world but it soon divided into partial sects, which in turn began to subdivide *ad infinitum.* Since each Gnostic or *Pneumatic* believed himself in possession of the supreme knowledge to which he had the same right as his brothers, and since it is a characteristic of heresy to change its dogmas whenever it sees fit in order to satisfy its theories, a multitude of new schools and secret associations emerged. Neither Epiphanius, nor Marcus or Heracleon followed faithfully on Valentinus' footsteps.

Even less so the Ophites [94] - so called for having adopted the serpent as their symbol, which they saw as a good spirit sent to the first man by celestial *Sophia* to encourage him to break the tyrannical law of *Jaldabaoth,* that is, the demiurge.

Dualism, Antithesis, and hatred for Judaic institutions escalate considerably with this sect but do not quite reach the delirium the Cainites reached when their proselytes launched a vindication of all the criminals in the Old Testament (Cain, the inhabitants of Sodom, Kora, Dathan, Abiron): victims all, they said, of the spite and vindictiveness of the vengeful demiurge of the Jews, Jehovah. Their morals (!) went hand in hand with their historical understanding. They boasted of committing every single act prohibited in the Decalogue, to them an imperfect law like any other law that emanated from an evil spirit and they paraded themselves as partisans of what they called "the law of nature".

The Carpocratians went even further. They advocated absolute community of property and women, and gave free rein to all appetites of the flesh. As for dogmas, the Carpocratians reduced all Gnosis to contemplation of the first monad, a Platonist leftover not quite in tune with the rest of their system.

Gnosis' decadence and ruin reaches its lowest point with the Borborius, Phybionites, Adamites and Prodicus schools, all starving in doctrine and brutally adrift in morals. The Adamites celebrated their cult in the nude. It is barely admissible to repeat in the vernacular what St. Epiphanius had to say about these groups. With great difficulty did imperial edicts managed to stop the nocturnal and tenebrous mysteries of the Cainites, the Nicholaites and the Carpocratians.

---

[94] The *Ophites* had a graphic representation, an anagram (or *schema,* as the pedantic Krausists say today) of the intellectual world according to their system. It was called *diagramma.* Origen writes of it, *Contra Celsum,* Bk. VI, and Matter has an illustration of it in his book.

And so, of course, Egyptian Gnosis died. Persian and Syrian Gnosis, on the other hand, unsullied by such abominations, "bequeath their black mantle" [95] to other heretics, if indeed these were heretics and not theosophists, for they were, after all, raised outside the Christian religion and Judaism.

Such were the Manichaeans of whom I shall say little because their system is not complex and everyone who has but leafed through St. Augustine's writings knows of them.

The slave Mani is accredited as having been the founder of this doctrine. He was not brought up in the magic arts but on the teaching of Zend-Avesta, whose principles he exchanged for those of Gnosis, which he had learnt from the writings of a Scythian. Like Simon Magus and other pseudo-prophets he called himself the "Paraclete" and "Sent by God", and proclaimed the purgation of Christianity, which he believed to have degenerated in the hands of the Apostles.

Manichaean theory comes down to an open and bold dualism: good contradicts evil, darkness contradicts light; Satan, prince of matter, is the opposite of the God of the spirit. Both principles are eternal. Satan is not a fallen angel but matter's *genius*, or rather, matter itself. In the Empire of Light, Mani establishes a series of spirits or *aeons* that in the last analysis are God, or his attributes, or modes of existence - infinite in number. The same happens in the Empire of Darkness. The champions of the Manichean *Ahriman* are interminably at war with those of Ormuzd. At one time conflict broke out amongst the evil spirits: some of them wanted to invade the Kingdom of Good and join its *aeons* (because the inclination for good and perfection is in-born even in the princes of Chaos). God, to stop them, produced a new emanation, the Mother of Life, to enter into contact with matter and correct its natural perverted tendency. The son of this mother, the first man (πρῶτος ἄνθρωπος), then begets the soul of the world, which animates matter; he impregnates her, and she gives birth to creation. The part of this soul that does not fuse with the visible world returns to the celestial regions and is the redeemer, the saviour, the *Christos,* seeking always to gather up the rays of his light strewn over all creation.

The body of man was the creation of demons. It was they who imposed on him the precept of the tree of knowledge which Adam broke on the advice of a celestial spirit (as in the Ophite system), and created Eve to chain him more and more to the stimuli of the flesh. As an unavoidable logical consequence of these preliminaries, the Manichaeans condemned Judaism as a religion full of errors, dictated by the spirits of darkness. Instead, they subordinated man to a sidereal fatalism whereby, from the stars wherein they dwell, both Primal Principles fight for absolute control of his mind and will.

There is no need to point out that the Manichaeans understood redemption from a Docetist perspective: Light, they said, cannot unite with darkness, that is why Darkness did not understand Light. The Cross was a

---

[95]   Poet Tom Moore's phrase, *Travels of an Irish gentleman in search of religion.*

symbol, an external sign for the Psychics (to use Gnostic terminology) but not for the elect, ἐκλεκτοὶ, who in the other systems we have discussed were called Pneumatics.

On the question of the soul's destiny in the after-life, Manichaeism is not without novelty and originality. The souls who through asceticism in this world have managed to loosen themselves from all earthly ties enter the region of the moon, where they are bathed and purified in a lake. From there, they pass on to the sun where they receive a baptism of fire. After this, it is easy to see how they will transit to the superior spheres and to intimate union with the divine. Impure souls, however, are condemned to transmigration until sanctified. Mani denies the resurrection of the body and limits considerably the *palingenesis* of the spirits. Matter is totally annihilated.

The Manichaean morality was ascetic in the highest degree. Marriage was forbidden, as was the use of meat. The ecclesiastical hierarchy was made up of twelve so-called apostles and seventy-two disciples soon warring among themselves, as one would expect. Some confused Christ with *Mithra*, or even Zoroaster, or Buddha. In the West, the Manichaean doctrine spread easily because, unlike Gnosis, it was not pure theosophical speculation but had a very practical aspect to it and tried to resolve the eternal and dreaded problem of the origin of evil. [96] Eminent minds like St. Augustine's were seduced at first by the apparent cohesion and clarity of the system, free now from the haziness in which Persian and Syrian imagination had previously enveloped it. They were soon convinced, however, of the inanity and scant scientific worthiness of

---

[96]   The Manichean doctrine was explained by its founder in the Letter *Fundamenti*, preserved for us by St. Augustine in his refutation. In another letter St. Epiphanius reproduces it (*Haeres.*, 66). There is a work by Faustus of Milevis quoted also by St. Augustine in his book against this heretic.

For the historical component, see also Beausobre, *Historie critique du Manicheisme*, and Matter, *Histoire critique du Gnosticisme*.

The following are also worth consulting:

Lewald, *Commentatio de doctrina gnostica*, Heidelberg, 1818.

Neander, *Desarrollo genético de los principales sistemas del gnosticismo* (in German), Berlin, 1818.

Bellerman, *Sobre las piedras abraxas* (in German), Berlin, 1820, and following.

All these works, including Matter's first edition, are prior to the discovery of what is now principal source on Gnosticism, namely:

Origenis Philosophumena sive omnium haeresum refutatio. E codici Parisino nunc primum edidit Emmanuel Miller. Oxonii; e typographeo academico, MDCCCLI, XII-348 pgs. Gnostics are covered from Book V onwards. Many attribute this work, not to Origen, but to St. Hippolytus.

[The find, in 1842, of Books 4 to 10 of this important work, the direct source of which was a book, today lost, by Theophrastus, leaves no doubt as to its author being the priest Hippolytus, from the early years of third century. [Editor, 1912]

Mani's dogma, of its hardly disguised fatalistic tendency, and of the moral consequences that, logically, were to be drawn from it.

The holy bishop of Hippo was to be this heresy's most fierce opponent, showing most clearly in his treatise *De libero arbitrio* and in a hundred places besides that evil proceeds from human will, and that human will alone is responsible for what it does. Providence on the one side and human liberty on the other have never been more eloquently defended than in the works of this African Father. All creation is good: sin, source of all evil in angel and man, cannot break universal harmony, because evil is perversion and degeneration, not *substance* but *accident*.

These preliminaries over (which I have attempted to condense as much as I could), let us now proceed to study the development of Gnosis and Manichaeism in Spain.

The First Spanish Gnostics. The Agapeae.

About the mid-fourth century, an Egyptian called Marcus, a native of Memphis, probably educated in the schools of Alexandria, came to Spain followed by a long train of admirers, mostly women, from Gallic Aquitaine. This Marcus (who should not be confused with other Gnostics of the same name, like Marcus of Palestine, a disciple of Valentinus), [97] was a Manichaean, a theurgist, and also practised the magic arts. He spread his doctrine, described as a "singular mix of pure Gnosticism and Manichaeism", [98] in Spain, but we have no exact or specific reports of this (St. Irenaeus' comments refer to the other Marcus), so we can only form an opinion of him from what we gather from Priscillianism.

Marcus attracted to his party several notable figures, most significantly Elpidius, one of those rhetoricians so abundant in the schools of Spain and the Gallia Narbonnensis, and a noble and rich matron by the name of Agape. The role of women is highly notable in the Gnostic sects. We remember Helena with Simon Magus, Philomena with Apelles, Marcelina with Carpocrates, Flora with Ptolomy; and outside of Gnosticism, Lucila with the Donatists, Priscilla with Montanus.

Marcus and Agape went on to found a sect called the *Agapetes*. If we go solely by the brief and obscure details that ecclesiastical writers have left us, these two appear to have devoted themselves to abominable excesses in their nocturnal frolicking, the lady founder herself being a prime example. This alone would prompt us to think that the Agapetes were Carpocratians or Nicholaites were it not for the fact that their kinship with the Priscillianists has been proven and confirmed. In any case, we do know that all Gnostic sects degenerated in

---

[97]   See in St. Irenaeus Appendix what he says about this theosophist Marcus, to compare his doctrine with that of the Spanish Gnostics.

[98]   The expression is Matter's (vol. 2, p. 311).

their last years ultimately to become secret societies, with all the difficulties and dangers attached to such gatherings, which also include all manner of rumours and gossip about them from those outside (often more than justified). "Qui male agit, odit lucem".

If Marcus' disciples were really Carpocratians, as Jacques Matter is inclined to believe, there is really nothing strange about their following the"law of nature" and the teaching that "everything is pure for the pure". But this is all we know of them, and I ought not to attempt to supplement or fill the silence left by ancient documents with my own conjectures. [99]

---

[99]   "Qui (gnostici) per Marcum Aegyptium Galliarum primum circa Rhodanum, deinde Hispaniarum nobiles feminas deceperunt". (*In Isaiam*, chapter LXIV). Says St. Jerome with reference to St. Ireaneus (Lib. 1, chapter IX), which undoubtedly refers to the other Marcus: "Talia autem dicentes et operantes…et iis quoque, quae sunt secundum nos regiones Rhodanenses, multas seduxerunt mulieres".

"Primus eam (gnosticorum haeresim) intra Hispanias Marcus intulit, Aegyptio profectus, Memphis ortus. Hujus auditores fuere Agape quaedam non ignobilis mulier et rhetor Helpidius. Ab his Priscillianus est institutus…" (Severus Sulpicius, *Hist. Sac.* Lib. XI).

"In Hispania Agape Elpidium, mulier virum, caecum caeca duxit in foveam, successoremque sui Priscillianum habuit" (St. Jerome, Ep. *Ad Ctesiphontem*, 43rd in the St. Maurus edition).

"Ostendens…Marcum quemdam, Memphiticum, magicae artis scientissimum, discipulum fuisse Manis et Priscilliani magistrum". (St. Isidore, *De viris illustribus*, chapter XV. The Doctor of all Spain said this in regard to Ithacius.

It seems to me that St. Jerome himself is not free from confusion in what refers to the two Marcuses;. The first lived in the second century, whereas Priscillian's master must have flourished at the beginning of the fourth century. It is obvious that St. Irenaeus could not have spoken about him, save in prophecy. All that he says of Marcus has to refer to Valentinus' disciple. Girves distinguishes them both well, and so does Ferreiro. If St. Jerome did not confuse them, we have no choice but to admit that the primitive Marcus had also been to Gaul and Spain. If not, see the following paragraph from St. Jerome's letter to Theodora, Lucinian's widow (number 53 of St. Maurus' edition):

"Et quia haeresos semel fecimus mentionem Qua Lucinus noster dignae eloquentiae tuba praedicare potest, qui spurcissima per Hispanius Basilides haeresi saeviente, et instar pestis et mortis totas intra Pyrenaeum et Oceanum vastante provincias, fidei ecclessiasticae tenuit puritatem, nequaquam suscipiens *Armagil, Barbelon, Abraxas, Balsamum*, et ridiculum *Leusiboram*, caeteraque magis portenta quam nomina quae ad imperitorum et muliercularum animos concitandos, et quasi de Hebraicis fontibus hauriunt barbaro simplices quosque terrentes sono, ut quod non intelligunt, plus mirentur? Refert Irenaeus, vir Apostolicorum temporum, et Papiae auditoris Evangelistae Johannis discipulus, Episcopusque Ecclesiae Lugdunensis, quod Marcus quidam de Basilides Gnoscici stirpe descendens, primum ad Gallias venerit, et eas partes per quas Rhodanus et Garumna fluunt sua doctrina maculaverit; maxime nobiles feminas, quaedam in occulto mysterio repromittens hoc errore seduxerit, magicis artibus et secreta corporum voluptate amorem sui concilians. Inde Pyrenaeum transiens, Hispanias occupavit, et hoc studio habuerit ut divitum domus, et in ipsis feminas maxime appeteret…" (And he is referring to the work *Adversus omnes haereses*).

[All traditional writings concerning Elpidius and Agape, disciples of Marcus of Memphis, must be a web of tall tales. Marcus, the Egyptian, a second century man, could not have been disciple of a heresiarch of the third century (Mani). In E.-Ch. Babut's opinion (*Priscillien et le*

Priscillian

It is a pity that almost the sole authority on this subject is the foreign-born rhetorician Sulpicius Severus, and that we find ourselves having to half-grope around rough edges and obscurities, unsure of both names and facts! I shall endeavour to sift my way through to the truth from the scarce reports we have.*

In the year 379, in the consulship of Ausonius and Olybrius, [100] a disciple of Elpidius and Agape, a native of Galicia, Priscillian by name, of the Hispano-Roman race (if we are to judge by his name which is as Latin as Priscus or Priscilla), gave himself to preaching a new heretical doctrine. The picture Sulpicius paints of him throws very little light - given that it is the work of a fifth century pedagogue who submissively copied it, sometimes down to the actual words, from Sallust's famous epic *Catilina.*

Priscillian was, according to how the Gallic rhetorician describes him, "from a noble family, of great wealth, daring, prolific, knowledgeable, much practised in oratory and disputation; happy, for sure (he adds), had he not thrown away great gifts of body and soul with his evil opinions. Frequently at vigil, he endured hunger and thirst; by no means covetous, extremely frugal. But to these qualities, he added vanity in great measure puffed up by his science, false and profane, for he had practised the magic arts since his youth". [101]

Priscillianisme, Paris, 1909), Elpidius has to be the rhetorician Delphidius; as for Agape, she is probably a product of someone's imagination, unless upon conversion to Christianity, Delphidius and his wife Euchrocia adopted the names Elpidio and Agape, in remembrance of the Christian virtues spoken of by the Apostle (πιστις, ἐλπίς, ἀγάπη (Editor, 1912)].

* On Priscilian, see Babut's book quoted above; *Histoire ancienne de l'Eglise*, volume 2 by Duchesne (Paris, 1908-1910), and A. Bonilla's *Historia de la Filosofía Española*, 1, 194, and 2, 462. Dr. Schepss found in a Baverian library, year 1885, eleven tracts of Priscilian, and published them in 1889, in volumeXVIII of *Corpus scriptorum ecclesiasticorum latinorum*, of Vienna. They are attached in the Apendices of the present volume, as also the articles, unfortunately incomplete, that Menéndez Pelayo started publishing in the Journal *Revista de Archivos* upon Swepss finding, re-writing his study on Priscilianism. New works have not entirely solved the problem: while from Babut's study we surmise that Priscilian was not a heretic but a Catholic mystic and that his persecution was unjust, for Hilgenfeld (*Zeitschrift für wissenchaftliche Theologie*, 1892, p. 1 and flwg.), Priscilian was a gnostic and even a Manichean (Editor, 1912).

[100] This date is confirmed by the *Chronicle* of St. Prosper of Aquitaine.

[101] "Ab his Priscilianus est institutus, familia nobilis, praedives opibus, acer, inquirens, facundus, multa lectione eruditus, disserendi ac disputandi promptissimus. Felix profecto si non pravo studio corrupisset optimum ingenium: prorsus multa in eo animi et corporis bona cerneres. Vigilare multum, famen ac sitim ferre poterat, habendi minime cupidus, utendi parcissimus. Sed idem vanissimus et plus justo inflator prophanarum rerum scientia: quin et magicas artes ab adolescentia eum exercuisse creditum est." (Sulp. Sev., *Historia Sagrada*, lib. 2; in vol. VI of the *Bibliotheca Veterum Patrum*). I am following the Lugdunensis edition.

All we can really conclude in substance from this customary outline are two things: one, that Priscillian possessed that eloquence, easy wit, and varied doctrine necessary to every party leader; and two, that he was given to magic from an early age. We have no way of knowing today what kind of magic Priscillian knew and practised. Was it the Celtic or Druid superstition of which there were, and continued to be for a long time after, remnants in Galicia? Or was it the secretive doctrines of the East to which St. Jerome seems to allude when he calls Priscillian *Zoroastris magi studiosissimum?* [102]   Perhaps both, if we could venture that Priscillian practised first the magic of his native land and later learnt the magic arts of Persia and Egypt which, in essentials, did share some similarities with that of the Celts. Be that as it may, Sulpicius Severus maintains that Priscillian, intent on propagating Gnosis and Manichaeism, not as he had learnt them from Marcus but with substantial variants, recruited to his party a great number of nobles and plebeians who were swept along by the prestige of his name, his eloquence, and the glitter of his gold. And so they were drawn to him, women especially, eager always for novelty, victims of curiosity, and attracted by the poise and gloss of the Galician heresiarch who was tender in words and meek and unassuming in demeanour and attire: good means to captivate love and adoration from a retinue of devotees.[103]

But not only women: bishops, too, among them Instantius and Salvianus, whose dioceses the historian of these diversions does not mention. Priscillianism spread rapidly from Galicia to Lusitania and from there to Betis. As a result, the bishop of Córdoba, Adyginus or Higinus, Hosius' successor, [104] suspicious of what he was witnessing, issued a formal complaint to Idacius or Hydacius, Metropolitan of Mérida, if we read in Sulpicius' text *Emeritae civitatis*, or, as others claim, *emeritae aetatis* - an elderly priest. According to Sulpicius Severus, who in this one fact merits little faith because we know he was a capital enemy of this particular bishop, Idacius started proceedings against the Priscillianists of Lusitania with such an overly excessive zeal that he actually caused the fire to spread, and made Instantius and the other Gnostics resolute on helping Priscillian, and swore to do so.

After long and hard-fought battles and in order to curb advance of the new doctrine, it became necessary to convene a council (year 380) in Saragossa. Two bishops from Aquitaine and ten Spaniards attended, among them, Idacius, whose signature appears last. This synod excommunicated the prelates Instantius and Salvianus and the laymen Helpidius and Priscillian.[105] The eight

---

[102]   Ep. *Ad Ctesiphontem adversus Pelagium.*

[103]   Priscillian gave them symbolic names, i.e. Balsamo, Barbelon, Treasure, Leusibora.

[104]   Regarding this bishop, see vol. X of *España Sagrada*, pp. 208-212.

[105]   So says Sulpicius Selverus, but it is not found in the canons that have come down to us and today possess (Vid. *Collectio Canonum Ecclesiae Hispanae*, ed. 1808, p. 303, a sure sign that some have been lost. [Or that there was no excommunication, as Babut believes. (Editor, 1912)].

canons we know of today promulgated at this Council of Saragossa, on 4th October, refer more to the external manifestation of the heresy than to its dogma. Canon I bans women from preaching and teaching doctrine, as well as attending readings, speeches, and meetings *vivorum alienorum*. Canon II prohibits fasting carried out on Sunday "by persuasion or superstition" in order to absent oneself from Church during Lent, or to "celebrate obscure rituals in caverns and on hills". Canon III anathematises those who receive the Eucharist but do not consume It in church. The fourth says that no one is to abstain from going to church from the 16th of the kalendas (17th December) until Epiphany, or remain hidden in his house, or go to the hamlet, or "up to the hills", or walk barefoot… on pain of excommunication. No one shall arrogate to himself the title of "doctor" [106] except those persons to whom it has been granted. Virgins shall not keep vigil before their fortieth year.

Do keep all these points in mind, we shall return to them at the appropriate moment. But for the time being, let us keep our eye firmly on these facts: the secret meetings that were taking place between men and women together; the sacrilegious fraud with which many received Communion; teaching that was entrusted to laymen and women, as the Agapetes had done. Severus Sulpicius pointed out another canon whereby bishops were forbidden to receive into communion with the Church anyone who had been excommunicated by another bishop: a literal copy of one of the Elvira canons. Number six is directed at the affected asceticism of the Priscillianists, and separates from the Church those clerics who adopt monastic rules and austerities for the "vanity and conceit of being held in higher esteem than the rest".

The *Acta* are signed by Fitadius, Delfinus, Eutiquius, Augencius, Lucius, Ithacius, Splendonius, Valerius, Symphosius, Carterius, and Idacius. Notification and implementation of the decree excommunicating the Priscillianists with express mention of their names, as the Fathers of the First Council of Toledo are quoted in the text, was entrusted to Ithacius, the bishop of Lusitania, not to be confused with Idacius of Mérida despite the similarity of their names and neighbouring dioceses. [107]

---

[106]   Teacher

[107]   The date of the Council of Saragossa is stated in the collections of Loaysa and Labbé of 380 (418 of our era), though they appear in neither the *Code Emilianensis* nor in *Vigilianus*. Binio and Girves place it in 381; Mansi in 379. Pagi, Tillemont and Risco (*España Sagrada*, vol. XXX) follow common opinion, which seems plausibe because Priscillian started propagating his heresy in 379, in the consulship of Ausonius and Olybrius (*S. Prosperi Aquitani Chronicon*). Ambrosio de Morales doubted, for no good reason (our great century's historians were also able to sin of excessive doubt) that this Council, the *Acta* of which we do have, was the same one celebrated against the Priscillianists. It is true that in the preserved canons (which undoubtedly are not complete because it is impossible that the Saragossa Fathers would leave the doctrinal part of the heresy untouched) Priscillian is not mentioned by name. But they most certainly allude to his errors if we go by the information we have of them. (Vid. Morales, Bk. X, chapter XLIV). The

Higynius, bishop of Córdoba, the first to raise the alarm against the Priscillianists, wavered in the Faith. He prevaricated in their favour - the reason why Ithacius excommunicated him and deposed him from his see, basing his decision on the conciliar decree. We do not know the motive behind the fall of the prelate from Betis: a natural symptom, perhaps, of the weakness of our human condition, and not difficult to explain if we believe Priscillian to have been as persuasive and eloquent as his own enemies describe him to be.

If with Higynius's deposition the Priscillianists lost a bishop, the Gnostics Instancius and Salvianus were manipulating to gain another. They riotously and anti-canonically raised their leader, Priscillian, to the see of Avila [108] convinced of the following that their doctrines would gain if the savvy and skilful heresiarch was armed with sacerdotal authority. Chaos ensued. Idacius and Ithacius redoubled their persecuting zeal, determined to weed out the perverted seed, and appealed to the imperial judges (*parum sanis consiliis*, says Severus) who proceeded to throw some Priscillianists out of their churches. The reigning emperor Gratian enacted a mandate (in 381) intimating exile "extra omnes terras" for the Spanish heretics. Some gave up, others hid while the storm was brewing, and for a while it seemed that Priscillianism was over and the community of its followers dispersed.

However, Priscillian, Instancius and Salvianus were not men to be frightened easily at some imperial decree mandated by a fickle court where justice could be bought and sold. [109] They were confident in their ability and knew the power of their art and wealth, as events prove. Their error had become an obsession now, and on no account would they return to the Catholic fold. So the party left Spain with the firm plan to obtain revocation of the edict and, as they went, took the opportunity to spread their doctrine throughout the Aquitaine and the Italian Peninsula. They won many new believers to their cause in the Elusa region and in Bordeaux [110] perverting, especially, Euchrocia and her daughter Prócula in whose estate they stayed and dogmatised for many days. Both ladies accompanied them on their journey to Rome, and with them a whole legion of women ("turpis pudibundusque comitatus", says Sulpicius) with whom the Priscillianists engaged in more than platonic or spiritually edifying relations. Priscillian himself, founder and fomenter of the sect, had a son by Procula, among whose many ascetic virtues continence does not appear

---

bishops that Sulpicius mentions as Priscillian's persecutors, sign the *Acta* of Saragossa, as did also some from the Aquitaine: which also conforms to the narrative of the ecclesiastical historian (Vid. Risco, vol. XXX, p. 234).

[108]   *Abulensi*, not *Labinense*, as Sulpicius Severus's text reads, full of errors on Spanish nomenclature, for example, Sossubensi instead of *Ossonobensi*, etc.).

[109]   *"Cuncta venalia erant"*, says Sulpicius.

[110]   The bishop St. Delphinus refused to receive them and so they went to Procula's house instead.

to have shined particularly brightly, even after she was crowned with a sacred *infulae* by the grace of her Lusitanian patrons. [111]

In this grand style, the new bishop arrived in Rome. They could have saved themselves the journey. The great pontiff St. Damasus, who was a Spaniard and must have had some news of what they were up to, refused to hear their excuses and grant them audience. Only one who is ignorant of the disciplines of the times will find it strange that the pope limited himself to doing this and did not pronounce a new anathema against them. But why should he interject his authority on a matter that had already been judged and decided by the Spanish Church gathered in council, when he knew of the truth and wisdom of their decision, and when Priscillian was notorious for trying to bring back the grave errors of Gnosticism?

New disappointments awaited our heretics in Milan where they met with firm opposition by St. Ambrose who closed the doors of the church to them, as he would later do to Theodosius. But Priscillian and his devotees held a golden key to Gratian's fortress and soon enough managed to bribe Macedonius, *magister officiorum*, who obtained a new ruling from the emperor, according to which the first mandate was made void and the Priscillianists restored to their churches. So miserable were the times, such are the disastrous consequences the intrusion of civil power has always had on matters ecclesiastical! The new decree was implemented almost before the ink was dry. The Galicians' gold managed to tame Volentius, proconsul to Lusitania - staunch Priscillian antagonist that he had been. Both Priscillian and Instantius were restored to their churches (Salvianus had died in Rome) and an outright anti-Catholic persecution began. Ithacius, the fiercest and most determined of the heresy's foes, ran the greatest danger. He wisely fled to Gaul where he appealed to the prefect Gregorius who, because of the authority he had in Spain, called the authors of these outrages to appear in court, having previously acquainted the emperor with the details of the case, as well as the bad faith and unscrupulous greed with which his counsellors were operating in their dealings with the Priscillianists.

But the Priscillianists parried the blow in time. Priscillian's treasure and Macedonius' willingness to please him could open doors everywhere. Gratian issued a new mandate withdrawing judicial responsibility for the case from the hands of the Gallic prefect and referring it to the Vicar of Spain, in whose *forum* the sentence would not long delay. Macedonius, the Priscillianists' meek and mild servant, went further. He sent envoys to Trèves to arrest Ithacius who had taken refuge in that city under the aegis of bishop Pritanius (or Britanius), but he skilfully evaded them. While this was going on, new events were taking place in Brittany that were to prove of immense benefit to the Priscillianist cause.

---

[111]   We are told (and Sulpicius records it) that Procula used some herbs to abort so as to hide her shame ("Fuit in sermone hominum...partum sibi graminibus abegisse").

Military anarchy, the never-ending plague of the Roman Empire, contained in the East by Theodosius' strong hand, befell the West once more during Gratian's last tragic days, different indeed from his laudable beginnings. The legions of Brittany hailed the Spaniard Clement Maximus as emperor. After a short-lived and feigned vacillation, he accepted the purple and crossed over to Gaul at the head of one hundred and thirty thousand soldiers. Gratian fled to Lugdunum (Lyon) with some of his men and was killed in an ambush, perhaps at Maximus' bidding who was by now blinded with ambition though sufficiently adorned with the finest of laurels. The "Spanish tyrant" entered Trèves victorious, and his compatriot Theodosius, who was too far away to claim Gratian's inheritance, had to agree to a pact with him, ceding him Gaul, Spain and Brittany, to avoid greater evils. It was the year 384, under the consulship of Ricimer and Clearchus.

Maximus was watchful of purity in orthodoxy but too prone, as all emperors of the decadence, to lay his sword on the Theology scale. Ithacius was well aware of this virtue and this failing. He tried to use both for his own ends – a laudable undertaking, had it not been spoiled by the means. He submitted a report to him against Priscillian and his associates "full of ill will and recriminations" says Sulpicius Severus, with his usual animosity towards this bishop.

A list of the truly serious anti-Catholic and antisocial errors that were taking place would have been enough for Maximus to decide in favour of punishment but, more prudent than Ithacius, he remitted the finding of the case to the synod of Bordeaux, before which Instantius and Priscillian were summoned to appear. Instantius responded to the charges *in causa propria* and was condemned and deposed by the Fathers of this Council, who judged his defence unsatisfactory. Up to this point, procedure had been in accordance with canonical rules. But Priscillian, fearful now of a similar verdict, opted instead (unhappily for him as it turned out) to appeal directly to the emperor whose ministers he was hoping to buy, as he had Gratian's.

And the French bishops "with the inconsistency proper of their race" (in the words of Sulpicius, who was French) actually consented to hand over the hearing of an ecclesiastical case to a royal tribunal, the judicial competence of which extended only to implementation of conciliar decrees, and this only as a last resort. Fortunately, Maximus was Catholic, and this short lived subservience of the Church to the temporal power was not ultimately for ill though it did cause more scandal and strife. Severus says: "What the French Bishops should have done was to pass sentence of insubordination against Priscillian, or if there were grounds for the accused to consider them suspect, to trust the decision to other bishops, but never to allow the emperor to interject his will on a cause so evidently ecclesiastical" and, we add, so far removed from civil jurisdiction.

St. Martin of Tours protested against such an innovation, but in vain. He exhorted Ithacius to desist from the accusation and appealed to Maximus against the shedding of Priscillianist blood. He managed to stop it while he was in Trèves - he even obtained a formal promise from the emperor that this would not happen. But as soon as he was outside the city gates, bishops Magnus and Rufus redoubled their efforts with Maximus, and the emperor bade the Prefect Evodius, an "implacable and grave man," to judge the case.

Priscillian was convicted of common crimes, to wit, casting spells, obscene secret meetings at night with women, praying naked, and other excesses of this kind (those engaged in by the Carpocratians and Adamites alike). Evodius sent Maximus the report of the Proceedings. The emperor opened a new trial, the prosecuting counsel this time being not Ithacius but Patritius, official to the Treasury. In the end, Priscillian and two new converts to his doctrine, the clerics Felicissimus and Armenius, and proselytes Asarivus, deacon Aurelius, Latronianus and Euchrocia were sentenced to death and decapitated.

We know very little about any of them, and Sulpicius' swift narrative is not enough to satisfy the curiosity excited by some of these names. The report in the *Chronicon* attributed to St. Prosper of Aquitaine is even briefer though it has, at least, the advantage of pointing out the date: "In the year of our Lord 385, during the counselship of consuls Arcadius and Bautus... in Trèves, was beheaded Priscillian together with Euchrocia, wife of the poet Delphidius, Latronianus and other accomplices of his heresy". [112]

If only we had some more facts about who this Latronianus (or Matronianus) was! St. Jerome devotes to him these brief and honourable words in his book *De viris illustribus* (chapter CXXII): "Latronianus, from the province of Spain, a greatly learned man, comparable in poetry to the classics of old, was decapitated in Trèves with Priscillian, Felicissimus, Julian, Euchrocia, and others of the same party. We have works of his genius, written in a variety of metres". All the more pity that poetry so enchanting to St. Jerome, a fine judge in matters of taste, has been lost!

Of Euchrocia, mother of Procula (she who was Priscillian's Thaïs) and wife of Delphidius, the poet and rhetorician from Bordeaux, we have notices in two other writers, Ausonius and Latinus Pacatus. Ausonius, in the fifth of the elegant eulogies he dedicated to the Bordeaux masters, calls Delphidius a fortunate man because he died, he says, before he could witness his daughter's error and his wife's execution:

> minus malorum munere expertus Dei,
>
> medio quod aevi raptus es,
>
> errore quod non deviantes filiae,

---

[112]   I reproduce passages from Sulpicius, St. Jerome, St. Prosper, etc. in an Appendix of documents relative to Priscillianism, thus avoiding additional notes and references that may overly distract the reader's attention with footnotes.

poenaque laesus conjugis. [113]

In a *Panegyric to Theodosius*, Pacatus used Euchrocia's execution as an opportunity to praise the clemency of Theodosius and contrast it with the cruelty of Maximus, who had by now been defeated in battle and killed at Aquilea. "Exprobabatur mulieri viduae", he says, "nimia religio et diligentius culta divinitas". [114] This religious and ascetic affectation, so resplendent to the eyes of a pagan orator like Pacatus, was much prevalent with the Priscillianists.

Instantius and Tiberianus Beticus were exiled to *Sylina*, one of the British Isles [115]. The former was fortunate to have been sentenced by the church synod or he would have shared Priscillian's fate. Tertulus, Potamius, Juan, and other Priscillianists less well known were subjected to temporary exile in Gaul. Villagers in Bordeaux stoned Urbica, another of Priscillian's pupils. [116]

Tiberianus Beticus has a paragraph in St. Jerome's *Illustrious Men* (CXXIII). "He wrote" - says the Saint – "an Apologia in overblown and verbose style to defend himself against the accusation of heresy; but crushed by the weariness of exile, he changed his mind, and married off one daughter who had already offered her virginity to God". This passage is obscure, even when we dismiss the rendering of those who read, absurdly, *matrimonium 'sibi' copulavit*. Since Priscillianists condemned marriage, it would appear that by marrying off his daughter, Tiberianus wanted to show he had turned his back on his old errors though incurring a new one in not respecting her vows. That is why St. Jerome said that he "came back like a dog to his vomit" (*canis reversus ad vomitum*). But the Priscillianist firestorm did not die out with the blood shed at Trèves.

However, before we proceed with the history of this heresy, reasons of chronology and logic demand we give some notices about the Ithacians, their radical adversaries, and of the grim events that followed the execution of the Spanish Gnostics in Gaul.

Anti-Priscillianist reaction: The Ithacians. St. Martin of Tours

The *vox populi* accused Ithacius of being the cause and the principal instigator of Maximus' heavy hand against the Priscillianists. The bishops who had convened at Trèves, however, continued *communicating* with him and

---

[113]   *Decimi Magni Ausonii Burdigalensis Opera, Jacobus Tollius recensuit… Parisiis, 1693.*

[114]   *Panegyrici Veteres… Parisiis, 1767* (ed. Baune), p. 334, number 29 of Latinus Pacatus' *Panegirico*. Worth reading in its enterity.

[115]   We do not know which one, perhaps due to the corruption of the names in Sulpicius' text. He says it was *ultra Britanniam*.

[116]   *S. Prosperi Chronicon.*

approved of his conduct, Theognostus' protests notwithstanding. [117] But as soon as St. Martin of Tours became aware of the punishment that had been inflicted on the heretics and of Maximus' violation of the pledge he had made to him, he set out for the imperial court, causing alarm and terror in all simply by his coming.

The emperor had signed a prescript the day before for special adjudicators to go to Spain (Sulpicius calls them *tribunes*) to investigate all remaining heretics and do away with their lives and property. The confused and frenzied harshness of these decrees would no doubt affect many good and innocent Catholics, which often happens with universal dictates. Nor were the emperor's ministers the most ideally suited judges to decide who was and who was not a heretic, or what punishment they should get. Maximus and the *Ithacian* bishops (Ithacius' supporters were already so-called) were afraid that St. Martin might distance himself from their communion and tried by every possible means to persuade and reassure him. As he approached the city gates, palace officials (*magisterii officiales*) came to urge him enter only "in peace" with the other bishops. The saint replied that he would enter "in peace with Christ", and moved past them. He spent the night at prayer. In the morning, he presented the emperor a list of petitions, the principal one being to stop the tribunes leaving for Spain and to lift his hand off further persecutions. Maximus took two days to reply. Meanwhile a number of bishops came to him accusing St. Martin not just of defending the Priscillian heretics but of avenging their cause, and beseeched the emperor to exercise his authority and put a stop to such audacity. The Ithacians pleaded, wept, threatened, and supplicated, prompting Maximus to condemn the holy bishop of Tours, but the emperor was hesitant to consent to their unjust requests. Instead, he called Martin and tried to convince him that the sentence against the Priscillianists had been passed by a pertinent judicial authority and not solely at Ithacius' instigation, whom only a few days before the synod had declared innocent. Martin would not give in. Then Maximus arose, took leave of his presence, and sent the tribunes to Spain.

St. Martin's charity towards his fellow men was too sincere for him to persevere in fruitless obstinacy. He quickly returned to the palace and agreed to all, if only that bloodthirsty mandate were withdrawn. Maximus granted his request without further difficulties, and St. Martin communicated with Ithacius and his followers though he refused to sign the Synod's Report. The following day he fled the city ashamed of this first weakness, and going deep into the woods, he cried bitterly. Sulpicius says: "There he heard an angel's voice, saying: You do well, O Martin, to be remorseful, but you could not have won this battle any other way: go, restore your virtue and perseverance; and never put your salvation – rather your life! – in danger again". ("Merito, Martine, compungeris, sed aliter exire nequisti. Repara virtutem, resume constantiam, ne

---

[117]   This bishop Theognostus was later to excommunicate Ithacius and his followers.

jam non periculum gloriae sed salutis incurreris"). And they say that in the sixteen years he was yet to live St. Martin never attended a council or a bishops' gathering again. [118]

Now here we touch on an important issue. It is one my pen will have to contend with more than once in the course of this history and it is this: the temporal punishment of heretics (*punition*, to use Fray Alfonso de Castro's expression). This is not the right place to debate it, but we must have the circumstances of the facts so far narrated clear in our minds, lest we wander off into erroneous misunderstandings.

Priscillian's execution is the first case of bloodshed for heresy that we read of in ecclesiastical Annals. Now when we take into consideration the laws of that time, was punishment for heresy *itself* unjust? ? It was definitely not. The crime of heterodoxy is of a twofold character: as a *social* crime, it breaks the unity and harmony of the State and attacks the social foundations upon which the State is built. Consequently it was, and still is, penalised in Catholic countries by civil laws, more or less strict according to the times, certainly, but of its being subject to punishment there is no doubt. The Priscillianists had been charged with common - or public – crimes, if we care to read what it is written of them; and capital punishment, which today we judge excessive in all things, was not considered so in the fifth century, or for many centuries after. As a *sin*, heresy naturally is subject to spiritual rectification. What exactly did Ithacius and his backers' error actually consist of? Of course it is harsh to say, as they did, that "heretics should be exterminated by the blade or by the flame", but words, I think, leave room for exoneration. St. Jerome says: Priscillian "was condemned by the sword of the law and on the authority of the whole world". The punishment was legitimate and lawfully sanctioned, even though it was being applied for the first time. On what, then, was the charge of illegality brought by St. Martin of Tours and his passionate biographer Sulpicius Severus based? On this: the fact that Idacius and Ithacius had asked the Crown to pass judgement on matters of the Church. Even more, it was based on the fact that the bishops gathered at Bordeaux and Trèves consented to having the emperor, from his own law court, judge a case that the ecclesiastical authority had not yet ruled on - obviously a violation of the rights of the Church, the only body that can define on questions of dogma and separate the heretic from the communion of the faithful. In all else, however, it was the emperor's duty to punish, as he did, the followers of a doctrine that, as St. Leo the Great put it, "damned all decency, was actively advocating the breaking of the sacred bond of matrimony, and trod over all law - human and divine - with their fatalist principles". The Church does not invoke the support of temporal power; it accepts it when it is offered to punish so-called *mixed* crimes ("Etsi sacerdotali

---

[118]   Sulpicius Severus, dialogue 3 (p. 369 of *Bibliotheca Veterum Patrum*, volume VI), and in our Appendix to this chapter.

contenta judicio cruentas refugit ultiones, severis tamen constitutionibus adjuvatur", says St. Leo).

St. Martin's courageous stand in favour of those unfortunate Priscillianists is a most honourable attribute of his evangelical charity; but it proves nothing against the legitimacy of the temporal punishment imposed on the heretics. He could have also asked pardon for a criminal, a murderer, or an adulterer, but we would not conclude from this that he was condemning laws against common delinquents. Of course we all wish that not a drop of blood had ever been shed in the name of religion or anything else, but that does not make capital punishment unlawful or unnecessary. Society has a right to defend itself as the individual has a right to defend himself. And, perchance, is he not an enemy of the health and well-being of society at large, who solely of his own volition, or based on some fanatical stand, rips its womb apart with the dagger of heresy and scatters her children to the winds?

We shall soon see in the pages that follow whether the Priscillianists did or did not do this, when we talk about their beliefs.

Having said that, I have no doubt that Ithacius (also known as *Clarus*) proceeded against the Priscillinists with a rage, passion and hostility that was personal, visceral, and unworthy of a bishop, and for which he was in fact later excommunicated in 389 (according to St. Prosper' *Chronicon*), deposed from his see (we know not by which council), and exiled during the reign of Thodosius the Great and Valentinian II, as Severus and St. Isidore tell us. [119] Chronologically, we have to set his exile and death as having occurred between 388, that is, between the death of his protector Maximus, and 392 when Valentinian died. We know nothing else about our bishop. St. Isidore attributes to him a book "in quo detestanda Priscilliani dogmata et maleficiorum ejus artes libidinunque ejus probra demonstrat", but it has unfortunately been lost. It would have been of great help today. His diocese was the *Ossonobensis* (Osúna), in Lusitania, jurisdiction of Beja, not *Sossubensis* or *Oxomensis*, as Sulpicius editions state erroneously.[120] (He also calls the episcopate of Avila where Priscillian intruded *Labinensis* instead of *Abulensis).

The second of Priscillianism's fearless persecutors was Idacius. The *Chronicon* of St. Prosper and the Latin translation of St. Jerome's *De viris illustribus* call him *Ursatius*, but in the Greek text of the same treatise, the *Acta* of the First Council of Toledo, and in Sulpicius Severus' book, one constantly reads *Idacius*. We cannot identify clearly where his bishopric was because the *emeritae* of Sulpicius' text seems to agree with *aetatis* and not with *urbis* or *civitatis*, as some have read. Unlike Ithacius, whose name obscures his own in later anti-

---

[119]   "Ob necem Priscilliani... Ecclesiae communione privatus, exilio condemnatur, ibique die ultima fungitur, Theodosio Majore et Valentiniano regnantibus" (St. Isidore, *De viris illustribus*, chapter XV).

[120]   On Idacius and the Ossonobense Church, see volume XIV of *España Sagrada*.

Priscillianist efforts, he was not deposed but resigned his episcopate voluntarily. "Nam Idacius, licet minus nocens, sponte se Espiscopatu abdicaverat". Many editions read *Nardatius,* but this, like *Trachio* in another passage dealing with Idacius, must certainly be an erratum. Anyhow, his contrition did not last long, apparently. Sulpicius Severus tell us that he tried to get his see back but gives no further explanation. [121]

The third of the Ithacian bishops we have some news of was Rufus, the one who, together with Magnus, managed to triumph over the emperor's scruples and make him break his pledge to St. Martin. He couldn't have been a man of much intellectual acumen: apparently he let himself be misled by some swindler who claimed to be the prophet Elijah and had deceived many with some false miracles: in return for his inane credulity, he lost his mitre. [122]

The state of religious confusion that Priscillian had thrown the Peninsula into must have been grave indeed for such impostures to take place and be believed.

I do not believe it correct to call the Ithacians, this group of intolerant anti-Priscillianism extremists, a "sect". The Church excommunicated them later because of their personal excesses, but we do not know of any error of dogma or discipline they professed that qualifies them as heretics or schismatics, as with the Luciferians, for example. Far be it for me to hold them up as models of exemplary conduct! But error of judgement and actual heresy are two different things and very far apart. They acted badly. They did not dogmatise.

What a sad portrait of poor Ithacius Sulpicius left us! He describes him as "an intrepid man, a bigmouth, reckless, extravagant, a slave to gluttony and to his belly. He was so stupid (he adds), that he accused every one he saw fasting or reading sacred Scripture of being a Priscillianist. He even dared call St. Martin a heretic. St. Martin! A man who should be compared to the Apostles!" And this is what hurts Sulpicius most. But does this messy inkblot on his picture merit any points? Could this perchance be the same Ithacius " 'Clarus' in doctrine and eloquence" of whom St. Isidore speaks? Who knows! If Sulpicius has told us the whole truth, let us at least admire the judgement of God who made use of such a miserable instrument to bring down the Priscillian pride.

Priscillianism after Priscillian. Councils and Abjurations. The Luciferian Schism. Letter of Pope Innocent. Letter of Toribius and St. Leo. The Council of Braga. End of this heresy.

The Priscillianists saw Ithacius' deposition from his see as a victory. Galicia, Lusitania and one or two other regions in the Peninsula were swarming

---

121   Idem Idacius, see *España Sagrada* vol. XIII.

122   Severus, *De Vita B. Martini*, number 25.

with devotees of his doctrine. They brought Priscillian's remains and those of the other heresiarchs executed with him at Trèves to Spain and began a cult to them as martyrs and saints. The secret night gatherings did not stop but now an inviolable oath was taken never to reveal what went on inside, even if that meant committing perjury, something that many doctors of the sect, Dictinius among them, declared justifiable. "Jura, perjura, secretum prodere noli", was their maxim. Thus joined by the same bonds as all other secret societies, they came to exercise complete control over the Galician Church. They altered the liturgy, made anti-canonical elections of bishops from their own faction and, in sum, brought about a true schism. The other Spanish bishops excommunicated the prevaricators, and a brief period of anarchy ensued. The One Church became the churches, and it did happen that at one time there were two, sometimes more, prelates in one diocese, and even bishops appointed to sees that did not exist. The main accomplice in all these altercations was Simphosius (the pretender bishop of Orense), a staunch proselyte of the heresy though he had formerly signed the proceedings of the Council of Saragossa. His son, Dictinius, a writer of merit to his partisans, followed in his father's footsteps and promoted the same errors. His father made him bishop of Astorga with the approval of the other Priscillianists. Paternus, another heretic, was raised to the see of Braga.

Confusion grew and, eventually, the sectarians themselves, fearful of the consequences or remorseful, perhaps, of the fire that was scorching Galicia on their account, sought to find a point of compromise and submitted it to St. Ambrose, the great bishop of Milan. Their hope was that his conciliatory words might persuade our Catholic prelates to agree to a compromise so that peace and harmony might be restored. The Galicians were to accept certain conditions of submission, the first being to retract their error. St. Ambrose had witnessed the painful scenes at Trèves. He himself had refused to communicate with the Ithacians and wrote about the distressing sight of watching, with great anguish of heart, Higinius, Córdoba's old bishop, leaving for exile.[123] He found himself, therefore, well disposed to clemency, and judging the Priscillianists' words to be sincere and their conditions acceptable without doctrine or discipline being compromised or weakened in any major way, he wrote to the bishops of Spain (this letter has not been preserved) asking them to receive back into communion the Gnostic and Manichaean converts. One of the chapters of the concord St. Ambrose proposed was the deposition of Dictinius and, most probably, of the other riotously elected bishops, who would have to remain in the order of presbyters. [124]

---

[123]   "Dolore percitus quod Hyginum Episcopum senen in exilium duci comperi, cui nihil jam nisi extremus superesset spiritus. Cum de edo convenirem comites ejus, ne sine veste, sine plumatis paterentur extradi, extrusus ipse sum" (St. Ambrosii *Opera*, ep. XXXVI).

[124]   Circumstances recorded, as the following are, on the definitive decree of the first Council of Toledo (Vid. this chapter's Appendix). In them we read vague references to a Council

In accordance with the bishop of Milan's letters and the counsel of Pope Siricius, our prelates convened a Council in Toledo. It was the year 396. However, Simphosius and his group refused to attend. He said, cautiously, that he had moved on from the errors of Priscillian and the other "martyrs" (those executed in Trèves). He did not, however, make a formal retraction or gave any another sign of repentance, nor did he carry out any of the conditions proposed by St. Ambrose. The Council Fathers knew that his conversion was calculated, because Simphosius and his allies continued to use the apocryphal books and clung stubbornly to their old opinions. So nothing was achieved at this Council. But the disappearance of the Acta and the silence of other testimonies do not prevent us from knowing something about its concerns.

Though attempts at reconciliation had been frustrated, Priscillianism was nonetheless losing favour and devotees by the day, no doubt due to the unitary and Catholic inclination of our generous race. Only in this way can we account for the fact that four years later, in 400, those who a little earlier had shown themselves adamant and hostile, now retracted en masse and with evident signs of sincerity, without being forcefully compelled or obliged in any way to do so by any higher power. This memorable event occurred during the First Council of Toledo - so called because all we know of the real first Council of Toledo is that it took place. This synod is as important, perhaps more important than the Third Council of Toledo but (inexplicably to me!) has not gained the same degree of recognition. Because, if in the year 589 we see an invading barbarian race bow their heads before the conquered peoples, accept their superiority, worship their God, and surrender to the civilising supremacy of the Hispano-Roman race, the true and only Spanish race, we should never forget that one-hundred-and-eighty years earlier, another Council of Toledo bound the will of this mighty race with an indissoluble bond. This Council gave us unity in doctrine, a unity that was later to ensure victory not only against Visigothic Arianism but against each and every other heresy the Catholic Church has ever had to contend with in our land. Unity in discipline, too, which put a stop to anarchy. And "churches" became The One Church, a model of wisdom and virtue to the entire West.

The Toledo Fathers knew well that it was unity that was needed at the time. That is why Patruinus, bishop of Mérida, presiding, opened the Council with these memorable words: 'Since everyone of us has began doing *diverse things in our churches* thus creating scandal that borders on schism, let us here determine, if you will, the norm that all bishops should adopt in the ordination of clerics. My opinion is that the Constitutions of the Nican Council should be kept in perpetuity and that we should never separate from them". And the

---

of Saragossa, which Simphosius attended for one day only, he and his companions being excommunicated by the synod. Ferreiro thinks it was convened in 396.

bishops responded: "It is our will, and let him be excommunicated who acts against what is set forth in the Canons of Nicea".[125]

Mark this: "In the Canons of Nicea" that is to say, in the universal (Catholic) discipline of both the East and West. Our great Spanish Church, faithful to our great Hosius' tradition, has never aspired to any of those semi-schismatic autonomies that other churches are constantly dreaming about and longing for.

The First Council of Toledo, as it has come down to us, comprises four clearly distinct sections: the *Canones disciplinares*, the *Assertio fidei contra priscillianistas*, the abjuration formulas pronounced by Simphosius, Dictinius, etc., and the *Sententia definitiva* that admits them back into the fold of the Church. The authenticity and link between all of these documents has been invincibly demonstrated by the most learned Father Flórez (*España Sagrada,* vol. VI).

The canons are twenty in number. I shall refer to them very briefly.

a) Number XIV is directed against the Priscillianists who received Communion sacrilegiously - not consuming the sacred Host. Number XX decrees that only the bishop, not presbyters (as was done in some provinces) consecrate the Chrism. As for the other canons, some concern avoiding irregularities in ordination (I, II, III, IV, VIII, and X): number II bans public penitents from advancing beyond the orders of porter and lector (and this only in cases of absolute necessity), unless they had already been sub-deacons before falling into sin; others deal with clerics' attendance at their churches and to the daily Sacrifice; it prohibits moving from one diocese to another unless they are returning to the Faith from heresy; they separate from the fold of the Church he who communicates with the excommunicated (can. V, XII, and XV). Number VI seems to be indirectly addressing customs held by Priscillianists: for example, virgins consecrated to God must not attend gatherings or assemblies or maintain excessive familiarity with their confessor nor with laymen or priests. We saw a similar prohibition in the Council of Saragossa.

b) After the canons comes the *Regula Fidei contra omnes haereses, maxime contra priscillianistas* - a precious document that, for our Church, has had the same or comparable importance as the Nicene Symbol has had for the Universal Church. It is a brilliant testimony to the purity of the Spanish Church in that troubled century, a symbol of glory and immortality for the bishops who

---

[125]   "Quoniam singuli coepimus in Ecclesiis nostris facere diversa, et inde tanta scandala sunt quae usque ad schisma perveniunt, si placet, communi consilio decernamus quid ab omnibus Episcopis in ordinandis clericis sit sequendum. Mihi autem placet constituta primitus Nicaeni Concilii perpetuo esse servanda, nec ab his esse recedendum. Universi Episcopi dixerunt: Hoc nobis placet, ita ut si quis, cognitis gestis Nicaeni Concilii, aliud quam statutum est, facere praesumpserit...hic excommunicatus habeatur..." (*Collectio Canonum Ecclessia...Hispanae,* ed. Biblioteca Real, 1808, p.321)

authored it. The *Regula fidei* is a work of such importance and meaning for this present work, that I consider it appropriate to translate it whole and *de verbo ad verbum*, [126] while adding some comments on its clauses later.

"We believe in one only Omnipotent God, Father, Son, and Holy Spirit, Maker of all things visible and invisible, of heaven and of earth. We believe there is one only God, and one Trinity of the divine substance: that the Father is not the Son; that the Son is not the Father; but the Son of God is of the nature of the Father; that the Holy Spirit, the Paraclete, is neither the Son nor the Father, but proceeds from the Father and the Son. Hence: the Father is not begotten, the Son is begotten, the Holy Spirit is not begotten but proceeds from the Father and the Son. The Father is He Whose voice was heard in the heavens: "This is my beloved Son, with Whom I am well pleased: listen to Him". The Son is He who said: "I am of the Father and came from God to this world". The Paraclete is the Holy Spirit, of Whom the Son spoke: "If I do not return to the Father, the Spirit will not come". We affirm this Trinity, distinct in persons, one in substance, indivisible and with no distinction in virtue, power or majesty. Aside from this, we accept no other divine nature, neither of angel nor of spirit, nor of any virtue or power that claims to be God. [127] We believe that the Son of God, God born of the Father before all beginning, sanctified the womb of the Virgin Mary, and from her He took, with no act of man, true body, not imaginary or fantastical, but solid and true. [128] We believe that two natures, the divine and the human, concurred in one sole person, our Lord Jesus Christ, who was hungry, and thirsty, and felt pain, and cried, and suffered all our physical pains, until He was crucified by the Jews and buried, and rose on the third day. And later He conversed with his disciples, and forty days after the Resurrection He ascended into heaven. This Son of Man we also call the Son of God, and Son of God and of Man jointly. We believe in the future resurrection of the flesh; and we say that the soul of man is not of the divine substance or emanated from God the Father, but God's creation, created of His free will. [129]

If anyone says or believes that the world was not created by God Omnipotent, let him be anathema.

If anyone says or believes that the Father is the Son or the Holy Spirit, let him be anathema.

If anyone says or believes that the Son is the Father or the Holy Spirit, let him be anathema.

---

126 Latin text included in Appendix.

127 The Gnostic *aeons*.

128 Condemnation of Docetism.

129 Condemnation of Pantheism and of the system of emanation.

If anyone says or believes that the Holy Spirit is the Father or the Son, let be him anathema.

If anyone says or believes that the Son of God took flesh only and not a human soul, let him be anathema;

If anyone says or believes that Christ could not have been born, let him be anathema.

If anyone says or believes that the Divinity of Christ was *convertible* and *passible*, let him be anathema.

If anyone says or believes that the God of the Old Law is one, and the God of the Gospel another, let him be anathema. [130]

If anyone says or believes that this world was made by any other god than Him of Whom it is written: "In the beginning God created heaven and earth", let him be anathema.

If anyone says or believes that the human body will not rise after death, let him be anathema.

If anyone says or believes that the human soul is a part of God, or of the substance of God, let him be anathema.

If anyone says or believes that any scriptures are to be accepted and venerated other than those the Catholic Church holds and venerates, let him be anathema.

If anyone says that Divinity and humanity form one sole nature in Christ, let him be anathema.

If anyone says or believes that the Divine Essence can be extended outside of the Trinity, let him be anathema.

If any one gives credence to astrology or the science of the Chaldeans, let him be anathema.

If anyone says or believes that matrimony celebrated in accordance to divine law is execrable, let him be anathema.

If anyone says or believes that the flesh of birds or fish that has been granted to us for our nourishment is execrable, let him be anathema.

If anyone follows Priscillian in these errors, and having been baptised believes anything against the See of Peter, let him be anathema".

And this valiant condemnation of Pantheism, anti-Trinitarianism, Docetism, and Marcion's Antithesis reverberated from beneath the vaults of the ancient Basilica of Toledo. These Canons, proposed by Potruinus and approved by the other bishops, were then transmitted to all churches

---

[130]   Marcion's Antithesis.

throughout Spain, which has preserved this faith since then with inviolate purity.

Observe that this was the first Council to define the procession of the Holy Spirit, from both the Father and the Son. The opinion of Pagi, Quesnel and other critics who say the *Filioque* particle was added later simply does not hold. [131]

What was now missing was the compliance of the Galician Bishops attending the Synod. God moved them to repentance and good judgement, for in the third session, Dictinius rose, as we read in the Acta, and spoke these words: "Hear me, good priests, correct me in all that I am wrong. I shall accept your correction for it is written: "Vobis datae sunt claves regni coelorum". I ask that it be the gates of heaven, not those of hell, that be opened to me. Forgive me, I shall lay all before your eyes. I repent of having said that the nature of God and that of man are the same. I do not only subject myself to your correction: I retract and impeach all other errors in my writings. God is my witness that I speak the truth. Where I erred, correct me. A moment earlier I said this and repeat it now: all that I wrote in my first paper I reject and condemn now with all my heart. With the exception of the name of God, I anathematise all of it. All I have said against the Faith, I condemn it all, including its author."

After Dictinius spoke Simphosius: "I condemn the doctrine of the two principles – the doctrine that affirms that the Son could not have been born, expressed in the Paper we read earlier. I anathematise this sect and its author. If you wish, I shall do so in writing". And he wrote these words: "I reject all heretical books and especially the doctrine of Priscillian where he says that the Son could not have been born *(innascibilem esse)*".

Presbyter Comasius spoke next, saying: "No one will be in doubt that I am of one mind with my prelate, and I condemn all that he condemns, because I hold nothing superior to his wisdom but God. Be certain that I shall do or think nothing other than what he has said, and so as my bishop whom I follow has spoken, whatsoever he has condemned, I condemn".

In one more session, all of them confirmed their retractions, Comasius adding: "I do not hesitate to repeat what at another time I stated, for my own salvation: I abide by the authority and wisdom of my elderly bishop Simphosius. I am of the same mind I was yesterday: if you wish, I shall so state in writing. Let all those who wish to participate in your communion, follow this example". And he read out from a scroll: "Since we all follow the Catholic faith of Nicea, and here we have heard read a document brought by presbyter Donatus wherein Priscillian said that the Son could not have been born, which is against the Symbol of Nicea, I anathematise Priscillian, author of this perverse statement and condemn all the books that he wrote". And Simphosius added:

---

[131]   See Flórez's fine-tuned observations, *España Sagrada*, vol. VI

"Whatsoever wrong books he wrote, I condemn". And Dictinius ended: "I follow the example of my father, progenitor and master, Simphosius. With what he has spoken, I concur. It is written: If anyone evangelises you contrary to how you were evangelised, let him be anathema. Therefore, all that Priscillian taught and wrote erroneously, we condemn".

Concerning the irregular elections of Dictinius and other Priscillianist bishops, Simphosius confessed to ceding to the almost unanimous will of the people of Galicia ("totius Galiciae plebium multitudo"). Paternus, prelate of Braga, said he had long ago abandoned Priscillianist errors through the reading of St. Ambrose's works. Two other bishops, Isonius, recently consecrated, and Vegetinus, which had appeared before the Council of Saragossa, subscribed to Simphosius' retraction. [132] However, Herenas, Donatus, Acurius, Emilius and several other presbyters refused submission and reiterated in a loud voice that Priscillian had been a Catholic and a martyr, persecuted by the Ithacian bishops. The Council excommunicated and deposed the rebels convicted of heresy and perjury by the testimony of three bishops and many presbyters and deacons. [133]

The *Sententia definitiva* admits Vegetinus and Paternus, who did not relapse into heresy to full communion. Simphosius, Dictinius and the others would keep their sees, but not enter into the fold of the Church until receiving the opinion of the Pontiff and that of St. Simplicianus, bishop of Milan and successor to St. Ambrose, whom the Fathers had consulted for their final judgement. Whilst this final absolution was pending they would abstain from conferring orders, and this included other Galician bishops that had adopted the *Rule of faith*, an indispensable condition for accord. Apocryphal books and "meetings in the houses of women" were banned, and it was ordered that Ortigius be restored to the see from which he had been removed by the Priscillianists.

The ills and discord in our Church however did not end suddenly with this Council. Many bishops disapproved of the absolution granted to the Priscillianists, and more particularly, that Simphosius, Dictinius and others were allowed to remain in their dioceses. And this is how the Luciferian schism began and became entrenched. Galicia remained isolated once more; as for the rest of the Peninsula, Tyrians and Trojans pushed on with their reciprocal anti-canonical consecrations and depositions of prelates. Those of the regions of Betis and Carthage were the most adamant in not communicating with the Galicians.

---

[132]   Isonius had been made a bishop by Simphosius while still a catechumen.

[133]   The signatures of this Council appear in the following order: Patruinus, Marcelus, Aphrodisius, Licinianus, Iucundus, Severus, Leonas, Hilarius, Olympius, Orticius, Asturius, Lampius, Serenus, Florus, Leporius, Eustachius, Aurelianus, Lampadius, Exuperancius.

In the thick of this general confusion, a man named Rufinus, a turbulent man, who had been pardoned once before by the Council of Toledo for his excesses, started ordaining bishops in every small town he could find and "filled the churches with scandal". The same was being done in Cataluña by Minicius, bishop of Gerona, while in Lusitania, Gregorius, Patruinus' succesor, was deposed of his Mérida see.

This chaos had to be stopped, and so the bishops of Tarragona on the one hand and Hilarius, one of the Fathers of the Council of Toledo on the other, and with him the presbyter Helpidius, asked Pope Innocent to intervene (circa 404). The Pope addressed a famous Decretal [134] to all Spanish bishops pleading for unity and reconciliation stating that "in the bosom of the Faith itself peace has been violated, discipline confused, the canons trodden over, law and order forgotten, unity torn asunder by the usurpation of many churches". [135] The Pontiff has harsh words for the Luciferians' obstinacy and intolerance. "Why does it hurt them that Simphosius, Dictinius and the others who have retracted their heresy have now been received into the fold of the church? Do they perchance think they have not lost enough of their previous honour? If this pricks and mortifies them, read how the Apostle St. Peter came, after his tears, to being what he had been. Consider that Thomas, after his doubt, lost nothing of his former merits. See that the prophet David, after confession of his sin, was not deprived of the gift of prophecy...Promptly, you who are dispersed, come together at once to form only one body in the wholeness of the Catholic Faith. It is when the body splits into parts that it is exposed to all manner of afflictions". [136] He then mandates deposing the bishops chosen by Rufinus and Minicius against the Canons of Nicea and to separate from the communion of the faithful all Luciferians who refuse to vow to the consensus reached at the Council of Toledo. We also see by this letter that some of the interloping bishops had been soldiers, attorneys, and even leaders of public games.

---

[134]   Jacob Sirmond published it complete for the first time. It can be read in Appendix III, vol. VI, of *España Sagrada*, p. 325-30

[135]   "Et in ipso sinu Fidei violatam intra provinciam pacem, disciplinae rationem esse confusam, et multa contra Canones Patrum, contempto ordine, regulisque neglectis, in usurpatione Ecclesiarum fuisse commissa".

[136]   "Quaero enim, quare doluerint Symphosium atque Dictinium, aliosque qui detestabilem haeresim damnaverunt, receptos in fidem Catholicam tunc fuisse? Num quod non aliquid de honoribus amisserint quos habebant? Quod si quos hoc pungit aut stimulat, legant Petrum Apostolum post lacrymas hoc fuisse quod fuerat, considerent Thomam post dubitationem illam nihil de prioribus meritis omisisse; denique David Prophetam egregium post manifestam confessionem suam, prophetiae suae meritis non fuisse privatum. Quare...in unitate Catholicae Fidei omnes qui dispersi sunt congregatur, et esse inexpugnabile unum corpus incipiat, quod si separetur in partes, ad omnes patebit lacerationis injurias".

The emperor Honorius included the Priscillianists in the edicts he passed against the Manichaeans, Donatists and pagans on 15th November 408.[137] On 22nd February 409, in the consulship of Honorius and Theodosius, he made the punishment even more severe, convinced that "this type of people shall have nothing in common with the rest neither in custom nor in law" and that "heresy will be treated as a public crime – something against the security of all". Every convicted Priscillianist was to lose his property (which was to be passed on to his heirs as long as they did not incur the same crime), and be disabled from taking possession of inheritance or rewards, entering into contracts, and losing the right to bequeath. The servant who informed on his master was to be freed; he who followed him in his errors would be under obligation to the Treasury. The administrator who acquiesced in it was condemned to perpetual hard labour in the mines. Prefects and other officials, remiss in the persecution of this heresy, would pay fines ten or twenty pounds of gold.

In 409, the barbarians invaded the Peninsula. Galicia was subjugated by the Swabians remaining isolated from the rest of the Iberian land. Priscillianism continued.

In deference to logic though violating chronology, I shall take the history of this heresy now to its end.

About the middle of the fifth century, St.Turibius, usually called "of Liebana" who, as he himself relates, had been on pilgrimage to various places, even to the Holy Land, returned to Galicia where he was elected bishop of Astorga. He would devote his efforts from then on to eradicating all vestiges of Priscillianism still remaining, starting by taking the apocryphal books out of the hands of the faithful. With this aim in mind, he wrote an epistle to bishops Idacius and Ceponius *De non recipiendis in auctoritatem Fidei apocryphis scripturis, et de secta priscillianistarum,* which I transcribe in the Appendix. [138] But he did not think this remedy sufficient and appealed to the Apostolic See. He sent St. Leo the Great two writings, lost today: *Commonitorium* and *Libellus*. The first was a list of the errors he had found in the apocryphal books; the second a refutation of the Priscillianists' principal heretical errors. In both books, says Montanus, bishop of Toledo, "hanc sordidam haeresim explanavit (Thoribius), aperuit, et ocultam tenebris suis perfidiaeque nube velatam, in propatulo misit". The deacon Pervincus delivered Turibius' epistles to the Pope, who replied on 21st July 447 (consulship of Alipius and Ardaburus). His letter is a long exposition and refutation of Gnostic errors divided into sixteen chapters. I insert it in the Appendix as a most precious document, and we shall bear it in mind when making an exposition of Priscillianist doctrine later.

---

[137]   *Cod. Theod.* Lib. XLIII.

[138]   Sr. López Ferreiro includes it too, and translates into Spanish, *Estudios histórico-críticos sobre el Priscilianismo…* Santiago, 1878. An excellent work that reached my hands just when I was reviewing this chapter. It is more exact and complete than Girves' book.

As an ultimate remedy, St. Leo asks for a national council, if indeed it were possible to convene one, or at least a synod of the bishops of Galicia, to be presided by Idacius and Ceponius. There can be no doubt that this provident event took place. The celebration of a General Council would have been impossible due to the on-going wars between Swabians and Visigoths, but the bishops of Betis, Carthage, Tarragona and Lusitania did gather in Council to confirm the *Rule of Faith* and probably add some additional clauses. We do not have the Acta of this Synod but we do know that the *Assertio fidei* was sent to Balconius, Metropolitan of Braga and to the other Galician bishops, gathered, perhaps, in provincial synod at the same time. All accepted it, as well as St. Leo's decretal, though some of them in bad faith ("subdolo arbitrio", reads Idacius' *Chronicon*). This is the synod referred to as *De Aquis-Celenis*. [139]

During a whole century the Church in Galicia fought and struggled heroically, unassumingly, against two heresies at the same time: the Arianism of the Swabians (a foreign heresy therefore not as alarming) and against Priscillianism which lingered on with satanic doggedness backed by some bishops. One would expect some memorials of this long struggle to have been preserved, but there are none. Regrettably, wars of the mind and of human conscience are those that occupy the least space in history books. Personally, I cannot even express how many long narratives of wars, how many catalogues of dynasties, how many listings of noble lineage I would forego just to know exactly how and when the Priscillian heresy died in Galicia! But we can, at least, share and rejoice in the final Victory Hymn: the last, the final anathema that in 567, more than a hundred years after St. Leo's Letter, the Fathers of the First Council of Braga pronounced over both their enemies, victorious at last. Victorious not by force of arms or intolerant executions but by the incontestable fortitude of Truth and the supremacy of the Christian Faith, which moves mountains.

With what joy they speak of Priscillianism as a thing of the past! And not satisfied with the *Rule of Faith*, they add seventeen canons more, against just as many errors held by our Gnostics!

"Should anyone deny that the Father, the Son and the Holy Spirit are three Persons, of one substance, virtue and power, and recognises only one Person, as Sibelius and Priscillian said, let him be anathema.

Should anyone introduce other divine persons other than the Most Holy Trinity, as the Gnostics and Priscillian said, let him be anathema.

Should anyone say that the Son of God and our Lord was not born of the Virgin, as asserted by Paulus de Samosata, Fotinius and Priscillian, let him be anathema.

---

[139]   Father Flórez doubts its existence. Ferreiro, always inclined towards a multiplicity of Councils, accepts it.

Should anyone stop celebrating the birth of Christ according to the flesh, or pretend to do so by surreptitiously fasting on that day and on Sunday, meaning by this that they do not believe Christ took true human nature, as Cerdo, Marcion, Mani and Priscillian said, let him be anathema.

Should anyone believe that the human soul or angels are of the divine substance, as Mani and Priscillian said, let him be anathema.

Should anyone say with Priscillian that the human soul sinned while in its celestial dwelling and that this is the reason it is locked in the body, let him be anathema.

Should anyone say that the devil was not at first a good angel created by God, and that its nature is not a work of God but has come from the darkness and the eternal principle of evil, as the Manichaeans and Priscillian affirmed, let him be anathema.

Should anyone believe that the devil created some abhorrent creatures, and that it is the devil that brings about thunder, lightning, storms and drought, as Priscillian said, let him be anathema.

Should anyone believe, with the pagans and Priscillian, that the human soul is subjected by fate to the stars, let him be anathema.

Should anyone affirm, with Priscillian, that the twelve signs of the Zodiac have influence over diverse parts of the body, themselves marked with the names of the Patriarchs, let him be anathema.

Should anyone condemn matrimony and procreation,[140] let him be anathema.

Should anyone say that the human body is a work of the devil, and that conception in the maternal womb is a sign of diabolic operations, not believing therefore in the resurrection of the flesh, let him be anathema.

Should anyone say that creation of all flesh is not a work of God but of evil angels, let him be anathema.

Should anyone, judging as filthy the flesh that God granted us for our nourishment, abstain from it, except out of mortification, let him be anathema.

If a cleric or monk lives in the company of women that are not his mother, sister or near relative, as the Priscillianists did, let him be anathema.

If anyone in the fifth day of Holy Week, which is called the Lord's Supper, at the legitimate hour after *None*, has not fasted before celebration of the Mass in Church but (as with Priscilian's sect) celebrates this festivity after

---

[140]   I omit the customary formula *as the Manichaeans and Princillian said* because it does not vary from here on.

the hour of Terce with a Requiem Mass breaking the fast, let him be anathema.

If someone reads, follows, or defends the books that Priscillian altered to suit his error; or the treatises Dictinius wrote before his conversion under the names of the Patriarchs, Prophets and Apostles, let him be anathema".

Canon XXX of the disciplinary decrees of this Council bans the singing of hymns in church other than Psalms from the Old Testament.

I think we can firmly state that the Council of Braga buried Priscillianism forever. J. Matter says that "this heresy went on as a secret sect until the Arab invasion" but he produces no proof for this opinion. However secret it may have been, is it conceivable that the following Councils of Toledo did not anathematise it at any time? Everything leads us to conclude that by the seventh to eighth centuries Priscillianism belonged to the annals of history, even if some superstitions lingered on as the last smouldering symptoms of this epidemic.[141]

This is really all I know about Priscillianism from an historical perspective. [142] Let us now in the following paragraphs look at its literature and dogmas.

---

[141]   For example, the Fourth Council of Toledo condemns Lectors in Galicia who were not tonsured and who wore long hair with a small crown in the middle of the head "as was the custom of the heretics."

The Third Council of Braga (AD 713) speaks of those who consecrated with milk or grape juice, not with wine, and of those who profaned the Mass to the point of serving themselves food in sacred vessels, all of which was expressly qualified as being an after-taste of Priscillianism.

Toledo IV speaks of the custom observed in "some churches in Galicia" of closing the doors of the Basilicas on Good Friday, and of not celebrating the Offices, or fasting, but rather eating as sumptuously as one could at the hour of None. In other churches, candles or Paschal lamps were not blessed (canons VII, VIII, and IX). St. Braulius wrote to St. Fructuosus who was in Galicia "Cavete autem ilius patriae venenatum Priscilliani dogma" (*España Sagrada*, vol. XXX, Apend. III, ep. XLIV).

[142]   Sources I have consulted for the history of Priscillianism:

❖   Sulpicii Severi, *Historia Sacra, Dialogi.* (in vol. VI of *Collectio Maxima Veterum Patrum*, Lugduni, 1677.

❖   *S. Prosperi Aquitani Chronicon*, in vol.VIII of the works of St. Jerome, ed. Vallart, Verona, 1738.

❖   *S. Hieronymi Opera*, ed. cited, vol. I, *Epistolar, clas.* 3, letter 75. *De viris illustribus*, chapters CXXI, CXXII, CXXIII (vol. 2) and in vol. II, *Dialogus adversus Pelagianos*, etc.

❖   *Idatii Chronicon*, in vol. IV of *Historia Sagrada*.

❖   *Concilios de Zaragoza, Toledo y Braga*, in vol. II of *Collecta Maxima*, Aguirre, or in vol. III of the Catalani edition (Roma, 1753).

❖   St. Isidore, *De viris illustribus*, chapter XV (Ithacius). In ed. Arévalo.

❖   Decretal of Pope Innocent (Ep. XXIII *ad Toletanos*), in vol. III of the *Colección de Concilios*, Mansi, and in VI of *España Sagrada*.

Priscillianist Literature.

Under this title, I include not only works composed by the devotees of this heresy but also the apocryphal books they used, and the challenges and refutations others wrote to combat them.

Of the writings of the father and dogmatiser of the sect himself, even the titles are lost. We know nonetheless of several tracts of his thanks to St. Jerome's account *(De viris illustribus)* and the *Acta* of the First Council of Toledo.

A most curious fragment of a letter by Priscillian himself is preserved in Orosius' *Commonitorium.* It reads: "This is the first wisdom: to recognise in different types of divine souls the virtues of nature and the disposition of bodies. Through which heaven and earth join, and all the principalities of the world work, to win the dispositions of the saints. Patriarchs occupy the first circle, and carry the divine stamp *(chirographum)*, designed by the assent of God, the angels and all the spirits. It is imprinted on the souls that will have to come down to earth, and serves them as a shield in battle". ("Haec prima sapientia est, in animarum, typis divinarum [143] virtutes intelligere naturae et corporis dispositionem. In qua obligatum videtur coelum et terra, omnesque principatus saeculi videntur astricti sanctorum dispositiones superare. Nam primum Dei circulum et mittendarum in carne animarum divinum chirographum, angelorum et Dei omnium animorum consensibus fabricatum patriarchae tenent, quae contra formalis militiae opus possident")[144]. I will come back to this brief but notable fragment of the works of the Galician heresiarch a little later.

The second Priscillianist fragment we know of is the *Apologetico* of Tiberianus Beticus, mentioned also by St. Jerome *(De viris illustribus)*, and also lost. The saint said he found the style "puffed up" and full of affectation.

Nor do we have Latronianus' poetry, praised by the hermit of Bethlehem as equal to the classics of old.

❖ Girves, *De secta Priscilliaristarum dissertatio* (*Romae*, 1750), the best work on the subject.
❖ Flórez, *España Sagrada*, vols. VI (*Iglesia de Toledo: Concilios*), XIII (*Iglesia de Mérida*), XIV (*Iglesias de Avila, Ossonoba*, etc.) XV (*Iglesia Bracarense*), XVI (*Iglesia de Astorga*), touching also on those of Orense, Lugo, and others.
❖ Risco, *España Sagrada*, vol. XXX (*Iglesia de Zaragoza*).
❖ La Fuente, Vicente, *Historia eclesiástica de España*, vol. I, 2nd ed. Excellent work.
❖ Murguía: *Historia de Galicia*, vol. II (The Appendix in this book is Honorius' mandate).
❖ Matter, *Histoire critique du Gnosticisme*, vol. II, 2nd ed.
I will omit Tillemot, Baronius and other general historians.

I add the recent work by Sr. D. Antonio López Ferreiro, titled *Estudios histórico-críticos sobre el Priscilianismo*, by D... canon of the S.I..C. of Santiago, Santiago, 1878, 4°, 254 pp. This precious tract was first published serially in *El Porvenir*, a Catholic journal of that city.

[143] Some read *divinarum virtutem intelligere naturas,* which changes the meaning considerably.

[144] This closing is obscure, and the reading varies in the several editions. The one above seems to me to be the best.

We have more sources on the literary output of Dictinius, bishop of Astorga, who repented of his errors and came to die in the odour of sanctity. During his Priscillianist phase he wrote a treatise that he entitled *Libra*, as it was divided into twelve questions in the same way that a Roman pound, or *libra*, is divided into twelve ounces. This book maintained, among other absurdities, that it was lawful to lie for religious reasons. St. Augustine tells us of this in his book *Contra mendacium* which he wrote in order to refute this part of Dictinius' work. [145] Dictinius' heretical writings were still read with great veneration by the sect's adepts around the time of St. Leo the Great, who said referring to them: "They are not reading Dictinius, but Priscillian; they approve of what Dictinius wrote when in error, not of what he rectified in repentance; they follow him in his fall, not in his reparation".

Dictinius had offered in support of his main error this passage from St. Paul: "loquimini veritatem unusquisque cum proximo suo" (Eph 4:25), concluding from this that one is under the obligation of telling the truth only to one's "neighbour", that is, one's co-religionists. In support he proffered the fictions and simulations of Rebecca, Thamar, the midwives of Egypt, Rahab of Jericho, and Jehu, and even St. Luke's "finxit se longius ire" when speaking of the Saviour. St. Augustine responds that some of these cases are related as *facts* that took place but are not recommended for replication; that in others, while the truth is silent, no falsity is being said; and finally, that others are allegorical and figured forms of speech.

About the year 420, a Galician bishop, Consentius, sent a letter with the *Libra* and other Priscillianist writings to St. Augustine via the cleric Leonas together with some Catholic refutations, and gave him an account of what Fronton, Servant of God, had confided to him about the Priscillianists. This letter, which would have been most important to us, has also been lost. One of the things he asks the Saint in this letter is if it is licit to pretend to be a Priscillianist in order to discover the wicked things these sectarians were up to. He himself thought it was permissible but other Catholics disapproved of it.

St. Augustine (in the above-cited book *Contra mendacium, ad Consentium* divided in twenty-one chapters) [146] vigorously reproves such immoral tactics, though he does praise Consentius' zeal, his eloquent style, and his knowledge of Sacred Scripture. "Never!" – he exclaims – "how can it be licit to combat lies with lies? Are we to be the Priscillianists' accomplices precisely in what they are worse than other heretics?...Lying is more tolerable in Priscillianists than in Catholics: they blaspheme not knowing, we, knowingly; they against *scientia*, we against *conscientia* ...Let us not forget the words: "Quiqumque me negaverit coram hominibus, negabo eum coram Patre meo..." Where did Jesus say: Dress yourselves in wolves' clothing to capture wolves though you may be sheep? If

---

145   *"Occultandae religionis causa esse mentiendum"*.

146   Vol. VI of the Maurus edition.

this is the best way to bring them out, it is better that they remain secret". He adds that in matters of religion especially, even the pettiest lie is not licit; there are other nets to catch heretics, to wit, the preaching of the Gospel and the continuous refutation of their errors. He advises him, above all, to combat Dictinius' *Libra*.

Consentius consulted St. Augustine again later on five points which had some remote connection with Priscillian's doctrines:

1) If the body of Christ preserves the bones, blood, and other forms of the flesh.
2) How is the passage from the Apostle "caro et sanguis regnum Dei non possidebunt" to be interpreted.
3) If each part of the human body was created by God.
4) If faith is sufficient for the baptised to obtain eternal salvation.
5) If the breath of God on Adam's face created his soul, or was the breath the soul itself.

To the first question, the bishop of Hippo answers that it is the doctrine of the Faith that Christ's body in heaven is the same body He had on earth; to the second, that the "works of the flesh" are the vices; to the third, that nature works and generates itself directed by the Creator; to the fourth, that faith without works is a dead faith; to the fifth, that to state that the soul is not a particle of the divine substance should suffice, and all else is idle debate.

There is another letter from Consentius asking about some doubts on the mystery of the Trinity.[147]

The Priscillianists differed from other Gnostics in that they admitted the whole of Sacred Scripture, the Old Testament and the New. But, as St. Leo said, they would introduce the most bold and daring variants into the texts: "Multos corruptissimos eorum codices...invenimus: Curandum ergo est et sacerdotali diligentia maxime providentum ut falsati codices, et a sincera veritati discordes, in nullo usu lectionis habeantur". St. Braulius saw some of these books still in use as late as the seventh century. As for the alterations they contained, we find no available data to determine. What is known is that each Gnostic sect amended the Bible according to its own particular teachings; the reason being, in fact, that they held it to be a collection of esoteric books, much inferior to the apocryphal ones they used.

The label of *apocryphal books* has been used to refer to works of very different origin. As chaff among wheat, innumerable writings appeared in the first century of the Church comingled with the Gospels, the Acts, and canonical Epistles. Sometimes their aim was to give wholesome nourishment to the faithful's devotion; others, to spread unnoticeably a multitude of errors. Leaving aside works written by Jews under the name of Patriarchs and Prophets

---

[147]   St. Augustine, Letters CCV and CCX.

of the Old Law, like *The Book of Enoch, The Life of Adam, The Testament of the twelve Patriarchs,* etc., the apocryphal books of Christian origin can be summarised into four classes:

1) Canonical books completely altered, for example, *The Gospel of St. Luke* and the *Epistles of St. Paul,* as Marcion rewrote them. All these falsifications were the work of heterodox sects.

2) Apocryphal books, wholly heretical, and with a distinctly marked propagandist intention. Almost all of them have perished, i.e. *The Gospel of Judas Iscariot,* written by the Cainites; the *Gospel of perfection,* the *Long and the Short interrogation of Mary,* etc.

3) Books that contained errors though they were non-doctrinal books and had certainly not been intended as expositors of the dogmas of the heterodox sects. To this genre belong almost all those we know of today. Let it be noted that some of them went through several rewritings as they passed from one sect to another, or even from heterodox to Catholics sources, to the point of containing today very few heresies. One of the best known works in this group is the *Acts of St. Paul and Thecla,* written especially to give credence to the doctrine of those who wanted to attribute to women the faculty of preaching and of conferring baptism. But the ripest fruit in this group of apocryphal literature is the book *Clementines* or *Recognitiones* written, or altered, by the Ebionites, and one that could be qualified as a true literary jewel.

4) Orthodox apocryphals written with the aim of satisfying the curiosity of the faithful on points the Gospel narrative or the *Acts of the Apostles* touch only in passing. They are generally of a later date than heretical books with whose scraps they arrayed themselves more than once. The best known and least worthy of these Christian apocryphals is the compilation of the false *Abdias,* carried out, most probably, in the sixteenth century.

The historical and literary appeal of all these books, even the mediocre, was great indeed. There one finds the seed of all the legends and pious traditions that enchanted the fantasy of the Middle Ages: it was there that, for the first time, Christian sentiment was poured into art, at times with a splendour and gusto that truly astounds us today.

The Priscillianists of Spain took over many of the apocryphals of earlier sects and reinflated them with added falsifications. As a general summary, the Epistle of St. Turibius to Idacius and Ceponius, and that of Orosius to St. Augustine will serve to list them, as best one can:

1. *Acts of St. Andrew.* Cited by Toribius. These are the ones attributed to Leucius. Today we know of a text of these *Acts* written in Greek that can be read in the collection of Tischendorf (pp. 105 to 131), [148] but it is different from

---

[148]   *Acta Apostolorum apocryphal ex triginta antiquis codicibus graecis.* Leipzig, 1851.   I continuously follow this edition which seems the most complete in what relates to Greek

the one by Leucius, or at any rate, rewritten by some Catholic author who distilled from them their Manichaean flavour and saved the narrative. The variance in the different editions is proved by the fact that those we do possess lack that singular passage quoted by St. Augustine (*Contra Manichaeos*, chapter XXXVIII), where he tells the story of a Maximilla who, not wanting to pay her husband her conjugal duty (for she judged it to be a sin), incurred in nothing less than "procuring", or "third-party accommodation." We know the Manichaeans and Priscillianists condemned marriage and the propagation of the species. The rewriting of these *Acts,* well proven today, must be rather ancient since St. Beatus of Liebana and Eterius of Osma quote a passage from it with praise in their refutation of Elipandus' heresy.

2. *Acts of St. John.* In the same collection of Tischendorf (pages 266 to 276), one reads the text of these *Acts* in Greek which must be that attributed by Toribius to Leucius, and agrees in little or nothing with the narrative of *Abdias*. St. Augustine, in the treatise *In Joannem, CXXIV,* quotes and censures a passage in these *Acts* where it is stated that the Apostle did not die like the rest of men but sleeps in his tomb awaiting the coming of the Saviour, and sometimes, with his breath, removes the dust covering him. The author displayed great imaginative creativity in these *Acts.* Here we encounter for the first time the story of the fugitives' captain converted by St. John, as well as another of more literary importance and worth, namely, the story of Callimachus of Ephesus, furiously enamoured of the Christian maiden Drusilla, to the extreme of disinterring her body with sacrilegious intent in mind. It was from here that the famed Hroswitha, a nun from Gandersheim, took the main argument for one of her dramas, *Callimachus* - a true literary jewel from the tenth century were its writing authentic, which many doubt.

3. *Acts of St. Thomas.* We know of two texts, one Greek, the other Syriac. The latter has many more traces of Gnosticism than the first and was not printed until 1871, when W. Wright made room for it in his *Apocryphal Acts of the Apostles, edited from Syriac manuscripts in the British Museum and other libraries.* [149] These *Acts* seem to have been translated from the Greek, but from a more ancient and a more Gnostic text than the one we have today. In the Greek there are two very curious hymns missing, notably one about the "pearl of Egypt", one of those beautiful fables sectarians so liked to use, and not dissimilar to *Sophia.* Nor is there any trace of this hymn in the barbarous Latin rendering that goes by the name of *Abdias.*

This *Acts of St. Thomas* refers to the preaching of the Apostle in India and seems to have been written to advocate the most absolute continence. Christ

---

apocryphals . See also: J. Alberti Fabricii, *Codex Pseudepigraphus Novi Testamenti,* Hamburg, 1703, and the *Nova Collectio,* by Thilo, Leipzig, 1832.

[149]   London, 1871. Volumen 1: Syriac texts. Volume II, English translation, pp. 146-298, are the *Acts of Judas Thomas.*

appears to two spouses and exhorts them to persevere in chastity. The ascetic sects of the Apoctatists or Cathars (pure), one of the Enchratist branches or Tatian's disciples used these *Acts* a great deal. Because of their shared principles, they were adopted also by the Manichaeans, Priscillianists and many other factions of Gnosticism. But since every sect interfered and meddled with the text, it ended up seeded with doctrines that some admitted and others rejected. "In the Acts they called *of St. Thomas*" - writes Toribius – "it is worthy of note, and of execration, to say that the Apostle baptised, not with water but with oil, which is what the Manichaeans adhere to, but not the Priscillianists." ("Specialiter in illis actibus, quae Sancti Thomae dicuntur, prae caeteris notandum atque execrandum est quod dicit eum non baptizare per aquam, sicut habet dominica praedicatio, sed per oleum solum: quod quiden isti nostri non recipiunt, sed manichaei sequuntur").

The passage that seems to have given St. Toribius reason for censure says (in the Greek text of the Tischendorf collection) [150] after mentioning the conversion of a king of India and of his brother: "Καί κατάμξον αύτους είς τήν σήν ποίμνην καθαρίσας αύτους τώ σω λουτρώ καί άλειψας αύτους τψ σψ έλαιψ" ("Receive them in your fold having purified them with your baptism and anointed with your oil"). Thylus, relying on the authority of the holy bishop of Astorga, believes that the reference here is to baptism. Others understand it as relating to Confirmation. The text seems to favour the latter because it clearly separates *baptism*, which washes, from *oil*, that anoints. What follows is even clearer. The neophytes ask the Apostle to imprint the "divine stamp" on them after being baptised, and εκελέυσε προσενεγκείν αύτος έλαιον, ίνα διά του έλαιου δεξονταί την σφραγίδα: ήνεγκαν ουν έλαιον ("He asked them to bring oil, that through oil they may receive the divine sign. And they brought the oil"). It seems evident that it is Confirmation according to the Greek rite that is being alluded to here. But let us not rush into saying that St. Toribius misunderstood the passage or made a mistake here, because we are dealing with a text he actually had in his own hands and must have known quite well. It is possible that the one that has come down to us is a later re-writing of the passage to better fit orthodox teaching. [151] The *Pearl* hymn, for example, and St. Thomas' prayer in prison, have also disappeared despite the latter being of sufficient Catholic flavour.

These were not the only apocryphal *Acts* known to the Priscillianists. St. Toribius adds: "et his similia". Among them, no doubt, those of *St. Peter and St.*

---

[150]   Also in Thylo's, and in the *Dictionnaire des Apocryphes* of Abbot Mignet, an ample compilation but incomplete and one that unfortunately does not include the original texts but French translation only.

[151]   In another publication of Tischendorn, apocalypses Apocryphae Mosis, Esdrae, Pauli, Joannis, etc. Lipsiae, Mendelssohn, 1866, pp. 156-161, are inserted fragments of another Greek text of the *Acts of St. Thomas*, preserved in the Code of the Library of Munich and of another in the Bodleian.

Paul which together with the other three mentioned make up the book that Focius in his *Mirobiblion* called περιοδος τών αγιών Άποστολων, and attributes to Leucius.

This Leucius, or Lucius Charinus, whom Pope Gelasius calls in his Decree against apocryphal books a disciple of the devil himself, was a Manichaean of the fourth century who, as far as I can make out, did not actually write anything but collected, corrected, and added several apocryphals that had formerly been popular with the Gnostic community. He was, let us say, the Homer of all these rhapsodies.

From the same *Leucian* source seems to have come the *Acts of St. Andrew and St. Mathew in the city of the Anthropofagi Cannibals* which, if you are interested, you can find in the collection of Fabricius. They are very Gnostic and very Manichaean. I am not sure if the Priscillianists read them.

4. *Memoria Apostolorum*. Undoubtedly a most interesting read, if it were not also lost. St. Toribius says of it: "Id quo ad magnam perversitatis suae auctoritatem, doctrinam Domini mentiuntur: qui totam destruit Legem Veteris Testamenti, et omnia quae S. Moysi de diversis creaturae factorisque divinitus revelata sunt, praeter reliquas ejusdem libri blasphemias quas referre pertaesum est." ("In which, to give more credence to their perverse doctrine, they pretend a teaching from our Saviour that destroys the whole of the Old Testament Law and all that was revealed to Moses about creatures and their Maker, in addition to all the other blasphemies that would take too long to mention").

Orosius, in his letter to St. Augustine, is a little more explicit: "And this they confirm with a book they call *Memoria Apostolorum* where, the apostles having pleaded with the Saviour to show them the "Unknown Father", he answers them that, in line with the Gospel parable "Exiit seminans seminare semen suum" (the sower went to sow his seed), this sower was not a good sower (the creator or demiurge). Had he been, he would have not shown himself so reckless: going about scattering seeds along the roadside, between rocks, or on unfruitful ground! What he wanted to convey was his doctrine, i.e. that the true sower is one that casts chaste souls in the bodies he chooses". Curious passage, this, rich in anecdotes like all of Orosius' *Commonitorium*. We see clearly that the Priscillianists copied Marcion's *Antithesis* between the Old and the New Law, between Jehovah and the God of the Gospel, a doctrine we saw condemned in the *Regula fidei* of the Council of Toledo.

5. *De principe humidorum et de principe ignis* (On the principle of water and the principle of fire). We have no other news of this book either save for what Osorius tells us: "God, wanting to give rain to men, showed the "virgin light to the prince of the humid" who, enkindled in love ran after her, but was unable to reach her. And his profuse sweat turned into rain and with a horrendous growl it begot thunder". A book that contained such raw and clumsy meteorological theories had to be the offspring of Priscillian, much like the *Memoria Apostolorum*.

We saw also that the Council of Braga prohibited the tracts written by Dictinius under the names of the Patriarchs and Prophets, and of which nothing remains. Nor can we confirm with certainty if the *Acts of St. Andrew, St. Thomas and St. John* circulated in Greek or in Latin among the heretics of Galicia. The latter seems more probable.

It was St. Toribius' observation that only a small part of Priscillianist theories was actually taken from the apocryphals, and adds: "Quare unde prolata sint nescio, nisi forte ubi scriptum est per cavillationes illas per quas loqui Sanctos Apostolos mentiuntur, aliquid interius indicatur, quod disputandum sit potius quam legendum, AUT FORSITAN SINT LIBRI ALII QUI OCCULTIUS SECRETIUSQUE SERVENTUR, solis, ut ipsi aiunt, PERFECTIS paterentur". We shall infer, then, that they had access to *esoteric* teaching and *occult* books, like all sects derived from Gnosis.

These heretics altered the liturgy of the Galician Church too, introducing such a multitude of hymns that the Council of Braga prohibited everything but the Psalms from being sung in church. A pity that these Priscillianist hymns are lost! If Latrotianus and other poets of merit composed them, they would have surely been curious and interesting for the history of our literature. Would they have resembled the beautiful hymns of Prudentius, perhaps, or the Visigoth *Hymnarius*? I would venture that our Gnostics' songs would compare to those by Bar-Daisan and Harmonius. Who knows! Maybe even to the odes of the Neoplatonist Synesius. Both were pantheists of course, though they got there by different routes. Maybe ours cried out with the sublime disciple of Hypatia:

> From your earthly existence,
>
> O human intelligence, you shall return
>
> the iron ties broken
>
> with mystical embraces
>
> to fuse in the essence divine [152]

St. Jerome, speaking of these sectarians' night-gatherings says that, when they embraced their women, they recited verses from the *Georgics* (Libro II):

> tum Pater omnipotens foecundis imbribus Aether
>
> conjugis in gremium laetae descendit, et omnes
>
> magnus alit, magno conmixtus corpore, foetus…

But this is rather an erudite interpretation coming from the pen of St. Jerome, who is a saint. I happen to think the Priscillianists' songs were probably a little less classical. [153]

---

[152]   Synesius, Hymn I. This author's translation.

One of the most noted relics of the Priscillianist liturgy and the only indication we have of their chants is the hymn of Argyrius. St. Augustine left us some extracts of it in his letter to Ceretius. [154] It reads like this, *verbatim*:

"This is the Hymn that the Lord said to his Apostles in secret, according to what is written (26:30) in St. Mark's Gospel: "Having said the hymn, he went to the mountain". This hymn has been left out of the Canon because it was so decided by those who act according to their whim and not according to the spirit and truth of God. For it is written, (Job 12:7): "It is good to conceal the *sacramentum* (mystery) of the king; but it is also honourable to reveal the works of the Lord:

1. I want to untie, and I want to be untied.
2. I want to save, and I want to be saved.
3. I want to be begotten.
4. I want to sing: all of you, leap.
5. I want to cry: all beat your breasts.
6. I want to adorn, and I want to be adorned.
7. I am a lantern to you who see me.
8. I am a door for you who knock on me.
9. You who see what I do, be silent about my works.
10. With the word I misled all, and I was not wholly misled."[155]

---

[153] In a recent Paper on Religious Poetry read at that Athenaeum in Madrid, where so many promising minds shipwreck and go down, I heard the Church being criticised for having made the heterodox hymns vanish, above all, it was expressed, those of the Gnostics in their Montanist, Manichaean and Priscillianist branches. I have devoted more than a little time to this type of research but I never knew, until I heard this, that there had actually been Montanists in Spain, and more, that they were Gnostics, when, in fact, Tertulian, the most famous of them all, was actually Gnosticism's greatest enemy. I did not know, either, that we had had Manichaeans in Spain other than the Priscillianists, for Pacentius was a foreigner and had no followers. One learns new and stupendous things each day. What Spanish Montanists were there, pray, that had any hymns to speak of? I have said this many times, I repeat it now. The *Ateneo* is the greatest impediment our culture has. It distracts the spirit of our youth, accustoming them to speak and give opinions about anything and everything in open forums without sufficient preparation. I am saying this in general, not just refering specifically to the author of that particular Paper, a friend, to whom I am doing the greatest favour I can by not naming him. He, who has written the history of our sanctuaries and images is now converted to echoing impiety and foreign Voltairianism. May God come to our aid and guide us! Note: This piece of advice is meant to be friendly.

[154] Epistle CCXXXVII, ed. S. Maurus, vol. II.

[155] "Hymnus Domini, quem dixit secrete Sanctis Apostolis discipulis suis, quia scriptum est in Evangelio (S. Mat. XXVI, 30): Hymno dicto ascendit in montem, et qui in Canone non positus est propter eos qui secundum se sentiunt et non secundum spiritum et veritatem Dei; eo quod scriptum est: Sacramentum Regis bonum est abscondere, opera autem Dei revelare honorificum est.

I. Solvere volo et solvi volo.
II. Salvare volo et salvari volo.
III. Generari volo.

The explanation the Priscillianists gave as to the meaning of this enigmatic composition could not be more innocent. The "solvere" alluded to untying oneself from carnal ties; the "generari" to spiritual engendering, in the sense St. Paul said "donec Christus formetur in nobis"; the "ornare" came to be, also, in the words of the Apostle "vos estis templum Dei". In short, all words in the hymn were concordant with Holy Scripture.

But the secret, hidden meaning they attached to it was very different. That which wants to untie is the one substance: *divinity*; that which wants to be untied is the same substance as humanity, and so forth with the rest: the one that wants to save and be saved, to adorn and be adorned, etc., etc. The "Verbo illusi cuncta" involves perhaps a profession of Docetism.

Argyrius, a Priscillianist, explained the interpretation of this hymn and other Priscillianist apocryphals in two books. Bishop Ceretius sent a copy to St. Augustine for him to examine and refute, and the Saint did so in a long epistle. [156] If all that was contained in the hymn was holy and good, why make it the subject of secret teachings? Argyrius' explanations (St. Augustine felt) did not serve to clarify but rather to hide its true meaning and dazzle outsiders. The bishop of Hippo deals only with one of Argyrius' volumes, the other he had misplaced, the saint said, he knew not how.

To keep their doctrine alive in the minds of their fellow-believers, Gnostic sects adopted means other than books and chants, namely, *abracas* or amulets, about which many scholars have written extensively already. In Matter's copious collection I find few that could refer specifically to the Priscillianists. The most striking, and one that undoubtedly belongs to our heretics, depicts a Celt-Iberian warrior under the protection of the twelve signs of the Zodiac. The sidereal superstition of Priscillian's disciples is well documented. [157] The figure is carefully crafted. Other talismans relating to astrology could well be associated with Spain but with less probability. [158]

IV.   Cantare volo, saltate cuncti.

V.   Plangere volo, tundite vos omnes.

VI.   Ornare volo et ornari volo.

VII.   Lucerna sunt tibi, ille qui me vides.

VIII.   Janua sum tibi, quicumque me pulsas.

IX.   Qui vides quod ago, tace opera mea.

X.   Verbo illusi cuncta, et non sum illusus in totum.

[156]   Epistle CCXXXVII, ed. Maurus, vol. 2

[157]   *Histoire critique du Gnosticisme, Planches, Planche VIII, fig. VIII.*

[158]   The so-called *Cruz de los Angeles* of Oviedo has two of these amulets or *basilidic* or Priscilianist stones, according to a most plausible opinion (Vic.*Monumentos arquitectónicos de España*).

So then, are we all to start criticising the Church for destroying all these literary and artistic monuments, the books and the stones of the Priscillianists, as many accuse her of doing?

First, we do not know, and I can find it nowhere recorded or mentioned, that the Church did actually destroy them. Second, if Priscillian's works are lost, so are those of Ithacius and of others who refuted him. Third, if she did destroy them, she was absolutely right to do so. Because unity is and should be the priority here, and the fancies and literary curiosities we might all have today mean nothing, especially when we consider them alongside the constant danger those repertories of error meant to the traditions and faith of the Christian peoples, nor could they have meant anything to those ancient bishops battling there on the ground, if indeed they could even guess at them.

I will say little about the works of Priscillianism's opponents because practically all of them are lost. Ithacius' book is nowhere to be found. Bishop Peregrinus, cited by some as the author of many canons against Priscillianism, has to be identical to Patruinus, bishop of Mérida, who presided at the Council of Toledo and proposed all the canons there approved, that is, the *Bachiarius Peregrinus* I shall refer to later. The *Communitorium* and *Libellus* of St. Turibius of Liébana are lost; all we have is his brief letter to Idacius and Ceponcius, which deals explicitly with the apocryphal books. The two most curious documents relating to this heresy are the *Communitorium*, that is, Osorius' letter to St. Augustine, and the epistle of St. Leo the Great to Toribius. Both are included in the Appendix. St. Augustine's book *Contra Priscillianistas et Originistas*, says little or nothing about the former and much about the latter, as we will see in a moment.[159]

Orosius and St. Leo, the *Regula Fidei* and the Canons of the Council of Braga together with a few other remnants, will be our sources, then, in the

---

[159]   Lucinius Beticus, who must be Theodora's husband, a leading persecutor of the Priscillianists, consulted St. Jerome around the year 396 on whether 1) it was obligatory to fast every day; 2) the Eucharist should be received daily, as it was done in some churches. The doctor of Stridon answers that each province should follow its own tradition, and that "the Eucharist must be received only when we have no remorse of conscience" (Vid. Epistle LII.t.v.). Ferreiro thinks that Lucinius' questions had to do with Priscillianist issues.

There is only thing on which I disagree with the present-day historian of this heresy. He believes that Casulanus, Januarius and Maximus were Spanish. They had consulted St. Augustine on fasting on Saturday (Vid. Epistle XXXVI, volume II, Maurus ed., and LIV and LV, *Ad inquisitionis Januarii*, and XXLXIV), on frequent communion, the offices of Maundy Thursday, the day of the celebration of the Pasch, "evangelical fortune-telling" or divination by means of the pages of the Gospel, and the dogma of the Incarnation. There is no allusion whatever to Spain in St. Augustine's replies, and the Priscillianists are mentioned only once, and that in passing. Nor were these questions debated only by them. As far as Casulanus is concerned, we know that his question was based on a tract written by the Manichaean Romanus. Manichaeans and Priscillianists shared the same principles on fasting.

following paragraphs, which aim to explain the dogmas and influence of Gnosticism in Spain.

Exposition and Critique of Priscillianism.

The origins of Priscillian's doctrine are known and unequivocal. His challengers made good efforts to reveal them. "The Priscillianists mix Gnostic and Manichaean dogmas", says St. Augustine (*De haeresibus*, chapter LXX), adding that to this heresy flowed "as into a sewer" all the follies of the previous ones. "Quamvis et ex aliis haeresibus in eas sordes, tanquam in sentinam quandam, confusione confluxerint". It is a thought that St. Leo the Great echoes and elucidates further in his famous epistle: "Nihil est enim sordium in quorumcumque sensibus impiorum, quod in hoc dogma non confluxerit: quoniam de omni terrenarum opinionum luto, multiplicem sibi foeculentiam miscuerunt: ut soli totum biberent, quidquid alii ex parte gustassent". Again and again the Pontiff insists on the *syncretic* character of Priscillianist teachings: "If we remember" - he says – "how many heresies had preceded Priscillian in this world, we will hardly find one error with which he had not been infected". ("Denique si universae haereses, quae ante Prisciliani tempus exortae sunt, diligentius retractantur, nullus pene invenitur error, de quo non traxerit impietas ista contagium"). Sulpicius Severus limits himself to saying that Priscillian resurrected the Gnostic heresy, but does not specify which one. St. Jerome (Dialogue *Adversus pelagianos*, Prologue) places our heresiarch shoulder to shoulder with the Manichaeans and the Massalians, and in the treatise *De viris illustribus* supposes him a disciple of Basilides and Marcus, acknowledging that not everyone agrees with him on this.

From all of this we can deduce that Priscillianism was, in essence, Manichaean doctrine reworked by Egyptian Gnosis. This curious syncretism, a sort of blending together of doctrines from Memphis and Syria, is important enough in the history of theosophical thought for us to attempt to distinguish, as best we can, what its doctrine really consisted on.

Fortunately, the testimonies we have, while not numerous, are thoroughly trustworthy: that of Orosius, because like them, he was Spanish and their contemporary; the Fathers who decreed the *Regula fidei*, for the same reasons; and St. Leo's because he faithfully and accurately reproduces the notices Turibius communicated to him, who we assume was well informed, if on nothing else at least on the *externals* of Priscillian doctrine, for he says that they held initiation and secretive rites. St. Augustine, in *De haeresibus* chapter LXX, relies for the most part on data provided to him by Orosius. Philastrius of Brecia does not mention any of Priscillian's disciples by name but alludes clearly to the Gnostics of Spain. The Council of Braga faithfully follows St. Leo's letter down to the number and order of the anathemas.

Let us begin, then, with the treatise *De Deo*. There is no doubt that

Priscillianists were anti-Trinitarian and, St. Leo adds (and with him the Braga Fathers), Sabellians as well. They admitted no distinction of Persons, only attributes or modes of the divine essence manifesting itself: "Tamquam idem Deus nunc Pater, nunc Filius, nunc Spiritus Sanctus nominetur". This is why the *Regula Fidei* insists continually on the dogma of the Trinity. But should we really attribute a Sabellian origin to the Priscillian heresy on this point? I do not think it necessary: all Gnosis did away with the Trinity, a mystery irreconcilable with the pantheism and dualism that all these sects professed to a greater or lesser degree, as well as with that indeterminable succession of their *aeons*. How can the understanding of a God *Uno et Trino*, hence a personal, active, and creator God, ever be reconciled with systems that place an "unknown father" up there in some inaccessible region, who never communicates with the world (which he did not create anyway) except through a succession of emanations which are, and at the same time are not, his own essence, or reflections of it, and which are always at odds with their rivals, the malefic principles, also emanated from some power, sometimes independent, sometimes subordinate, often confused with matter itself? When the Priscillianists denied the Trinity they really were no different from other heretics of the same stock, save perhaps in their being Patripassionists (as St. Leo states), that is to say, on teaching that the Father had suffered death on the cross. Which, by the way, is contradictory to the Docetism all Gnostic branches embraced, for they all saw the crucifixion, not as something real, but purely figurative and symbolic. But when was human delirium consistent! [160]

The Priscillianists taught that there was a succession of aeons, all emanating from the divine essence and inferior to it in dignity and in time ("De processionibus quarumdam virtutem ex Deo, quas habere coeperit, et quas essentiale sui ipse praecesserit"). The Son was one of those aeons - the reason why St. Leo qualified them as Arians ("Dicentium quod Pater Filio prior sit, quia fuerit aliquando sine Filio, et tunc Pater coeperit quando Filium genuerit"). "As if from eternity there could be something wanting in the divine essence," the same Pope said.

We have no data to show the origin of the *virtues* or *powers* Priscillian claimed. Two of them might have been "the prince of the humid" and "the prince of fire" we saw in one of the apocryphal books.

The Priscillianists told us the devil was *essentially* and intrinsically bad: he was the principle and substance of all evil, not created by God but born of the Chaos and of the Darkness. *The Valentinians* and particularly the Manichaeans of Persia attached to him the same origin, as we saw earlier. St. Leo refutes this

---

[160]   Orosius confirms Priscillianist Antitrinitarianism: "Trinitatem autem solo verbo loquebatur, unionem absque ulla existentia aut proprietate asserens, sublato et Patre et Filio et Spiritu Sancto, hunc esse unum Christum dicebat." (Commonitorium)

system of the two principles and of eternal evil with his customary sobriety: "It is repugnant and contradictory to the divine essence to create anything evil, and there can be nothing that is not created by God".

The *cosmology* of our heretic's followers was simple, simpler than that of the Manichaeans because they were neither intimidated by the rigour of logic nor afraid of its consequences. The world, according to them, had been created, not by a demiurge or any secondary agent of Divinity, but by the devil himself who kept it under his dominion and who was the cause of all physical and meteorological phenomena ("A quo istum mumdum factum volunt", says St. Augustine). Very few Gnostics, save for the Ophites, Cainites and other thinkers of the same ilk, dared accept this principle outright, even when this was where their system ultimately and irremediably led them. No modern-day pessimist has gone that far. Ignorance, nay, amnesia about universal harmony could go no further.

Priscillian's anthropological doctrine was an unavoidable consequence of these foundations. The soul of man, like all spirits, is a part of the divine substance from which it originates via emanation ("Animas ejusdem naturae atque substantiae cujus est Deus", says St. Augustine). But it is not one, as indeed it should, and must be, in all pantheist thinking, but multiple: error, again, inevitably contradicting itself. God imprints his stamp (*chirographum*) on these souls when he is about to eject or dislodge them from his essence - which Priscillian compared to a depot (*promptuario*) of ideas, or of forms. [161] Thus stamped, the spirit promises to wrestle vigorously in the arena of life, and starts its descent down the celestial circles and regions - which are seven - each inhabited by one intelligence, until it reaches down and goes beyond the boundaries of the inferior world and falls under the power of the prince of darkness and his ministers, who then lock up these souls in different bodies. Because bodies, like all matter, are a demonic creation.

This peregrination of the soul was generally accepted by all the Gnostic schools. What affords Priscillian some originality is his sidereal fatalism, whose seed he found in Bar-Dasain's philosophy and on Manichaeism. But not content with saying that the body was subject to the influence of the stars, as his predecessors had done, he insisted on assigning a celestial power to each part of the human body, on which it was dependent. He distributed the influence of the twelve signs of the Zodiac in this manner: Aries for the head; Taurus for the neck; Gemini for the arms; Cancer for the chest, and so forth. But his physiological astronomy did not stop here. He went on to enslave the soul as well - to celestial powers this time: to angels, patriarchs, prophets... reckoning that to each faculty or, as he called it, each "member" of the soul, corresponded a person from the Old Law, to wit: Ruben, Judah, Levi, Benjamin, et al.

---

[161]   I am basing this exposition on texts by Orosius, St. Augustine, St. Leo, etc. which I attach in the Appendix and which I do not cite at each step to avoid prolixity.

Where was human liberty in all this? The body was a slave to the stars and the evil spirits, the soul in bondage to celestial influences. Dualism was left with no meaning, nor could that stamp or divine *chirographus* ever overpower the devil. Because even if the soul was induced to good by its patrons, not only was it joined and subjected to the body, but each of its faculties was subject to the member in which it dwelled, and that is why the head, for example, suffered the contradictory influence of Ruben and Aries! The Priscillianist man was a slave both to the twelve signs of the Zodiac and to the twelve sons of Jacob. He could move neither hand nor foot unless guided and governed by one and the other powers. Did the Priscillianists intend, when they took their dualism to this ridiculous extreme, to save even a mere inkling of free will and responsibility, and to give man even a diminished liberty of choice between these two ends so fatally imposed on him? I am not sure they did.

And where did this unbearable slavery come from? From original sin. But not an original sin committed here on earth, but an original sin committed up in celestial regions where intelligences dwell. The souls that, having emanated, went on to sin, were those same souls that, in punishment, descended to their bodies: a doctrine of Platonist flavour common to all Gnostics. Down here on earth, they were condemned to *metempsychosis* until washed and purified of their sin, after which they returned to the substance whence they came.

Priscillianist Christology does not differ in anything essential from Docetism. For them, Christ was a fantastical or imaginary person, an aeon or attribute of God which showed itself to man *per quandam illusionem* to destroy or nail down on the cross the *chirographum,* or sign of slavery. However, at the same time they are charged with saying that Christ did not exist until He was born of the Virgin. This apparent contradiction becomes clear when we remember that the Gnostics distinguished between the aeon Christos, power and virtue of God, and the man Jesus, to Whom the *Pneuma* was communicated. The Priscillianists called the former *ingenitus* (ἀγεννητος), and the latter *unigenitus,* not because He was of the Father, but because He was the only one born of the Virgin.

Hateful of matter, they denied the resurrection of the body. Hateful of Judaism, they opposed any doctrine of the Old Testament, accepting only its allegorical interpretations.

About their stand on morals there is much uncertainty. Certainly, they affected much outward asceticism. Like the Manichaeans, they condemned marriage and the eating of meat. Certainly, they professed a principle, lofty and generous in appearance, but one which has led many a noble soul astray: they believed that human virtue and understanding can reach perfection, not only similitude but equality with God. [162] This maxim contains the seeds of all moral

---

[162]   St. Jerome, Dialogue *Adversus Pelagianos*

aberration. The Priscillianists believed that when one reaches this sovereign perfection, sinning, whether knowingly or ignorantly, was impossible. Now if you add to this belief the poisonous fatalist theory referred to above, you will understand why our Gnostics were so remote, in practice, from the actual severity of doctrine they affected. M. Matter proffers that the "secret licence of customs the Priscillianists are accused of is one of those hateful accusations typically thrown at people who put themselves up as examples of a special kind of purism". But Matter is a little too optimist and prone at every turn to side with the Gnostic sects, as if in love with their cause. An accusation repeated unanimously by Sulpicius Severus, ardent enemy of the Ithacians (the Priscillianists' foes), by St. Jerome, St. Turibius and St. Leo the Great is not just idle talk by the vulgar mob. It is one that was juridically proven twice, one at Treves by Evodius and again in Rome by St. Leo who recounts the matter in this way: "Sollicitissimis inquisitionibus indagatam (OBSCOENITAS ET TURPITUDO) et Manichaeorum qui comprehensi fuerant confessione detectam ad publicam fecimus pervenire notitiam: ne ullo modo posset dubium videri quod in judicio nostro cui non solum frequentissima praesentia sacerdotum, sed etiam illustrium viroroum dignitas et pars quoedam senatus ac plebis interfuit ipsorum qui omne facinus perpetrarent, ore reseratum est... Gesta demonstrant". ("Having with solicitude inquired and uncovered through the testimony of many Manichaeans (who had themselves been imprisoned) about their obscenities and turpitude, we brought these testimonies to public notice, that what our tribunal uncovered might in no way appear doubtful (held before many priests, illustrious gentlemen and a great part of the Senate of the people) from the lips of the aforementioned who had perpetrated this wickedness... The proceedings of the trial prove this"). So tales about the Manichaeans' and Priscillianists' moral depravity was more than gossip after all! The secrecy of their gatherings, the oath of "jura, perjura, secretum prodere noli", the hold which women had on the sect, in short, a thousand and one particulars must have led people to suspect what St. Leo calls the "execrabiles misterios e incestissima consuetudo" of Priscillian's disciples, comparable to those of the Carpocratians, the Cainites, and all those other degenerate branches of the Gnostic tree.

Of their rites, we know little or nothing. They fasted out of time and season, actually on days of jubilation for Christians. They took oaths on the name of Priscillian. They sacrilegiously pretended to receive Communion and kept the Host for unknown superstitions. [163] As regards ecclesial hierarchy, they

---

[163]   The Church, despite the frankness with which in her first days she permitted the faithful to touch the Sacred Eucharist and to take It home, and anointing their forehead and eyes with the Blood of Christ upon receiving it, as St. Cyril attests (*Cathech. Mystag.*, V), seeing the abuse the Priscillianists and other heretics made of this practice with their enchantments and superstitions, stopped it entirely, to the point of not even showing the Blessed Sacrament during the Sacrifice, especially in the West, where St. Gregory of Tours says (lib. VII, chapter XXII) that once the consecration was over, the Host was concealed under the corporal: a practice that was

took the principle of revolutionary equality to the utmost. Neither laymen nor women were to be excluded from the ministry of the altar, according to Priscillian. The Consecration was performed not with wine but with grape juice or even milk, superstitions still existing in 675, the date of the Third Council of Braga which condemned it in its first canon.

There is little need to underline the importance of astrology, magic, and theurgic practices in their system. All testimonies agree on attributing to Priscillian great skills in the goetic arts, though no one specifies which ones. In the only fragment of his we know of, we see clearly how much he esteemed astrological observation, which for him must have substituted for all other science because it supplied the key to all anthropological phenomena.

This is the scarce information we can give of Priscillianist opinions conforming to all data we have gathered and collated. If it proves insufficient to satisfy one's curiosity, at least it gives us a general idea of the character and basis of this heretical speculation. It remains for us now to interpret the influence it had on the subsequent meanderings of Iberian thought. But before we do this, it might be worthwhile to inquire why Priscillianism became so profoundly entrenched in Galicia, and remained unreservedly and openly so for nearly three centuries. [164]

A recent opinion put forward by D. Manuel Murguía in his *Historia de Galicia* may provide some clues to this question. His thesis is that Celtic pantheism had not been totally eradicated in the western regions of the Peninsula even after the conversion of the Galicians. As a result, Egyptian Gnosis, also a pantheistic system, found spirits ready to welcome it. But a difficulty springs to mind here: the pantheism of the Celts was a materialistic pantheism inspired by a vivid and dynamic sense of nature; as for the human spirit, we cannot be sure, nor is it plausible, that they identified it with God. The pantheism taught by Priscillian on the other hand was an idealist pantheism: it despised and hated matter, created and governed by the infernal spirits.

I find that other factors have more in common. For example, the Celts accepted transmigration, as did the Priscillianists. Both practised necromancy - evocation of the souls of the dead. Astrological superstition, more developed in Priscillianism than in any of its sister sects, must have been favoured by the residue of a sidereal cult that was deeply ingrained in Celtic rites: priestesses would not have seemed a radical novelty to those who had venerated

---

still observed in part well into the twelfth century. A celebrated author of that time notes it, saying: "statim post... elevationem demitti Sacramentum a Sacerdote solitum, et opereri sindone" (Guilbert, de Pignor, Sanct., chapter II). (Note of D. Joaquín Lorenzo de Villanueva, in volume I of *Viaje Literario a las Iglesias de España*, from his brother Fr. Jaime, p. 64).

[164] Some attribute the diffusion of Priscillianism to the widespread cult to Mithras in the Peninsula. The wise Father Fita agrees with this plausible opinion.

druidesses. Moreover, what of those night gatherings carried out *in latebris*, in the woods and on the hills, to which the Council of Saragossa seems to allude - unknown to other Gnostics? Their origin is clear, if our reading of the canon is not mistaken.[165]

Leaving aside these coincidences, it is a rather singular case that in one tiny corner of the Latin world there emerged and developed one of the many brands of Greco-Oriental theosophy, and to such a degree. It is an acknowledged fact that almost by instinct the West rejected all heresies of a speculative or abstract nature, opening its doors only to dialectic subtleties like those of Arius; and it is no less certain that if, indeed, the West engendered some heretical concepts, these were always wholly practical and directed to resolving problems such as grace and free will: that of Pelagius, for example.

If in some way we are to account for the phenomenon of Priscillianism, we have to turn to one of the laws governing Iberian heterodoxy, for like any other subject, there do exist providential laws, though they may look like aberrations and accidents. The Iberian race is a *unitary* race. This is the reason why (even from the viewpoint of human reasons alone) our people find their natural home and rest in Catholicism. And those rare individuals among us who at one time or another have had the misfortune of severing themselves from it, or were born in another religion or belief, nonetheless always seek an ontological unity, however vacuous or fictitious that may be. This is why in every non-Catholic Spaniard, if he really follows the inclination of his race and does not just limit himself to imitating foreign teachings, there is always a pantheist seed, more or less developed, more or less active. In the fifth century, it was Priscillian; in the eighth Hostegesis; in the eleventh Avicebron; in the twelfth Aben-Tofail, Averroes, Maimonides. Indeed, who was it that broadcast to Christian schools all over Europe the erroneous doctrines of Avicebron and Averroes but the archdeacon Domingo Gundisalvus, and later, "Spanish Marutitius"? This same pantheist yeast can be seen, inescapably, in one of the boldest and most determined thinkers of the sixteenth century, and one who followed the Reformist tides: I am speaking of Michael Servetus. The following century saw the rebirth, in different forms, of the same spirit urged now by David Nieto, Benito Espinosa (Spinoza), Spanish by origin and language, and Miguel de Molinos. The differences among these authors are radical and profound. On rare occasions would any one of them know of the others. But can one possibly avoid noticing that invisible bond weaving together all these seemingly discordant books, such as *Fuente de la vida, Guia de Extraviados, El Filosofo autodidacto,* the treatise *De la unidad del pensamiento, De processione mundi, Zohar, Christianismi Restitutio, Naturaleza naturante, Etica, Guia Espiritual* ? Even in a century like the last, so little given to speculations of this kind, did we not see

---

[165]   "Nec habitent *in latibulis cubiculorum aut montium qui in suspicionibus* (perhaps *superstitionibus*) perseverant." Canon II.

a resurgence of the *Kabbala* and the emanist principle in the *Tratado de la reintegracion de los seres* by our theosophist Martinez Pascual? One is keenly aware of the widespread dissemination that several idealist pantheisms have had in our land, Hegel's and Krause's, for example, whereas Positivism, which is ransacking Europe today, barely manages to secure a little credence among us, in spite of the enthusiasm of its devotees.

This, my dear compatriots, is because we, Iberians, even when we are totally blundering and shooting off the mark, have sufficient nobility to reject that base, vulgar, and petty empiricism that sees only effects, not causes; never laws, only phenomena. At least Idealism (in any one of its phases), or Naturalism (when founded on an ample and robust conception of nature as entity), have some nobility (though of course they are misguided), and are not lacking in that scientific rigor that so easily dazzles minds bereft of the True Light.

What merit does Priscillianism have in the eyes of science? Little or none, because it lacks originality. Priscillianism was a leftover, the *substratum* of all Gnostic delirious ravings. If it has any redeeming quality that sets it apart from the others, it is the sound rigor with which it was willing to accept all its consequences, even the most absurd. It is Fatalism taught more crudely than any sect could have possibly taught it; a Pessimism more caustic and disconsolate than any disciple of Schopenhauer could ever have dreamt of.

What does it mean to the eyes of history? It is but the last mutation of Gnosticism and Manichaeism, degenerate by then in dogma and morals. Viewed this way, Priscillianism is important as the only Gnostic heresy that actually took hold in a small corner of the Western world, and it could be argued that the miasma it left behind helped later father the plague of the Cathars and Albigenses in the twelfth and thirteenth centuries. I do not think this impossible (though I am not here affirming it); after all, Priscillian did have disciples in Italy and in Gallic Aquitaine, and God only knows through what invisible weft the good and the bad remnants of ancient civilisation came to be preserved and fused in the haze of the Middle Ages. More than Manichaeans from Bulgaria and Thrace would have been needed to enkindle that firestorm that threatened to devour Southern Europe in its trail.

And when it comes to Spanish heterodoxies in particular, we are going to see a close affinity between this tenebrous sect and the *Iluminados* and Alumbrados of the sixteenth century because both of these held that man could reach a state of perfection such that it was impossible for him to commit or be responsible for sin: a doctrine we are going to see reproduced later in the seventeenth century by Miguel de Molinos. Nor is it necessary to point out that the magic and astrology Priscillian adopted was not buried alongside his dogma but has stayed on among us as a constant temptation to human weakness and curiosity, be it in its most vulgar form of demonological superstitions or reduced to a *scientific system* in books like those by Raimundo de Tárrega or the pseudo-Virgilio Cordobes, as we shall see in later chapters.

It must be emphasised that Priscillian, as far as we can make out by the excerpt preserved by Osorius, also attached a scientific meaning (as people say today) to an Astrology not dissimilar to what the Alexandrian Neoplatonists and their Renaissance Italian disciples gave to Theurgy. As for the *chirographum*, the sign of servitude the devil impresses on bodies, it is easy to see its similarity to the characters and symbols that the Middle Ages supposed to be inseparable from the demonic symbol.

Furthermore, and looking for every analogy in the course of this history, Priscillianism as an anti-Trinitarian sect precedes Arianism, Adoptionism, and the opinions of Valdés, Servetus and Alfonso Licurio, all smothered at birth by the salvific Catholic spirit that has informed our civilisation since the Council of Elvira. Let us add to this that Priscillianism opened the history of secret societies in the Peninsula[166] and that, due to its doctrine on transmigration and other sidereal voyaging, it must be counted among the precursors of Spiritualism. Finally, those Neo-platonist relics entangled in the theories of aeons, identical in the final analysis to those of Ideas, do represent something in the history of our philosophy. And here Priscillianism links up afresh with Michael Servetus who in the sixteenth century resuscitated this Alexandrian notion, placing it also at the service of a pantheistic and anti-Trinitarian system.

But these and others analogies are usually fortuitous. I think we can say, with no danger of error, that Priscilliasnim itself drew its last breath at about the end of the sixth century and has, since then, been completely forgotten.

For us Spaniards, this and other heterodoxies are accidents, aberrations - a passing cloud that will inevitably clear away with no one having to disperse it. This is precisely what happened here. Heresy is repugnant to the Spanish character, and if proof were needed of this, Priscillianism would provide such proof. It did not originate in Spain, it never took hold on the country at large but quickly retrenched to a small part of the territory and there it died, asphyxiated by our national conscience, which is Catholic and universal. No, not by our *intolerance,* which in any case would have been rather difficult to exercise in the midst of the division and anarchy prevalent in the fifth century. The execution of Priscillian and four or five of his cohorts in Treves proves nothing because it was precisely after that event that the heresy returned with much more vigour and force, and was then to last for nearly two hundred years more: in this long period there was not one single Priscillian execution. There were no threats and there were no burnings. The people themselves started coming back to the fold of the Church, until the last offshoots of that heretical branch withered and dried up all by themselves, up there in the beaches and mountains

---

166   So has the most erudite Dr. D. Vicente de la Fuente estimated in his *Historia de las Asociaciones secretas*, vol. 1.

of Galicia, on whose soil never again has the seed of error taken root since those ill-fated and unhappy days. And this in spite of Priscillian's doctrine being a pantheist doctrine interwoven with Celtic rites and having therefore a chance of life due to its affirmations being ordered and consistent.

What were the consequences of Priscillianism? Directly, dire of course, as with all heresies; indirectly, perhaps even good - a storm that purified not just the physical but the moral world as well.

God is not the author of evil. He allows it, because from the bad he brings out the good, and from poison its antidote. This is why the Apostle said: "Oportet haereses esse ut qui probati sunt manifesti fiant in vobis". And the benefits that Priscillianism left behind are so many that they oblige us to view that temporary disruption as something well employed. Our Church, who had shown herself great from its beginnings, adorned with the triple halo of her martyrs, sages, and councils, was deeply divided when Priscillian appeared on the scene. He was to contribute to the confusion and discord, increasingly separating Iberian peoples along dogmatic lines whereas, until then, they had been separated only on questions of discipline. But with this danger in sight, a wholesome reaction began to take place. Those bishops who were each doing *diverse things* in their dioceses came together and allied themselves against the common enemy. They understood the necessity of unity in all and above all, and gave the Christian peoples of the *ultima hesperia* this unity with the *Regula Fidei* and with their unconditional submission to the Canons of Nicea. And the Spanish Church was henceforth definitely established: the Church of Leander, Isidore, Braulius, Tajón, Julian, Eugenius... never to divide or separate again, be it at times of barbarous invasions, territorial collapses, change of rite, or downright religious infernos like the Reformation.

Our Church is the golden axis of our culture. When all other institutions fall, she alone remains standing. When unity breaks down, be it because of war or conquest, she restores it. And in the midst of the darkest and most turbulent centuries of our national life, she arose, like that column of fire that guided the Israelites on their wanderings through the desert. With our Church all becomes clear; without it, the history of Spain would be reduced to fragments.

In addition to this precious unity arrived at by the First Council of Toledo, Priscillianism contributed also to the extraordinary intellectual upsurge that flourished in Spain in the last century of the reigning Roman empire and during the whole of the Visigoth period. In the previous chapter, we looked at the works of Priscillian himself, and those of Latronianus, Dictinius, Tiverianus, and some others, worthy of literary note in St. Jerome's opinion. Apocryphal books and hymns, all that I call "Priscillianist literature", brought out responses and retorts, most of them lost now, but writings that ennobled the names of Ithacius, Idacius, Patruinus, Turibius, the two Aviti, Orosius himself - that outstanding author of the *Tristezas del Mundo (Moesta Mundi)*, he whose name is seen next to St. Augustine and Salvianus of Marseille among the architects of the *Philosophy of History*. Perhaps the first essay of this Bragan presbyter was his

Commonitorium, the letter on the errors of Priscillian and the Origenists. It was in this battle that he first exercised his robust mind and that hard-hitting, unbecoming, yes, and melancholic style with which he later explained Providential law on human events.

And who knows! Maybe Latronianus and his followers' heretical chants encouraged the great poet from Aragón, Prudentius, to write his immortal verses! We would certainly have something to thank Priscillian for if, however indirectly, he was the reason for the first of the Christian poets to grace Spain. More probable still, because of its proximity to Galicia, is that Conantius of Palencia was inspired to dethrone these chants and so wrote his *melodías.*

But where would we end if we went down the wide and open field of conjecture! [167]

---

[167]   Sources for Priscilianist doctrine:

❖   *S. Aurelii Augustini Episcopi operum, tomus VI, continens* τά πολεμικα… *Coloniae Agrippinae, suntibus A. Hierati, 1606.*

❖   The treatise *De haeresibus,* dedicated to deacon Quod-vul-Deus; *Consultio* or *Communitorium,* of Orosius (pp. 253-col. I), and St. Augustine's treatise *Contra priscillianistas et Origenistas,* which is his response.

❖   *S. Leonis Magni Pape Primi opera omnia…auctiora.* Lugdini, 1700 (ed. Quesnel), pp.226-232. (Epist. to Toribius, followed by his to Idacius and Ceponius).

b) Here we have to note two unbelievable errors from distinguished French writers: first, Rousselot, in his book *Les Mystiques Espagnols,* which would be worthy of praise if only we could tear out the 73 pages of Introduction which are full of serious errors about our scientific history. He says, literally (let readers be amazed!) the following: "It would be futile to remember here the old errors of *Félix de Urgel* and of Priscillian, *prior to the conversion of Arian Spain to Catholicism".* First, Priscillian dogmatized before the barbarians brought their Arianism with them; second, *Spain has never been Arian.* Because the Visigoths were not Spaniards, and the Hispano-Roman race never adopted their religion. As for Felix de Urgel, he was not *prior* (!) to Recared's conversion: he lived in the eighth century, after the Arab conquest.

Matter, in his Histoire du Gnosticism (volume II) speaks highly of the Priscillianism that appeared when Theology, he says, was becoming petrified in Spain and our theologians were falling into the most deplorable ignorance. It was not becoming petrified; rather, what our theological science had was an over-abundance of life. The tendency was not to ossification or immobility, it was rather to anarchy and disorder. Now about that deplorable ignorance of Spanish theologians, does he mean the deplorable ignorance of Hosius, St. Gregorius Beticus, Olimpius, Patruinus, St. Damasus, Pacianus, Carterius, Audencius …? This seems to be yet one more of those bouquets of flowers clever foreigners are always presenting us with. Those deplorable theologians signed the first Ecumenical Councils; one of them wrote the Symbol of Nicea; another was charged with resolving the Donatist question; another filled St. Jerome with terror when he had to reply to his letters, et sit de caeteris. We have no evidence of any Frenchman or German coming to Spain to deliver us from that ignorance. In any case, may God forgive the good faith those learned and grave gentleman are always showing towards us, a faith that makes them infringe continually the eighth commandment of the law of God!

c) I decided not to include here the fables that the *Cronicones* contain about Priscillian and his disciples, especially Dextrus'. Nicolas Antonio reduced them to dust in chapter V, lib. II, of his *Bibliotheca Vetus.*

Origenism. The two *Aviti*.

At a time when Galicia was infested throughout with Priscillianism, two presbyters of the diocese of Braga left Spain, one for Jerusalem, the other for Rome. The latter adopted the opinions of Marius Victorinus. Victorinus was a Platonist orator and philosopher who had converted during Julian's time and authored a critical work - *De Trinitate* - against the Manichaeans. But Avitus soon abandoned Victorinus to follow Origen whose books [168] and doctrine the other Avitus had also brought from the East. Back in Spain, both begun to challenge Priscillianism firmly and vigorously, teaching wholesome doctrine on the Trinity, the origin of evil, and creation *ex nihilo*. With this and the good use they made of Scripture they converted many Gnostics, who showed some reluctance only on the issue of creation from nothingness.

Unfortunately, books by Origen, the great Alexandrian presbyter, which were the two principal Aviti texts, contained some mistakes, or rather (to agree with his apologists), contained opinions that could easily be twisted to mean something else. This is not the place to enter into an already much debated question. Suffice it to say that Origen's errors, if indeed he made them, were never based on an antagonistic doctrinal stand but due to the obscurity still reigning in the first centuries of the Church over points of dogma which had yet to be defined.

The two Spanish Origenists concurred with the Platonist theory of Ideas, but in a less orthodox sense than Origen. They said, for example, that all things "were concretely (*factae*) in the mind of God" before they appeared in the external world. To this extreme realism they added pantheist notions, such as the affirmation that the nature and substance of angels, principalities, powers, souls, and devils, was one and the same, in spite of which they assumed a wide-ranging angelic hierarchy based on differences according to merit. Their theory about the world was thoroughly Platonist. They saw it as a place of expiation for souls that had sinned in prior existences. They challenged eternal punishment, too, insisting that there was no other hell but that existing in one's own conscience, and that the devil himself could eventually be saved *quoad substantiam* because his essence was good, once the accidental or malefic part had been consumed by fire. They admitted a series of different redemptions for angels, archangels, and the other superior spirits prior to human redemption, pointing out that Christ had taken the *form* of each of the hierarchies he was about to redeem. Celestial bodies were held to be incorruptible, alive, and rational.

The new heresy spread rapidly in the regions dominated by Priscillianism, but we have no other indication of its progress than a letter from Orosius, who was also from Braga, like the two Aviti. (The fact that Galicia was Orosius'

---

[168]   Mainly *Peri-archon* and Scripture commentaries.

home is proved by a letter of St. Braulius to St. Fructuosus of Braga). Orosius left Spain carried by "an invisible force", as he says ("occulta quadam vi actus"), to visit St. Augustine in Hippo. He presented to him his *Commonitorium*, or consultation, on the errors of the Priscillianists and Origenists where he relates all that was said above and attests to the truth ("Est veritas Christi in me"). Orosius wrote this in the year 415, and was answered by St. Augustine in the treatise inappropriately entitled thereafter *Contra Priscillianistas et Origenistas*. On Priscillian's doctrine, he barely says anything at all, pointing to what he had already written on his works against the Manichaeans. He takes issue with those who denied creation *ex nihilo* on the basis that God's will was *aliquid*, a sophism easy to dispel, as St. Augustine did, by distinguishing between the *fiat creator* and the *materia subjecta*, between *active* power and *passive* nothingness. He then moves on to defend, with authoritative and rational arguments, the question of eternal punishment, clear and manifest in Scripture *("ignis aeternus")*, conformable to the intrinsic malice of sin as an offence to the supreme good and disruption of universal harmony. Nor can remorse of conscience, so debilitated and obscured in many, be seen as the sole punishment, as our Origenists maintained and some 'moderns' of today echo.

As to the theory of ideas St. Augustine seems happy enough. He was a Platonist himself but denies that in God are the things themselves *(res factae),* but rather the types, forms or reasons of all things *(rationes rerum omnium)*, much like an architect has in his mind the idea of the house he is about to build, not the house itself. Perhaps this was really what the two Aviti had in mind but since they could not express it with the same lucidity and scientific rigor as the prelate of Hippo, what they said led to serious errors, denying, even, creation or the individuality of beings, which outside the divine mind would have only an apparent existence.

From Africa Osorius passed over to the Holy Land to consult St. Jerome on the origin of the rational soul. He was a man who craved knowledge and would not let long and arduous journeys stand in the way if they would enable him to satisfy this longing. And there, "at St. Jerome's feet", he says, he lived in the cave of Bethlehem, growing in wisdom and "fear of God". And though "unknown, foreign, and poor", he took part in the Council convened at holy Jerusalem against the errors of Pelagius.

At about this time the remains of the protomartyr St. Stephen were found, of which presbyter Lucian wrote a brief account in Greek, translated into Latin by yet another Avitus from Braga who was then living in Jerusalem, different from the other two, as Dalmases and Father Flórez have clearly proved. The translator Avitus could not have known, in 409, of Origen's book *De Principiis* because St. Jerome sent it to him that same year, accompanied by a letter that pointed out the errors that had been inserted in that book by those who called themselves Origen's disciples, much against the will and judgement of Origen himself.

After Orosius's time we hear nothing about Origenism in our Peninsula. Nor are we aware of any heresies during the Roman era other than those already mentioned, because it is a well known fact that Vigilantius, whom St. Jerome refuted, was not born in Calahorra but in Gallic Aquitaine,[169] just as it is a fact that he preached his errors in areas of Barcelona, albeit without much fruit.[170]

Theological Polemics in Roman Spain. Challenges to several heresies.

The religious framework of the period that I have presented (in which I include the arduous period of transition to the Visigothic monarchy) would be incomplete were I not to mention the refutations made by Iberian theologians to several heresies: new incontrovertible proof of the literary splendour of that age, unknown or forgotten now. It will console us also to see that the Spanish Church never ceased to prepare and move her unyielding champions for combat when confronted with error, be it propagated at home or abroad.

The first in this glorious series of controversialists was St. Gregorius Beticus, bishop of Elvira, who wrote an elegant treatise - *De fide seu de Trinitate* - against the Arians and Macedonians, according to St. Jerome *(De viris illustribus,* chapter 105). The identification of this work with the seven books *De Trinitate* published by the learned Portuguese humanist Aquiles Estazo in 1575 claiming them all for Gregorius is more than doubtful. They seem, rather, to be the work of Faustinus, a Luciferian presbyter, who dedicated them to Queen Flaccila, Theodosius' wife, not to Gala Placidia as the text printed by Estazo reads. [171]

Idacius Emeritensis, the Priscillianists' foe, is not the Idacius who authored a small tract, *Adversus Warimadum Arianum*, found in volume IV of the *Bibliotheca Veterum Patrum*.[172] The tract is exclusively an explanation of difficult passages in Scripture on the Trinity, and the author tells us he wrote this small work "in Naples, city of Campania".

In Gennadius, *De scriptoribus ecclesiasticis*, chapter 14, we find the following: "A Spanish bishop, Audentius, wrote a book, *De fide adversus omnes haereticos*, against the Manichaeans, Sabellians and Arians, but above all against the Photinians, now called Bonosiacs, where he showed the Son of God to be co-eternal with the Father and that His divinity did not commence when the Man-Jesus was conceived by the work and grace of God and born of the Virgin Mary".

[169]   Vid. Orosius' *Commonitorium* and St. Augustine's letter, already cited. Dalmases y Ros, *Disertación histórica por la patria de Paulo Osorio*, Barcelona, 1702, pp. 157-179. Flórez, *España Sagrada*, vol. XV, *Iglesia de Braga*, pp. 306-328. Morner, *De Orosii vita*, 1844.

[170]   Vid. following paragraph.

[171]   Nicolás Antonio, *Biblioth. Vetus*, lib. II, chapter II, insists on attibuting this book to Gregorius. Father Florez in *España Sagrada*, treatise XXXVII, provides definite reasons to deny it.

[172]   Ed. Paris

One who also battled against the Arians was Potamius, Bishop of Ulisea (Uguíjar, north of Granada), a friend and disciple of Hosius, accused like him of prevarication by those who protected the schism of Lucifer. We have an epistle, *Potamii ad Athanasium, ab Arianis impetitum, postquam in Concilio Ariminense suscripserunt*, published for the first time by the Benedictine D'Achery. [173] The subscription establishes its date - after 359. The style is overly resonant, obscure and in bad taste; but the author shows himself to be a discerning theologian and learned in the Holy Scriptures. Father Maceda has written about him extensively.

St Jerome recorded[174] that Carterius, one of the prelates at the Council of Saragossa, wrote a treatise against Helvidius and Jovinianus, who denied the perpetual virginity of Our Lady. Of Carterius, we know (by testimony of a letter from St. Braulius to St. Fructuosus) that he was Galician, and that he lived a long life famed for his learning and holiness. "Laudatae senectutis et sanctae eruditionis Pontificem". From one of St. Jerome's [175] letters written about the year 400 and addressed to the patrician Oceanus, we see that Carterius was in Rome about this time, and that the Priscillianists held him unworthy of being a priest because, prior to his ordination, he had been married twice, contravening St. Paul's words: "Unius uxoris virum". To which St. Jerome replies that Carterius' first marriage had taken place before he was baptised and should not, therefore, be counted. [176]

Much more lucid in the history of Christianity and that of literature is the name of Pope St. Damasus, glory of Spain, as Pérez Bayer has demonstrated. This Pontiff convened five Councils against various heretics. The first rejected the Formula of Rimini and the doctrines of Auxentius, bishop of Milan, who had fallen into Arianism; the second, those of Sabellius, Eunomius, Audeus, Photinus, and Apollinaris, who was anathematised again in the third; the fourth confirmed the synod of Antioch's decision regarding the Apollinarists; and the last, the Second of the Ecumenical Councils, known as the Council of Constantinople (equally famous with Nicea) was held in 381 against the heresy of Macedonius who denied the divinity of the Holy Spirit [177]. It was a Spaniard who wrote the Nicene Creed affirming the consusbstantiality of the Son, and it is to another Spaniard that we owe the celebration of the Synod that defined the

---

[173]   *Spicilegium, etc.* Vol. III, Paris, 1723, p. 299. Florez: *España Sagrada*, volume XIV, pp. 386-389. Maceda, *Hosius*, pp. 383 and following.

[174]   *Contra Helvidium*

[175]   Epist. LXXXII *ad Oceanum*

[176]   "Nunquam, fili Oceane, fore putabam ut indulgentia Principis calumniam sustineret reorum, et de carceribus exeuntes, post sordes ac vestigia catenarum dolerent alios relaxatos... Carterius Hispanae Episcopus, homo aetate vetus et sacerdotio, unam antequam baptizaretur, alteram post lavacrum, priore mortua, duxit uxorem, et arbitraris eum contra Apostolii fecisse sentemtiam", etc. rtc.

[177]   Masdeu, *Historia crítica*, vol. VIII

consubstantiality of the Holy Spirit. Hosius and Damasus are the two great figures of our ancient ecclesiastical history.

Not far from them shines also St. Pacianus, bishop of Barcelona, among whose works, fortunately preserved, are three epistles against Novatian and his disciple Sempronian. [178] Novatian, the third century anti-Pope, had maintained the error concerning the *re-baptised*, condemning second marriages and not admitting to penance those who had sinned after Baptism unless they received the Sacrament again. St. Pacianus challenged the growth and advance of this heresy with his writings *Paraenesis*, or exhortation to penance, and *Sermon to the faithful and cathecumens on Baptism*, truly elegant and ingenious works. But he refuted it more directly in the two letters cited above, in answer to two of Sempronian's tracts, *De Catholico nomine*, that is, *Cur Catholici ita vocarentur*, and *De venia poenitentiae sive de reparatione post lapsum*.

Olimpius, believed to have been Pacianus' successor to the see of Barcelona, wrote a tract (since lost) *Against him who denies the free will of man and those who suppose eternal evil.*[179] St. Augustine (*Contra Julianum*) praises this refutation of Manichaean fatalism in laudatory words, referring to Olimpius as this "most glorious man of the Church and of Christ". It is certain that the bishop of Barcelona's tract was aimed especially at the Priscillianists - the only Manichaean branch that managed to make any inroads in Spain.

How sweet it is to call to mind now the name of our glorious Prudentius, "a lyrical poet, the most inspired the Latin world saw after Horace and before Dante". [180] I shall not remind the reader of all of the wondrous hymns where he celebrates the triumphs of confessors and martyrs, as Pindar had exalted those triumphant on the arena and the chariot. Nor shall I evoke now his poem against Symmachus, rich in lofty and majestic beauty of thought and expression. One is astonished to find this in an ignored author. Nor shall I refer to his *Psychomachia* which, apart from its philosophical value, places Prudentius among the fathers of allegorical art. I shall refer only to two other theological poems, the *Apotheosis* and *Hamartigenia*, both formal refutations of heretical systems.

The *Apotheosis* could be divided into four parts. The first (v. 1 to 178) is directed against the Patripassionists who did not accept any distinction between the three persons of the Trinity, and hence attributed the Crucifixion to the Father. The passage below, where Prudentius elucidates the union of the two natures in Christ, shows the vigour with which this poem is written, with the theological argumentation in no way damaging or weakening the valiant inspiration of the poet:

...pura, (divinitas) serena, micans, liquido praelibera motu
subdita nec cuiquam, dominatrix utpote rerum;

---

[178] *Paciani quae extant opera, nimirum Paraenesis, Epistolae ac de Baptismo.* Valencia, 1780, with Spanish translation and an erudite preliminary address by D. Vicente Noguera y Ramón.

[179] Vid. Gennadio: *De Script. Eccl.*, chapter XXIII.

[180] Villemain.

cui non principium de tempore, sed super omne
tempus, et ante diem majestas cum Patre summo,
immo animus Patris, et ratio, et via consiliorum
quae non facta manu, nec voce create jubentis,
protulit imperium, patrio ructata profundo.
his affecta caro est hominis, quem foemina praegnans
emixa est sub lege uteri, sine lege mariti.
ille ...fel potat, et haurit acetum,
ille pavet mortis faciem, tremit ille dolorem.
dicite, sacrilege Doctores, qui Patri summo
desertum jacuisse thronum contenditis illo
tempore, quo fragiles Deus est illapsus in artus:
ergo Pater passus? Qui non malus audeat error?
ille puellari conceptus sanguine crevit?
ipse verecundae distendit virginis alvum? [181] (V. 87)

(It is pure, serene, shining, utterly free and unconstrained in movement, not subject to any power, for it is master of all things, having no beginning in time, but beyond all time and before the days began it is the majesty that resides with the Father supreme, Yea, the spirit of the Father, His thought, the channel of His designs, which not made by His hand nor created by the voice of His command, but emitted from the depths of the Father, carried out His will. This therefore no scourges can cut nor spittle defile, nor hand hurt with buffeting nor nail-pierced wounds fasten upon a cross. It was the flesh of man that felt these things, flesh that a woman with child brought forth according to the law of birth, without the law of wedlock. He it is that suffers hunger, that drinks the gall and drains the vinegar. He it is that fears the shape of death and trembles at the pain. Tell me, ye blasphemous teachers, who maintain that the supreme Father abandons His throne at the time when God entered into a mortal body, was it the Father, then, who sufffered? What would not evil error dare? Was the Father Himself conceived and did He flow from a maid's blood? Did He Himself swell a modest virgin's womb?)

The second section of the poem defends the dogma of the Trinity against the Sabellians or Unionites. It begins with the verse:

cede prophanator Christi, jam cede, Sabelli... (V. 178)

(Yield, thou desecrator of Christ, yield now, Sabellius...)

A few pages later one encounters this blissful expression with Aristotle's dialectic in mind:

---

[181]   *M. Aurelii Prudentii Opera omnia*, vol, I., ed. Arévalo, pp. 410-411

texit Aristoteles torta vertigine nervos... (V. 202)

The third is directed against the Jews (vs. 321 to 552); it is the one with most poetic colour, though of no direct interest to us here. Nevertheless, let me record here the brief and lively strokes with which the Celtiberian poet describes the propagation of Christianity and the ruin of the old superstitions:

audiit adventum Domini, quem solis iberi

vesper habet roseus, et quem novus excipit ortus.

laxabit Scythicas verbo penetrante pruinas

vox evangelica, hyrcanas quoque fervida brumas

solvit, ut exitus glacie, jam mollior amnis

caucassea de cote fluat Rhodopejus Hebrus.

mansuevere getae feritasque cruenta Gelont...

libatura sacros Christi de sanguine potus...

delphica damnatis tacuerunt sortibus antra:

non tripodas cortina regit, non spumat anhelus

fata sibyllinis fanaticus edita libris.

perdidit insamos mendax Dodona vapores,

mortua jam mutae lugent oracula Cumae.

nec responsa refert Lybicis in syrtibus Ammon.

ipsa suis Christum capitolia Romula moerent

principibus lucere Deum, destructaque templa

imperio cecidisse ducum: jam purpura supplex

sternitur Aeneadae rectoris ad atria Christi

vexilumque crucis summus dominator adorat! (V. 424)

(He that dwells under the western sun of evening has heard of the Lord's coming, and he that welcomes anew the rosy dawn. The sound of the gospel with its piercing word has loosened the frosts of Scythia, and its warmth unlocked the Hyrcanian winter, so that Rhodopeian Hebrus, freed from ice, is now a kindlier stream as it flow from the rocks of Caucasus. The Getans have a peaceable frown and the bloody, savage Gelonian, when thirsty, fills bloodless cups with pure milk, for he will taste the holy draught of the blood of Christ. The once treacherous land of Moorish Atlans has learned to dedicate its long-haired kings at Christ's altar. Since the Spirit, that Spirit who is God, touched a moral womb and God entered into a mother's body and by a virgin made himself man, the cavern of Delphi has fallen silent, its oracles condemened; no longer does the cauldron direct responses from the tripod. No longer does a priest possessed utter with foaming mouth and panting breath fates drawn from Sibylline Books. Lying Dodona has lost its maddening vapours. Cumae is dumb and mourns for its dead oracles, and Ammon returns no answer in the deserts of Lybia. The very Capitol at Rome laments that Christ is the God who sheds light for her emperors and her temples have fallen in ruins at her leaders' command. Now the successor of Aeneas, in the imperial purple, prostrates himself in prayer at the house of Christ, and the supreme lord adores the banner of the Cross).

He who in the midst of an arid theological debate finds accents such as these could not possibly be a "poeta de escuela", as Comparetti had the audacity to opine, but actually the First Western Christian poet, as Villemain acknowledged. He who "at times compares with Lucretius" in Ozanam's estimation. The *Christian Horace*, as Renaissance scholars believed. He of whom Vives said that he "had things equal to the ancients, and in some surpassed them".

The purpose of the fourth part of the *Apotheosis* is to combat the error of the Ebionites, Marcionites, Arians, and all heretics who deny the Divinity of the Word. And who would believe that even when touching upon these arduous doctrinal issues, not only does the poet retain his qualities, but can display true greatness, sparkle and grace, as these verses show:

estne Deus cujus cunas veneratus Eous

lancibus auratis regalia fercula supplex,

virginis ad gremium pannis puerilibus offert!

quis tam pennatus, rapidoque similimus Austro

nuncius Aurorae populus, atque ultima Bactra

attigit, illuxisse diem, lactantibus horis,

qua tener innupto penderet ab ubere Christus? (V. 608)

(Is He not God to Whose cradle the East does reverence, offering on bended knee before the Virgin's lap kingly gifts on gilded platters for the child in swaddling clothes? What winged messanger, swift as the rushing wind, came to the peoples of the morning in farthest Bactra to tell them a day had dawned whose hours were full of richness, the day on which the babe Christ hung on an unwedded breast?)

While illustrious Greek Doctors like Synesius tripped over Pantheism and held the soul to be a particle of the divine essence; while others judged it to be corporeal, if of the finest matter, Prudentius skilfully avoids both hurdles in little more than one verse:

> ...Speculum Deitatis homo est. In corpore discas
> rem non corpoream... (V. 834)
> (..man is a mirror of Godhead. In the body we may come to know something that is not bodily...)

Against Pantheism he argues:

> ...absurde fertur (anima) Deus, aut pars esse Dei, quae
> divinum summumque bonum de fonte perenni
> nunc bibit obsequio, nunc culpa aut crimine perdit,
> et modo supplicium recipit, modo libera calcat. (V. 884)

> (...it is irrational to say that the soul is God or a part of God, for at one time by obedience it drinks in the divine and supreme good from its everlasting source, and at another by sin and wickedness loses it and now must submit to punishment, only to tread it under foot again freely).

On the origin of the soul, a matter of some hesitation for St. Augustine, Prudentius shows no doubt. He combats the idea of those who supposed it to be derived from Adam by generation, in like manner with emanatist doctrine. His explanation of how original sin is transmitted conforms strictly to orthodoxy:

> quae quamvis infusa (anima) novum penetret nova simper
> figmentum, vetus illa tamen de crimine avorum
> dulcitur: illuto quoniam concreta veterno est. (V. 921)
> (Yet though it is always a new soul that is infused into the new body, it is nevertheless said to be old after the sins of its fathers, since dirt unwashed is caked hard upon it).

In the last section of the *Apotheosis*, the Docetism of the Manichaeans is challenged:

> Aerium Manichaeus ait sine corpore vero
> Pervolitasse Deum, mendax phantasma, cavamque
> Corporis effigiem, nil contrectabile habentem. (V. 957)

> (There moved about, says the Manichaean, a phantasmal God without real body, a false apeparance, an empty likeness of body, having nothing tangible).

Against the dualism of Marcion and a vast majority of other Gnostics, Prudentius wrote the poem *Hamartigenia* or *On the origin of sin*. Against the error of those who divide and distinguish between the God of Moses and the God of the Gospel, our poet says the Son is the form of the Father, understanding by *form*, the *logos*, or *word* in the manner of some Peripatetics. For Prudentius, form is inseparable from essence:

forma Patris veri verus stat Filius, ac se

unum rite probat, dum formam servat eamdem. (V. 51)

(He is a Real Son, the likeness of a real Father, and properly
proves His unity by keeping the same likeness).

Form, then, implies not only similitude but also identity of existence.
Prudentius elaborates on this fine concept and then moves on to speak of the
origin of evil, due to sin of angel and man, and draws a beautiful picture of the
disorder that was brought by sin into the natural and the spiritual world. He
ends this long description with verses that seem imitated from a well-known
passage of the *Georgics*:

felix qui indultis potuit mediocriter uti

muneribus, parcumque modum servare fruendi!

quem locuples mundi species et amoena venustas,

et nitides fallens circumflua copia rebus

non capit, ut puerum, nec inepto addicit amori,

qui sub adumbrata dulcedine triste venenum

deprendit latitare boni mendacis operto. (V. 330)

(Happy the man who has been able to use with temperance the
gifts granted him and to keep frugal measure in his enjoyment of
them, whom the world's rich display with its pleasant attraction
and its flowing abundance of lying baubles does not charm like a
child, nor enslave to a foolish love, who detects the deadly poison
lurking under the feigned sweetness, in concealment under what
falsely claims to be good!)

With expressive imagery he shows the absurdity of presupposing a
Primal Principle that is evil, substantial and eternal:

Nil luteum de fonte fluit, nec turbidus humor
Nascitur, aut primae violator origine venae,
Sed dum liventis liquor incorruptus arenas
Praelambit, putrefacta inter contagia sordet. (V. 354)

(There is no muddy flow from the fountain-head, the water is not
turbid at its rise, nor made unclean as it springs from its source;
but as the pure stream washes the dirty sand along its banks it is
befouled by contact with decay).

Man's free will is vigorously defended in this poem, which the Aragonese
poet/theologian closes with a fervent prayer to Christ asking humbly not for the
joys of glory of which he considers himself unworthy, but for the flames of
purgatory:

O Dee cunctiparens, animae dator, O Dee Christe,
cujus ab ore Deus subsistit spiritus unus:
te moderante regor, te vitam principe duco,
Iudice te pallens trepido, te iudice eodem
Spem capio fore quidquid ago veniabile apud te,
Quamlibet indignum venia faciamque loquarque.
confiteor; dimitte libens et parce fatenti.
Omne malum merui, sed tu bonus arbiter aufer
quod merui; meliora favens largire precanti
dona animae quandoque meae, cum corporis huius
liquerit hospitium nervis, cute, sanguine, felle,
ossibus exstructum, corrupta quod incola luxu
heu nimium conplexa fovet, cum flebilis hora
clauserit hors orbes, et conclamata iacebit
materies oculisque suis mens nuda fruetur,
ne cernat truculentum aliquem de gente latronum
inmitem, rabidum, vultuque et voce minaci
terribilem, qui me maculosum aspergine morum
in praeceps, ut praedo, trahat nigrisque ruentem
inmergat specubus, cuncta exacturus ad usque
quadrantem minimum damnosae debita vitae.
multa in thesauris Patris est habitatio, Christe,
disparibus discreta locis.   non posco beata
in regione domum: sint illic casta virorum
agmina, pulvereum quae dedignantia censum
divitias petiere tuas, sit flore perenni
candida virginitas animum castrata recisum.
at mihi Tartarei satis est si nulla ministri
occurrat facies, avidae nec flamma gehennae
devoret hanc animam mersam fornacibus imis.
esto, cavernoso, quia sic pro labe necesse est
corporea, tristis me sorbeat ignis Averno:
saltem mitificos incendia lenta vapores
exhalent aestuque calor languente tepescat;
lux inmensa alios et tempora vincta coronis
glorificent: ne poena levis clementer adurat.   (V. 931)

(O God, the Father of all and giver of the soul, O God Christ,
from Whose mouth proceeds the Spirit, God in unity, by Thy
governance I am directed, under Thy leadership do I live my life,
under Thy judgment I pale and tremble, under Thy judgment too
I take hope that what I do will find pardon with Thee, however
unworthy of pardon be my act of speech. I confess my sin; be
Thou ready to forgive me and spare the confessor. I have
deserved all ill, but do Thou, Who art a kindly judge, take away

what I deserve and in gracious answer to my soul's prayer bestow better gifts one day upon it, when it shall have left behind this bodily lodging buillt up of sinews, skin, blood, gall, bones, to which its indweller, corrupted with indulgence, clings, alas! too fondly, and when the doleful hour shall have closed these eyes and the material body shall lie dead and the bared soul have the use of its natural vision, may it not see one of the race of robbers, fierce, ruthless, raging, with frightful, threatening look and voice, that shall drag me down headlong, as a brigand his captive, spotted as I am with the stains of my conduct, and send me plunging into black caverns, there to exact from me to the last farthing all that is due for my wasteful life. Many dwellings are there in the Father's treasure-city, O Christ, and set appart on sites that differ. I do not ask for a home in the region of the blessed. There let the companies of pure men dwell who have disdained earthy possessions and sought after Thy riches, and the unspotted virgins whose flower has never faded and who have cut off the appetites of the heart. Enough for me if the features of no minister of hell meet me, and this soul of mine be not plunged in the depths of the furnaces and devoured by the flames of greedy Gehenna. And let it be that the grim fire swallow me in the chasm of Avernus because for my bodily stain it must needs be so; yet at least may the flames be gentle and the heat of their breath be mild, may their fury die down and their burning moderate. Let others enjoy the glory of infinite light and crown-encircled brows: as for me, may my punishment be light, my torment merciful).

From a literary standpoint, the *Hamartigenia* is even better than the *Apotheosis*. But let a comparative study of both books, as well as the philosophical relationship between them, remain for that time when I can publish them, translated and illustrated, together with Prudentius' other magnificent inspirations.

Let us now face those accusations of heterodoxy levelled against our Saragossan poet. Petr Bayle and others say that when Prudentius refers to the soul as *liquid* and calls it an *element* (hymn X of the *Cathemerinon*, book II *Contra Simmaco* and elsewhere), he holds it to be material and mortal. Such outlandish interpretation is based on these verses:

humus excipit arida corpus
animae rapit aura liquorem   (Cath. X v. 11)

(The dry earth receives his body, the breath of air carries off the pure spirit)

But who is not able to see that this *liquid soul* and the *aura* that carries it are figurative expressions on the lips of a poet, who in the same hymn says:

sed dum resolubile corpus
revocas, Deus, atque reformas,
quanam regione jubebis
animam requiescere puram?

(But till Thou dost recall the mortal body, O God, and makest it
new, in what region wilt Thou bid the pure soul rest?)

This is the poet whom we saw in the *Apotheosis* distinguishing "in corpore
rem non corpoream" How could Bayle say, unless drawn to this assertion by his
love for paradox, that our poet's doctrine here differed little from that of
Lucretius, when the poet said :

Nec sic interimit mors, res, ut materiae
Corpora conficiat, sed coetum dissipat ollis,
Inde aliis aliud coniungit, et efficit omnes
Res ut convertant formas, mutentque colores...

(Luc. Bk II, v. 1001)

(Nor does death so destroy things as to annihilate the bodies of
matter, but it disperses their combination abroad; then it conjoins
others with others, and brings it about that thus all things alter
their shapes and change their colours...)

As for the word *element*, how can anyone doubt that Prudentius applies it
to every principle, not just the material, as Lactantius did in book three, chapter
six, of his *Institutiones divinas*: "Ex his duobus constamus elementis quorum
alterum luce praeditum est, alterum tenebris", where one sees clearly that he is
alluding to the union of rational principle and matter? Did not Cicero say in his
Questiones Academicas that the word *elementa* was synonymous with *initia* and
translations both of the Greek αρχαί?

One is hard-pressed to believe, with Jean Le Clerck, that Prudentius
inclines to the Manichaeans' error on the question of the absolute prohibition
of meat. Even though in Hymn 3 of the *Cathemerinon* he says

absit enim procul illa fames
caedibus ut pecudum libeat
sanguineas lacerare dapes.
sint fera de gentibus indomitis
prandia de nece quadrupedum... (Cather. III 58)

(Far from us be the appetite that would choose to slay cattle and
hack their flesh to make a bloody feast. Let uncivilised tribes
have their savage meals from the slaughter of four-footed
beasts...)

We can only deduce from this that he is here recommending the abstinence
practised in those centuries by innumerable Christians as means to greater
perfection, but nothing beyond that.

Some have seen as impious the final oration in the *Hamartigenia* that I have quoted above. They thought our poet was asking for the fire of hell, not of purgatory, which would then not be a humble prayer, said Bayle, but an impious and desperate one, similar to that of Filippi Strozzi who, before killing himself, asked God to put his soul next to Cato of Utica's and other ancients who had committed suicide. Between this and the "Moriatur anima mea more philosophorum" attributed by the Schools to Averroes there is little difference. But as Prudentius is not speaking of Tartarus but of purgatory all difficulty fades away, and all we are to see in his words is the modest expression of a spirit that does not consider itself worthy of entering the celestial dwelling, without first passing through the cauterising flames that will purify it. If there is some excess here, it is excess of devotion, or perhaps, simply, poetic licence.

Cardinal Bellarmine so qualified the singular doctrine of Prudentius in Hymn 5 of the *Cathemerinon*, where he says that in the night of Holy Saturday the damned themselves rejoice and feel some relief in their torments:

marcent suppliciis Tartara mitibus
exultatque sui carceris otio
umbrarum populus, liber ab ignibus...(Cather. V v.133)

(Hell's force abates, its punishments are mild, and the people of the dead, set free from the fires, rejoice in the relaxation of their imprisonment, nor do the sulphuruous rivers boil as hot as they are wont...)

This opinion, untenable today, was not rare in Prudentius time. St. Augustine (*De civitate Dei*, book, XXI, chapter XXIV) dares not reject it, for though punishment is eternal (he says), God may consent to it being less severe at some given times, and some degree of mercy and consolation might come to the infernal regions. The *Index expurgatorio* of Rome (1607) said that at the margin of these verses the note *Caute legendi* be written.

While some held a few of Prudentius' concepts and phrases suspect, others agreed with the heretics he attacked. Petr Bayle accuses him of begging the question posed by the Manichaeans. "Why does God not prevent evil?" - they asked. "He who does not prevent evil, causes it". To which Prudentius does *not* answer, as Bayle misreads, "because man sins freely" but "because man was created free that he might be worthy of reward". And since it is more worthy of Providence to create free than fatalist beings, Prudentius' answer is neither *petitio principii* nor as easy to resolve as the sceptic of Amsterdam imagines. [182]

When fighting Manichaeans, Marcionists, Patripassionists, etc., it is almost certain that Prudentius had in mind the Priscillianists as well, who (as Krausse's followers would say today) *communicated* with these heretics' opinions.

---

[182]   See, as Prudentius' vindication, chapters XV to XX of Father Arévalo's excellent *Prudentiana*, which precedes Rome's edition, 1788, which is the one I am following.

In *Hamartigenia,* however, he mentions only Marcion, and in *Apotheosis,* Sibbelius; this is why I have not included him among Priscillianism's direct adversaries.

Against the Frenchman Vigilantius who denied the intercession of the saints, the veneration of martyrs' relics, etc., and preached these doctrines in the country of the Vectons (others read Vascons), Arevacos, Celtiberians, and Laletans, there arose Riparius, a presbyter of Barcelona, who passed on news of this heresiarch's errors to St. Jerome. The saint replied with a letter asking him to send as many of Vigilantius' writings as he could. Riparius together with another presbyter, Desiderius, did so and St. Jerome made use of these data in his hard-hitting and wounding *Apologeticon adversus Vigilantium.* Riparius and Desiderius' letters have not been preserved, nor are we aware that this heresy had many proselytes in Spain.[183]

I dare not include Philastrius, bishop of Brescia, and author of a well-known *Register of Heretics* among our Spanish controversialists, however much Ughelli in his *Italia Sacra* and other foreigners regard him as one of us.

Orosius valiantly wielded his pen against the Pelagians in his apologia *De Arbitrii libertate,* though some, Jansenius among them, doubted this work belonged to him.

It has become clear now that a monk, Bacchiarius, author of two celebrated tracts, *De reparatione lapsi* and another that could be titled *Confessio Fidei,* was not English or Irish, but Spanish, and Galician at that, as Francisco Flori, canon of Aquilea and Father Flórez have proved.[184] Baccharius left his motherland on pilgrimage to Rome. Because of his origin, he was suspected of Priscillianism, and so he wrote the above-cited Confession of Faith. He protests against those who defamed him because of his native land ("Suspectos nos facit non sermo, sed regio: qui de fide non erubescimus, de provincia confundimur"), and manifests his Catholic sentiments concerning the Trinity, Incarnation, resurrection of the flesh, rational soul, origin of sin, marriage, use of meat, fasting, etc. He constantly contrasts his doctrine with that of the Priscillianists, though he does not specifically refer to them by name, and he duplicates, sometimes to the letter, the words of the Council of Toledo's *Regula Fidei,* as anyone curious enough to leaf through them will notice. He also rejects the errors of Helvidius and Jovinianus. Ferreiro is of the opinion that Bacchiarius could well be that *pilgrim* cited by Zaccaria, because our monk sometimes refers to himself as such: "Peregrinus ego sum...."

---

[183]   Vid. About Vigilantius and his challengers the precious dissertation of Cervera's Cancelario, D. Ramón Lázaro de Dou, *De tribuendo cultu SS. Martyrum reliquiis, in Vigilantium et recentiores haereticos...Accessit praevia de Vigilantii patria, vita et haeresibus dissertation.* Cervariae, 1767, typ. Acad. Also, *España Sagrada,* vol. XXIX, number 200.

[184]   The first edition of *Confessio Fidei* was made in Milan by Muratori, 1698. The second by Flori in Rome, 1748. The third by Father Flórez in volume XV of *España Sagrada* (Appendix), together with *De reparatione lapsi,* which is in the *Bibliotheca Veterum Patrum.*

Book 1
Chapter 3

Heresies during the Visigothic epoch

Arianism among the Vandals: persecutions.

A Glimpse of Nestorianism. Letter of Vitalis and Constantius.

Manichaeism in Galicia and Extremadura. Pacentius.

Remnants of Priscillianism. Letters of Montanus and Vigilius.

Arianism among the Swabians. Their conversion to Catholicism by St. Martin of Braga (year 560).

Arianism among the Visigoths until Leovigild.

Arianism in Leovigild's time. The last struggle.

Apocryphal writings. One bishop's materialism.

The Visigoths renounce Arianism. Third Council of Toledo. Heterodox coup attempts and Witeric's reaction.

The heresy of the *Acephali*.

The Councils of Toledo and their relationship with the Holy See.

Theological polemics in Visigothic Spain.

Witiza's heterodox politics. End of the Visigoth Empire.

Arianism among the Vandals. Persecutions

When the hand of God, in order to punish the Roman world for its abominations cast upon it a swarm of barbarians from the woods of Germania, the banks of the Volga, the Tanaïs and Borysthenes, the onslaught that followed was to produce a considerable amount of religious confusion to the invaded peoples. Gnostic fantasies had by then given way to other beliefs, more dialectical than theosophical in character, almost all derived from an anti-Trinitarian basis, and prominent among these was *Arianism*: a doctrine that, by seeming clear and straightforward, found a good reception in the West and sooner or later infected the majority of the barbarian tribes.

The mysteries of the Trinity and the Incarnation, even when looked at from a distance with the eye of our deficient human reason, are concepts so lofty, so sublime, that without them we would lose the key to the world of ideas and sever all relationship between God and the world - between man and God. That unitarian god of Gnosis, the god of Socinianism, can be identified only in two ways: either with creation (an absurd pantheism to which our conscience and our intimate inner sense vigorously revolt against in order to cry out our human individuality and free will), or else it must be independent and detached from the spirit and from matter, 'far from our world and its pain', like the gods of Epicurus and of Lucretius. These systems do not explain creation: in them, the essence of God remains inactive. God's unity for them, having no distinction of Persons and lacking both variety and unity, neither creates nor does it ever touch its creation. This is why the Gnostics needed a series of emanations between creator and the thing created, as Kabbalists do.

In contrast, see how much light the concept of a God *Uno et Trino* sheds over the shadows of human reason! The Father creates through his *Logos,* his Word, and infuses all things created with his *Pneuma,* the Holy Spirit, with the infinite unity of essence being in no way impaired. Instead of a cold and dead unity, we have here a living, palpitating unity, the spirit of God running through the waters, the Word of God becoming flesh, shining in the darkness, though the darkness did not know Him.

What a beautiful dogma this is, beaming with truth and life! God, our God, condescends to come down to man by an act of endearing love for him, and in so doing joins heaven and earth in a tight, firm, and indissoluble bond, lifting redeemed humanity to God and God Himself becoming the exemplar and model of humanity, whose flesh he assumed, and in whose pain he shared.

These mysteries cannot be explained; if they could be, they would cease to be mysteries. Human reason has limitations, a fact that human reason itself acknowledges at every turn. But the light of this mystery is such that it illumines all things by pointing to their final consequences, while our complete understanding remains impossible.

But man, having lost faith and with his mind blinded by the devil of arrogance, often aspires to offer explanations about the infinite and, with an impertinence bordering on dementia, goes on to deny what his understanding cannot reach, as if his human mind was the rule and measure of the absolute.

Arius was careful to distinguish his own anti-Trinitarian rejection from that of Valentinus, Mani, Hierax and Sabellius, in spite of which he copies the Gnostics, and more than once, especially the Alexandrian neo-Platonists. The eternal generation of the Word appeared contradictory to Arius' petty *common sense.* He did not stop to consider that in the Divine essence there had to be, from eternity, plenitude of being and existence, because to suppose it incomplete at any time would be to deny the infinity of his Being. To my mind, Arius, the skilled debater, the learned theologian, does not show a first-class analytical ability in his arguments. It is said he used to go about asking women: "Can you have children before giving birth? Well, neither can God".

When orthodox theologians made him face the above argument, he dodged it, and to get out of it he went on to deny the divinity of the Word whom he nonetheless continued to call the Son of God. His challengers objected that the Son is of the essence of the Father and, therefore, God. And Arius responded weakly with the mediocre differentiation of the Word not being *homousios,* or consubstantial with the Father, but *homoiousios,* that is, similar. Yet it is explicitly clear in Scripture: 'Ego et Pater unum sumus". And Arius, who explained everything in terms of similitude, could never explain what this similitude actually consisted in, or in what way it differed from complete identity.

The *Word* of Arius is not God and is not man either. It is something in between, a sort of demiurge that God created to effectuate his *ideas* of creation and redemption in the world.

118

Though caught up in this vicious circle, [185] Arianism had nonetheless features that appealed to the masses, because it brought dogma down to the level of common reasoning. That is why it was able to resist stubbornly and vigorously the efforts of Hosius and St. Athanasius, the anathema of Nicea and Sardis, and the first edicts of Constantine.[186] And to make matters worse, the emperors/theologians of the decadent epoch sided with Arius, Aecius, Acacius, and Eunomius; and then, from the Arians sprang the Macedonians who accepted the divinity of the Son but denied that of the Holy Spirit.

The imperfect Christianity that was taught to the barbarian races of Northern Europe (most of their missionaries were Arians) was the tragic outcome of emperors meddling in matters of the Church.

We do not know precisely when Christianity reached the Vandals. The Goths were catechised by Ulphilas who made a version of the Bible in his own tongue. This is how these poor barbarians, due to Valens and other *Emperors of Theology*, came to be heretics without even knowing it. "Haeretici sunt sed non scientes", says Salvianus of Marseille (*De gubernatione Dei*): "errant, sed bono animo errant", and goes on to reflect on whether those poor innocents would be punished for their error on the Day of Judgement... *"nullus potest scire nisi judex"*. These new souls, eager to receive any teaching that would uplift them from the earthly soil their old idolatry had tied them to, must have surrendered easily to a system that freed their crude understanding from having to deal with theological thorns such as consubstantiality; and all they saw in Christ was a Prophet.

The first sons of the North that descended upon Spain were far from sharing in that religion, however. They were Vandals, Swabians, Alans and Silingos who in the year 409, led by Gunderic, Atace and Hermeric, came to cause such horrendous slaughter and devastation in our Peninsula, an absolute wreckage followed by hunger and widespread pestilence of which Idacius' *Chronicon* speaks at length. The Vandals and the Alans were partly Christian, partly followed their old idolatry. The Swabians, on the other hand, were all idolaters. They occupied Galicia, then infested with Priscillianism. The Alans took over the Lusitanian and Carthaginian territory, and the Vandals the Betis region, which they laid waste with incredible ferocity. The Hispano-Roman race, the Catholic peoples, were the victims of hordes who, having shortly before embraced Arianism, added to their natural bloodthirsty zest that fanaticism so characteristic of sects - a terrible thing in uncultivated spirits! The African bishop Victor Vitensis wrote the history of this persecution, which started in Spain and then moved on to Mauritania.[187]

---

185   On Arianism see Moelher's work, *Athanasius the Great and the Church of His Time against Arianism, (Maguncia, 1827)*.

186   Vid. Chapter 1.

187   *Historia persecutionis Vandalicae in Africa, cum notis Theodorici Ruinart*, Paris, 1694. Vid. also, St. Isidore, *Vandalorum historia*.

Genseric, or Giseric, one of the more notorious barbarian leaders was, St. Isidore notes, the first Vandal king to embrace Arianism.[188] According to Victor, he spurred persecution against Spanish Catholics, beheading a beautiful and noble lady who had refused to be re-baptised according to the Arian rite. In 427, Genseric crossed the Strait and after conquering Africa thanks to Count Boniface's treason, he doubled his harshness against the church. Many Africans were to gain the palm of martyrdom, and among them Spaniards, too, such as Arcadius, Probus, Eutychius, Pascasius and Paulus. Honoratus Antoninus, bishop of Cosantina, wrote to them an admirable and most eloquent letter heartening them to withstand persecution: [189]

"Take heart, faithful soul" - he wrote to Arcadius – "rejoice, confessor of the Divinity, in the wrongs you are now enduring for Jesus Christ, as the apostles rejoiced in the lashes and chains they themselves received. See the dragon prostrated at your victorious feet....raise your eyes to heaven: see the host of martyrs weaving the crown of your victory from their own laurel wreaths ... remember how brief is the time of affliction, how long the eternity of reward... though a woman, the mother of the Maccabees, sensing God's aid within her, had the courage to be present (oh immovable column!) at the martyrdom of her seven children, and to encourage them on to their death. With fortitude she deprived herself of them. Behold, now she sees them radiant at her side, crowned for evermore ... It was God Who formed you in the womb of your mother, God Who created your spirit as He created all things in the world. God, Who adorned you with reason and understanding. Can you deny Him now the martyrdom He is asking of you? Will you dare deny Him, with harm to yourself, the longing He has to glorify you? The earth, the sun, the moon, the stars, all beauty on earth, all will end...oh but you will live eternally...what a joy to gaze at Jesus with your soul, very soon now, and to know that one day you will see Him with the eyes of the flesh!".

If we follow Antoninus' words closely, Genseric's persecution seems more Patripassionist than Arian. He alerts Acacius most of all to keep persevering in his confession of the Word Incarnate. He continues:

"The Father, the Son and the Holy Spirit are one God; but only the Son incarnated, not the Holy Spirit, or the Father. So it is with us: though the soul is one, and the understanding is in it, and is *it*, the souls acts in one way, the understanding in another; life is the property of the soul, but knowing is of the reason, as in one same ray of sun there is heat and there is light, and though they cannot be separated, it is heat that warms and light that illumines, and radiating warmth is the property of heat and not of light, and radiating light is the property of light and not of heat... When one strums the zither, three things come together to create the sound: art itself, the artist's hand, and the

---

[188]   "Qui ex Catholico effectus Apostata in Arianam haeresim primus effertur transiisse"

[189]   Translation into Spanish by Masdeu, *Historia crítica de España,* Ilustration 12, volume 11.

string. Art inspires, the hand strums, the string makes the sound, and though three things concur to produce the same effect, it is the string alone that produces the sound. Likewise, the Father, the Son and the Holy Spirit co-operated in the Incarnation, the Son alone was incarnated".

Thus reflected a fifth-century African bishop! Chroniclers of power and might will keep on recording invasions and conquests, but let us be allowed to commemorate some of these forgotten testimonies of learning, and the fidelity shown by the conquered Latin race.

Persecution by the Vandals was fierce but it did not last long in Spain. Those barbarians abandoned Betis and moved on to Africa; in our seas they kept only the Balearic Islands. In 484, King Uneric exiled all Catholic bishops, among them those of Majorca, Minorca and Ibiza, whose names were Elias, Macarius and Opilius. Another among the persecuted was Maracinus, who signed the *Acta* of the Second Council of Toledo as "exiled because of my Catholic faith". The people of Taves, a city of Africa, embarked for Spain with their wives and children rather than accept a heretic bishop.

We know of no apostasy having being caused by this first Arian storm. Nor can we confirm that our poet Dracontius, author of the *Hexaemeron* or *Work of the Six Days*, had been persecuted because of religion; all that we know is that he was imprisoned by order of king Guntheric, Genseric's predecessor, not yet Arian.

First signs of Nestorianism. Letters of Vitalis and Constantius

The Vandal persecution in the regions of Betis and Carthage was not the only danger Christians were facing. Around the year 439, two Spanish presbyters, Vitalis and Constantius (others read Tonantius) wrote a letter to St. Capreolus, bishop of Carthage:

"There are some people here who maintain "Deum innascilibem esse". In their opinion, the man Jesus was born of the Virgin Mary, and it was only later that God lived in Him. We, your humble servants, oppose such affirmation, for we think it contrary to Holy Scripture. We ask that you may elucidate our deficiencies and instruct us as to what the Catholic Church maintains as truth on this point". [190]

It was a humble request, accompanied by pertinent texts from the Bible - a sure sign of Vitalis and Constantius' solid instruction in dogma. St. Capreolus hurried to answer this letter which had been delivered to him by Numinianus,

---

[190] "Quia sunt hic quidam qui dicunt non debere dici Deum natum; nam et haec est fides eorum, hominem purum natum fuisse de Maria Virgine, et post haec Deum habitasse in eo. Quorum nos, humiles pueri tui…resistimus affirmationi…Exoramus ut informetis parvitatem nostrum in his, quod rectum habes fides catholica…" *Bibliotheca Vet. Pat.*, vol. VII, fol. 5, ed. Lugdunense).

with the epistle *De una Christi veri Dei et hominis persona contra recens dammatam haeresim Nestorii.*[191]

This error of two persons in Christ was a leftover from Gnosticism, which separated the *aeon - logos* or *Word* - from the man Jesus. In Spain, it could well have sprung from Priscillianism. But the person who gave shape and form to this new heresy in the eastern world was Nestorius, Patriarch of Constantinople.

Difference of natures led him to assume difference of persons. For him, the Christ born of Mary was only a man; Divinity joined to this man, as clothes to a body. That is why he called the Virgin not *Theotokos,* that is, Mother of God, but *Antropotokos,* mother of the man. Nestorius' error was based on the obvious confusion of the terms *person* and *nature.* Our own Fray Alfonso de Castro [192] elucidated this point: "This same difference we can see in all things created. Man is one sole person: nonetheless he receives various denominations according to his diverse natures: in regards to his body he is mortal, immortal as regards to his soul. In the same way ("si licet parvis componere magna") Christ, in unity of Person, combines natures, the human and the divine."

Against Nestorius' heresy arose St. Cyril of Alexandria with his book *De recta fide ad Theodosium,* and, later, Pope Gelasius with *De duabus naturis in una persona.* The great Theodoret however allowed himself to be seduced. The Council of Ephesus, convened in 431, anathematised those who called Christ theophoros, *he who carries God,* and set in precise terms what the Catholic word *theotokos* means: "Not because the Divine nature took its origin from the Virgin, or because it was necessary that the Word be born a second time which would be a futile and ridiculous belief, since the *Logos* precedes all time and is co-eternal with the Father, but because, for our salvation, He joined human nature to Himself, and proceeded from woman. The Christ-Man was not born of Mary first and then the Word inhabited in Him, but rather He made himself flesh in the virginal womb".[193]

Nestorius was censured and deposed but the heresiarch's doctrine did not die. His adherents withdrew to Persia and Mesopotamia, eventually reaching India where they still exist today or have existed until recently though in small numbers, under the name of *Christians of St. Thomas.* In 1599, many of them rejoined the Latin Church keeping communion under both species and

---

191   Included in vol. VII, *Bibliotheca Vet. Pat.*

192   *De haeresibus,* lib.IV, tit. *Christus,* p.136 of vol. I, ed. 1773. *Opera Alphonsi a Castro Zamorensis.*

193   "Non quia divina ipsius natura de Sacra Virgine sumpsit exordium, nec propter seipsam opus habuit secundo nasci post illam nativitatem quam habebat ex Patre (est enim ineptum et stultum hoc dicere, quod is qui ante omnia saecula est et cumsempiternus, secundae generationis eguerit), sed qui propter nostram salutem naturam sibi copulavit humanam, et processit ex muliere. Nec enim primum natus est homo communis de Sancta Virgine et tunc demum inhabitavit in eo Verbum, sed in ipsa vulva atque utero virginali secum carnem conjunxit". Carranza, *Summa Conciliorum,* ed. 1570, fol. 134 v.

the marriage of priests. Those from Ottoman Asia remained separated from the two Churches, the Roman and the Greek, though they joined the Jacobites and other sects with their own two Patriarchs. No heresy in the Annals of the Church has lasted so long.

But let us come back to Spain. Vitalis and Constantius did not know of any council having been called at Ephesus or of Nestorius' heresy when they wrote to St. Capreolus – which makes their zeal and clear intelligence on theological matters deserving of double praise. The bishop of Carthage, in his reply, informs them of what had taken place in the East, exhorts them to persevere in the Faith and combat all prevarication, and sets out the New Testament passages that confirm the unity of Person in Christ.

In the eighth century we shall see Nestorian doctrine make a comeback under the name of *Adoptionism*, sparking off grave conflicts within the Spanish Church supported by Felix of Urgel and Elipandus of Toledo.

Manichaeism in Galicia and Extremadura. Pacentius

Soon after this event, there appeared in Galicia, then subject to the two-fold calamity of Swabians and Priscillianists, a Manichaean called Pacentius or Pascentius, a Roman, who attracted a good number of proselytes - not a difficult task, there being so many supporters of *Dualism* in the western regions of the Peninsula. News of his teaching came to the ear of St. Turibius of Astorga and of Idacius both of whom brought proceedings in 448 against the new heretics. Pacentius took refuge in Lusitania but Antoninus, bishop of Mérida, informed of his prior condemnation by the proceedings Idacius and Turibius had sent him, banished him from that province. We owe news of this event to Idacius' *Chronicon*. [194] Pacentius must have been one of the Manichaeans judged at Rome by St. Leo, of whom he speaks in the letter to Turibius.

Remnants of Priscillianism. Letters of Montanus and Vigilius

To this incident of relatively little importance is linked however something of a Priscillianist comeback. In the previous chapter, we noted St. Turibius' efforts in combating this heresy, which resulted in the celebration of two provincial councils. Idacius related that the submission of many Galician bishops to the Church in the synod called *Aquis Caelenis* was false-hearted to say the least. In the years 525-530, Montanus, bishop of Toledo, was still sending letters about it to a monk by the name of Turibius and the faithful of the

---

[194]   "In Asturicense urbe Gallaeciae quidam ante aliquot annos latentes Manichaei gestis Episcopalibus detenguntur, quae ab Idatio et Turibio Espiscopis, qui eos audierant, ad Antoninum Emeritensem Episcopum directi sunt… Pascentium quemdam urbis Romae, qui de Asturica diffugerat, Manicaeum. Antoninus Episcopus Emeritae comprehendit, auditumque etiam de provinciali Lusitaniae facit expelli". Flórez, *España Sagrada*, Vol. IV.

Palencia region, warning them against that "detestable and foolish Priscillianist sect" and repeating St. Leo's anathemas. One can see from the Metropolitan's words that Gnosticism had taken deep roots in Palencia: "Praeterea perditissimam Priscillianistarum sectam tam actis quam nomine a vobis praecipue novimus honorari". This monk, Turibius (not the one from Astorga) was doing his utmost to uproot it; for this reason Montanus did not hesitate to give him the glorious title of "restorer of divine worship" in that province. ("Jure etenim auctorem te divini cultus in ac praesertim provincia nominabo. Putasne quanta tibi apud Deum maneat merces cujus sollertia vel instinctu, et idolatriae error abscessit, et Priscillianistarum detestabilis ac pudibunda secta contabuit").[195]

In 538, in the consulship of Volusianus and Joannes, Pope Vigillius addressed an epistle to Profuturus, bishop of Braga, who had consulted him on diverse points of dogma and discipline such as the use of the word *filioque* which some were suppressing in the *Credo*, the abstinence of meat taught by the Priscillianists, the baptism of Arians, and the time of commemorating Easter.[196]

The last decrees against Priscillianism, i.e. those of the Council of Braga, have already been mentioned in their appropriate place. I bring this incident to mind now not to break the chronological thread or pass over any signs of heterodoxy during this period.

Arianism among the Swabians.
Their conversion by St. Martin of Braga in 560.

It is really quite astonishing! An idolatrous people who turn to Christianity, from Christianity to heresy, from heresy back to orthodoxy (every old error gone) and all of this in the space of less than 150 years! It is a pity that we have so little information about these prodigious happenings! This is because, unfortunately, the Swabian monarchy has been mostly ignored by our historians, who are largely only interested in the splendour of the Visigoths.

The Swabians were pagans when they landed in Galicia [197] and remained so until the time of Rechiarius who reigned from 448 to 456 and who received baptism before marrying one of the daughters of the Goth King Theodored.

---

[195]   Vid. these letters in volume 1 of the *Toledo Fathers*; Flórez's vol. V; *Ambrosii Morales Opuscula Historica...*, vol. 3, Madrid, 1793. Montano's letters are in pp. 82 to 89, in *Excerpta* of the Vigilianus and Emilianensis codex.

[196]   "Ac primum de his quos Priscillianae haeresis indicasti vitiis inquinari, sancta et convenienti religione catholicae detestione judicas arguendos, qui ita se sub abstinentiae simulatae praetextu, ab escis videntur cranium submovere, ut hoc execrationis potius animo quan devotionis, probantur efficere". Collectio Canonum; ed. *Biblioteca Real*, col. 154.

[197]   *Suevorum Historia, España Sagrada*, vol. VI, p.504.

"*Catholicus factus*", St. Isidore said.[198] His people followed him in his conversion but their Catholicism, probably only half understood, did not last long.   In Remismund's time, a certain Ajax, Galatian by nationality and Arian by religion, came to Galicia sent by the Goth King Theodoric. This was enough for all Swabians, from the king downwards, to accept the new Arian dogma imposed by Theodoric as a condition for Remismund marrying his daughter, and this they did with the same ease with which they had accepted the previous dogma.[199] This apostasy took place in 502 (era), A.D. 464

Arianism lasted for ninety-six years among the Swabians with little change until Charraric's reign, according to the account given by St. Gregory of Tours, or until Theodomir's time, if we follow the chronicle of St. Isidore.

Gregory of Tours relates their prodigious conversion in the style of something like a pious legend. I transcribe it literally below only because I think it adds something that the arid language of history cannot convey. [200] It reads like this:

> "Oh, my tongue cannot begin to tell of so many wondrous and prodigious events! It happened that the son of Charraric, King of Galicia, was very seriously ill ... and the region was full of lepers. The king and all his subjects [201] followed the fetid Arian sect. But when the king saw his son in grave danger, he spoke to them, saying: 'That Martin of Gaul who is said to have shone in virtue, of what religion was he? Do you know?' And they answered, saying: 'He watched over his flock in the Catholic faith, believing and affirming the equality of essence and omnipotence between the Father, the Son, and the Holy Spirit, and that is why he is now in heaven and watches continually over his people.' And the monarch responded: 'If your words are true, go, my faithful friends, to his temple; take with you many gifts, and if my son regains his health, I shall learn the Catholic faith and I shall follow it.' So he sent to the saint's grave as much silver and gold as the weight of his own son. But oh! love for his old sect remained deep in the King's heart and he did not obtain what he had hoped for! When the envoys returned, they spoke of the wondrous things they had seen at the tomb of Blessed

---

[198]   The Swabian kingdom encompassed, in addition to Galicia, the regions of Asturias, the present-day Portuguese provinces of Tras de Montes and Entre Douro e Minho, and a good part of the kingdom of León and Old Castille.

[199]   "Hujus tempore Ajax natione Galata affectus Apostata Arianus inter Suevos Regis sui auxilio, hostis catholicae fidei et divinae Trinitatis emergit. De Gallicana Gothorum regione hoc pestiferum virus afferens, et totam gentem Suevorum lethalis perfidiae tabe inficiens". *San Isidori Chronicon.*

[200]   *De miraculis Sancti Martini Turonensis*, Lib. 1, chapter 11, in the Turonensis edition by Ruinart, Paris, 1699. See in Appendix the chapter dealing with the Swabians conversion. [Menéndez y Pelayo failed to include this in Appendix. Editor, 1912].

[201]   Swabians only should be read in this remark. The Hispano-Romans in this region were either Catholics or Priscillianists.

Martin and said to the king: 'We do not understand why your son has not been cured'. The king, realising that his son would not be well until he confessed the divinity of the Word, built a temple in honour of St. Martin, and said: 'If I am deemed worthy of receiving the relics of this holy man, I shall believe all that the Catholic priests teach'. And once more he sent his servants with great offerings to sollicit the relics, which were given them, as was the custom. But they said: 'Give us permission to leave them here and take them tomorrow'. And they spread a silk mantle over the grave, and on it they placed the relics. And having kissed them, they said: 'If we meet with the grace of this patron saint, they will weigh twice their weight tomorrow and shall be placed for blessing – asked for with faith'. And they spent the night in vigil. The next morning they weighed them again and the saint's grace had been so copious that their weight had risen as far as the scales could show. The relics were lifted amidst much rejoicing, and the people's songs of praise reached the ears of the city prisoners who, in awe of the soft melody coming from their lips, asked the guards what was the occasion for such jubilation. And the guards said: 'The relics of St. Martin are being taken to Galicia: this is the reason for the singing of hymns'. And the prisoners wept and pleaded with St. Martin to deliver them from their chains. Then the guards, frightened, fled impelled by a supernatural force, and the chains were broken, and a multitude of people were freed from prison to kiss the relics of the saint who had deigned to save them...The envoys carrying the relics, seeing this prodigy, rejoiced in their heart and said: 'Now we know that this holy bishop is benevolent to us, wretched sinners'. So amidst songs of thanksgiving, they sailed in favourable wind, the heavens as their shield, the waves gentle, the air at rest, the sails unfurled, the seas calm, and joyously they reached Galicia. Miraculously, the King's son was made well and came out to receive that treasure... and then, from distant regions and moved by divine inspiration, came a priest called Martin... The King, with his entire household, confessed the unity of the Father, the Son, and of the Holy Spirit, and received the Chrism. And the people were freed from leprosy and so they remain to this day; and all the sick were cured... and the people of Galicia now so burn in the love of Christ that they would all gladly suffer martyrdom if the times of persecution were to come again".

Such is the beautiful tradition that in the sixth century accounted for the sudden conversion of the Swabians to Catholicism. History, through St. Isidore's lips, tells us much less. The convert king was not Charraric but Theodomir, and the catechist was St. Martin Dumiensis (or *Bracarensis*, from Braga), glory of our church though born in Pannonia and educated in the East. He wrote of himself:

Pannoniis genitus, trascendens aequura vasta
Galliciae in gremium divinis nutibus actus.

Father Flórez tried to resolve this contradiction by allowing for two conversions: the King's and his court in times of Charraric, and the other by the entire people during the reign of Theodemir, thanks to the exhortations of the Hungarian St. Martin.[202] Nonetheless St. Isidore's text is straightforward and alludes to one sole conversion: "Multis deinde Suevorum regibus in Ariana haeresi permanentibus, tandem regni potestatem Theudemirus suscepit. Qui confestim, Arianae impietatis errore destructo, Suevos catholicae fidei reddidit, innitente Martino Monasterii Dumiensis episcope, fide et scientia claro: cujus studio et pax ecclesiae ampliata est et multa in Ecclesiasticis disciplines Gallaeciae regionibus instituta".

In any case, St. Martin Dumiensis is the apostle of Galicia. Not only did he convert the Arians (and we can easily assume he had his battles with the Priscillianists too), but he also kept people's superstitions at bay with his most remarkable tract, *De correctione rusticorum*.[203] He was learned in Greek Letters and human philosophy, translated and compiled the sayings of the Egyptian Fathers, and wrote a good number of moral treatises (*Formula vita honestae*, *De moribus*, *Pro repellenda jactancia*, *Exhortatio humilitatis*, *De ira*, etc.), woven in large part with many of Seneca's ideas and dictums. [204] He is the most ancient Senecist of the Iberian Peninsula.

In honour of his apostolic zeal, Venantius Fortunatus from Trevis sang:

Martino servata novo, Gallicia plaude,

sortis apostolicae vir tuus iste fuit.

qui virtute Petrum, praebet tibi dogmate Paulum,

hinc Jacobi tribuens, inde Joannis opem.

Pannoniae ut per hibent veniens e parte Quirinis

est magis effectus Galli-Sueva salus.

St. Martin founded the *Dumiensis* (Doma) monastery, near Braga. The conversion of the Swabians advanced so rapidly that in the aforementioned Council of Braga it was no longer necessary to pronounce new anathemas against Arianism, the Fathers limiting themselves to reading out Vigillius' decree, and from it extract their Canon V which declares the formula for the administration of baptism, "in the name of the Father, and of the Son, and of the Holy Spirit."

The abjuration of the barbarians in Galicia had been so complete! It was a natural triumph of the culture of the Hispano-Roman peoples who, after all, made up the majority and best educated part of the population, especially in that particular region where Priscillianism and its challengers came from (all signs of a vigorous intellectual movement), and where Orosius, Bacchiarius, the Aviti,

---

202   *España Sagrada*, vol. 15, fols. 111 and folwg.

203   Vid. following chapter.

204   The best edition of the works of St. Martin of Braga is that which forms part of volume 15 of *España Sagrada*.

Idacius, Turibius - all worthy predecessors of St. Martin - had written. The Swabians, too, with the innocent candour of neophytes, wished to draw near the Light. King Miro was regarded as a person "with an insatiable thirst for knowledge, running to the fountain springs of moral science", and begging the bishop of Braga for the teachings and consolations of the wisdom of old. [205]

By the time Andeca's usurpation and Leovigild's weapons put paid to the small Galician kingdom, the Roman-Swabian fusion was almost complete. Catholicism, classical-ecclesiastical knowledge and the giant Latin spirit were soon to confront a new and much disputed battle.

Let us turn our attention now to the Arianism of the Visigoths.

Arianism among the Visigoths until Leovigild's time.

When Ataulph entered Barcelona in 416, all Visigoths with him professed unanimously the Arianism they had learnt from Ulphilas. But less barbarous than other invaders, or distracted perhaps by conquests and alliances that took them away from religious persecutions, they did not try to impose their dogmas on the conquered, or follow the Vandals' bloodthirsty example.

In Andalucía, on the other hand, blood ran in torrents everywhere. Their bishops, writes St. Augustine, were "firm and hard at work safeguarding and protecting their flock: they left their churches only after the last of their faithful had evacuated them; many had to abandon their homes, others endured persecution to the point of death, some died through starvation in their besieged cities, others were made prisoners and slaves". In Catalonia and the Gallic Narbonne, however, people enjoyed a relative amount of freedom during the reigns of Ataulph, Sigeric, Walia, Theodored, Turismund and Theodoric, all of whom were working actively on the building of the new empire.

In time, Euric was to see the whole of our Peninsula fall under his crown (save for Galicia and neighbouring lands where the Swabians were to remain for another hundred years, and Aquitaine). But King Euric, the first legislator of their barbarian race, remembered the conquered only to persecute them. In Aquitaine he killed, imprisoned and banished large numbers of clerics and priests.

Alaric, his successor, was more moderate in his severity. He honoured many Roman people with high posts and had the codex *Breviario de Aniano* compiled for his own use. From that moment on, there were laws for both peoples, different for each: one for the Barbarian conqueror, the other for the conquered Latin. However one might criticize them, they did bring some relief when compared to the outright anarchy that had followed the first invasions.

---

[205] "Non ignoro, clementissime Rex, flagrantissimam animi tui sitim sapientiae insatiabiliter poculis inhiare, eaque te ardenter quibus moralis scientiae rivuli manant, fluenta requirere" (Prologue, *Formula vitae honestae*, by St. Martin).

However, Alaric's moderation did not hold back another barbarian leader, the Frank Clodoveus or Clovis, who soon before had converted to Christianity and had begun, under the pretext of religion, to strip the Goths of their possessions in Gaul. Alaric then exiled two bishops, Volusian of Tours and Quintian of Rodez, as suspects of intelligence with the Franks. Clovis swore to banish all heretics from Aquitaine, and in spite of the conciliatory efforts of Theodoric King of Italy, war was declared and Alaric was defeated and killed in Vouglé, near Poitiers.

Amalaric came to the throne following Gesalaic's brief reign and Theodoric's regency. His marriage to Clotilde, Clovis' daughter, was to be a new seed of much discord and misfortune for the Visigoth kingdom. Clotilde was Catholic, and Amalaric was determined to harass her on account of her faith. He forbade her to worship and maltreated her verbally and physically. According to French tradition, the offended Queen sent a cloth stained with her own blood to her four brothers Childebert, Clotarius, Clodomir and Thierry as an indication of the blows, violence and abuse she had endured at the hands of her husband. Childebert, King of Paris, and Clotarius of Soissons, moved to her aid and retaliated. Procopius relates that Amalaric was crushed in battle and killed, we know not where; or ran through by a lance when he was going to take refuge in a church, as Gregory of Tours believes; or decapitated by his own soldiers in Narbonne, according to St. Isidore. Childebert returned to Paris with his sister as well as a rich booty (not an insignificant part of which was silverware taken from churches).

Two wretched wars had by now taken Visigoth might to the edge of ruin. Cities in the Narbonne region were opening their doors to the Franks because, as Catholics, they were seen as liberators. Theudis' strong hand managed to contain the tearing apart of the kingdom, and neither he nor Theudisel, Agila, or Atanagild - who referred to Spain as 'the Imperial Greeks' and of whom St. Isidore says "Fidem Catholicam occulte tenuit, et Christianis valde benevolus fuit" [206] - committed acts of hostility against the Spanish faith.

Up until the year 570, at the start of Leovigild's reign, there were no persecutions by Arians against Catholics beyond that initially carried out by Euric, and this one limited to the Aquitaine, as far as we can now gather. Nor did those monarchs inhibit the celebration of numerous provincial councils such as those at Agde, Tarragona, Lérida, Valencia, Gerona, and the Second Council of Toledo. The Visigoths were not fanatics. They were, moreover, too small in number to counter the unanimous beliefs of the conquered people who, little by little, were impressing upon them their customs and their language.

---

[206]   Some suppose these words were added later to the *Chronicon* because they are missing from many other manuscripts.

Arianism in Leovigild's time. The last struggle

Leovigild was a man of lofty mind and firm will, but he found himself in the worst possible situation a leader of his people could have the misfortune to face. On the one hand, he aspired to unity, and this he certainly obtained, territorially speaking, with the conquest of the Swabian kingdom and the submission of the Basques. He understood well however that political unity could not come from the conquerors who, as all barbarians, were people prone to disunity and extremist individualism. For this reason, Leovigild organised his mighty state on the lines of Roman organisation which in time brought about the assimilation of both races.

The empire, in the manner of Diocletian or Constantine, was the ideal that impelled Leovigild to copy its pomp and circumstance in his court: the palace hierarchy, the purple and the crown, the title *'Flavius'* with which his son Recared was the first to adorn himself and which was preserved diligently by all his successors. It is truly an odd title because of its classical reminiscences: suffice it to indicate that the barbarians, far from destroying ancient civilisation, as those who would see an abyss between the Roman world and our own suppose, were in fact overcome, subjugated, changed by a civilisation that dazzled and overwhelmed them, even in its most lamentable decadence. The empire, the last expression of the classical world, was an arbitrary, even absurd institution; but it had fulfilled its providential mandate by extending unity of civilisation to the ends of the known world, and by approving through the tyrant and fratricidal Caracalla, the unity of rights and duties, and the universal right to citizenship.

Another type of unity, more intimate, was at the same time being carved out by Christianity. The two tendencies came together in Constantine's time and the empire embraced Christianity as its natural ally. Julian strove to separate them and was defeated. Theodosius placed his sword at the service of the Church and put an end to paganism. The empire perished soon after - its dream greater than its reality. But the classical spirit regenerated by Christianity's influence - that spirit of law and of unity in culture - lived on through the darkness of the middle centuries, informing in southern countries all civilising culture which in the essential is Roman civilisation, in law as it is in science and art, and not Germanic, or barbarian, or chivalrous, as it was fashionable to imagine it. This is why both Renaissance periods, the thirteenth and the fifteenth centuries, were most *natural* events and did not overturn but rather aided the flow of ideas. And in fact, this idea of Renaissance was served by all the great men of the Middle Ages, from the Ostrogoth Theodoric to Charlemagne, from St. Isidore who recompiled ancient knowledge to St. Thomas who tried to Christianise Aristotle, from Gregory VII to Alfonso *El Sabio* (the Wise). There have never been *solutions to continuity* in history.

Leovigild, his eye fixed on political unity and, who knows, perhaps on social and racial matters as well, stumbled across an invincible obstacle: religious differences. In trying to do away with this difference and overpower it from an

Arian stand, he set himself up as champion of the minority, of the barbarian and uncultured element, going backwards rather than forwards. Not only did he lose the battle, something to be expected, but he lived to witness the germ of doubt and discord penetrate his own palace, and soon after his own family turn against him in open rebellion. Finding himself caught in the middle, Leovigild, who was not a tyrant, nor an oppressor, nor a fanatic, but who on the contrary had more magnanimity than any of his people's princes, found himself forced into much bloody violence. Such violations have, with the passing of time and with the concrete social conditions of his era now forgotten, made his memory execrable, although he was much respected by St. Isidore and other writers closer than we are to that wretched struggle which indirectly (and as a reaction) brought about his son Recared's official disavowal of Arianism and religious unity to the Peninsula.

The history of this last conflict has been written many times, and I shall touch upon it here only briefly.

Hermenegild, Leovigild's first-born and heir to the crown, married Ingunda, a Catholic princess, daughter of our own Brunechilda and the Frankish King Sigebert. Frankish marriages, as we know, were always open to calamities. Ingunda endured the same insulting treatment Clotilde had received, but not from her husband this time, but from her mother-in-law, Queen Gosuinda, a fervent and zealous Arian, who stubbornly persisted on re-baptising her daughter-in-law and, as Gregory of Tours writes, perhaps with some exaggeration, hit her and even trod and trampled over her. However, these outrages yielded the opposite results Gosuinda had hoped for. Not only did Ingunda persist in the faith, but her husband Hermenegild was also moved to embrace it, touched by the exhortations and teaching of the great prelate of Seville, St. Leander, Severianus' son, of the province of Cartagena.

Leovigild came to know of his son's conversion with much grief. Hermenegild had taken the name of John in baptism wanting to do away with any traces of his barbarian lineage, even in name. His father summoned him to appear before him, but he did he not come. Instead, he rose in arms against him helped by the Byzantine Greeks who lived in the Cartagena region and the Swabians of Galicia. To this act of "rebellion and tyranny" (the *Biclarensis'* words), [207] Leovigild responded in the year 583 by gathering up his people and surrounding Seville, where his son held court. The siege lasted until the following year. Miro, king of the Swabians, who had come to Hermenegild's aid, died during this siege. [208] The *imperiales* deserted their camps and finally,

---

[207]   "Leovigildus Rex exercitum ad expugnandum tyrannun filium colligit...Leovigildus Rex civitatem Hispalensem congregato exercitu obsidet, et rebelem filium gravi obsidione concludit" (*Chronicon*, Biclarense, *España Sagrada*, vol. VI)

[208]   "Anno primo Mauricii Imperatoris, qui est Leovigildi regis XV an. Leovigildus Rex civitatem Hispalensem congregato exercitu obsidet, et rebellem filium gravi obsidione concludit; in cujus solatio Miro Suevorum Rex ad expugnandam Hispalim advenit, ibique diem clausit extremum..." Biclarensis.

Leovigild, aggravating the plight of the besieged from Italica whose walls he had rebuilt, procured the city's surrender partly due to hunger, partly to force, and partly by bending the course of the Betis river.[209] All other cities and garrisons under Hermenegild's command surrendered, and finally Córdoba itself, where the prince had taken refuge. It was there at Córdoba that Hermenegild, trusting his brother Recared's word, placed himself in his father's hands. Leovigild banished him to Valencia (according to the Abbot of Valclara, whose account I prefer to follow here, because he was a Spaniard himself and a contemporary of the time he is writing. St. Gregory of Tours places this exile in Osset). But Hermenegild would not rest. Once again he rose up on a seditious war supported by the Hispano-Romans and Byzantines until, again, he was defeated by his father at Mérida and imprisoned in Tarragona. He expatiated his sins in 585. He was to receive from the hands of Sisbert the palm of martyrdom because of his refusal to receive communion with an Arian bishop. 'Hermenegildus in urbe Tarraconensi a Sisberto interficitur', notes the chronicler from Velclara dryly as he relates this war, scandalous on both sides, with an impartiality worthy of a true Catholic. But the martyrdom Hermenegild suffered by confessing the faith erased his early misdeeds in the mind of the Hispano-Roman people who soon after started venerating the memory of this Gothic prince who, though not of their race and family, had generously embraced the cause of the oppressed against the oppressors. This veneration was confirmed by Pontiffs; Pope Sixtus V extended the feast of St. Hermenegild to all Spanish Churches to be celebrated on 14th April. [210] It is singular however that St. Isidore remembers the King of Seville only to say in praise of Leovigild that he subjugated his son, who "tyrannised" the empire ("Filium imperiis suis tyrannizantem, obsessum superavit"). To me, this shows how little preoccupied and how little fanatical were those Doctors of our Church: not even in aid of doctrinal accuracy would they consent to the slightest deviation from the moral law!

Ingunda, Hermenegild's wife, now in hiding, crossed over to the African coast where she died, and her son Amalaric was taken by his father's servants to Hermenegild's old ally, Mauritius, King of Constantinople. Hermenegild's rebellion allowed Leovigild two victorious wars: one against the Swabians whose dominance he thoroughly crushed, and another against the Franks, inflicting upon their king Gontran many defeats on land and sea.

Leovigild's persecution of Catholics was harsh. But let us nonetheless recognise that he had sought to find, albeit erroneously, a reconciliation similar

---

[209]   "Interea Leovigildus Rex supradictam civitatem nunc fame, nunc ferro, nunc Baetis conclusione, omnino conturbat…Leovigildus muros Ithalicae antiqua civitatis restaurat: quae res maximum impedimentum hispalense populo exhibuit". Biclarensis, *ut supra*.

[210]   In addition to the Biclarensis' account of St. Hermenegild, see St. Gregory the Great, *Dialogues*, lib. 3, chapter 31; the Turonensis' *Historia eclesiástica*, books 5 and 6, and *Milagros*, etc., book 3 chapter 12. All these events, as those mentioned in the previous chapter, are well known to us so I will not prolong the narrative here.

to the *Interim* that the emperor Charles V was to promulgate in the sixteenth century for his States in Germany. Attempts by secular kings and princes to meddle in theological issues and matters of the Church have always been useless and futile, if not dangerous. In the year 580, Leovigild called a meeting of Arian bishops. They proceeded to make some changes to their sect's beliefs in order to make them more acceptable to Catholics; for example, ordering not to re-baptise those who might have come over to the sect, but to *purify* them (as they called it) by the imposition of hands and Communion. Moreover, instead of the old formula of glorification they used without the conjunction, i.e. "Gloria Patri, Filio, Spiritui Sancto" [211] (to do away with the equality between the three divine persons), they substituted another, also erroneous, but one they fancied would sound better, "Gloria Patri per filium in Spiritu Sancto". Accordingly, they wrote a confession of faith with this Arian and Macedonian formula which Leovigild obstinately insisted on imposing to all his subjects by fair means or foul.

But the Catholic Hispano-Romans resisted it, and heroically so. The most illustrious bishops of that time were thrown out of their sees: St. Leander of Seville who sought asylum in Constantinople; St. Fulgentius, of Ecija; Licinianus, of Cartagena; Fronimius, of Egde, in the Languedoc; Mausona, finally, the most famous of the Mérida prelates. His biographer, [212] the deacon Paulus, gives us a lengthy account of what happened to this holy man: he refused to subscribe to the *Formula fidei* of the Arian meeting held in Toledo, and not intimidated by fear or threats, when Leovigild sent a heretic and impostor bishop called Sunna to Mérida, he did not hesitate to challenge him to a public disputation in the church of St. Eulalia.

Sunna, as Paulus of Mérida describes him, was a "homo funestus, vultu teterrimus, cujus erat frons torva, truces oculi, aspectus odibilis, motus horrendus, eratque mente sinister, moribus pravus, lingua mendax, verbis obscoenus, forinsecus turgidus, intrinsecus vacuus, estrorsus elatus, introrsus inanis, foris inflatus, interius cunctis virtutibus evacuatos, utrobique deformis, de bonis indignus, de pessimis opulentus, delictis obnoxius, perpetuae mortu nimis ultroneus". In a word, Lucifer himself.

Mausona was at prayer before the Virgin of Mérida for three days and three nights before entering into battle and "armed with celestial consolation" he went down to the portico where the Catholics gathered on one side, and Sunna and his Arians friends on the other. The disputation commenced (the *debate,* as we say today) "ingens verborum certamen", Paulus says; and Mausona, a genius in eloquence as well as doctrine, easily reduced his adversary to silence. A prayer as sweet as honey was on the lips of the bishop of Mérida: "Nam tantam gratiam in ejus labiis eo die Dominus conferre dignatus est, ut nunquam

---

[211]   Vid. Letter of Vigillius to Profuturus.

[212]   Vitae Patrum Emeritensium, *España Sagrada*, vol. 13, pp. 335 and following, chapters, 10-15

eum quisquam viderit prius tam claro eloquio facundum…licet semper docuerit ore eloquentissimo". Then, as Holy Scripture says and Paulus happily repeats, "the righteous saw and rejoiced and all iniquity sealed their lips, for the Lord closes the mouth of those who speak iniquity". And whilst the Arians went numb, the Catholics prostrated themselves and raised voices of jubilation to the Lord, singing: "Quis similis tui in Diis, Domine? Quis similis tibi, et non est secundum opera tua?" And with this triumph, they entered the Basilica praising the holy virgin Eulalia for so exalting her servants and reducing their enemies to nothingness ("Qua in sublime erexerat famulos, et ad nihilum suos redegerat inimicus").

The evil spirit (Paulus continues to tell us) moved Leovigild to call Mausona to Toledo and to demand from him St. Eulalia's mantle, to which the bishop vigorously replied: "Compertum tibi sit quia cor meum sordibus Arianae superstitionis nunquam maculabo: tam perverso dogmate mentem meam nunquam inquinabo: tunicam Dominae meae Eulaliae sacrilegis haereticorum manibus polluendam, vel etiam summis digitis contrectandam, numquam tradam". In vain did Leovigild command his people to go to Mérida and search for the tunic in the treasure of the church: they could not find it because Mausona was wearing it himself concealed in his own body. When the king threatened him with exile he replied: "If you know of any place where God is not, send me there" ("et ideo obsecro te ut si nosti regionem aliquam, ubi Deus non est, illic me exilio tradi jubeas"). Then they mounted him on an untamed steed to break him, but the brute quieted down as it felt his weight. Leovigild, frightened by this prodigious event, allowed him to retire to a monastery, and it is noted that after three years he let him return to his see, warned by a voice in his sleep that warned him: "Redde servum meum".

These and many other beautiful oral traditions are written in the *Leyendarium* of Paulus of Mérida, and though no one holds them to be articles of faith, they are however from an eighth-century author [213] and give us a living and faithful view of the times: of that last and desperate struggle between the two religions and the two peoples. It is pleasant to attend in spirit to that kind of theological duel in the atrium of Roman Mérida.

Leovigild barely shed any Christian blood save for that of his own son. Gregory of Tours accuses him of having tormented a priest whose name he does not mention. He enriched the Treasury by confiscating the revenues of churches and, seeing that this was an easy way of taxation, he applied it to all, Catholic and Arian alike.

The Spanish Church remained immovable in the midst of this squall. Only one bishop apostasized, Vincentius of Saragossa.[214] The other bishops did not look kindly on this apostasy. Severus, bishop of Malaga, whom we shall

---

[213]   However, he ends his history with Renovatus, a prelate from the seventh century.

[214]   "Vincentium Caesaraugustanum de Episcopo Apostatam factum et tanquam e coelo in infernum projectum". *St. Isidori Chronicon*, era 606.

soon see with Licinianus combating the materialist ideas of another bishop, wrote a book, now lost, against the Saragossan bishop reprimanding gravely him for prevaricating in the hour of trial.[215]

The tenacity of the resistance, the remorse, perhaps, for the death of Hermenegild, brought the Visigoth king to a better understanding in the last days of his life. He died a Catholic in 587 having repented for his past errors, as Gregory and the (*Gesta Francorum*) relate. The public disavowal of Arianism by his son and successor Recared seems to confirm this. Our historians say nothing of his father's conversion but Hermenegild's blood proved to be fertile irrigation for the soil of our Church.

Apocryphal writings. One bishop's materialism.

People's faith may have been purified in persecution but Christians were nonetheless being constantly exposed to real dangers, often due to the levity and gullibility of some of their prelates. We know of the errors of two of them, though only one name has come down to us through Licinianus' precious letters – one of the most curious monuments of Spanish learning from that time.

Licinianus, bishop of *Carthago Spartaria*, that is, Cartagena, not Carthage of Africa as some have imagined, [216] was one of the bishops Leovigild sent to exile. It is known that he died tragically in Constantinople, poisoned by his enemies.[217] Only three of this illustrious gentleman's letters have come down to us: the second and third are of interest for our study here.

The second of these letters was addressed to Vincentius, bishop of Ibiza, who had accepted as authentic a letter "signed by Christ" - supposedly fallen from the sky. This type of fiction is not unique in the history of the church. It belongs to the same genre of apocryphals as the *Letter from the Redeemer to Abgar of Edessa*, or the *Letter from the Virgin to the citizens of Messina*. There were Gnostic sects actually founded on fictions such as these, notices supposedly fallen to earth from the heavens by express providence. The author of this particular one, the knowledge of which spread fast throughout Ibiza, could not however have been a Gnostic: more probably a Jew, or perhaps a Judaizer or a pharisaic Christian, because the document continually exaggerates the precept of rest on Sunday and extends it even to necessities such as preparation of daily food; it prohibits travelling anywhere or even performing an act of generosity on Sundays. The bishop of Cartagena, right on the mark, quipped: "Let us hope that Christians, since they no longer frequent church as they should on that day, do at least something of benefit for their souls by doing good works, and not just go dancing!" The letter from heaven above, said to have fallen on the altar

---

[215]   "Edidit libellum unum adversus Vincentium" St. Isidore, *De viris illustribus.*

[216]   "Licinianus Carthaginis Spartariae Episcopus" says, expressly, St. Isidore, the only ancient writer to speak of him.

[217]   "Veneno, ut ferunt, extinctus ab aemulis" St. Isidore, *De scriptoribus ecclesiasticis.*

of St. Peter at Rome, was read by this bishop from the pulpit in order to reach all the faithful. Licinianus, of course, reprimands Vincentius for the foolish ease with which he had accepted this writing, in which to boot, he says, "one finds neither wholesome doctrine nor one single grammatically correct sentence". [218]

Of greater significance is the third letter, *in qua ostenditur Angelos et animas rationales esse spiritus sive totius corporis expertes* [219] addressed to the deacon Epiphanius and signed by Licinianus jointly with Severus, bishop of Málaga. It happened that one bishop whose name his challengers had the courtesy or the reverence to omit, had denied the spirituality of the rational soul and of angels, asserting that everything outside of God was corporeal. A materialist assertion could hardly go any further. Those who now consider this materialist approach as the new rationale for looking at the world can count a sixth century anonymous Spanish bishop in the sad catalogue of their predecessors. Of course, to be fair, the question was not as clear then as it is now. For though all the Fathers of the Latin and Greek Church agreed on the spirituality and immortality of the soul, one cannot deny that some had explained it without the necessary degree of clarity and scientific precision, and this could offer not only a pretext for error but a weapon of attack. Both Tertullian and Arnobius got lost on this question. [220] But when others speak of the *matter* of the soul, this should be understood always as referring to a most *fine* substance, different in any case from physical matter. Moreover, for them the soul was not the rational principle they called *pneuma* but the vital principle referred to as *psyche*.

The bishops of Cartagena and Málaga offer two types of arguments to counter the error of this unknown bishop, the first based on authority, the other on rational argument. I shall draw attention to the second.

"Every living body", says Licinianus, "consists of three elements: it is absurd to say that the substance of the soul is made up of something else. If the soul is made in the image of God, it cannot be body". The materialists of the day maintained that 'the soul is corporeal because it has to be contained physically in some place" and Licinianus and Severus counter this belief with this admirable reply:

> "Pray tell us where the soul can be contained. If it is contained in the body, the containing body has to be of a quality higher than the soul contained. It is absurd to suggest that the body exceeds the soul in excellence; consequently, the soul is what contains and the body is what is contained. If the soul is the one governing and vivifying the body,

---

[218] See Licinianus' letter in *España Sagrada*, vol. 5, appendix 4, p. 425, and a summary in the Appendix to this chapter.

[219] See Flórez, vol. V, Appendix 4, p. 421, and our Appendix .[Note from Editor, 1912: Neither this letter by Licinianus nor the previous one, were included in the Appendix by Menéndez y Pelayo. See A. Bonilla's *Historia de la Filosofía española*, I, 426, where epistle 3 can be read].

[220] Tertullian resolutely affirms the corporeality of the soul (*De anima*)

then it must the one that is doing the containing. It cannot be limited by the body it contains, as is the case with a barrel full of water... it is all outward and inward as much in the superior part of the body as in the inferior. If you touch with a finger another extremity of your body, the whole of the soul feels the touch. The physical senses are five but the soul is not divided by senses: the whole soul hears, the whole soul sees, the whole soul smells, the whole soul touches, the whole soul tastes, and when it moves the body from one place to another, it is not moved itself. For the same reason, we distinguish clearly three natures as well: the nature of God, which is neither in time or place; that pertaining to the rational spirit, which is in time but not in place; and that of matter, which is in time and in place. But one might retort to this: 'The soul cannot exit outside the body: its *quantity*, therefore, is limited by it'. 'If that were so (Licinianus continues), the taller and more physically developed one is, the wiser he ought to be, and what we often see is the contrary: because the quantity of the soul is not measured by that of the body. If the soul were according to the body's size, how, being so small, would it contain such great ideas? How can we contain in our mind images of cities, mountains, and rivers, of all things created of heaven and earth? What space is there big enough for the soul to encompass and condense such a large space? But since it is not body, it contains all places (*inlocaliter*) in a non-localised way. If a glass is contained in another glass, the smaller has to be the one inside, the bigger the one outside. How then can the soul which contains such greatness be smaller than the body? Hence, we affirm that the soul has *a given* quality but no quantity; and that God has neither quantity nor quality. Since the soul is not equal to God, it has quality; since it is not body, it lacks quantity. And we believe with the Holy Catholic Faith that God, an incorporeal Being, made some things incorporeal and others material, and subjected the irrational to the rational, and the non-intelligible to the intelligible, the unjust to the just, evil to good, and mortal to immortal".

Where can we find in the whole of the sixth century a page on psychology that is comparable to the one I have just translated faithfully word for word? Such was the anthropological doctrine professed by what we now identify as the Fathers of Toledo and the School of Seville. What were the sources of these doctrines? Licinianus and Severus tell us: first, St. Augustine, who had defined the soul as a substance endowed with reason and disposed to govern the body; second, and with more clarity, bishop Mamertus Claudianus, a learned scholar, who in his book *De incorporalitate animae* stated that "the soul is the life of the soul", and that *reason* "is its substantial being". But these were seeds. The sum and substance of this doctrine we owe to Licinianus and Severus themselves, just as we owe them that clear and peremptory demonstration of the unity and subjectivity of sensation, and that admirable division of Being according to the categories of time and place, of quantity and quality; as we owe them, finally, the great spiritual concept of the "containing, uncontained, soul", a kind of rational *atmosphere* in which the body lives and by which it is governed.

This concept, preserved by the Spanish Doctors, will pass later to the Scholastics of the Middle Ages. St. Thomas will formulate it again, albeit subject to a Peripatetic criterion, according to which the "soul is the first *entelechia* of a physical body which has life potentially", or as the Angelic Doctor from Aquin said, "the act, or the substantial form" of the body – ultimately a concept identical to that of Licinianus but more open to misinterpretation, conforming almost to Plato's in his *Primer Alcibiades*.[221] But let it be plain that for St. Thomas, as for Licinianus, the non-localisation of the soul is an axiom, and one and the other consider the spirit as cause of all phenomena and principle of life.

Cartesianism broke this harmony when it divided the human being in two and took the opposition of matter and spirit to extremes. From then on they were to form two separate kingdoms. Indeed, to explain their interaction it was necessary to conceive of new systems, and there emerged theories that localised the soul in the brain or some of its parts, ignoring or completely disregarding the qualities of the spirit. The logical outcome was that materialism began to throw out the soul, that uncomfortable guest, and though immaterial, they subjected it to the condition of matter. Then came what is now called *Positive Philosophy* affirming the existence of two parallel orders of phenomena but neither acknowledging nor denying the existence of the essences they are to be referred to. And to this day, if we are to avoid the logical consequences of this so-called *modest* science (though it is both the haughtiest and at the same time the lowest, poorest and most contemptible science human thought has ever come up with), we shall have to retrace our steps and go back to our wise compatriot Licinianus, and with him see in the *containing* and *uncontained, substantial form of the body*'s animical substance the principle and basis of all our change. Only then shall we become convinced that there is something, much in fact, to be learnt from Spanish scholarship, and from the most obscure period at that!

Licinianus in his reply showed himself to be a learned and profound Biblicist as he gathered together and elucidated texts relative to the rational soul from the Sacred Scriptures, and on this as on the other points gained a marked victory over the *ignotus patriarch* of our Spanish materialists.

The Visigoths renounce Arianism. Third Council of Toledo.
Heterodox coup attempts and Witeric's reaction.

The radical changes soon to take place in the religious conditions of the Visigoth people were evident from the first days of King Recared's reign.

---

[221]   Αὐτό γε τό τοῦ σώματος ἄργον ὡμολογήσαμεν ἄνθρωπον ειτναι...

Catholicism by this time counted innumerable proselytes inside the palace, such as ambassador Agilan, converted in France by the Saint of Tours. Recared himself must have been inclined to the True Faith in his father's lifetime, and if Leovigild died a Catholic - which is credible -, along with the bitter wound left by Hermenegild's torture, it was natural that the exhortations of the catechist St. Leander should now illumine Recared's spirit with the light of grace. He attended lengthy controversial debates between Catholic and Arian bishops before receiving baptism (which took place ten months into his reign), so in no way must we judge his conversion hasty or abrupt. The king's abjuration carried with it that of the whole people, and for added solemnity in 589 (627) a Third Council of Toledo was called. Sixty-three bishops and six vicars attended this national synod, five from Spanish provinces (Tarragona, Cartagena, Betis, Lusitania, Galicia) and one from Narbonne. The venerable Mausona, from Mérida, one of the prelates who had the most influence over the monarch's decision, presided. The council opened on 4th May, and Recared addressed the Fathers in this way:

"I believe you are mindful, reverend priests, that you are here assembled to re-establish the discipline of the Church. And since of late the heresy that has threatened the Catholic Church did not allow for synods to be celebrated, God, Whose Will it is to put this obstacle behind us, is counselling and exhorting us to restore the canons and the ecclesiastical tradition of old. Let us all rejoice in seeing that by the grace of God and for our glory, discipline may return to its initial source. I would advise and exhort you, before you commence, that you prepare yourselves with fasting, vigil and prayer, that canonical order, gone astray in the course of time and forgotten in our age may, by divine grace, be made manifest to your eyes".[222]

When the Fathers heard the king - a heretic until then - speak in this way, they broke into words of thanksgiving and acclamation. And having fasted for three days they gathered on the 7th of May. Recared, after accompanying the bishops in prayer, addressed them once more with these words:

"We believe it is not unknown to your excellencies how long the Arian error has been dominant in Spain, and that not many days after the death of our father we joined the Catholic Faith, from which you

[222]   "Non incognitum reor esse vobis, reverendissimi Sacerdotes, quod propter restaurandam disciplinae ecclesiasticae formam, ad nostrae vos serenitatis praesentiam decoraverim, et quia decursis retro temporibus haeresis inminens in tota Ecclesia catholica agere synodica negotia denegavit, Deus cui placuit per nos ejusdem haeresis obicem depellere, admonuit instituta de more ecclesiastica reparare. Ergo sit vobis jucunditatis, sit gaudii quod mos canonicus prospectu Dei per nostram gloriam ad paternos reducitur terminos. Prius tamen admoneo pariter et exhortor, jejuniis vos et vigiliis atque orationibus operam dare, ut ordo canonicus, quem a sacerdotibus sensibus detraxerat longa ac diuturna oblivio quam aetas nostra se nescire fatetur, divino dono vobis rursum patefiat". (Aguirre, *Collectio*, etc. vol. II).

would have derived much joy. It is for this reason, reverend Fathers, that we have brought you together in synod, that you may thank God for a new flock coming into the fold of Christ. What we have to say to you of the faith, and hope you will embrace it, is written here in the document we put before you. Let it be read and examined in council, that our glory, illumined by the testimony of faith, may shine forever".[223]

In a loud voice a notary lector read Recared's profession of faith by which he declared to follow the doctrine of the four General Councils of Nicea, Constantinople, Ephesus and Chalcedon, and reproved the errors of Arius, Macedonius, Nestorius, Eutyches and all other heresiarchs condemned by the Church until that time. The Fathers approved it with fervent thanksgiving to "God the Father, the Son and the Holy Spirit, Who deigned to concede peace and unity to His Church, bringing all into one only flock with one Shepherd through the apostolic Recared who marvellously glorified God on earth". The king's abjuration was then followed by that of Queen Badda, and the Arian bishops and clerics present declared that "following their most glorious monarch, they anathematised the old heresy with all their heart". The council pronounced the following condemnations:

"Whosoever persists in preserving the Arian faith and communion, or does not reject it with all his heart, let him be anathema.

Whosoever denies that the Son of God and our Lord Jesus Christ is eternal and consubstantial with the Father, begotten of the essence of the Father without beginning, let him be anathema.

Whosoever does not believe in the Holy Spirit, or denies that he proceeds from the Father and the Son, and is co-eternal and consubstantial with the Son and the Father, let him be anathema.

Whosoever does not make a distinction of Persons between Father, Son and Holy Spirit, or contrariwise, does not recognise the unity of essence in God, let him be anathema.

He who asserts that the Son and the Holy Spirit are inferior in divinity to the Father, or that they are creatures, let him be anathema.

He who says that the Son of God does not know that which the Father knows, let him be anathema.

---

[223]   "Non credimus vestram latere sanctitatem, quanto tempore in errore Arrianorum laborasset Hispania et non multos post decessum genitoris nostri dies, quibus nos nostra beatitudo fidei sanctae catholicae cognovit esse sociatos, credimus generaliter magnum et aeternum gaudium habuisse; et ideo, venerandi Patres, ad hanc vos peragendam congregari decrevimus Synodum, ut de omnibus nuper advenientibus ad Christum, ipsi aeternas Deo gratias deferatis. Quidquid vero verbis apud sacerdotium vestrum nobis agendum erat de fide atque spe nostra, quam gessimus, in hunc tomum, conscripta atque allegata, nota facimus. Relegatur enim in medio vestri, et in judicio synodali examinatus, per omne successivum tempus gloria nostra ejusdem fidei testimonio decorata clarescat".

He who supposes a beginning in the Son and the Holy Spirit, let him be anathema.

He who dares assert that the Son of God, in his divinity, is visible or passible, let him be anathema.

He who does not believe that the Holy Spirit is God, true and omnipotent, as are the Father and the Son, let him be anathema.

Whosoever follows another faith and communion from that of the Universal Church defined in the Canons of Nicea, Constantinople, Ephesus, Chalcedon, let him be anathema.

Whosoever separates and distinguishes the Father, the Son and the Holy Spirit in honour, glory or divinity, let him be anathema.

Whosoever shall not say: 'Glory be to the Father, and to the Son, and to the Holy Spirit', let him be anathema.

He who judges as good the sacrilegious act of re-baptising, or practices it, let him be anathema.

Whosoever shall not reject and condemn with all his heart the *counciliabulum* held at Rimini, let him be anathema.

Therefore, let all things that the Roman Church condemns be condemned in Heaven as on earth, and let there be admitted on earth and in Heaven all things that she admits, under the reign of our Lord Jesus Christ, to Whom with the Father and the Holy Spirit may honour and glory be given for ever and ever. Amen."

Upon this profession of faith, signed by all, the converted bishops were admitted to the last deliberations of the council, almost all on issues of discipline.

We shall here point only to a few: canon II, which establishes the recitation of the Creed during the Mass; canon V, which forbids converted Arian clerics to cohabit with their wives; number IX, according to which the Arian churches and their wealth were to be under the control of the bishop of whose diocese they were parishes; and canon XVI, which asks priests, judges and nobles to bring an end to the idolatrous cult which had burgeoned in large parts of Spain, above all in Galicia or, as some read, in Gaul (Narbonne). In the following chapter we shall see what this return to idolatry meant, taking into account two other canons linked to this one, and explain it.

Eight Arian bishops signed the abjuration with Recared. All have Gothic names, not one single Hispano-Roman among them. They were Ugno, Murila, Ubilisgiculo, Sumila, Gardingo, Becilla, Argiovito y Froisclo, and occupied the sees of Barcelona, Palencia, Valencia, Viseo, Tuy, Lugo, Oporto and Tortosa. Five of them were intruders since there were Catholic bishops in those dioceses. They too signed at the council, which respected everyone's privileges, the Arians preserving their titles for the sake of peace, until there new sees fell vacant.

Recared validated the decrees of the council which was brought to a close with a homily by St. Leander, a fragment of eloquence worthy of St. John

Chrysostom which corresponds to the magnitude and gravity of the event being celebrated.[224]

"The novelty of the feast itself," said the Metropolitan of Seville, "indicates this to be the most solemn of all… Many have been newly converted, and just as in other festivities celebrated by the Church we rejoice for the benefits already received, here today she rejoices for the inestimable treasure she has just procured. New people have been born to the Church. Those who before troubled us with their harshness, console us now with their faith. A past calamity is now an occasion for gladness. When they oppressed and confronted us, we wept; but our weeping turned what before their conversion was a weight on our shoulders into what is now our crown... the Catholic Church grows throughout the whole world; it advances through the society of all peoples… of her can the divine words be said: "Multae filiae congregaverunt divitias, tu vero supergressa es universas…" Be glad, rejoice, Church of God; be glad and rise to form one whole body in Christ. Dress yourself with fortitude. Fill yourself with jubilation, for your sorrows have now turned into joy, your habits of pain into rejoicing. In danger, you grow; in persecution, you flourish. Your beneficent Bridegroom will not let you be dishonoured without giving you back, many times over, what has been taken from you in bringing your enemies to your feet … Weep not, neither be sad that some have temporarily separated themselves from you, for you shall regain them aplenty. Have hope and a robust faith, and you will see the promise fulfilled. For it is written in the truth of the Gospel: "Oportebat Christum mori pro gente, et non tantum pro gente, sed ut filios Dei qui errant dispersi, congregaret in unum". The Church knows from the foretelling of the Prophets, from the evangelical oracles and the apostolic documents, how sweet charity is, how delectable unity. She preaches concord among peoples and sighs for the unity of all. She sows goods of peace and charity. Rejoice in the Lord, for your longing has come to an end. You are now seeing the fruits that for so long, amidst tears and prayer, you had dreamed of. And after frost, rain and snow, you now contemplate, in the sweetness of spring, the fields full of flowers, and in the vine, clusters of grapes… The Lord said: "I have other sheep that are not of this flock and it is good that they come in, that there may be one flock and one shepherd". You are now witnessing this promise being fulfilled. Can anyone doubt that the whole world will be converted to Christ and enter the One and only Church? "Praedicabitur hoc

---

[224] *Collectio Canonum Ecclesiae Hispaniae*, ed. Of Biblioteca Real, col. 359. Some have expressed doubts about the authenticity of this precious document, but only out of love for contrariety and without any plausible basis whatever. Cardenal Baronius writes a propos of this homily: "Stylo inculto, veluti rudi rastro vertit auri fodinam...simplici enim et impolito stylo (ut saeculi hujus barbarie silvescentes conditio ferebat) sed divina scientia valde referto et sapientia mirifice exornato, instar arboris, licet cortice durioris, tamen pomorum pendulorum foecunditate pulcherrimae." But *(in Baronius' peace)* the *inculto* in St. Leander' oration is not the *style* but the *terminology,* nor can the seventh century be called barbarous, least of all seventh century Spain. Mariana re-edited this homily, preserving the thoughts, into a more classical and elegant phrase. It can be read in his Latin *Historia* as well as his *Castilian.*

Evangelium regni in universo orbe, in testimonium omnibus gentibus..."
Charity will bring together those whom discord of tongues has separated...
There will be no part of the Earth, no barbarous people to whom the light of
Christ will not reach... One church, one heart, one soul! From one man did all
human lineage come that mankind may think and love and be *one*... Of this
Church said the Prophet: "My house shall be called a house of prayer for all
people" and "The mountain of the house of the Lord shall be made ready on
the top of the mountains, and it shall be exalted above the hills; and all nations
shall flow unto it. And many people shall go, and say: Come, let us go up to the
mountain of the Lord and to the house of the God of Jacob". The mountain is
Christ, the house of the God of Jacob is His Church where all people will
gather. So says Isaiah: "Arise, shine upon Jerusalem, because your light is
coming, and the glory of the Lord has shone for you; and the people will come
to your light, and the nations to the splendour of your Orient. Turn your eyes
and look: all are now gathered and have come to you, and the sons of the
strangers will build your walls, and their kings will serve as your ministers...'"

I have to shorten this sublime effusion - this song of triumph of the
Spanish Church. Unfortunately, in my slovenly critical style, I must add some
reflexions of what is now labelled *philosophy of history* on that marvellous episode
that was the conversion of the Visigoths to Catholicism. What words, and mine
at that, will not appear weak and pale after those of St. Leander, who in such an
exalted manner knew how to interpret the human, civilising, universal spirit of
Christianity?

From a religious perspective there is no need to underline the importance
of Recared's abjuration. True, the Visigoths were not Spanish and their heresy
had permeated little, if at all, into the indigenous population; but once
established in the Peninsula, they were a danger to the Catholic Faith if only as
persecutors and an antidote to unity, that unity of belief so vehemently praised
by St. Leander. This unity was achieved in the Third Council of Toledo when
the Hispano-Roman population was unanimous in doctrine and Galician
Priscillianism almost entirely extinguished. All that remained was submission
on the part of the invaders who, ignorant and unrefined, had followed a
doctrine that was destructive of the fundamental principle of Catholicism: the
immediate and continuous action of God in the world, a Divinity that is
personal, *alive*; the Father Creator, the Word incarnate. By debasing the Person
of Christ down to a human level, this unity, this link, was broken, God and the
world were once again left isolated, and creation and redemption the work of a
creature, of a demiurge. Such impoverished doctrine must have made the spirit
of the Visigoths themselves vacillate when they found themselves faced with the
beautiful *Regula fidei* of the Spanish Church.

The Church was victorious. Victorious because God and truth are with
her; and a victory it most certainly was, a triumph that was to continue for many
centuries until this wretched one we happen to live in. An inestimable treasure
of religious unity, never broken by Epilandus or Hostegesis, zealots of Oriental

pantheism in the twelfth century, the Albigensis and Valdenses, Pedro de Osma, sixteenth century Protestantism that threw the rest of Europe into commotion, the Illuminati, Alumbrados, Molinists, Jansenists, or the sceptics of the last century. Because in our land all these sects, all heretical manifestation eventually comes crashing down headlong on to that precious Wall that was built by the Councils of Toledo.

Some - very few - Spaniards may have gone astray, but the Spanish people has never apostasised. God willed that at one time or another all heresies might make their appearance on our soil so that this precious unity, sustained with titanic efforts throughout the ages against the spirit of error, could never be attributed solely to isolation or intolerance. And today, by the mercy of God, I can sit here and write this history, if nothing else to show that all heterodoxies have come and gone from our land but truth remains with the vast majority of Spaniards on its side, as even our own adversaries acknowledge. And if old errors have passed, so will the many dazzling and blinding errors of today. And once again we will be of one heart and one soul; and this unity in religion, not dead but temporarily being trampled, will again assert its claim, demanded by the unanimous will of a great people to whom a meagre herd of the irreverent and indifferent will mean nothing in the end.

The opposition that Licinianus, Fulgentius, Mausona, and Leander had to face was not a *negative,* an impotent opposition, one incapable of rising above itself, lacking in greatness and fecundity: the opposition of degenerates. It was, rather, the *positive* defiance of a young and fanatical race, the Visigoths, strong-willed and unperverted in body or spirit. This race had exclusive power, the command of the army, the administration of justice. It could apply and it did apply the laws of the conqueror to the vanquished. Yet, we triumphed. We converted them. We civilised them. We *hispanized* them, in short. And how did this miracle come to pass? Not by coercion or force of arms: Hermenegild's *coup* was an isolated attempt, perhaps as political as it was religious. We did so with patience, with persuasion, and with knowledge.

What were the social and political consequences of Recared's great deed? Prior to it, there were two rival communities, always suspicious and distrustful of each other, divided by religion, customs, language; one condemned to being the victim, the other the tyrant, ruled by distinct and contradictory laws. Such a state of affairs was totally unfavourable to cultural progress. One of the races had to cede to the other, and Recared had enough courage to sacrifice his own (if sacrifice it was, and not baptism and regeneration). And he, a Gothic monarch, head of a military empire, a descendent of Alaric who had poured the cup of the wrath of the Lord in Rome, came to bow his head to the Church, only to raise it to greater glory before her bishops, grandsons of those crushed by the first Visigoth hordes, their slaves, but loftier, because of the light of understanding and the incontestable spirit of the Faith.

The moment Goths and Spaniards were one in worship, fusion among the races began and, little by little, the former forgot their Teutonic tongue to adopt the sweet and mellow modulations of Latin speech. And after Recared

144

came Recesvint to abolish the race laws that prohibited mixed marriages, and there were barbarian kings married to Roman ladies and barbarian monarchs who wrote in the language of Virgil.

The coarse, unrefined, uncultivated and unpolished organisation of the State, arisen among a people born and raised in the wild, changed when it met with the admirable order of the councils. Thus, gradually, by the natural superiority of enlightenment over vulgarity, they began little by little to understand civic affairs, with this or that characteristic. Failings in the electoral system were considerably lessened; military despotism was restrained; the throne became strengthened by the walls and fortresses of law and advocacy ensuring litigation and defendants' rights as well as other barricades that did away with all arbitrariness; many elements of oppression and disorder were mitigated (extinguishing them altogether would have been impossible), and even the severity of penal laws was softened. Under this influence, the barbarian *Fuero Juzgo* came to excel all previous barbarian codices - barbarian only in part: barbarian only in what our bishops could not have abolished at the risk of annihilating the Visigoth race.

It has been said that the councils appropriated powers outside of their jurisdiction. Oh, please, who can possibly believe such nonsense! On which side was knowledge and on which side ignorance? To whom could the Church have ceded the charge of educating her new-born children? To Witteric? To Chindasvint? To Ergivius? To those who scrambled onto the throne by slaying their predecessors or on some other blundering pretext stripped them of their crown? As if humanity would have made much advance being guided by such principles! The councils' tutelage was not imposed or contrived. It was providential law sought and solicited by the Visigoth Kings themselves.

But not all Arians consented to detract, which proved unfortunate as much for them as for their monarchy. There was, in addition to intruding bishops, a hostile and intractable warring element that would not adjust to Hispano-Roman civilisation (something beyond their understanding), nor listen to the teachings of the Church. Instead, they persecuted her whenever they could with plots and uprisings against the monarchs she protected. This *military* and heretical opposition, first represented by Witeric, appears to a large extent impersonated in Chindasvint's usurpation, in Hildaric's and Paulus' war against Wamba and, above all, in Witiza and his sons, or whoever the traitors were that opened the Strait's gates to the Arab invaders. They certainly got their iniquitous revenge. For them, however, it meant disappearing as a nation - a just punishment for their perfidy. The race that rose to reclaim their native soil, inch by inch, was the Hispano-Roman race - faithful Visigoths having by now become totally intermixed with it. As for that *noble lineage* that sold out their homeland, well, God made it drown in the ocean of history.

But let us go back to Recared who had informed St. Gregory the Great, then occupying St. Peter's Chair, of his conversion. The letter of the Visigoth King was accompanied by a chalice made of gold and precious stones as an offering. The pope answered in 591 by remitting some relics and a discreet letter, highly honoured by Recared:

"I can barely express in words," the Pontiff said, "how very much your words and deeds have consoled me. A new miracle has occurred in our day. Thanks to you, the Gothic peoples have come from the Arian heresy to the truth of the Faith. I can well exclaim with the Prophet: 'This change comes from the right hand of the Most High.' What will I say on the Day of Judgement when I present myself empty-handed and you with a legion of believers who, because of you, have come to the grace of Jesus Christ?"

He then goes on to admonish him against vainglory, recommends purity of body and soul, and clemency and good governance for his subjects.[225] Recared kept up a good correspondence with the Pontiff and later sent more than three hundred garments in alms for St. Peter's poor.

It is said that in Toledo Recared threw all Arian books to the flames - an act much lamented now by our present-day *freethinkers*. I am not in the least tempted to start crying over such a loss – which may even be an imaginary one. What books, pray, could the barbarian Visigoths have? Some samples of the *Biblia Ulphilana* – a philological monument of significance, but not to Spanish culture. Is it not more sensible for us to lament the loss of so many works by Justus, Apringius, Licinianus and other Catholic and Spanish Doctors of the time? Listen here! No one burned them, all right? They were lost! There cannot have been so many when even their memory has been wiped out. We do not know of a single name of a Visigoth writer prior to Bulgaran or Sisebut. Who was writing and erecting that vast encyclopaedia of learning "devoured by the flames of fanaticism?" We have ample evidence of the works of Priscillianists and of other heretics. Are we to measure Recared's aim, which was to try to give social unity to his people, by the standard of some discontent palaeographer or archaeologist of today?

It remains for me to mention the Arian coup attempts against the reign of Leovigild's son.

In 587, Sunna, the aforementioned intruder bishop of Mérida, conspired with Segga, Witteric, and other nobles of the city government who had not taken kindly to Recared's conversion and that of his people. [226] The main aim of

---

[225] *'S. Gregorii Magni opera omnia ad manuscriptos codices emendata et illustrata, studio et labore Monachorum ordinis S. Benedicti e Congregatione S. Mauri' Lutetiae Parisiorum,* 1705, lib. I, ep. LXIII, and lib. VII, ep. CXXVI. Recared's letter to St. Gregory was publish for the first time in 1700 by Baluzio (*Miscellaneorum libri...,* vol. 5). Both these epistles as well as another and a fragment can be read in the Masdeu, Appendices to vol. 10, Illustrations 6 and 7.

[226] Anno VI Mauricii qui est Recaredi secundus annus, quidam ex Arianis, Sunna Episcopus et Segga cum quibusdam, tyrannidem assumere cupientes detenguntur...' *Biclarensis Chronicon.*

"Sunna namque Gothicus Episcopus...irritatus a Diabolo, quibusdam Gothis nobilibus genere, opibusque perquam ditissimis, e quibus etiam nonnulli in quibusdam civitatibus comites a Rege fuerant constituti, consilio diabolico persuasit, eosque de Catholicorum agmine... separavit". Pauli, *De vita Patrum Emeritensium,* chpt. XVII and XVIII. Paulus, on which my text is based, tells at length of this conspiracy.

the plotters was to assassinate Mausona and Duke Claudius who had the governance of Mérida and was a Hispano-Roman. *'Romanis parentibus progenitus'*, says Paulus. Witeric was the one assigned to get rid of Mausona and Claudius in the atrium of the church of Mérida, but however hard he tried he could not pull the blade out of the scabbard, as "if it were fixed there with iron nails". Repenting of his crime, he threw himself at the feet of Mausona and disclosed the whole plot to him. Thanks to this revelation, a new danger was avoided. Sunna and his partisans resolved to finish off Mausona, Claudius and other Catholics of Mérida by striking them on their way back from the procession they held on Holy Week from the city centre to the Basilica of St. Eulalia, outside the city walls. They hid their swords in wheat carts and promised to spare neither man nor woman, old or young. The attempt was thwarted. Claudius, forewarned by Witeric, fell on the assassins, seizing many and stabbing those who resisted. Sunna was offered pardon if he converted but he, with tenacity worthy of a higher cause, swore to die in defence of the religion he had learnt from his early years. Recared's judges did not want to make a martyr of him and exiled him to Mauritania. Segga was sent to Galicia with one of his hands chopped off. Witeric remained free, and Vacrila, who had taken refuge with his wife and children in the Basilica of St. Eulalia, was assigned as servant to that church - a sentence Mausona revoked, letting him go free and giving him back his property, with no other condition but to run a short distance, as a sign of obedience and vassalage, before the horse of deacon Redemptus. [227] Other Sunna accomplices suffered expatriation and confiscation of property.

At about this time, an Arian bishop called Athaloc and two *comites*, Granista and Wildigern, rose against the king in the Gallic Narbonne. Recared's army quashed the rebellion and Athaloc, who hated Catholics to death, died in a fit of anger.

A new conspiracy was forged in 588 against Recared by his stepmother Gosiunda, Ingunda's torturer, and bishop Uldila. Both feigned conversion and secretly profaned the consecrated Host. The king found this out and exiled Uldila. Gosiunda died shortly after.[228]

Recared prevailed over all his enemies at home and abroad. His right-hand in matters of war, Duke Claudius, crushed the Franks led by king Gontran at Carcassonne, instilling terror on them for many a day. The same degree of success with the other plots was enjoyed by the Duke and *cubiculario* Argimund, who had his hand cut off, his head shaved and had to go about mounted on an ass through the streets of Toledo in the year 589.

---

227   Vic. *Paulo Emeritense*, chp. 19.

228   "Anno VII Mauricii qui est Recaredi tertius annus, Uldia Episcopus cum Gosuinta regina insidiantes, Recaredo manifestantur, et Fidei catholicae communionem quam sub specie christiana quasi sumentes projiciunt, publicantur. Quod malum in cognitationem hominum deductum, Uldila exilio condamnatur, Gosuinta vero...vitae tunc terminum dedit" *Biclarensis' Chronicle*).

Recared's son and heir, Liuva, was weak to the point of jeopardising his father's work. Two years into the new reign, Witeric, the hired assassin at Mérida, was more fortunate: he cut his head and his right hand. There followed six years of Arian reaction in which that prince managed to make himself hated by his subjects both Goths and Spanish. He was stabbed to death at a feast. We have no more precise evidence of these events. In the year of Our Lord 610, Gundemar came to the throne.

The heresy of the *Acephali*.

At the second Council of Seville presided by St. Isidore in 619, in the ninth year of Sisebut's reign, there was present a bishop of Syrian nationality who denied the distinction of the two natures of Christ and affirmed that his Divinity had in reality suffered. The Monophysites and Eutychians, in avoiding Nestorianism, had fallen into the same error. But the *Acephali*, so-ca lled according to St. Isidore because it was not known who their cheif leader or *corypheus* was, or (as others suppose) because they denied the *impassibility* of the Father, were different from them in that they believed Divinity to be *passible*. The Fathers of the council of Seville refuted this heresy in the following terms:

Canon XIII: "Against these blasphemies, it is imperative that the two natures of Christ be shown, that He suffered only as Man, so that no one falls into this error again and severs himself from Catholic Truth. We confess that our Lord Jesus Christ, eternally born of the Father, born temporally of the womb of the glorious Virgin Mary, had in one Person two natures: a divine nature, engendered before time, and a human nature, produced in time. This distinction of the two natures is deduced: first, from the words of the Law, from the Prophets, the Gospel, and the Apostolic writings.

First, from the words of the book of Exodus (23:20-21): "Behold, I will send my angel who shall go before thee... and my name is in him". This speaks of divine nature; and from Genesis (22:18): "And in thy seed shall all the nations of the earth be blessed", to wit, in the flesh of Christ, who descends from the stock of Abraham. This speaks to his human nature.

Second, in the Psalms David speaks of the two natures in the person of Christ: Of divine nature in Psalm 109: "Ex utero ante luciferum genui te". Of human nature in Psalm 80: "Homo factus est in ea". Of the divine nature in 44: "Eructavit cor meum verbum bonuum". Of the human nature, in the same: "Speciosus forma prae filiis hominum".

Third, Isaiah affirms both natures in one and the same person of Christ. Of the divine, when he says: "Numquid qui alios parere facio, ipse non pariam?" Of the human: "Ecce virgo in utero concipiet et pariet filium". Of the divine: "Rorate coeli desuper, et nubes pluant justum". Of the human: "Aperiatur terra et germinet Salvatorem; Parvulus natus est nobis".

In the Gospel, the divine nature of Christ is affirmed: "Ego et pater unum sumus; and "Ego sum veritas et vita". Of the human: "Pater major me est; Tristis est anima mea usque ad mortem".

That Christ's humanity and not His divinity suffered, is shown in the words of Jacob: "Lavabit in vino stolam suam et in sanguine uvae pallium suum". What do this mantle and stole mean but the flesh of Christ adorned with the blood of His Passion?"

The bishop, convinced by these arguments, irrefutable I would say if one believes in the authority of Scripture (those who do not, do not enter into this type of argument), disavowed his error amidst great rejoicing from the Fathers of Seville. But the heresy did not die with him, still less the name. Two hundred years later, some sectarians who called themselves *Acephali* and *Cassians* reappeared in Mozarabic Andalucía. They were condemned, as we shall relate, in the Council of Córdoba of 839.

The Councils of Toledo and their relations with the Holy See

This will be a brief chapter. Its purpose is simply to show the dignity of the Spanish Church at that time, against those who have accused her of being rebellious to the supremacy of the Pontiffs - a favoured argument of the Jansenists, used by the blind critics or the ignorant of today to judge our most venerable prelates of the seventh century as nothing less than schismatics or precursors of the Reformation.

From the fourth Council of Toledo onwards, heresies condemned by Toledo synods were few. The Fourth was celebrated in 633, *imperante Sisenando*, and its seventy-five canons decreed and unified discipline, excommunicating in canon XVII those who would not acknowledge the *Apocalypse* as sacred. [229] From the LIX onwards, the Fathers are concerned with conduct to be followed vis-à-vis the Judaizers. The rushed and hasty conversions imposed by Sisebutus' decree, highly disapproved of at this council ("Sicut enim homo propria arbitrii voluntate serpenti obediens periit, sic, vocante se gratia Dei, propriae mentis conversione quisque credendo salvatur") had given occasion for relapses and apostasies that the Toledo Fathers wished to avoid. They called on the one hand for "no one to be obliged by force to believe" ("Nemini ad credendum

---

[229] "Apocalypsis librum multorum Conciliorum auctoritas et synodica sanctorum praesulum Romanorum decreta Joannis Envangelistae esse praescribunt et inter divinos libros recipiendum constituerunt. Et quia plurimi sunt qui ejus auctoritatem non recipiunt, eumque in Ecclesia Dei praedicare contemnunt, si quis eum deinceps aut non receperit, aut a Pascha usque ad Pentecostem Missarum tempore in Ecclesia no praedicaverit, excommunicationis sententiam habebit". *Canon XVI.*

vim inferre"), but at the same time that converts, even when suffering violence or necessity, may not blaspheme the faith they had received in baptism. [230]

We can deduce from canon LIX that many false Christians preserved circumcision and other Jewish rituals. The council prescribed that in case of transgression their slaves be given their freedom and their children separated from them, [231] but without their parents' prevarication being detrimental to their honour or property (canon LXI), for it is written: "Filius non portabit iniquitatem patris". Canon LXII prohibits interaction and familiarity between the convert Jew and the unbeliever, to avoid occasion to relapse. Canon LXIV forbids the Judaizer to be witness at a court of law, and LXVI to have Christian slaves. This was the only course that could lessen, at least in part, the disastrous consequences of Sisebutus' intolerance. Feigned conversions were scandalous enough - public apostasy even more so.

Then, in 676 *Spanish Era*, that is, A.D. 638, the second year of Chintilla's reign, the Sixth Council of Toledo was convened. A letter from Pope Honorius sent by the deacon Turninus was read which caused a great deal of pain and distress to our bishops: they were exhorted to be stronger and more spirited in defence of the Faith calling them, with great offence to all, "canes muti non valentes latrare". In response to these unjust accusations by an ill-informed Pope, the Fathers wrote an additional profession of faith condemning all heresies and especially those of Nestorius and the Patripassionists.[232] St. Braulius, on behalf of all the Fathers there gathered, addressed a grave and well drafted letter that shows both the profound respect of our Church for Rome, and the humble vigour with which he rejected every unjust accusation.

"It is laudable" - wrote the bishop of Saragossa – "that Your Holiness watches over all churches with vigilant solicitude and confounds, with the divine word, those who profane the mantle of the Lord: the scandalous prevaricators, the abhorrent deserters.... This, too, was what our king Chintilla had in mind, which is the reason for our being gathered in council when your letters were received.... It was undoubtedly divine counsel that in two distant lands zeal for the house of God inflamed, in unison, both Pontiff and monarch ... for which we thank the King of heaven and praise and bless His name. What can be

---

[230]   "Ne nomen Domini blasphemetur, et fides quam susceperunt contemptibilis habeatur".

[231]   "Judaei qui ad fidem christianam promoti abominandos circuncisionis et alios Judaicos usus exercuerint, pontificali auctoritate corrigantur... Eos autem quos circumciderunt, si filii eorum sint, a parentur consortio separentur; si servi, libertati...tradantur".

[232]   "Quod ex tribus personis divinis solum filium fatemur ad redemtionem humani generis propter culparum debita quae per inobedientiam Adae originaliter et nostro libero arbitrio contraximus resolvenda, a secreto Patris arcanoque prodiisse, et humanitatem sine peccato de Sancta semper Virgine assumpsisse, ut idem filius Dei Patris esset filius hominis, Deus perfectus et homo perfectus...in duabus naturis una persona, ne quaternitas Trinitate accederet, si in Christo gemina persona esset". (Aguirre, vol. III).

greater or more profitable for human salvation than to obey the divine precepts and turn those who have gone astray back to the path of salvation? Nor will the exhortation with which you entreat us to be braver in defending the faith and more inflamed in the fire of the Holy Spirit prove fruitless to your crown ... We were not asleep or unmindful of divine grace... if we have shown tolerance towards those we should have submitted to a more rigid discipline, it was to conciliate them with Christian gentleness and to win them back through long and continual teaching. We do not judge it harmful to delay victory in order to secure it. Nothing that Your Holiness says in reproof do we judge applicable, least of all the passage you quote from Ezekiel, or is it Isaiah? - "canes muti non valentes latrare" for, attentive always to custody over the flock of the Lord, we are constantly biting at wolves and frightening off thieves, vigilant night and day. Rest assured that the Spirit that watches over Israel does not sleep or slumber in us. At the opportune time, we decreed against prevaricators; we have never interrupted the office of preaching, and that Your Holiness may be persuaded, we remit the Proceedings of this synod and of those held in the past. Thus, Holy Father and most venerable Pope, with the reverence due to the Apostolic See, we protest our clean conscience and unfeigned faith. We do not believe that the pitiable lie of a falsifier may continue to find room in your heart, or that the serpent will leave its mark on the rock of St. Peter upon which Christ built His Church... Finally, we ask of you, first and most exalted among bishops, that when you turn to God in prayer for the whole Church, you may deign to intercede for us, that with the fragrance of incense and myrrh our souls may be purified from sin, for well we know that no man crosses this sea without danger..."[233]

Now what is so schismatic or rebellious about that? Nothing! Do St. Braulius and the other bishops not recognise the supremacy of Rome? Do they not submit the Acta of the council for his examination? Do they not restate that the Bishop of Rome is the "first among bishops" and that it is to the Chair of St. Peter that vigilance over all churches in entrusted? ("Cathedrae vestrae a Deo vobis collatae...cum sancta sollicitudine omnium Ecclessiarum"). The See of Rome had been ill informed, and it was incumbent upon our bishops to dissipate that error and defend themselves, as they did, with no less modesty than verve. (The condescension and tolerance to wich they allude refers exclusively to the question of relapsed Jews whose treatment in the same council has been published by Father Fita, with excellent commentaries).[234]

---

[233] I have summarised this letter somewhat. The original Latin, with all other epistles of St. Braulius, was published by Father Risco in the Appendices to volume XXX of *España Sagrada*, pp. 318 to 396.

[234] *Honorio y St. Braulio de Zaragoza*, collection of articles published in the Madrid journal *La Ciudad de Dios*, 1870-1871.

The following synods are of no direct interest to our history of heterodoxy (thanks be to God). Recesvint could say in 653 to the Fathers of the eighth synod that all heresy had been eradicated save for *Judaic perfidy*, that is, apostasy of the Judaizers. Against this the canons from Sisenand's time were renewed.

We must look to the time of Ergivius, therefore, to do justice to a serious controversy (or so we are told) that took place at that time between Rome and the Spanish church, of which the schismatic and Jansenist temperament, now relegated to history (though its odour lingers on), took full and miserable advantage.

First, I will summarise what others have written about it:

The Fathers of fourteenth Council of Toledo wrote a Formula against the heresy of the Apollinarists from which the Pope crossed out several non-Catholic expressions. The Spanish Church, instead of accepting these corrections, convened a national council that once again approved the Formula and the defence made of it by Julian, Metropolitan of Toledo, who had included in it expressions that were injurious to the Head of the Church, accusing the Pope of *shameful ignorance*. Further, the Spanish bishops openly declared themselves in schism, announcing that they would persist on holding on to their opinion even if the pope detached himself from what they held as being wholesome doctrine. And then, in obvious and glaring contradiction, Rome accepted Toledo's profession of faith and explanation.

This is, generally, what we read. From it, one would logically have to deduce either that Pope Benedict had erred gravely on a question of dogma to begin with, or that St. Julian and the whole Spanish Church who had approved his writing had fallen into heresy, and on nothing less than on the mystery of the Holy Trinity!

Neither conclusion is acceptable; the first because it is injurious to the Holy See; the second because it seriously compromises the good name of the Spanish Church in her Golden Age. But since historic truth is never at war with Catholicism, my history, which truly wishes to be both, can and must remove this stone of scandal, and tell the truth exactly as it was. The events occurred in the way I am here going to relate them:

At the time Agathus was Pope and Constantine Pogonatus emperor, the council of Constantinople, the sixth of the Ecumenicals, was convened against the heresy of the Monothelites or Apollinarists, who denied the distinction of the two wills corresponding to the two natures in Christ. Leo II, Agathus' successor, sent the Acta of this Synod to the bishops of Spain for them to see and acknowledge. To the Acta were attached individual letters for Quiricus, Metropolitan of Toledo, Count Simplicius, and Spanish prelates in general.[235]

---

[235] Cardinal Baronius (volume 8) denied the authenticity of these epistles; but his arguments carry no weight and in any case do not influence the principal question, since in the Conciliar Proceedings it is recorded that Leo II consulted our churches, in one form or another.

The pontifical letters arrived in Spain in the winter of 683, just after the thirteenth Council of Toledo had adjourned, and it was difficult, because of the snow blocking the highways, to convene the Fathers in council again. St. Julian, Quiricus' successor, did not deem it prudent to delay a reply to the pope and, without prejudice to what the council had agreed, addressed an Apologia to the Pontiff, conforming to the decisions of Constantinople. [236]

In November 684, St. Julian convened a council of the Cartagena prelates, with vicars of the other five metropolises attending. The heresy of Apollinaris was anathematised and the Apologia that St. Julian had submitted was wholeheartedly confirmed, with the request that it may carry the same weight as the decretal letters (canon XI).

Meanwhile, the Apologia had arrived in Rome. The Pope, now Benedict II, did *not* condemn it, as it is generally presumed. Nowhere is there any proof or hint of a condemnation having taken place. What he did, and this *orally* and not in writing, was to advise Julian's messenger to the effect that some expressions in the Apologia were rather abrupt and could be taken out of context or misunderstood, namely these two: "The Will engendered the Will, as Wisdom engendered Wisdom" ("De voluntate a voluntate genita, sicut sapientia de sapientia"); and, "there are three substances in Christ". He judged it prudent that the Metropolitan of Toledo explained and defended them as best he could, with testimonies from Holy Scripture and the Holy Fathers ("Quibus munirentur et solida fierent"). All of this is clear from the records of the fifteenth Council of Toledo. [237] The Pope did not define or condemn anything. He simply asked for explanations, and this he did not through public or even private documentation but *orally*. St. Julian duly submitted these explanations in another Apologia against which arose some detractors (those to which the word *ignorant* refers to, as we shall see). To silence them and give more authority to his reply, St. Julian was careful to convene a national council in 688 in which sixty-one bishops took part. This is the Fifteenth Council of Toledo.

The Fathers there assemled determined that it was indeed a Catholic proposition to affirm that "the Will engendered the Will, and Wisdom engendered Wisdom" since St Augustine used it, too, and that it was no different from these other expressions: "Essence engendered Essence; Monad engendered Monad; Substance engendered Substance; Light engendered Light", given that in none of these phrases one is meaning to say that there are two substances in God, or two essences, or two wills, or two wisdoms, but that substance, essence, will, and wisdom are equally in the three Persons that proceed among themselves by spiritual generation. Hence, the Father (Voluntas)

---

[236]   This Apologetic has been lost, but the fourteenth Council of Toledo, canon IV, makes reference to it: "Placuit proinde illo tunc tempore apologeticae responsionis nostrae...", etc., and Felix confirms it in *Vida de San Julián*.

[237]   "Pro quibus muniendies... Benedictus Papa monuerat...quae tamen non in scriptis suis annotare curavit, sed homini nostro verbo renotanda injunxit". Canon IX.

engendered the Son (Voluntas) with the Will of the Father not being in any way different from the Will of the Son. As for the three *substantiae* of Christ, they state that these are *body*, *soul*, and *divinity*, for although human nature comprises body and soul, it is advisable to express it clearly in order to move away from the error of the Apollinarists, who deny the soul in Christ, or the Gnostics and Manichaeans, who supposed his body *fantasmical* or imaginary. In support of their opinion, the Toledo Fathers cite texts from Scripture and from Sts. Cyril, Augustine, Ambrose, Fulgentius and Isidore. They end with these words: "Iam vero si post haec, et ab ipsis dogmatibus Patrum, quibus haec prolata sunt, in quocumque dissentiant: non jam cum illis est amplius contendendum, sed per majorum directo calle inhaerentes vestigiis erit per divinum judicium amatoribus veritatis responsio nostra sublimis: etiamsi ab ignorantibus aemulis censeatur indocilis". ("If after this and the sentences of the Fathers on which ours are based, some continue to dissent, we shall not debate them further. We shall follow the path set by our elders, secure in the knowledge of meriting the approval of lovers of truth, though the ignorant may call us disobedient). It is clear that *the ignorant* were not the Pope and his advisers since they had not debated anything, nor had they been opposed to the thinking of the Toledo Fathers, but had simply asked for explanations. And it is a fact that not only were they happy with these explanations but they received the Apologia with enthusiasm. The Pope ordered it to be read by all (unlikely, had the writing referred to him as *ignorant*), and sent it to the emperor of the East who received it with these words: *Laus tua, Deus, in fines terrae*....[238] What is more, Benedict II thanked Julian and the Toledo Fathers for this learned and devout writing.

Is it even within the realm of the possible that the injurious allusion was aimed at the Pope? [239]

In the Sixteenth Council of Toledo, held in 693 after the death of St. Julian, his doctrine was again ratified and included in the profession of faith.

Theological polemics in Visigoth Spain

Before we move on to speak of the wreckage and ruin of the Visigoth empire, we shall pause a while to contemplate the literary glory of this period, albeit from a partial and simplified perspective since we are going to deal only with issues of theological controversy.

---

[238]   "Quod Roma digne et pie recipiens, cunctis legendum indixit, atque Imperator acclamando: '*Laus tua, Deus, in fines terrae*', *lectum saepius notum fecit. Qui et rescriptum Domino Juliano...cum gratiarum actione et cum honore remisit*'. Archbishop D. Rodrigo, lib. III, chapter XIV. The Pacensis confirms this – an authority almost contemporary authority.

[239]   Mariana attributes the harshness of St.Julian's phrases to the ardour of the polemic. Pérez Bayer (notes to N. Antonio, *Bibliotheca Vetus*) defends him, as I have done. The Jansenists muddled up these and other questions, as we shall see when we come to speak of them. See the *Apologetico* in volume 2 of the *Toledo Fathers*, pp. 76 to 87.

The material is not vast. The remarkable learning of the Spanish Church during the sixth and seventh centuries had occasion to be applied in the long and arduous objections to heterodox doctrines and their tendencies, but these polemical works almost always disappeared with the circumstances that caused them. For this reason, though the number of monuments to our learning from that age is large, that of anti-heretical books is relatively small.

We have already spoken of the letter by Vitalis and Constantius against Nestorianism; the two letters by Montanus that refer to Priscillianism; of Severus' book against Vincentius of Saragossa, and of the tracts of Licinianus. Let us not forget *De Correctione rusticorum* by St. Martin Dumiensis which we shall study in detail in the following chapter. The same prelate from Braga sent a letter to bishop Boniface defending the rite of triple immersion at baptism against those who judged it an Arian superstition. This Apologia is written with great ardour: it even accuses those who practised simple immersion of being Sabellians and Anti-Trinitarians. [240] St. Martin bases his judgement on the aforementioned decree of Pope Vigilius to Profuturus.

Euthropius, abbot of a Servite monastery and bishop of Valencia, a brilliant mind at the third Council of Toledo, also merits our mention for his book against those who challenged the monastic life *(De distractione monachorum)*, addressed to Petrus, bishop of Ercávica; also his letter to Licinianus about the Sacrament of Confirmation and the controversy surrounding it. These two tracts have been lost but are cited by St. Isidore [241] who also confirms that Licinianus sustained a long correspondence with Eutropius.

St. Isidore, in chapters 33 and 34 of his interesting book *De viris illustribus*, preserved the memory of Justinianus, prelate of Valencia, brother of Elpidius, Justus, and Neridius, all bishops and all writers: a family similar to that of Severianus. Our bishop wrote a book of answers to five questions that one Rusticus had addressed to him: the first about the Holy Spirit; the second, against the Bonosiacs who called Christ the 'adopted' Son of the Father; the third, saying that "it was not licit to repeat baptism", as did the Donatists; the fourth, on the difference between the baptisms of John and of Jesus; the fifth, on the "indivisibility of the Father and the Son". Justinianus flourished at the time of Theudis.

All these are overshadowed by St. Leander of Seville, [242] catechist to Hermenegild and Recared, the heart and soul of the Goths' conversion in 589. During his exile in Constantinople, St. Leander wrote two books against the

---

240   See this epistle in *España Sagrada*, vol. XV, pp. 422 to 425

241   *De viris illustribus*, chapter XLV, of the Toledo Fathers edition.

242   I will say nothing about the ridiculous genealogy that links the Spaniards Leander, Fulgentius, Isidore and Florentinus with the Goth royal family. Not only is there no trace of this in writings contemporaneous with these saints, it is also contrary to all known data. As if their glory did not shine enough without having to link them to royal nobility, acts performed only for the adulation of kings. *Vanitas vanitatum...* N. Antonio has already mocked this absurdity.

Arians: one extensive, the other briefer, where he starts by quoting the words of his adversaries first in order to refute them all. Both are rich in scriptural erudition and written in a vehement style, according to St. Isidore. They have not been preserved, just as none of the refutations of Arianism have been preserved, though they were not burned like the supposed Toledo books. Why are so many tears shed for the former but no one remembers the latter? Judging by his homily, St. Leander's writings must have had great merit. Nor do we have the epistle *De baptismo* in which he consulted St. Gregory the Great on the rite of single or triple (*una* or *trina*) immersion. The Pope, as St. Leander sensed, answered that one or the other rite could be practised according to the custom of each province. Both were Catholic; the Western Church had opted for *trina* immersion, but since this was the rite practised also by the Arians who wished to signify the distinction of rank between the divine Persons, he advises St. Leander to opt for the one single immersion. The Fourth Council of Toledo was later to confirm this. In defence of the rite of the Greek Church, which was also the rite of the Spanish Church on this point, Joannes, Patriarch of Constantinople, wrote the treatise *De sacramento baptismatis*, dedicated to St. Leander. It is now lost but St. Isidore cites it. St. Gregory's letter, written in a spirit of tolerance, different from St. Martin Dumiensis (Doma monastery, near Braga) is numbered XLIII in the collection of his works where several others also addressed to Leander can be found.[243]

---

[243]   In the early years, it was the practice of the Spanish Church to immerse the cathecumen three times in the water. But when Arianism appeared, and as its followers were trying to distinguish with the triple immersions the diversity and inequality of natures between the Father, the Son and the Holy Spirit, Catholic bishops started adopting, little by little, the rite of one sole immersion, which St. Gregory the Great approved in consideration of these motives, as one can see in Epistle 41, book 1, to St. Leander. "De trina mersione baptismatis, nil responderi verius potest quam quod ipsi sensistis, quod in una fide nil officit Sanctae Ecclesiae consuetudo diversa. Nos autem quod tertio mergimus, tridunae sepulturae sacramenta signamus; ut dum tertio infans ab aquis educitur, resurrectio triduani temporis exprimatur; quod si quis forte etiam pro summae trinitatis veneratione existimet fieri, neque ad hoc aliquid obsistit baptisando semel in aquis mergere; quia dum in tribus personis una substantia est, reprehensibile esse mullatemus potest, infantem in baptismate vel ter, vel semel inmergere, quando et in tribus mersionibus personarum trinitas, et in una potest divinitatis singularitas designari. Sed qui nunc hucusque ab haereticis infans in baptismate tertio mergebatur, fiendum apud vos esse non censeo; ne dum mersiones numerant, divinitatem dividant; dunque quod faciebant, faciunt, se morem vestrum vicisse glorientur".

In spite of this ruling by St. Gregory, some bishops retained the triple immersion rite until the Fourth Council of Toledo (633, Sisenand's reign) to avoid appearances of schism and scandal to the people (Canon VI). "De baptismi autem sacramento propter quod in Hispaniis quidam sacerdotes trinam, quidam simplam mersionem faciunt, a nonnullis schisma esse conspicitur et unitas fidei scindi videtur; nam duas partes diverso et quasi contrario modo agunt, alii alios non baptizatos esse contendunt...".

They then cite St. Gregory the Great's text and add: "Quia de utroque sacramento quod fit in sancto baptismo a tanto viro reddita sit ratio, quod utrumque rectum, utrumque irreprehensibile in sancta Dei ecclesia habeatur, propter vitandum autem schismatis scandalum vel haeretici dogmatis usum simplum teneamus baptismi mersionem, ne videantur apud nos qui tertio

And then St. Leander's brother, St. Isidore, the brilliant *Doctor of all Spain*. The name alone says it all. His learning was the most prolific, universal and prodigious of his century. In his encyclopaedic treatise *Etymologies* he covers the history of heretical manifestations, reflecting and deliberating on *Heresy and Schism, the heresies of the Jews and Christians* in chapters III, IV, and V of Book VIII. His list is founded on those by Philastrus of Brescia and St. Augustine's, with small additions. But it is certain, on St. Braulius' testimony, that Isidore wrote a book, *De haeresibus*, in which he compiled, briefly, as much information on heresy as was known at the time. The book is missing in all collections and codices so far examined. The two books *De fide catholica* are not addressed to heretics but to Jews.

Neither the forty-four epistles of St. Braulius nor the *Sentences* of Tajón, truly the Master of this approach to theological teaching (rather than Peter Lombard) belong appropriately to this catalogue. [244]

The presbyter Aurasius' letter against the Judaizer Froya, or Froga, is included. He had built a synagogue in Toledo and openly favoured his co-religionists backed by his power and wealth. Aurasius' invective is preserved in a codex in the *Bibliotheca Toledana*. We also hear about Froya in Tajon's letter to Quiricus.

Also lost is the book *De Trinitate* by St. Eugenius of Toledo which he wrote to be circulated in *parts of Libya and the Orient*, as St. Ildephonsus confirms. It was probably a polemical book and would have included refutations of all errors on the dogma of the Trinity up to that time.

Fortunately we do have St. Ildephonsus' treatise *De virginitate S. Mariae* against "three infidels", which was approved in an admirable and exceptional

---

mergunt haereticorum approbare assertionem, dum sequuntur et morem, et ne forte cuiquam sit dubium hujus simpli Ministerium sacramenti videat in eo mortem et resurrectionem Christi significar nam in aquis mersio quasi in infernum descensio est, et rursus ab aquis emersio resurrectio est. Item videant in eo unitatem Divinitatis et Trinitatem personarum ostendi, unitatem dum simul mergimus, Trinitatem dum in nomine Patris et Filii et Spiritus Sancti baptizamus".

It is true, however, that St. Martin of Braga did not agree with the practice of one immersion on the basis that, by trying to avoid Arian error, we could easily fall into the Sabellian or Anti-Trinitarian error. "Per hoc dum quasi vicinitas fugitur ariana, sabelliana ignorantibus subrepet pestis; quae dum sub uni nomine unam solummodo retinet tinctionem, eundem Patrem dicit esse quam Filium, eundem quem Filium et Spiritum Sanctum dicit esse, et quem Patrem; et dum nullam distinctionem trium Personarum in sacramento Baptismi monstrat, trium vocabulorum unam sacrilegus contingit esse personam... Nunquid quia Ariani Psalmum, Apostolum, Evengelia et alia multa ita ut catholici celebrant nos errorum vicinitatem fugiendo, haec sumus omnia relicture? Absit, quia illi ex nobis, ut scriptum est, exeuntes, praeter minorationem Deitatis Filii Dei et Spiritus Sancti, cetera ita penes se retinent sicut nos". Letter to bishop Boniface, *De Trina mersione, España Sagrada*, vol. XV, pp. 423-426. By the eighth century, when all danger of Arianism had ceased, the Spanish Church returned to the general rite of three-time immersion. (Vid. Villanueva, *Viaje literario*, vol. V, pp. 13-17).

[244]   Father Risco provided an eminent service to our letters by publishing the works of St. Braulius and Tajón in volumes XXX and XXXI of *España Sagrada, (Iglesia de Zaragoza)*.

way by Our Blessed Lady herself according to a beautiful, ancient, and time-honoured Toledan tradition related by Cixila, St. Ildephonsus' biographer.[245] The three infidels refuted here by St. Ildephonsus were not Spaniards or even contemporaries - an erroneous impression given by archbishop Rodrigo [246] and repeated by Alonso in his *Estoria d'Espanna*. Helvidius and Jovinianus had been two well-known heretics during St. Jerome's time; this saint wrote more than one treatise against them. The third *infidel* in St. Ildephonsus' book is a Jew who appears here as representing his sect. Obviously, we must not get the impression that it was simply a liking for oratory that made St. Ildephonsus pick up his pen to write in defence of a dogma that had no antagonists in Visigothic Spain! The fervour with which it is written reveals not an exercise in rhetoric, but a real controversy that was continuing and very much alive. Jews and Judaizers in Spain were already likely to erupt into blasphemies (as they always did) against the virginity of Our Lady. It is highly probable that Helvidius and Jovinianus likewise had some partisans, and Rodrigo's text might well be alluding to this, while getting the names wrong. Jovinianus denied Our Lady's Virginity during birth; Helvidius after birth; the Jews categorically denied both.

St. Ildephonsus devoted a series of chapters against each of these sacrileges. The challenge to the Jews is the most extensive and animated because the denials of Helvidius and Jovinianus were included in it as well. Once the divinity of Christ was shown against the anonymous Hebrew, he logically and naturally deduces the dogma of the virginity of Mary, since in the Mother of the Word Incarnate there can be no impurity either before or after birth. In the words of Isaiah: "Ecce virgo in utero concipiet et pariet filium". He explains the correct meaning of the only two texts in the Gospel on which Helvidius and Jovinianus (and "moderns" after them) placed special emphasis, to wit: "Ecce mater tua et fratres tui", and "Non cognovit eam Joseph, donec peperit filium suum" - showing it to be a common and well known Hebraism to call blood relatives "brothers", and adding that *donec* does not properly or necessarily have to mean 'until the end'. The book is written with fervour, eloquence even, [247] though soiled at times by a choice of words in bad taste nowadays and a clear abuse of synonymy. Quiricus, bishop of Barcelona, wrote two letters to St. Ildephonsus congratulating him on this work and praising its merit; they are preserved together with the saint's replies. We should also note *De proprietate personarum Patris et Filii et Spiritus Sancti* as a polemical tract, attributed to St.

---

[245]   Vid. Volume V of Flórez's *España Sagrada*, from page 594.

[246]   "Hujus tempore cum Helvidius et Pelagius, e Gallis venientes plerasque partes Hispaniae infecissent..." *De rebus Hispaniae*, lib. XI.

[247]   It can be found, along with St. Ildephonsus' other works, in volume I of *Colección de Padres Toledanos*, by Cardinal Lorenzana. Also to be found there are the letters of Quíricus and St. Ildephonsus.

Ildephonsus but lost today. [248]   Thirteen sermons on the Virgin go also under the name of the holy prelate of Toledo but they are generally considered apocryphal. Juan Bautista Poza confirms this. [249]

St. Julian, in addition to his two Apologiae (cited above) compiled extracts from the six books of St. Augustine against the Pelagian Julian.

Finally, we ought to mention King Sisebut, a fervent Catholic. In order to convert the Lombard monarchs Adualicald and Theodelinda, he addressed them a letter refuting Arianism and showing the equality of the divine Persons with texts from Sacred Scripture and theological arguments.[250]

Witiza's heterodox politics.   End of the Visigoth Empire.

Historical tragedies, as well as historical glories, always centre on one or two persons, prototypes of heroism or turpitude, as the case may be. Such is the case of Witiza, penultimate King of the Goths, the sum total of the miseries and moral aberrations of that very sad age.   Perhaps he is not deserving of such loathing and rancour, but the unanimous voice of the centuries accuses him of being a tyrant and oppressor of his people, of being lascivious and schismatic; and it is true that it was during his reign, more than in the brief period of his successor Roderick, that the decadence and decay of a flourishing empire finally came to ruin.

Witiza is today enveloped in that tenebrous shadow that often accompanies myths of mercilessness and unbridled frenzy. There is, of course, an historical Witiza, of whom little can be said because there is barely any available data. The nearest authority to his time, Isidore Pacensis, shows him to be a just prince, liberal and benign, who redresses the grievances and injustices of his father Egica, and throws into the flames falsified documents which favoured the Treasury. But let us bear in mind that these good notices refer to his first years as king, and it will not surprise us therefore that from the *Chronicon Moissiacensis* written in the ninth century, the figure of Witiza begins to change. According to the foreign author of this chronicle, Witiza (and this is credible) maintained a veritable harem of concubines and, crossing from practice to theory, sanctioned polygamy in a ruling that was to be extended to all his subjects, laymen and clerics. And if from the *Moissiacensis'* we pass on to the *Chronicon* by Sebastián of Salamanca (interpolated although this interpolation is not Pelayo's), Witiza becomes a "homo probosus et moribus flagitiosus" "comparable to a horse or a mule", not only sinking to public and scandalous

---

[248]   The false *Cronicón* of Julian Pérez (a work by Román de la Higuera) names the heretics that attacked in St. Ildephonsus' times the virginity of Our Lady: *Teudio* and *Hellado*. Needless to explain that these two personages are *entes of the mind*, invented to explain the text of archbishop Rodrigo.

[249]   Vid. N. Antonio.

[250]   Flórez, *España Sagrada*, vol. VII, pp. 318 and following.

polygamy but actually rendering councils void and hindering the implementation of their canons, thus both "king and priests ignoring and scorning the law of God". [251]

The Chronicler of Silos tells us a little more about him. But Witiza's legend does not seem to be fully established until the thirteenth century through the works of the Tudensian (Tuy) archbishop Rodrigo, the groundwork for the now acknowledged *General Chronicle*. Witiza appears here not only as an abominable tyrant but a schismatic and rebellious king who protects and favours the Jews, convenes a *conciliabulum* in Toledo, promulgates scandalous decrees on discipline and responds to the Pope's reprimand by separating his kingdom from communion with Rome and prohibiting anyone, by decree, to recognize the authority of the Sovereign Pontiff. Witiza insults the Church with the scandalous imposition of a relative of his, Oppas, to the see of Toledo occupied then by Sindered; he murders Favila, Duke of Cantabria, and puts Theodofred's eyes out. He brings down city walls and turns weapons into ploughshares, not because of his love for the art of peace making, as some lover of paradox has been wont to maintain, but to prevent and obstruct uprisings against his tyrannical rule.[252]

Of all these statements one could, and ought to, express much doubt. Let his support for the Jews stand as tolerance and generosity on the part of the monarch - a tolerance that was to be fatal, as we will see. Nor is the levelling down of fortifications unbelievable, at least for the reason given above. There is nothing strange about Witiza exercising barbarous severity on his subjects, probably rebels; the same could be said of all Gothic kings, even the better ones. The nepotism manifest in the sacrilegious election of Oppas should surprise no one either, in those wretched times. But the Toledo 'council' as well as the schism are facts of such gravity and significance that it is impossible to accept them unless they are accompanied by documentary evidence prior to the thirteenth century. We do know that Witiza called a council (Toledo XVIII) but the Acta are nowhere to be found. But who will contend that canons were approved in that council that went against the good order and discipline of the Church? Archbishop Rodrigo, though one of Witiza's accusers, explicitly says the opposite. As for separation from Rome, though affirmed by the Tudensian archbishop, this is not an event that earlier chroniclers could have forgotten for over four centuries. To my mind, these accusations are more than doubtful and Mayans can, I think, base his defence of King Witiza on solid grounds.

---

[251]   "Cum uxoribus et concubinis plurimis se inquinavit: et ne adversus eum censura ecclesiastica consurgeret, Concilia dissolvit, Canones obseravit, Episcopis, Presbyteris et Diaconibus habere praecepit..." (*España Sagrada*, vol. XIII, p. 477, *Chronicon Sebastiani*)

[252]   Practically all these facts (because some were added in the sixteenth-century) can be seen in Lucas de Tuy, *Chronicon*, era 744, and in D. Rodrigo, *Rerum in Hispania gestarum*, lib. III, chapters XV and XVI.

But all sinful and decadent generations need to unload their crimes on someone else's shoulders, and Witiza, who was undoubtedly licentious and cruel even if he did not actually authorize concubinage and polygamy by decree, has become for historians of the *Reconquista* the symbol of the Visigoths' moral disgrace, rather than a man. Witiza is the *expiatory victim*.

How did this powerful dynasty come crumbling to the ground? A question we must touch upon, if only incidentally. For those who see "justitia elevat gentes: miseros autem facit populos peccatum" as the formula of history's moral law, and with St. Augustine, Orosius, Salvianus, Fray José de Siguenza, Bossuet and other *providentialists* (adherents all to the only true philosophy of history), consider original sin as the source of disorder in the universe, individual sin as the cause of all human misery, and social sin as the explanation of the waste and ruin of nations, they cannot but point to heterodoxy, and to ignoring the moral law as the first and decisive factor in the fall of the Visigoth empire. Let us see how these factors influenced that fall.

It would be a mistake to assume that both races, the Gothic and the Hispano-Roman, had mixed completely at the time of the catastrophe of Guadalete. Unity had advanced much with Recared and not insignificantly with Recesvint, but it was far from being thoroughly accomplished. True, they all spoke the same language and mixed marriages were more frequent each day; but there were other more intimate, more radical differences that separated them still, and I would not hesitate to place difference of religion among them. It matters not that Arianism, at least in name, had perished, and that Recesvint presumed all heretical doctrine extinguished. The Goths' conversion was too swift, too *official*, if we may put it so, to be sincere for all of them. Not because they held some special attachment to their ancient cult; on the contrary, I believe that once the time of more or less overt conspiracies and strife were over during Recared's reign, all or almost all abandoned Arianism *de facto* and *de jure*. But for many (and it pains one to admit it), this was not in order to become Catholics, but rather, *indifferent*, or at least dissenting non-practising Catholics, haters of the Church and her institutions. What we could call 'the people' among the Visigoths, and that includes the clergy, embraced for the most part the new and salvific doctrine with true and unfeigned faith. But, I repeat, that military aristocracy which constantly busied itself in the making and unmaking of kings was not very Catholic at all. From Witeric to Witiza, examples abound. The councils tried in vain to bridle this arrogant faction which was irritated with the rapid ascendancy of the indigenous population, but this could have been accomplished only by supporting a Hispano-Latin to the throne, and they did not dare go that far, perhaps to avoid greater ills. In fact, the Visigoth kings themselves understood that the support of the Church was necessary against these defiant magnates who could raise them to the throne and bring them down with equal ease. We actually see Sisenand, Chindavist, and Ergivio basing themselves on councils' decisions to provide some stability to their power, which was often usurped, and to secure the crown for their children or kin. The councils, for the sake of order and stability accepted some *faits accomplis,* the results of which were impossible to keep in check. [253] But rebellions did not cease, and what we would now call *militarism* or *pretorianism* found its last and most befitting representative in Witiza.

Witiza is for us the symbol of Visigoth aristocracy, neither Arian nor Catholic, but sceptic, hostile to the Church because the Church moderated royal might and opposed its excesses. [254] The conduct of the Gothic nobility was lax: cruelty and lasciviousness soil the pages of its history at every turn; adultery and repudiation were frequent. Many of Gothic stock had entered the clergy, who in turn caught the infection. The prelates of Galicia bled their churches dry, as we see from canon IV of the seventh council. The eighth Council, in canons IV, V, and VI, had to call a halt to the moral incontinence of bishops, presbyters and deacons, and even then the harm did not stop: it was necessary to declare the sons of sacrilegious unions as servants.[255]

Potamius, Metropolitan of Braga, came before the tenth Council of Toledo to confess himself guilty of impurity. Simony bordered on scandal: sacred objects were sold for a pittance (canon VIII of Toledo XI). Kings founded dioceses to place their handpicked bishops in them. Wamba chose one for Aquis whom Toledo XII deposed. Witiza crowned his son, or brother, Oppas with two mitres, and Toledo was at one time under obedience to two bishops at the same time. Discord among ministers of the sanctuary got to such a dismal point that it was not unknown for a cleric to put out the lamps, strip the altars, and suspend offices so as to satisfy some personal rancour. [256] Even the heinous sin of sodomy had to be anathematised for clerics and laymen in canon III of Toledo XVI!

It is painful to read the last Acta. Not because the Fathers allowed themselves some laxity or had stopped watching over discipline; on the contrary, we see in opposition to these disorders prodigies of virtue and austerity in bishops, monks and abbots, copiously fruitful with God's blessing in charity and doctrine. But who were the saints and who were the sinners here? Who the wise and who the prevaricators? Here are the names of some: Isidore, Braulius, Tajón, Eugenius, Ildephonsus,[257] Julian, all of them Spaniards, all of them Latin, save the last, of Jewish descent. And what do we find on the other side? Sigbert, who treacherously conspires against his King Ergivio, Sindered, Oppas. Note that not one bears a Roman name.

---

[253]   See, as proof, Canons XI and XII of the sixth Council of Toledo.

[254]   Another element of disorder were the Byzantine Greeks brought by Atanagild who stayed in Cartagena until the time of Suintila. The few that remained always appear boisterous and insubordinate. Ergivio was Greek, he dethroned Wamba.

[255]   Vid. Canon X of Toledo IX.

[256]   Canon VII of Council of Toledo XIII.

[257]   The name Ildephonsus might appear Gothic. But that of his parents – Esteban and Lucía – leave no room for doubt as to his Latin ancestry.

An infantile fairy tale, this so-called *innocent virginity* of the barbarians! It provokes nothing but hilarity. Perhaps they were innocent once, in the woods of Germania, but as soon as they made it to the South and saw and touched the then decadent imperial civilisation, they certainly acquired a taste for it - for that unbridled and infernal longing for treasures and pleasures. They revelled in all with the lack of foresight and the abandonment of a savage. Their lechery was as cruel and furious as that of a soldier storming and pillaging a besieged town. Barbarism is always worse in the vulgar than in the refined. That individualism, or rather, excess of personalism that the tribes of the North brought with them, impelled them to frequent and scandalous rebellions, to a discord that was visceral, and worse, to betrayals, treason, and perjuries against their own people and race. They could not cherish the great ideals of *the fatherland* and *the state*, proper to the Helenic and Latin peoples, since they had no conception of such things. This is why the Visigothic nobility, led by Witiza's sons and his "archbishop" Oppas, sold their land to the Muslims, deserted at the battle of Guadalete, and Theudomir, after a brief resistance, surrendered to Abdalassis in a most dishonourable way.

The Visigothic race had much to attone for, not the least of which was their total incapacity to establish a stable regime and culture. And yet there was such greatness in that period! Mark, however, that science and art, the canons, the laws, all these are glories of our Catholic Church, they are Spanish glories. The Visigoths left nothing: not a stone, not a book, not a souvenir, except perhaps Sisebut and the Bulgoran letters, probably written by Spanish bishops anyway, and signed under the name of these high personages. Let us not deceive ourselves: our peninsular culture is thoroughly Roman, from top to bottom, with a pinch of Semitic salt thrown in. There is absolutely nothing Teutonic about us, thank God! What the Goths brought us can be reduced to some barbarian laws (that clash with the rest of our codices) and a disorder and lack of discipline that eventually was to dissolve the empire they had built.

I am well aware that the Hispano-Romans were not exempt from this contagion, for God never sends calamities but when all flesh has gone astray. But those who up to the last minute had battled against corruption in the councils rose from the fall to face the Arabs with a new spirit. Eulogius, Alvarus, Samson and Abbot *Spera-in-Deo* gave undying glory to the School of Córdoba, and martyrs and confessors were to prove both their faith and the sturdy mettle of their soul under the Muslim tyranny that followed. And then the Asturians, the Cantabrians, the Basques and the *Marca Hispanica* began, all from different starting points, an heroic, mad resistance against the Arab invaders which, aided by God from Whom all great inspiration comes, cleansed us off the Gothic grime, did away with difference among the races, and brought us all together to re-conquer our soil and to become one people. The *Pelagio* (leader) that took on such enterprise had a Roman name. There are Goths among his successors: Falfilla, Froyla - a proof of unity in danger. Soon after, Gothism was no more, lost completely amid the Asturian, Navarrese, Catalan and Mozarabic peoples. Recesvint's law had been accomplished. What had not been achieved in times of plenty had to be done now in a blustery hailstorm. There were no more Goths and Latins, only Christians and Muslims, and among these more than a few apostates.

It is a fact proven beyond doubt that the Arab invasion was iniquitously sponsored by Jewish people living in Spain. It was the Jews who opened the gates of the main cities to them. The Jews were numerous, and they were wealthy. They had already conspired before during Egica's reign, putting the security of the kingdom in grave danger. The seventeenth Council of Toledo punished them harshly reducing them to servitude (canon VIII). But Witiza favoured them in turn, and to this protection they responded by plotting together with all the other dissidents. The indigenous population could have resisted a handful of Arabs crossing the Strait, but Witiza had disarmed them, fortifications were down, lances had been turned into rakes. History does not recall a swifter and more rapid conquest, one that was aided, almost on a wager, by Goths, Jews, political dissidents, personal revenges, and religious hatred.

Quid leges sine moribus vanae proficiunt? How could a society survive when mortally injured by irreligion and scandal, even if its laws were good and administered by prudent men? What is there to hope from a people "for whom infidelity was common in contract and in word?" as Toledo XVII painfully states in canon VI. Then add to this the poison of the *magic arts*, mistresses of royal and plebeian consciences, and that last sign of despair and dejection: *suicide*, anathematised in canon IV of Council XVI.[258]

The vices of the elective monarchy, or the lack of racial unity, are not enough to explain the Arab conquest. We shall have to dig deeper for its root, and with the holy author of the Proverbs repeat: "Justitia elevat gentem: miseros autem facit populos peccatum".[259]

---

*   On this question see *Estudio sobre la invasión de los árabes en España*, by Eduardo Saavedra and *Leyendas del último rey godo*, by Juan Menéndez Pidal. [Editor, 1912]

[258]   Father Tailhan, his love for the Visigoths notwithstanding, confesses that suicide was unknown among us until the barbarians arrived.

[259]   I wish to be allowed here to object with all the energy I can gather to those utter absurdities found in Rousselot's book *Les Mystiques Espagnols*. He says:

"The Visigoths do not appear to have serious inclination for study; the protection granted by some of its kings to the works of Braulius, Bishop of Saragossa, and to Isidore of Seville, is an isolated event and without consequence. Spain, at the time of its fall, was not at the level of France; in vain would you find there an Alcuin, never mind a Scoto Eriugena. Ignorance reigned everywhere... In France, Charlemagne immense personality granted great liberty to man, and consequently, to reason. From this, there was a favourable push to the development of intelligence of which Spain offers not the slightest vestige during the Goths time'.

How very daintily is expressed here all that is contrary to truth! Neither France nor any other nation in the West was, culturally, Spain's equal during the Visigoth epoch. Not because the Visigoths were cultured, but because Spaniards were. M. Rousselot seems to know nothing about our history and forgets that the Hispano-Roman race was the most literate and most numerous: that is, Licinianus's race from whom the French scholastics learnt the doctrine of the *containing and contained soul*, the race of St. Leander, St. Isidore, St. Braulius, Tajón, the true *Master of the Sentences*,

Book 1
Chapter 4
The Magic Arts and Divination. Astrology.
Superstitious practices in the Roman and Visigoth worlds.

Preliminaries. Magic in the ancient world. Greece and Rome.
Superstitious practices of both indigenous and nonindigenous people on the Peninsular. Vestiges preserved until our time.
Journey of Apollonius of Tiana to Betis. Extracts from Hispano-Latin writers concerning the magic arts.
Reports by Saints Lucianus and Martian. Superstitions anathemathised at the Council of Elvira. Efforts of emperor
Theodosius against magic.
Superstition in Galicia under Swabian domination. Treatise *De correctione rusticorum* of St. Martin of Braga.
Magic arts and divination among the Visigoths.

---

and teacher and predecessor of the Peter Lombards of this world – the best synthesisers of Scholastic Theology; the race of St. Eugenius, St. Ildephonsus, St. Julian... One would need to be bold indeed to say that barbarism reigned in Spain during these men's time! What was it that they knew in France then that we did not? Where can one find any great French writer during the seventh century? Would M. Rousselot please point them out - I fail to spot them anywhere. Give us a list of names, such as those that we can offer, for the whole of that century! Then we can have a debate!

Of course he cannot name a single one. There are none! And please, let us not get on to the Carolingian renaissance. Does M. Rousselot really expect us to believe that Alcuin is to be compared to St. Isidore, whom, by the way, he continuously copies and clumsily abbreviates? Will he, perchance, try to convince us that Scotus Eriugena was *French*? Does he not know that he was refuted by the *Spaniard*, Prudentius Galindus? Is he unaware of the part that in that *Renaissance* played by the *Spaniard* Claudius of Turín, the *Spaniard* Theodulphus, the *Spaniard* Felix? But how can he know that! He thinks that Felix was *prior to Recared's conversion*!

With lightweight authors such as this, a debate would be a waste of time and effort. When will the French cease to possess that blind animosity towards all things Spanish, that systematic desire, it would seem, to put us down, in bad faith and against all the laws of truth? Thankfully, there are some honourable exceptions. It is pleasing to be able to counter Rousselot's aberrations with a phrase from the great scholastic historian Hauréau on his dissertation about our compatriot Theodulphus: 'Christian Spain was, around the mid-eighth century, one of the most civilised regions of the ancient world. Like Italy and like Gaul, she had her barbarians, but in less disastrous circumstances' *(Singularités historiques et littéraires)*.

Has not Rousselot even leafed through the pages of his compatriot Abbé Bouret on the *School of Seville at the time of the Visigoths*? It would be futile to insist on it. But maybe we can convince the author of *Les Mystiques* with an argument *ad hominem*. After having said that 'ignorance reigned everywhere', he adds: 'However, the Goths had attained a high degree of culture'. Which opinion shall we opt for?

On the issues discussed in this chapter, the works of Dahn and Helfferich on *Visigoth Arianism and Spanish heterodoxy* shed a great deal of light. [The exact title of Helfferich work is *Geschichte des Westgotischen Arianismus*, Berlin, 1860, Editor, 1912].

Preliminaries. Magic in the ancient world. Greece and Rome.

Let us now turn our attention (and in so doing bring this First Book to a close) to an altogether different class of religious disorder – one not particularly exclusive to any one time or nation, but a sure and permanent calamity to all.

But first, a question. Should the *goetic* arts, divination, and all that other entourage of superstitions and fears from them derived be included in the type of history I am writing here? Are these practices important? Are they consequential? Are they so intrinsically real that they should in fact be accepted as a subject worthy of serious research?

It is undeniable that the demonic arts, a perpetual temptation to human free will, do exist. As for their real or actual impact, there the issue varies. Theoretically, we cannot ignore them. Historically, not always so. In the Holy Books we read of the prodigies carried out by the Magi of Pharaoh, and the calling up of the spirit of Samuel by the seer of Endor. But these indisputable facts aside, as well as one or two others sufficiently corroborated so as to leave no room for doubt, one must be mindful, of course, not to fall into petty credulity in this field.

God can, for His own high ends, consent to a disruption of natural laws by the powers of the abyss, more apparent than real, as happened in Egypt. In solemn circumstances such as those preceding the loss of Saul, He could make the dead answer the questions of the living. Everything is possible to Supreme Omnipotence. But it would be childish, nay, demented, to suppose that the prince of hell is under some kind of obligation to satisfy every absurd question the inane and the idle happen to think up every time they fancy calling on him via magic spells and ridiculous mediums. The devil has never been known to be an idiot. He has more than ample means at his disposal, and with hideous consequences at that, to lead human weakness astray without any need of all this absurd paraphernalia proper to outlandish and eccentric parodies. Moreover, it is sacrilegious and conducive to Manichaeism to presume a continual action by an evil spirit who enslaves man with magic spells and enchantments, and that God would consent to such tyranny.

In Spain, thank God, we find very few serious cases, if any, of people coming forward as corroborating witnesses to such events in the history of magic and the superstitious arts as I am now about to relate. Mere curiosity on one side, plain bad faith on the other, is what we will find. But it is obvious from a mere enumeration of such arts that they are heretical and forbidden by all law, human and divine.

To invoke the devil with this or that aim in mind, by whatever means, constitutes a real act of apostasy even if the devil does not answer, as is usually the case. Astrology is fatalism, pure and simple, because it ties and subdues the free will of a human being to planetary influences. All divination suffers from this and similar ills. Superstitions, from whatever source, are as contrary to true faith as darkness is to light; this is why all authors who have treated of sorcery and necromancy consider their adherents *ipso facto* heretics, and Fray Alonso de Castro in his book *De justa haereticorum punitione* (lib. 1, chapters, 13, 14, 15 and 16) holds them subject to the same spiritual and temporal pains, allowing only for some exemptions in favour of fortune-tellers and other predictions that do not call up the devil in their invocatory practices. In reality superstition is not formal heresy; but it is *sapit haeresim* and consequently comes within the bounds of heterodoxy.

From an historical perspective, nothing seems broader or, let us say, more muddled than the study of Magic and Astrology. But this is only at first sight. When we consider that these arts are more or less the same in all epochs and for all races and cultures, it becomes easier to reduce them down to three main principles - sources of all human aberration. These are, as I understand them, Naturalist Pantheism, Manichaeism or Dualism, and Fatalism.

From Pantheism, we get that multitude of spirits and emanations that live and palpitate throughout the whole of creation, begetters of engaging images and nocturnal terrors. From Dualism, the theurgic formulas, demonic cults, sanguinary and obscene goetic arts, pacts, witchcraft, that one particular *sabbath*, all of them the offspring of the deification of the prime principle of evil. Finally, Astrology: all auguries, spells and curses result from a rejection or lack of understanding of human liberty - instruments all dreamed up by man to pretend knowledge of the future, all of them laws to enslave the free exercise of his actions. All illicit superstition derives from one of these three roots. To these of course we must add ignorance (still with us, unfortunately) on what the agents of natural forces are, and how they operate.

We shall speak here only of black or goetic magic and exclude the so-called white or naturalistic magic, which in any case was a kind of recreational physics – comparable to necromancy only in the mystery with which it used to wrap up its operations. The famous statute of Memnon is one of the most poignant works of this type of magic among the ancients.

All this aside, there would be nothing easier for me now than to start flaunting about borrowed erudition and speculate on the magic of the Egyptians and Chaldeans - a knowledge always in the hands of the schools or priestly casts who saw Divination, Astrology and Theurgy as true sciences to be applied to worship. For me, by no means an Egyptologist, it is enough to go to Exodus, chapter 7, where we have all read: "And Pharaoh called the wise men and magicians; and they also by Egyptian enchantments and certain secrets did in like manner." ("Vocavit autem Pharao sapientes et maleficos et fecerunt etiam ipsi per incantationes Aegyptiacas et arcana, quaedam similiter").

Magic among the Egyptians came to assume something of a zoolatrical and somewhat fetichist character. Astrology reached absurdities such as those held by our Priscillianists, with each star influencing diverse parts of the body -

never fewer than thirty.[260] These doctrines were to change during Alexandrian times through contact with the doctrines of Greece. The book *De mysteriis Aegyptiorum* attributed to Jamblicus gives us a faithful idea of this particular type of theurgy, where the crucial part of the magic spell was in the actual secret words themselves.

Astrology and Chaldean (or Syrian) sciences were terms that became almost synonymous, at least for the Greeks. Indeed Astronomy owes many positive developments to this not-altogether-futile knowledge of the Chaldeans, though under its cloak there also lay a devastating fatalist outlook. "For the Chaldeans" - writes Diodorus of Sicily – "the stars have absolute dominion over the good or ill fate of man. Celestial phenomena become the symbols of the happiness or misfortune of nations". And in another passage: "the Chaldeans dedicate themselves to divination science, predict the future, perform purifications, sacrifices and incantations. They interpret the meaning of a bird's flight, dreams, and prodigies...they examine the entrails of victims... their science is transmitted from father to son".

In the Book of Daniel, the Chaldeans appear also as seers, magi, haruspices and interpreters of dreams: modes of divination identical to those used in Rome. But the area where Syrian knowledge predominated above all others was in the formulation of a person's specific horoscope (a genethliac theme) in relation to how the stars were positioned at the time of a person's birth.

Magic, which for the Chaldeans was derived from Sabianism, was in Persia the offspring of Mazdeist dualism. It evolved to a stage such that the name *magi*, or priests, came to be associated with that of sorcerers. The methods of divination practised in Persia were more numerous that those practised in Babylon. A book attributed to Osthanes mentioned hydromancy, magic spheres, aeromancy, astrology, necromancy and the use of lanterns, mirrors and smooth and shining surfaces. "Ut narravit Osthanes" says Pliny "species ejus plures sunt, namque et aqua et sphaeres, et aere, et stellis, et lucernis ac pelvibus, securibusque et multis aliis modis divina promittit: praeterea umbrarum, inferorumque colloquia".

Also from Persia came Catoptromancy, the knowledge of *specularii*, that is, divination by means of magic mirrors, according to Varro and quoted by St. Augustine (*De civitate Dei*, lib. VII). This was a kind of lecanomancy, or art of evocation of images by means of a cup, an emblem, the blade of a sword, or a vessel filled with water.

Divination by means of willow stalks, on the other hand, was characteristic of the Scythes, as we read in Heredotus (Book IV): "There is no wanting of diviners among the Scythes, whose manner of foretelling by willow stalks I shall henceforth describe: they bring canes stacked up high to the place

---

[260]   Vid. Origen, *Contra Celsus*, lib. VIII and, among contemporary authors, Lepsius' *Todtenbuch der Aegypter*, cited by Maury in *La Magie et l'Astrologie dans l'Antiquité et au Moyen Age.*

where they are going to perform the ritual, lay them on the ground, and proceed to untie them; then, one at a time, they take each stalk and put it aside, all the while foretelling. As they continue murmuring, they tie them back together and re-stack them again. This type of divination they have inherited from their forefathers". "The so-called *Enarees* believe that the goddess Venus grants them the art of divination. They use the inner crust of the *tilia* plant, make three stalks of each thin layer, roll them up around their fingers and, as they unroll them, they foretell". [261]

The Scythes held augurs in great esteem but burned them alive if their predictions failed.

Julius Caesar tells of the Celts of Gaul and Germania in chapters V and VI of Book VIII. He does not say much about the magic arts specifically except when he mentions the existence of a druidical priestly college among the Gauls (but not among the Germanic tribes)[262]. Tacitus, in his book *De situ, moribus, populisque Germaniae* is a little more explicit, and what he says concurs fully with the news Heredotus gives us about the Scythes. The Latin historian writes: "The people of Germania consecrate woods and forests and name the secret places they venerate after the names of their gods. They observe foretelling... their fortune-telling is without artifice. They cut a stick from a tree, cut it into pieces and put signs on each one. Then they throw the sticks onto a white garment. The village priest (if the ceremony is public) or the *pater familias* (if private) after praying to the gods, raising his eyes to heaven, takes three sticks, one at a time, and proceeds to foretell according to the signs drawn on them. If fortune is seen to be contrary they stop for that day, but if favourable, they verify it with the foretellers. They can also divine by means of the flight and the song of birds. But what is singular about this nation is the use of horses to foretell fortune. These animals are kept at public expense in the same sacred woods and forests. The horses are white and have served in no human endeavour... and when they carry the sacred carriage they are accompanied by the priest or the king of the town all the while carefully considering their neighing and snorting. No other oracle is given more credit than this one, not only the people but the nobles and high born as well, as also the priests who see themselves as ministers of the gods, whose will they believe is known to horses".

Little more than this is what the ancients left us on the superstitions of the people of Gaul, Germany and Brittany. But since the cult of the Celts was a naturalist cult, and the Druids, as Julius Caesar tells us, also taught Astronomy, we can easily conclude that astrological superstition had to be a part of their cult; and since they believed in metempsychosis (again, on his authority), they were probably more than a little inclined to necromancy and other evocations.

---

261   Translation into Spanish by Father Bartolomé Pou, Madrid, 1846, vol. 1, p. 337.

262   Cicero attributes them with great skill in the divination arts (*De divinatione*).

Customs still currently in existence tell of other practices not mentioned by the classics.

Celtic veneration of sacred fountains, hydromancy included, continued after the coming of Christianity. In several places in Great Britain and in Brittany, at St. Ellian's font in Denbigh, in particular, divination was practised until relatively recent times by means of throwing pins and needles into the water. In Scotland, enchantments and spells to facilitate childbirth also continued for a long time after. [263] The cavern called *St. Patrick's Purgatory* in Ireland had undoubtedly been a *necyomanteion* intended for evocation of the souls of the dead in ancient times. [264]

In Gaul, the *tempestarii* (so called because they brought about thunder and hailstorms), were sorcerers, haruspices, and interpreters of dreams. To Celtic divinities dethroned by the Faith, there succeeded in Northern lands a throng of gnomes, kobolds, trolls, etc., i.e. enchanters, goblins, elves, nymphs of the sea, of rivers, fountains and mountains. These remnants of ancient mythologies have steadfastly resisted change, as have solstice festivities, the verbena, and the four-leaf clover: reminiscences both of the sacred mistletoe.

But let us leave the barbarians (of whom I can speak only by reference) and come back to the Greeks and Latins from whom our culture evolved.

Magic, in Greece as in Rome, was of two types: one public and official, associated with worship; the other, popular, heterodox, oftentimes punished by law. The oracles - the centre of Helenic political life - are a brilliant expression of the first. Their history does not concern us here for they played little or no part in the superstitions of the Christian peoples, and even less so in the Iberian Peninsula. Augural art, not as important to the Greeks as it was to the Latins, and less respected by them, had been predominant in times prior to the consolidation and political influence of oracles. We remember in the *Iliad* the magician Calchas who reveals to the Achaeans the causes of the plague sent by Phaebo: that same Calchas who in Aulide had announced the will of the gods in regard to Iphigenia's sacrifice. Observation of dreams appears in Book II of the same poem, if the reference is not one of those interpolated texts. But scepticism about divination must have been prevalent as early as father Homer's time if we are to judge by Hector's sublime reply: "the best augury is fighting for your land". The law of *fatum,* however, is inflexible for the Homeric heroes. In book XIX, Xanthus one of Achilles' sacred horses speaks, inspired by Juno, and foretells to the son of Patroclus of his early and forthcoming death. Then swift-footed Achilles answered: 'Why dost thou prophesy my death? Thou needest not at all. Well know I even of myself that it is my fate to perish here, far from

• Cons. P. Sébillot, *Le paganisme contemporain chez les peuples celto-latins.* Paris, 1908. (Editor, 1912)

263 I. Graham Dalyell, *The darker superstitions of Scotland.*

264 Wright, *St. Patrick's Purgatory*, London, 1844.

my father dear, and my mother; howbeit even so will I not cease, until I have driven the Trojans to surfeit at war."

In the *Odyssey*, a poem from a different time and culture, magic and divination arts are held in much higher esteem. In Book II Telemachus sees two eagles sent by Zeus and takes favourable augural portents from their flight. The prototype of the *pharmaceutria*, the sorceress, unknown to the author of the Iliad is, in the Odyssey, Circe, whose magic spear has transmutational powers and who, drawn by their chant, the sweet taste of Prammius wine, and the victuals mixed with cheese, flour and honey, turns Ulysses' companions into swine, "carminibus Circe socios mutavit Ulyssi", but not however the ingenious Ithacan who resisted the enchantments with the molly herb given to him by Mercury.

Circe, very much a product of Greek imagination, is a pleasant and peaceable enchantress - not a horrid and repugnant witch like those in *Macbeth*. Ulysses looks like an outright savage when, sword in hand, he seizes the *euplocama* goddess who, in love with him, regales him in her fine palace. All is colourful and rosy in the Odyssey save for the necromancy in Canto XI with its reminiscences of true goety. Ulysses goes to the land of the Cimmerians, digs a pit on the ground, fills it with the victims' blood, and having made the three libation, the souls from Erebus came thronging in crowds, thirsty for dark blood. Ulysses bids them not to come near until the shadow of the blind Theban diviner Tiresias rises to predict his return to Ithaca, among other things. In Book XX, Penelope's lovers are terrorised by a hideous curse, and Theoclymenus announces their forthcoming death.

The Orphic rites, the mysteries of Eleusis and Samothrace, and other varied expiation and purification practices played no small part in the diffusion of theurgic practices. A noble and beautiful *hyeratic* poem of which not one authentic relic remains must have been linked to the ceremonies to which Epimenides of Crete and other righteous of paganism owe their fame. The legend of Epimenides, he who at about the fifty-sixth Olympiad purified Athens, having been profaned by Cylon's crime, is singular indeed: this thaumaturge was fed by nymphs and could leave his body and come back to it whenever it took his fancy. The same is said of Hermotimus of Clazomenae.

Astrological auguries regarding agriculture, propitious and unpropitious days, and varied other superstitions occupy an eminent place in Hesiod's *Works and Days*. He points out moons propitious to marriage as well as those when the unrestrained Furies walk the earth. He does not overlook divination by flight of birds but pays little or no attention to transmutation or the goetic arts.

Athens' genius for tragedy took novel and beautiful types of minstrels to the stage - seers, prophetesses and wonder-workers. Aeschylus incarnated *manteía (second sight* or prophetic spirit) in Cassandra of Troy: a wondrous image high above, between heaven and earth, to announce the evils that were to befall Agamemnon and the royal house of Maecenas. We sense priestly inspiration palpitating throughout Eumenides' terrifying poem - immortal avengers of the crime and exemplar of so many other fantastical representations of every time and place. Nor is necromancy wanting with the Persians: the shadow of Darius, for example, when he presents himself before the ancients of Sussa to hear of Xerxes' disaster from the lips of Athos and pronounce grave and unhappy dictums on the fortunes and intransigence of human things.

Blind Tiresias, "knower of all things of heaven and earth" reappears in Sophocles' tyrant Oedipus only to see his knowledge scorned by the obstinate king of Thebes who, himself injured by unforeseen misfortune, becomes (in Oedipus in Colonna) a seer, a prophet, a sacred object announcing future victories and prosperity to befall upon the soil where his ashes will rest. A lofty and peregrine concept of the Greeks, this - to suppose divination powers inseparable from the calamities with which the gods oppress those who forsake serenity, temperance, *sophrosyne* – due to arrogance and pride! And he who is the living epitome of celestial rage, is himself the one who announces his decrees to mortals!

It is pleasant to remember the classics. Clytemnestra's dream brings indescribable horror to Electra - the omen of Orestes' revenge symbolised by the serpent that devours the breasts of Agamemnon's homicidal wife. In *Trichinias*, a magical and supernatural element of a different kind is represented by the tunic of the centaur Neso.

Euripides uses - and abuses - auspices. For him, the enchantress is Medea: her revenge and jealousy different from that of Circe, her passion mightier than her powers of witchcraft; contrary to the Spaniard Seneca's imitation of it - on this one point inspired by Ovid's *Metamorphoses*.

A Spanish scholar of the seventeenth century, Pedro de Valencia, in his *Discurso* (unpublished) on witches and sundry things relating to magic, found a parallel between the witches' *sabbath* and the nocturnal feasts held by the Bacchae, such as are described in the singular and terrifying tragedy of Euripides, which carries this title. The description Nuncio makes of some Bacchants transport us almost to Zugarramurdi's *aquelarre*. The only thing missing is the billy goat. But even this is not absent in the *Sabasias* or Bacchus Sabasius' feasts, a degraded sequel to the Bacchae and the real origin of that *sabbath*, even in name.

It took time for Dionysius' orgiastic and deeply naturalistic cult, for Cithaeron's abominations and nightly terrors, Adonis' Phoenician rites and other eastern superstitions to adapt to Greece; they never quite lost their mysterious and secret character, tolerated only in part by the legislators. This is how the cult to the tri-formed Hecate, which was invoked during the *trivios* at night with strange ceremonies capable of inspiring terror in the bravest of hearts, came to fuse with another occult and murky superstition practised above all by the women of Thessaly. Origen, or whoever the author of *Philosophoumena* was, preserved for us the formula of the magic spell.

"Hail, infernal, earthly, celestial (tri-formed Bombon! Come, Goddess of the *Trivios*, Guide of light, Queen of the night, Rival of the Sun, friend and companion of Darkness; Thou who rejoicest in the growling of dogs and, errant, blood dripping, walkest among sepulchres in darkness thirsting for blood! O Terror of mortals, Gorgon, Mormon, Moon of a thousand forms, watch over my sacrifice". No different from how fifteenth-century Castilian witches invoked the devil - if we are to believe our incomparable *Celestina*.

In *Pharmaceutria*, one of Theochrytus' marvellous idylls, the second in order, one sees a scene of incantations, modern-style. Sîmaetha, a young girl from Syracuse, wants to enchant Delphis, who flees. She prepares a philtre, wraps the cup in sheepskin, and invokes:

> shine brightly, Moon,
> this murmured spell is for you and Hecate
> dark of the earth, who scares the trembling whelps
> visiting the barrowed dead where blood rots blackly.
> hail, dreadful one, be with me till I've made
> this magic fiercer than any made by Circe
> Medea, or Perimede the yellow-haired.

After this supplication, she pours flour and salt into the fire, burns a bay leaf, allows for a wax figure to melt down, turns the magical rhombus-wheel round several times, and calls on to the bird Phyngx to bring Delphis back to her arms:

> Delphis has rent me. So I burn the bay
> for Delphis. See, it crackles. In a flash
> it burns away and leaves a ghost of ash.
> thus may the flesh of Delphis be burnt away.
> *bird-wheel, hither wind him, wind home my lover.*
> the spirits aids, the mammet melts above.
> may Myndian Delphis thus be drained by love.
> dizzy him, magic bronze, swung roaringly
> by Aphrodite, twirl him home to me.
> *bird-wheel, hither wind him, wind home my lover.*

The making of love potions, the *hippomanes* of Arcadia, mane pulled from a colt's forehead, these were some of chief arts of Thessaly's enchantresses who, in addition, had the gift of attracting the *empusas*, that is, monsters with asses' feet. To these Phylostratus refers more than once in his *Life of Apolonius of Tiana*. The witches of Thessaly had yet one more phenomenal power: Transmutations. We can see this in Lucianus' famed novel, *Lucian - or The Ass -* a sort of parody on Lucianus of Patras' *Metamorphosis*. Lucian's guest undresses; she then puts two grains of incense in a lantern, picks up an urn, smears herself with it from head to toe, turns into a bat and off she flies: much what our own Alava witches punished in the Auto of Logroño tried to do. Lucian wanted to do the same but got the magic potion's recipe mixed up and ends up as an ass instead, from which state, after sundry adventures, he comes out eating roses.

By Lucianus' time, the magic arts had reached a point of utter insanity, with all the sad consequences that brings with it. Love for superstitious and exotic practices was growing at the same rate old beliefs were dying down. Few, if any, believed in the power of the oracles, "now silent" says Plutarch. Yet the *necyomanteion* (or Trophonius' passageway) whose mysteries were pure goety was avidly consulted. Old seers, Calchas and Tiresias, had now given way to Chaldean *mathematicians*, to fortune-tellers and horoscopers; to travelling Assyrian sorcerers like the one who provided Theocritus' Simaetha with a lethal drink which could send the soul of any hated person to Orco; to the Magi, Osthanes' disciples, who could see the future on water or in a mirror, and traced repugnant and atrocious figures on walls which would suddenly become ablaze with the sinister flames of black grout and asphalt tar (vid. *Philosoph.*); to the *orpheotelests*, skilled in purification and exorcism; to the *psycharogs* who invoked the spirits; to the *pitons*, or ventriloquists; to the *goetas* who invoked the infernal gods with piercing howls; to the *ophiogenas,* or snake charmers, "frigidus in pratis cantando rumpitur anguis"*;* to pseudo-prophets like Alexander whose trickery Lucianus related. In sum, to all things supernatural, preposterous and absurd that could ruffle the mind of a society now hopelessly sick and lost. The enchanters could do it all: rotate crops, call up rain and hail, make themselves invisible. More! They could bring down the moon from heaven to earth, "carmina de coelo possunt deducere lunam…"

This was what the cult to Hecate had come to! Should the reader be interested in finding out more about these and other such practices, he would do well to leaf through the vastly entertaining works of the Samosata satirist; they will not prove to be a disappointing read.

All modern superstition has its ancient equivalent. If in Spain we had water diviners who could discover treasures under seven soils, Alexander the *Seudomantis* had done so already long ago. And from the *Philopseudes* tales, how can we forget the Egyptian Panchrates! This was a man who had a host of spirits ready to obey his every command; with magic spells he could turn sticks and stones into servants who would serve him meekly in all of his needs. What are these but those *familiar spirits* we are to bump into more than once in the course of this history?

Against this whole ensemble of popular superstitions, there arose a philosophic and "learned" magic that refused to be likened to goety and called itself *theurgy*. Its *hierophants* were the neo-Platonists of Alexandria, successors to the neo-Pythagoreans in the fashion of *Apolonius of Tiana.*

The basis of the theurgic systems of Plotinus, Porphyry, Proculus and Marinus was the belief in a series of demons, some good, others evil – intermediaries between God and man - who could be lured and appeased with purifications, spells, and magic rites. Platonist demonology appropriated what was left of the Egyptian and Orphic mysteries combined with reminiscences of oriental cults. It was then that those portentous biographies of Pythagoras came to be written, turning the ancient Italiot philosopher in something like a wonder-worker gifted with ubiquity: a diviner of dreams who turns up at the Olympic games displaying a golden thigh. Those Alexandrian imbeciles could understand the thinker only when coated with their theurgic gloss! Plotinus boasted that he had a god in the figure of a dragon for a relative of his [265] whereas Egyptian priests had one demon only. Porphyry evoked Eros and Anteros, and the statues of these little gods would come down from their pedestal to embrace him. One such Anthusus invented divination by means of clouds. Ammonius had a very erudite donkey who loved poetry, and so much, that it would forgo its fodder just for the chance to hear hexameter verses. Another Alexandrian theurgist managed through demonical arts to have a voice as strong as that of one thousand men... Things such as these were written by Proculus, Marinus, Damascius, men who to cap it all had a good head on their shoulders, significant figures in the history of philosophy! Sad, pitiable human reason!

In Rome, the supernatural arts followed the same course as they did in Greece. There was a divination art – an essential part of worship – as religious as it was political. One could look at it from two different angles: *augural* art, which was indigenous, and *haruspicina* art, learnt from the Etruscans. We remember the legend of Accio Nevio, who split a rock with a penknife, or the purchase of the sibylline books made by Tarquinius Superbus. The overwhelming Etruscan influence embodied in these myths illustrates the importance and rapid growth of divination among the Latin peoples. From then on, it will never be severed from their history. What the oracles were in Greece, the auguries will be in Rome - organised within a priestly college. No war was undertaken without assessing the omens first; the failure of an enterprise was attributed either to having neglected them or to sacrilege: consul Claudius Pulcher's defeat in Carthage, for example. Superstition will bring about horrendous deeds and ventures, like the consecration of the three Decius to the infernal gods, or throwing oneself from Curtius into the open pitch at the centre of the Forum. Each time we leaf through the works of Livy, we see singular prodigies such as these and expiatory exercises: showers of blood, sex mutations, statues sweating or brandishing a lance, eclipses and comets filling people with terror. Even today, divination through dreams is frequent in Rome – fatalist, horrifying practices woven into every aspect of daily life!

Contact with alien civilisations brought new and pernicious rites to Rome. We see this in the *Senatus-consulto* against the Bacchanals who had come from Etruria and Campannia. They carried all the marks of a secretive, lewd, and brutal society, the likes of which had never been seen in Greece, at least to the same degree. The cult to Hecate was universal, too, no doubt because of its similarity with the old italic goddess *Mana-Geneta*. Chaldean astrologers, known as mathematicians, did not take long to make their presence felt: sometimes tolerated, others banned, but seen always with a mixture of terror and curiosity by great and small. And on to the astrologers footsteps there followed the

---

[265]   I have said nothing about the *Socratic demon* because it was not, to my mind, a superstitious belief held by Socrates but rather a symbolic or figure of speech on his part.

chiromantics, or diviners, who specialised in palm-reading - a superstition of Egyptian origin.

The old Roman belief in *lemures* and *larvas* led them to accept necromancy willingly, and Thessalian sorceresses were identified with *lamias*, in all ways similar to modern witches.

One can find histories of all these aberrations in Roman literature. Augur Marcus Tulius in his discreet dialogue *De Divinatione* shows himself thoroughly sceptical of them all, as if wanting to paraphrase Cato the Elder's famous saying: "I am not sure two augurs could look at each other in the face and not burst out laughing".

This disbelief might well have been universal. The poisonous alien plant of the magic arts was flourishing as fast as old beliefs in past patriotic and heroic deeds and the life and survival of Rome was collapsing. The poets of the Augustan era are faithful chroniclers of this growth.

Virgil's *pharmaceutria,* or sorceress (*Eclogue VIII*) asks her maid to tie dressings to the altar and bring over incense and verbena; she offers three-coloured ribbons to the goddess; walks the effigy of her lover around the altar three times; smears the molly sauce, burns the bay leaf, buries Daphnis' garments on the doorway, and concocts a potion made up of venomous herbs from Ponto. This is more than just mere imitation of Theocritus - the rites used by the poets from Mantua and Syracuse are quite different.

The typical Roman sorceress - the *lamia* that frightens children - is here fierce *Canidia,* from Venice (*Epodes* V and XVII). For her malefic concoctions she draws from the same store as all *pharmaceutrias* and *veneficas* then known: funeral cypress boughs, feathers of a night-roving screeching owl smeared with the blood of a hideous toad, herbs from Ioldos and Iberia, and bones snatched from the jaws of a starving bitch, all these to be burned in the magic flames. She herself, gnawing her uncut nail, brags of her magic skills:

"And yet no herb nor root, lurking in rough places, escaped me"

The purpose for all this paraphernalia and the infanticide depicted by Horace was the usual one: to lure an unfaithful lover back into one's arms. "He lies asleep on perfumed couch, forgetful of all mistresses. Aha! He walks at will, freed by the charm of some cleverer enchantress. By no wonted potions, Varus, thou creature doomed bitterly to weep, shalt thou return to me; and, summoned by no Marsian spells, shall thy devotion be revived. A stronger draught I will prepare, a stranger draught pour out, to meet thy scorn; and sooner shall the heaven sink below the sea, with earth spread out above, than thou shouldst fail to burn in love for me, even as burns the pitch in the smoky flame".

Actually, Canidia was a real person. Her real name was Gratidia (or so those in the know at the time tell us), a perfumist from Naples who made love potions. Horace, who carried a personal grudge against her, retold in *Epode* some of the gossip about her. In the comical satire VIII of Book I, *Olim truncus erat,* he placed her at the Esquiline cemetery in the company of Sagana searching for bones at night and scratching out a hole with her fingernails to fill it with the blood of a black lamb so as to perform an act of necromancy - calling up the souls of the dead. But her invocations to Tesiphone and Hecate did not bring about the desired result and one such Priapus, who happened to be in the garden at the time, punished the witches in a manner such that no one who has read the satire can ever forget. Horace went on to make a mocking retraction of all his invectives against her. In *Epode* XVII, he humbly confesses to Canidia's skills, the power and might of her spells ("Libros carminun valentium"), her magical whirling wheel and wax images, and thoroughly laments the sad state she and her incantations left him in. The tone of mockery in all these compositions leads one to believe that Canidia was not actually infanticidal but rather a procuress of amorous affairs. She and Fernando de Rojas' heroine *Celestina* do surely come from the same stock.

Tibullus' beautiful *Delia* inclined to another kind of superstition - less villainous and offensive. But why should we be surprised at a poor freewoman being superstitious when we see ladies of stature surrendering meekly to the will of any augur or *venefica*? Tibullus must have been a little superstitious himself, or pretended to be so in order to please her. In Elegy II, Book I, he tells her of the magic song he has learnt from this wise sorceress who can bend the flow of the waters, the course of the stars, evoke the dark and rent it with libations made of milk:

> She speaks, and the Syrian summer turns to snow
> She speaks, and heavens irate becomes serene...

Tibullus practised magic. In Elegy III:
> three times in the fortunes my destine
>
> ....

The tertiary number was sacred among the ancients: "Numero Deus impari gaudet", said the poet.

On the Magic Arts, all *Erotics*, faithful sketchers of the customs of their time, agree. Propertius writes in *Elegy* XXVIII of Book II:
> deficiunt magico torti sub carmine rhombi,
> et iacet extincto laurus adusta foco,
> et iam Luna negat toties descendere caelo,
> nigraque funestum concinit omen avis. (V. 34).

> (Now cease the wheels whirled to the magic chant, the altar fire is
> dead and the laurel lies in ashes. Now the moon refuses to descend
> so oft from heaven and the bird of night sings ominous of death).

Ovid, even leaving his extensive *Metamorphoses* tale aside [266] abounds in allusions to this genre. Old Dipsas in Elegy VIII of *Amores*, made the following portents:
> cum voluit, toto glomerantur nubila coelo,
> cum voluit, puro fulget in orbe dies.

---

[266]   See especially the episode on Medea.

sanguine, si qua fides, stillantia sidera vidi;
purpureus Lunae sanguine vultus erat.
hanc ego nocturnas versam volitare per umbras
suspicor, et pluma corpus anile tegi,
suspicor, et fama est: Oculis quoque pupula duplex
fulminat, et gemino lumen ab orbe venit.
evocat antiquis proavos atavosque sepluchris,
et solidam longo carmine findit humum. (I:8 v.9).

(Whenever she willed it, the clouds are rolled together over all the
sky; whenever she has willed, the day shines forth in a clear heaven.
I have seen, if you can believe me, the stars letting drop blood;
crimson with blood was the face of Luna. I suspect she changes
form and flits about in the shadows of night, her aged body
covered with plumage. I suspect, and rumour bears me out. From
her eyes, too, double pupils dart their lightning, with rays that issue
from twin orbs. She summons forth from ancient sepulchres the
dead of generations far remote, and with long incantations lays
open the solid earth).

Let us not belabour the point: any Latin book we open will give us the
same results. Many have written on this subject already – Leopardi, in
particular, [267] who wrote a book on divination separating and classifying its
chapters according to dreams, *stornutto*, nocturnal terrors, and other superstitions
to do with the midday hour.

The Romans believed in apparitions and ghosts. Pliny the Younger
(*Epistle* XXVII, Book VII) and Tacitus (*Annales*, book XI, chapter XX) speak
with astonishing aplomb of a woman of "supernatural height" ("ultra modum
humanum") who appeared to Curtius Rufus, a poor and obscure man, under
the Adrumeto porticoes, and said to him: "Tu es Rufe, qui in hanc provinciam
pro consule venies". Which actually and literally came to pass, both writers tell
us.

None of these superstitions, however, was without its sceptics and
challengers. Petronius in one of his famous verses gave a natural explanation for
dreams where he denies that Jupiter sends them:

somnia quae mentes ludunt volitantibus umbris
non delubra Deum, nec ab aethere Numina mittunt
ad sibi quisque facit,

…and Pliny called Magic "intestabilem, irritam, inanem, habentem tamen
quasdam veritatis umbras, sed in his veneficas artes pollere, non magicas"
(*Natural History*, Book XXX).

The history of Astrology and the science of the Chaldeans is intimately
linked to that of the Roman empire: Livia questions Scribonius about the

267   *Saggio sopra gli errori popolari degli antichi…Quinta impressione*, Firenze, 1850.

destiny of the son she is carrying in her womb; Theogenes reads Octavius his horoscope. This fact notwithstanding, astrologers were driven out during the Triumvirate in 721, and Augustus later burned over two thousand Greek and Latin books on divination ("fatidici libri") on Maecenas' advice.

Everyone knows of the terrors Tiberius' spirit endured in Caprea and the way in which he proved his astrologer Trasilus' learning by making some jump over a cliff. Tiberius had learnt the art of the Chaldeans in Rhodes. Enlightened knowledge indeed for a tyrant to have! One of these luminaries foretold Nero's parricide to Agripina. Her answer was: "may he reign, and I die". Sabina Popea's house was filled with astrologers and diviners. Didius Julianus made use of *asteroscopy* and magic mirrors. Many others lent themselves to divination to find out when the reigning emperor would die in order to take over, more often than not proving themselves worse than the previous one had been.

One could easily prolong an historical account on magic simply by focusing on the writings and reminiscences of classical writers. The satirists - Juvenal particularly - tell of the hold astrologers had on people, especially on feminine hearts. Reading Petronius we become aware of the widespread belief in the power of "ligatures" and incantations. And, to conclude, Apuleius, both in his own *Apologia* and in *The Golden Ass* can be for us the last and most complete and reliable witness of the aberrations of the ancient world concerning witchcraft and transformations. [268] This delightful novel by the African rhetorician is a host of prodigies. See above all the description of magic acts performed by Pamphile, Milo's wife, in the Third Book. Apuleius, a neo-Platonist philosopher as he indeed was, was surely given to theurgy. St. Augustine speaks of him in the *City of God* where he writes at length on the magic arts (Lib. XVIII) and attributes them partly to demonic influence. Other Fathers, among them Tertullian (*De anima*), Arnobius (*Adversus gentes,* lib. 1), St. Cyprian *(De idolorum vanitate)*, Origen, and Lactantius, do not hesitate to qualify the magic of the Greeks and Latins as "fallacia, ludus, fraus" denying they have anything solid or true about them. "Ars magica", says Origen, "non mihi videtur alicujus rei subsistentis vocabulum".[269]

And so it was that the forbidden arts became the last bastion of polytheism, moribund by then. The 'vulgar' people of the countryside (*pagani*) clung to their obscure rites, while philosophy, represented by the Alexandrians, leaned towards theurgy, at pains to distinguish itself from goety. Christians, quite rightly, denied such differentiation. Imperial edicts came to support our controversialists, and later we shall see the role that emperor Theodosius, a Spaniard, played in this particular crusade. [270]

---

[268]   See my thesis *La novela entre los Latinos*, Santander, 1875.

[269]   *Apud Theophilum Alexandrinum* (St. Jerome's Latin translation).

[270]   On the struggle between Christianity and magic, see (though written from a heterodox and rationalist standpoint) chapter 6 of the scholarly, and rather disorderly book by Alfred Maury,

Superstitious practices of indigenous and nonindigenous people in the Peninsula. Vestiges preserved to our day.

Spain, I would submit, is the least superstitious country on earth. But Spain, too, paid its dues to humanity on this, and from the most ancient days of its history. Unfortunately, the evidence we have is so meagre, contradictory and obscure, that we can affirm little with absolute certainty. The study of folk superstitions is almost untouched in our country; however, if we add the little that we do know to the scarce testimonies left by some authors, to the Councils we shall be citing from, and other peoples' collections of their own rites and customs, we might be able to shed some light on this issue.

The Northern and Western parts of Spain are, undoubtedly, the regions that have preserved most of these ancient customs, though it is not easy to distinguish what corresponds to each of the individual Turanian, Iberian, and Celtic primitive peoples. Strabo saves this difficulty somewhat by assuring us that the Lusitanians, Galicians, Asturians and Cantabrians shared a common way of life, and he includes the Basques (Vascons) and peoples of the Pyrenees region on this as well. "Talis ergo et vita montanorum eorum qui septemtrionale Hispaniae latus terminant, Gallaicorum, et Asturem, et Cantabrorum usque ad Vascones et Pyrenem: omnes enim eodem vivunt modo". This same similarity applied to their beliefs on the magic arts and divination practices.

Let us start with the Basques – something demanded by their greater antiquity and difference in race. It was the Basques, not the Cantabrians, who were famed in antiquity for being highly skilled in the art of augury. Lampridius, in his *Life* of Alexander Severus, attributes this emperor with great ability in orneoscopy (divination by the flight of birds), to the extent that he was considered better at this than the "Vascons of Spain and the Pannonians".

Conversion to Christianity took longer for the mountain peoples of the Pyrenees: they held on to the solecism of auguries long after evangelisation. In the sixth century, St. Amandus worked hard to eradicate these practices, going as far as destroying idols himself in some places. (My most profound apologies here to those who insist on seeing the ancient Basques as monotheists). "Audivitque ab eis gentem quandam quam Vacceiam appellavit antiquitas, quae nunc vulgo nuncupatur Vasconia, nimio errore deceptam, ita ut auguriis, vel omni deceptam, idola etiam pro Deo coloret". We know of this saint's preaching through the testimony of his biographer, Baudemandus. The French Basques also, according to St. Rictrudis' biographer, were given at this time to the "cult to devils," that is, to magic.[271]

---

of the French Institute, *La Magie et l'Astrologie dans l'Antiquité et au Moyen-Age ou Étude sur les superstitions paiennes qui se sont perpétuées jusquá nos jours,* Paris, 4th ed. 1877.

[271]   'Cujus incolae licet illo tempore pene omnes demoniacis essent dediti cultibus, a Deo tamen praelecta Rictrudis, sic ex eidem impiis, et sine Deo, prodiit hominibus, veluti solet rosa de spinosis efflorere sentibus: quae ab ipsis incunabulis cum aetatis tenerae provectibus honestis est alta et instituta moribus' (Vid. *La Vasconia,* by Father Risco).

There are still a good number of ancient practices current in French "Vasconia" [Gascony], as listed on Michel's *The cursed races* [272] as well as other places. Relatively few of them remain in our own Basque countryside. Yet here, too, folk believed in *sorguiñas* (witches) who made pacts with the devil and cursed men and animals; in diviners and *saludadores* (mediums); in spells and the "evil eye" (*begui yecó miña*), averted by exorcisms or by making the sign of the cross on a cup water filled with molten tin. It is difficult, however, to pinpoint their precise origin since superstitions like these were prevalent throughout half of Europe. More curious and characteristic seem those of French Navarre, which curiously have a great deal in common with those of Galicia. On the other side of the Pyrenees people believed in the apparition of wandering expiating souls, in *laminiac*, ominous beings, in a monster that lived in the darkest of forests which they called *Bassa-Yaon*, or *wild lord*. In some places, the Eve of St. John (the morning, in others) was celebrated with oblations at some given fountains, while others washed themselves in the Biarritz sea on the Sunday after Assumption. I am pointing out these practices because it was actually from Spanish Vasconia that they travelled on to France. Our Basques would in time forget them thanks to the persevering and glorious struggle led by the Spanish Church against all manner of witchcraft and superstitions. [273] It is up to the Basques themselves now to engage in investigating their beginnings; research on the roots of their language by comparing it to other *turanio* dialects would help, I think. For these ancient peoples, linguistic Palaeontology must serve as history - we have nothing else to go by. Later we will be able to see the Basque Provinces and their neighbouring regions as being the principal home of Spanish witchcraft during the fifteenth and sixteenth centuries.

Moving on now from the Basque *escualherria* to the peoples of Celtic race we find, in descending order, few in Cantabria, more in Asturias, many in Galicia and Portugal. It is worth noting that these are fast disappearing. Most have by now been relegated to history, but not, let it be said, due to progress brought about by the Enlightenment as some innocent folk believe, but because of the active, spirited, and vigorous action of the Christian faith: the One and only True Light.

Superstitious beliefs held by our Cantabrian mountain folk regarding witches have not been totally eradicated. The Mountain Witch differs little from witches of other times and places, certainly from that of the Basque and the Rioja regions during the seventeenth century. But on this point I shall cede the podium to that extraordinary mind that in two cherished books has described the customs of our Cantabria region.

---

[272]   *Histoire des races maudites de la France et de l'Espagne*, par Francisque Michel.

•   On current superstitions against the *evil eye*, see R. Salillas' *La fascinación en España* (Madrid, 1905), and, also, on witchcraft, the critical edition of Cervantes' *El casamiento engañoso* and *El coloquio de los perros*, Agustín G. De Amezúa y Mayo (A.B.)

[273]   I take these data from *Los Vascongados* by Miguel Rodríguez Ferrer, Madrid, 1873.

"The Mountain Witch" - writes my good friend José María de Pereda – "is not a sorceress, or an enchantress, or a seer. People do believe in these three phenomena, too, but not as something to be hated; on the contrary, they are treated with a certain degree of respect, consulted even. This is because, though they are still members of the devil's family, they often use their arts for good; they bring the sick back to health,[274] for example, discover hidden treasures,[275] or let you know where missing cattle or a stolen purse can be found. The real witch, on the other hand, brings nothing but trouble: she sucks the blood of the young, goes around at night biting whomever she hates, gives the *evil eye* to children, gives "maldao" to expecting mothers, starts up fires, brings on storms, parches up cornfields, and triggers wars within the family. Everybody knows that on Saturday, at midnight, witches fly on their brooms. They do this because they have to attend a special gathering of their own. The Mountain witch attends these meetings, too, which are actually held in a small village in the province of Burgos called Cernécula. There, they all gather around a hawthorn: the devil himself disguised as a billy goat, presiding. Needless to say, the means of transport she uses for this trip is her broom. The mysterious force that propels her forward through the air is made up of two things: first, an ointment black as tar which she keeps under the stones of the kitchen's hearth and with which she spreads herself from head to toe, all over; second, the actual words she speaks when she is so anointing herself. The recipe for this ointment is in fact the witch's infernal secret. Nobody knows it. The words she says, we do know. They are:

> Without God or Holy Mary,
> up the chimney I go!

What these scheduled meetings at Cernécula basically come down to is a lot of merry dancing around the hawthorn; to more than a few amorous excesses on the part of the president who, by the way, is not accredited with much good taste on his choice of partners; and above all, and this is important, to an exposition of needs, accounts and reasons for deeds performed, as well as much learned counsel and advice from their horned lord and master to all there present ..." "If cattle were let loose from the stable at night and gored, you can be sure the witch was right there in the thick of things playing havoc with the animals; the following day, therefore, crosses are to be painted all over the stables. If a dog howls near a cemetery, that is the witch, for sure, calling one particular villager to his or her grave. If a barn owl flies around the belfry, that's the witch drinking up the lamp's oil – or maybe condemning the whole village to some curse". [276]

---

274   *Saludadores*

275   *Zahories,* or something similar.

276   *Tipos y paisajes,* Second series of *Escenas montañesas.*

To this sketch drawn by a most sagacious observer, we can add a few additional reports given by the *Montañés* writer who chooses to hide himself under the pseudonym Juan García:

"The Cantabrian imagination often turns to that mysterious and malefic being who lives in the worm-eaten trunk of an ancient cypress. As all creatures of her sort, the witch chooses the dark and quiet hours of the night to carry out her wicked deeds. Her most marked aggression, indeed her favourite revenge, is to take a woman she does not like or has a grudge against from her bed at night and leave her out there in the cold, stark naked and exposed to the elements, in whatever place she happens to choose. To avert such formidable contingency, a prudent *montañesa*, if she has any reason to suspect the witch and fear a nightly assault, will not go to bed without leaving a healthy string of garlic under her bed'.[277] Mountain folk believe also in *mengues* or *familiar spirits*; on the power of *saludadores* and the *evil eye*, against which we can protect ourselves by means of black lignite pendants hanging from our neck - the equivalent of small ivory tusks in Rome (a superstition more entrenched there than elsewhere).

Should anyone ask me where all these beliefs come from I would not hesitate to say they are of Latin origin. There are few Celtic traces here, unless we count the *verbena* which is or was gathered the morning of St. John's day as an antidote to snake bites or some other dangerous reptile. Cantabria was thoroughly romanised. There are even reasons to suspect that no trace of the original populations remains.

Not so in Asturias, where superstitions are more exotic and further removed from the classical mould, though charming enough and representative of that region. Needless to say, we find beliefs in witches and the *evil eye* here as well, but we know also of the following dignitaries, almost all of Celtic origin: *nuberos*, leaders and agent provocateurs of thunder storms - equivalent to the *tempestarii* of Gaul cited by St. Agobard and the Capitulars of Charlemagne; the *hueste* or *buena xente (good people)*, a night procession of errant souls, common to all northern peoples; enchanted moors, guardians of treasures, a tradition also of Germanic origin; the *cuélebre*, or flying serpent, charged with the same duty (this myth could be of classical origin, akin to Iolcos' dragon or to Hesperides' garden); the *xanas* or fountain nymphs, evil and treacherous, who steal and bewitch babies. If I chose to be as systematic about classical origin theories as the *Celticists* are about their Celtic ones, I would gladly asseverate the kinship of these *xanas* with those nymphs who stole the child Hylas, "Hylas puer", as we read in the Valerius Flaccus' *Argonautica* and other ancient poems. But mindful not to abuse parallelisms, I am quite willing to grant northern origin enthusiasts their wish to associate our *xanas* to Germania's water nymphs, or to whatever fantastical beings they choose to come up with.

---

*   Amós de Escalante. (Editor, 1912).

[277]   *La montañesa* (Vid. *La Tertulia*, Santander, number 3, 1876). The *montañesa* witch uses the wax statuette, the same as Canidia or any other classical sorceress.

Those known as *saludadores* in the rest of Spain are in Asturias called *ensalmadores*. Their job is to cure certain ailments of men and beasts with magical words and bizarre rituals. In *Antón de la Mari-Reguera,* an *entremés* [278] written by the *Bable* (Asturian) hilarious poet Antonio González Reguera in the mid-seventeenth century, we find a pretentious, puffed-up *ensalmador* with high claims exorcising the soul of a dead woman who goes around in the form of a starling.

> Isi estornin fatal que tanto grita,
> Ie l'alma de to madre Malgarita,
> Que ñon terná descanso nin folgura
> En Purgatorio ni ena sepoltura,
> Si el sábanu en que fora sepultada
> Non s'apodrez hasta que quede en nada.

There follows a burlesque recipe that goes on forever, with just about everything thrown into it: the fat of a bear, the hair of a fox, two pages from the priest's breviary, etc., etc., and goes on:

> Y diréis: "Estornin de la estorneya
> Los figos deixa ó dexa la pelleya;
> Si ves l'alma quiciás d'alfun difunto,
> Márchate de aquí al punto...
> Vete pal' Purgatorio, y si non quieres,
> De mim rezos y mises non esperes.
> ¿Serás acasu en estornin tornado
> L'alma dún aforcado,
> O la güestia que vien del otro mundo
> Y sal de los llumales del profundo?"
> Al decir esto fáite cuatro cruces;
> Y encendiendo dos lluces...
> Pondránsete los pelos respingados,
> Ahullidos oirás, verás ñublados,
> Un sudor frio moyará to frente,
> Pero aquisi estornin impertinente
> Non tornará a gridar nin comer figos,
> Y deixaránte en paz los enemigos. [279]

You will notice we are witnessing pure necromantic evocation here - not to attract, but to ward off spirits; this soul transmigrated into a starling is one of the few vestiges of Celtic metempsychosis in our northern regions.

As concerning her wicked deeds, the Asturian witch is no different from the *Montañesa.* In a beautiful *bable* (Asturian) composition, *The Sick Child,*

---

[278]   Theatre play interlude (Translator's note).

[279]   *Colección de poesías en dialecto asturiano,* Oviedo, pub. Denito González, 1837, in cuarto. Edited and Introduction written by Cavela.

anonymous but generally attributed to the learned archaeologist Sr. Caveda, we read:

¿Si lu agüeyará
la vieja Rosenda
del otru llugar?
Desque allá na cuerra
Lu diera en besar,
Pequeñin y apocu
Morriéndose va,
Dalgun maleficiu
La maldita i fai;
Que diz q'á Sevilla
Los sábados va,
Y q'anda de noche
Por todu el llugar,
Chupando los ñeños
Que gordos están. [280]

The witches of Galicia, there called *meigas chuchonas*, are said to cause tuberculosis, and the evil spirits (the Mountain's *mengues*) nervous disorders. The remedy against these ills is to inhale the smell of the ruddy nectar plant at midnight, or to bathe at the same hour in the six waves of the *La Lanzada* sea, much as the French Basques do in the Biarritz sea. Juan Rodríguez de Padrón in the fifteenth century alluded to this custom.

The *nuberos,* or Asturian *tempestarii,* are called *nubeiros* in Galicia; the *hueste* (errant expiating souls) become the *estadía* in some parts, *compaña* in others, and are believed to announce the death of those in whose fields they appear. Superstitions linked to man's final journey are numerous in Galicia, and rather strange. It is a bad omen, for example, to be gazed at by a dying person; *portelas* (doors) are never to be slammed shut in order not to hurt the souls purgating for their sins there; nor is anyone going to St. Andrés of Teixido's *romería* (festive procession) to kill any reptile found on the way for that could be someone's soul, in that form, going to fulfil the *romaxe* (pilgrimage) they failed to do when alive. It is also said, finally, that a person who sees a friend being taken to the cemetery for burial is cursed because the deceased person sends him an *air* that attracts him to his death. The person who *ten ó aire,* especially if she is a woman, will be freed from this pernicious influence by going to the cemetery at night in the company of three *Marias.* They will stand around the grave and plead with the deceased to give back *the air* he took from the cursed

---

[280]   *Colección de poesías en dialecto asturiano,* p. 234.

•   Comp. Jesús Rodríguez López, *Supersticiones de Galicia,* 2nd edition, Madrid, 1910 (Editor, 1912)

---

woman while she, prone on the ground, breaths deeply to change the malefic air into a wholesome one.

If more proof were needed of the Celtic origin of all these non-classical pagan rites, we would no doubt find it in their similarity with the Breton superstitions described by Brizeux in his poems. Murguía, Galicia's historian, who I am following here for I judge him knowledgeable and trustworthy regarding his country's customs, said this well before I did.[281] The *romaxe* of the Galician dead is equivalent to the Bretons' *Pardon*.

We do not know and it is recorded nowhere (in fact, the opposite could be the case) that there were priests among our Celts in the manner of the druids of Gaul. But the so-called druid cult took deep roots in Galicia - relics of which are the natural altars, dolmens, moats (in Galician *mamoas* or *medorras*), menhirs and, particularly, oscillating stones, the latter serving for divination purposes. Strabo tells us in a text from which I shall be quoting a little later that Galicians and their neighbours, the Lusitanians, were prime models of this type of divination. Among ancient Galicians, qualified as atheists by the same geographer, the forests served as temples and the rocks as altars. Celtic pantheism deified the waters and the woods. Justin says that the Pico Sacro *(Mons sacer)*, located not far from Compostela, had never been touched by the plough. The only sanctuaries Galicia knew outside druidism must have been the temples to *Cabyres*, situated on rough mountaintops like the one at Lemnos to which this fragment from the Latin playwright Accius who (as far as we can conjecture) translated it from Æschalus refers:

Lemnia praesto
Littora rara et celsa Cabyrum
Delubra tenes, mysteria quies
Pristina castis concepta sacris
Nocturno aditu occulta coluntur
Silvestribus sepibus densa

Murguía acknowledges and defends the existence of the cult of *Cabyrism* in Galicia - similar to that of Samothrace and the ancient Islanders. [282] This mysterious cult to fire, linked to sidereal worship and a naturalist trinity, a most ancient cult among the Pelagians, had to be the primitive religion of our Iberians, absorbed and overthrown later by Celtic pantheism.

---

[281]   *Historia de Galicia* (vols. 1 and 2, by Soto Freire). This work remains, unfortunately, incomplete.

[282]   Vid. Pictet: *Du culte des Cabyres chez les anciens Islandais*, Geneva, 1856.

Toubin, *Essai sur les sanctuaires primitives et sur le fétichisme en Europe*, Paris.

Villamil y Castro, *Antigüedades prehistóricas y célticas de Galicia*, part 1, Lugo, 1873. Also, several dissertations by the same author in *Museo Español de Antigüedades*.

More light is shed on Galician superstitions by some canons from councils dictated against the Priscillianist commotion, and by a treatise of St. Martin of Braga. We shall make use of these documents later.

Let us now move on from Galicia to Lusitania. Its people, Strabo tells us, were "much given to sacrifices and to foretelling of the future through observation of the entrails of victims and feeling out the veins on the outer sides of the body." [283] Vestiges of druid cult to helm and oak trees can still be found in some parts of Portugal. Near the town of Alcarrede, in a place called *Entre Cabezas*, there is a *carvalho* (oak tree) at the foot of which there is a cistern or deposit of rainwater from which villagers draw for many different uses, some natural, others superstitious - one such being for the purpose of thwarting witchcraft and killing the *piolho das fabas* (*beans' lice*) on Holy Saturday. "This fact" - says Teóphilo Braga – "is suggestive of the Germanic superstition of the Igdrassill oak and the *Urda* fountain". [284] However, we do know with certainty that many of the Peninsula's mineral waters were already venerated as holy by the Celts and the Celtiberians. The tradition of the *Mouras encantadas* is in Portugal identical to that of Galicia and Asturias. Gil Vicente has referred to this same belief:

> Eu tenho muitos thesouros
> Que lhe poderao ser dados
> Mas ficaron *enterrados*
> D'elles do tempo dos mouros
> D'elles do tempo pasado…[285]

The name *moors* notwithstanding, we should not rush to see this legend as one of Arabic origin. One of the most popular in Spain, it derived most probably from an equivocation of the Celtic word *mahra* or *mahr* to indicate some particular spirits, and sometimes the devil within. Quintana found it in Extremadura, and though he is the least romantic poet one could ever hope to find, he used it as the subject for a very pretty romance - *The Fountain of the Enchanted Mooress* – preferred by many to some of his splendid and chivalrous odes. [286] The Quintanesque Mooress resembles the Asturian *xana* in no small measure.

The "erva fabada" referred to in the Portuguese romance of Doña Ausenda:

> A porta de dona Azenda
> Está uma erva fabada,
> Mulher que ponha a mao n'ella

---

[283]   Strabo, book III, paragraphs 6-7.

[284]   *Epopeas de raça mosárabe*, p. 56

[285]   *Obras de Gil Vicente*, ed. Hamburg, vol. 2, p. 489.

[286]   *Obras inéditas de Quintana*, Madrid, 1872, p. 24.

Logo se sente pejada, [287]

...and in the Asturian romance of *Princesa Alexandra*

Hay una hierba en el campo
Que se llama la borraja, etc...[288]

...could be counted also among superstitions of primitive origin, though with
less certainty. Perhaps it came down to us with the poems of the Breton cycle
during the Middle Ages. There, Queen Isea's misfortune is attributed to having
eaten a lily. Many fountains were said to have erotic powers. In the Portuguese
romance of Doña Areria [289] collected in Coimbra by Teóphilo Braga, we note
the following belief:

A cidade de Coimbra
Tem una fonte de agua clara:
As mozas que beben n'ella
Logo se veem pejadas.

On the other hand, the *fadada camisa* we see repeated in *Poema de Alexandre*
is a Lusitanian superstition prohibited by the Constitutions of the Dioceses of
Evora. We find it also in French poems, whence we derive ours.

In San Miguel, one of the Azores Islands, there still persists a belief in
lycanthropy or incantation of men into wolves, [290] an omen that can be undone
only by the shedding of blood. This superstition is well known in northern
Europe, too. Cervantes placed it there in his *Persiles*. [291] The Portuguese witch
or sorceress does not differ much from those of the rest of Spain, but in the
Azores there are curious variants: witches go to India in an eggshell and when
the cock crows they dive under the sea. Teóphilo Braga quotes a Visit Report
from the Vicar Simon da Costa Rebello to St. Pedro de Ponta Delgada on 30th
March 1696: "In this island" - writes the visitor – "there are some women called
entreabiertas (half-opened) who, by diabolic arts, say that souls come from the

---

[287]   *Romanceiro*, Almeida Garret, vol. 2, p. 181

[288]   *Romances tradicionales de Asturias*, compiled by Amador de los Ríos.

[289]   *Romanceiro geral*, Theophilo Braga, num. 33, p.87

[290]   'The last male-born of an uninterrupted series of seven male children born of the same
womb is *lobis-homen*. There's no way to avert this fatality awaiting the new-born but by baptising
him with the name of Benito (Benedict) and having his eldest brother, the first of the seven, as his
godfather...on fatal nights and hours, a magical power forces the lycanthrope to wandering'. Vid.
Th. Braga, *Epópeas*, p.63. In Gaul they called these lycanthropes *Gerulfos* (*loup-garou* in modern
French); in England, *Were-wolf*, in Germany, *Wargus*.

[291]   For all I am here recounting of Portuguese witchcraft, I am following Theophilo
Braga's *Epopéas da raça mosárabe*. He does however commit a serious error: he supposes all these
superstitions to be of Gothic origin when in fact the Goths came in small number and their
influence on this is almost nil. Nor is there any evidence to show they held these beliefs. More
likely they are from Gaul and the Breton peoples.

after-life to torment the sick..." I think the link between these superstitions and those of the Galician *air* is clear. [292]

I could easily prolong this listing of superstitious beliefs and practices which in Spain *seem* prior to the preaching of Christianity, but we would find nothing other than repetitions. In Andalucía, where the Iberian race did not mix with the Celts, the continuous intermixing of different cultures was such that it is difficult for us to identify now what belongs to each. We need not point out that there are hardly any indigenous or ancient traditions left in the whole assemblage of popular sayings and tales the fantasy of the Andalucians is so prone to. The classical element, seemingly the predominant one, was overtaken by the Semitic and the Semitic by that of the Christian peoples of the Middle Ages. Of original Turdetan traditions not a trace remains. [293]

Rites in the Celtiberian regions must have been analogous to those of the Celts, but the few superstitions that remain among Aragonese and Old Castilians have little ancient colour and give no cause for particular observations. The pre-eminent Celtiberian cult - the fires of the Eve of St. John - a Christian modification of the festivities of the summer solstice, continue to burn now across the peninsula as they did during Strabo's time. To this same feast were linked other odd customs, almost all forgotten now. Yet even in the sixteenth century, young girls of marrying age, with their hair loosened and one foot inside a vessel of "cold and clear" water, waited attentively for the first voice they heard which would bring to them the name of their future spouse. In Cervantes' lovely comedy, *Pedro de Urdemalas* (Act I) Benita says:

> Tus alas, ¡oh noche! extiende
> Sobre cuantos te requiebran,
> Y a su gusto justo atiende,
> Pues dicen que te celebran
> Hasta los muros de allende.
> Yo, por conseguir mi intento,
> Los cabellos doy al viento,
> Y el pie izquierdo a una bacía,
> Llena de agua clara y fría,
> Y el oído al aire atento.
> Eres, noche, tan sagrada,
> Que hasta la voz que en tí suena
> Dicen que viene preñada
> De alguna ventura buena.

---

[292]   The Portuguese Theophilo Braga attributes to the *Goths* the origin of this custom. As if there were Goths in Spain during Strabo's time! This is the absurd point to which that Germanic over-enthusiasm can lead - a sin that God would never forgive a Latin for!

[293]   Western Betis and Southern Lusitania regions (Roman Spain), between the Sierra Morena mountains and the Betis river (Translator's note).

Catalonia preserves, or did until relatively recently, a similar custom though of a more Christian flavour if we are to judge by a romance by my own tutor Rubió y Ors:

> Enceneu, ninetas
> De Sans Joan los fochs
> *Perque Deu vos done*
> *Gentils amadors* [294]

How many strange and spectacular happenings do we not find in our *Romances* about the morning of St. John's day:

> Captiváronla los moros
> La mañana Sant Juane...
> La mañana de San Juan
> Salen a coger guirnaldas...
> ¡Que hubiese tal ventura
> Sobre las aguas del mar,
> Como tuvo el Conde Arnaldos
> La mañana de San Juan!
> La mañana de San Juan
> cuando se cogen las yerbas...[295]

The same is true of popular songs in Cataluña and Portugal:

> Por manhan de Sam Joao
> Manhan de doce alvorada...

There are vestiges of ancient superstitions in the tales and proverbs echoed by our people, but we should be mindful to separate these from the vast number of eastern and western imports of the Middle Ages. The power of sorceresses and omens is even in the popular tale *The queen who turned into a dove* of which Durán made good use for his tale *Las tres toronjas (Three grapefruits)*.[296] Classical influence is clearly marked in other tales. In Andalucía, Cantabria and a few other places, a tale is told, though shortened and depreciated, similar to Apuleius' Psychis. The Cyclopes of Greek mythology became the *ojancano* of our Mountain peoples; the events attributed to it have a great deal of similarity with those of Poliphemus in the Odyssey.

---

[294]   *La nit de San Joan*, Vid. *Lo Gayter del Llobregat*, p. 82.

[295]   On a footnote to this Romance, Agustín Durán (*Romancero general*, vol. 1, p. 58) points out that 'in some villages there are still people who pour an egg into a glass filled with crystalline water to get, at midnight, the figure of a ship which they think is going to appear miraculously under the protection of the saint'.

[296]   The *rondallas* of Cataluña, without doubt the richest and most varied in the Peninsula, have been partly compiled by F. Maspons y Labrós (*La Rondallayre*, etc.). Valera has paraphrased with marvellous ingenuity *El pájaro verde (The green bird)* and others, also from the Betis region. We owe to Trueba imitations and re-writings, generally well done, of some from Castile and Vizcaya. Theóphilo Braga has promised us a collection of some from Portugal. Is there no one from our Mountain region that can take on a similar undertaking?

The word *fada* in Castille (writes the eminent Milá y Fontanals), as for all other Romanised Celtic peoples, comes from the Latin *fatum* (pl. *fata*), taken as singular feminine. There are two proverbs: *Quien malas fadas tiene en la cuna, las pierde tarde o nunca.* [297] *Acá y allá malas fadas hay.* Archipreste de Hita (fourteenth century) writes *in coplas* 713 and 798:

> El dia que vos nacisteis
> *Albas fadas vos fadaron*
> Que las *malas fadas negras*
> Non se parten de mi...

and Rodrigo Yáñez, in his poem to Alfonso XI, copla 879:

> A vos fadó malas fadas
> En tiempo que naciemos...

In this same sense we find it in the fairy tales of other countries, though as *Parcas* or goblins. [298]

Milá himself, in his *Observaciones sobre la poesía popular* [299] gives this account of Catalan superstitions: "We had until not long ago... superstitious crude beliefs in witches – some which still linger on to this day. For instance, we have recently seen a painting done to celebrate the restoring of a child back to health; according to one of these customs, witches had tried to snatch him out of a window on the Eve of St. Sylvester... Witch doctors, also, equal in everything to ordinary folk doctors except on their having divination powers besides concerning illnesses; so-called *saludadores*, that is to say, persons born on Christmas night who, in addition to having a sign imprinted on their palate, had the gift of healing hydrophobia. Those who practised black or white magic were men of great power, though somehow they always ended up destitute... Ghosts, which could be seen through the mountain mist with each foot on one pine tree; and finally, the *follets* (goblins or elfs)... Actual fairies, however, beings of suspect origin, are not at all mentioned either in serious tales or even in the *rondallas de la vora del foch'*. Metamorphosis and incantations are never absent from these *rondallas* (serenades or night songs) of which Milá himself published some examples and Maspons y Labrós collected in an extensive edition.

Also in Catalonia, according to Milá, one hears of castles and ruins inhabited by spirits, of mysterious lakes like the one at Canigó, of the errant hunter with dogs howling through the bellowing wind called *hunter's air* by the *payeses* [300]. This legend, also found in Germany and France (which some have

---

[297]   Vid. *Memorias de la Academia Española*, vol. 1. Rubió y Ors has a very pretty Romance poem in Catalan on this same subject.

[298]   *De la poesía heroico-popular castellana*, p. 380. Milá considers, on good grounds, the *fadas* of Alexandre's poem to be of foreign origin.

[299]   *Observaciones sobre la poesía popular, con muestras de romances catalanes inéditos*, Barcelona, 1853, p. 175. A sold-out edition which one hopes will soon be re-published with much addenda.

[300]   Persons of rural origin in Catalonia and the Balearic Islands (Translator's note).

explained in relation to astronomical signs) provided Burger with material for one of his tales.

The Asturian *xanas* surface in Catalonia with various other names: *donas de'aigua*, (water ladies), *alojas* (because their drink is *aloja* water, that is, water with honey and herbs), *gojas (young ladies)*, and sometimes *buixas* (witches) or *encantadas (bewitched)*. Their life is a continuous merry banquet: they enjoy eternal youth, seduce and bewitch passers-by, and sing and dance on full-moon nights. They hide from ordinary mortals by a coarsely-woven web.

Maspons [301] who has collected a wide range of most curious details on these fast-disappearing beliefs is inclined to see them as being of Germanic influence. My own opinion is that their being of classical origin is a sustainable theory too and that they can be explained as part of a pool of Iberian-Celtic-Roman traditions that need neither Goths nor Franks. In the popular songs of Catalonia and Portugal, the Greco-Roman superstition of mermaids is still alive, as this romance collected by Milá shows: [302]

> Desperteu, vos, vida mía,
> Si voléu sentir cantar
> Sentiréu cant de *sirena*

In a song from the Azores Islands we read: [303]

> Chegae aquella janella,
> Ouvi un doce cantar;
> Ouvi cantar as *sereias*,
> No meio d'aquelle mar...

Among ancient beliefs are those about goblins and elves but of these hardly any trace remains in Spain. According to the author of the *Ente dilucidado* (a work we will soon discuss) "these are neither good or bad angels nor souls separated from their earthly bodies, but rather *familiar spirits* much like the pagans' *lemurs*" says Fr. Feijoo.

If the reader is still with me, patiently, he might have noticed the Celtic-Roman origin of this new aberration. In fact, he might be persuaded the more if he knew that in the Mountain it is an age-old superstition to catch these spirits in the form of *ujanos* (worms) under ferns at midnight. He who succeeds in catching one of these *ujanos* will be able to make all manner of magic spells and "keep the scales on everyone's eyes" except on those who are equipped with a snake *respede* (tongue) [304] - an antidote akin to Ulysses' molly herb.

---

[301] *Tradiccions del Vallés, ab notas comparativas,* Barcelona, 1876, pp. 77 and following. This section covers all things relative to the *encantadas de Vallderros,* the *alojas* of *the estany de Bayolas,* the *gojas* of *St. Jordi Desvalls, encantadas de la siglera de Parets, etc.*

[302] *Romancero catalán,* p. 108.

[303] Theóphilo Braga, *Cantos do Archipelago açorano,* p. 273.

[304] *Tipos y paisajes,* by José María Pereda, p. 113

Also of ancient classical origin is the belief in *zahoríes* (finders) even if the name seems Arabic: changing names is easier than changing customs. The fact is that there were already *zahoríes* among the Greeks, that is to say, the Greeks too had their magician treasure hunters: Alexander the *Pseudomantis*, for example – one of Lucian's characters. The Spanish *zahorí* had the power to fathom hidden treasures under seven layers of soil, and owed this spectacular faculty to having been born on Good Friday. Before Christianity, of course, it had to be due to something else. This superstition was still around during Feijoo's time who wrote a long tract to combat it.

All I have said so far is but a rough draft of *conjectural* history (if the words are not at war with each other) on Spanish beliefs, practices and rites which could in some way be admitted as being prior to the preaching of the Gospel, but which continued later in a more or less altered form. Of actual positive history, we hardly have anything to go by save for Strabo's notes on the Lusitanians, Lampridio's on the Basques, and the fact that Silus Italicus calls Galicians "fibrarum et pennae divinorunque sagaces".

Phoenicians, Greeks, Carthaginians and Romans brought their respective magic and divination arts to our soil with them. Many inscriptions tell of augurs and haruspices. Without needing to go to the Hübner collection in the early Masdeu, we find mentioned men such as Marcus Aurelius, Pius Reburrus, an augur in the province of Tarragona, Lucius Favius, aruspice, [305] and Lucius Minucius, augur. In the wake of Roman cult, came the Egyptians and Orientals. Recent excavations in Cerro de los Santos seem to have revealed the existence of a Magi and Chaldeans' temple [306] and of a *hemeroscope,* or night observatory.

Journey of Apollonius of Tiana to Betis.

Extracts from Hispano-Latin authors concerning the Magic Arts.

In Nero's time, when Christianity first came to our country, a most unusual person made it to Betis who was to influence, directly or indirectly, the expansion of the magic arts in Spain. He was the famous Pythagorean Apollonius of Tiana, a prototype, if you will, of the ravings and moral derangement of his time. We owe his biography to Philostratus the rhetorician - if a novelette full of fantastical wondrous happenings and long declamations can properly be called a biography! It is based on anecdotes and accounts (probably

---

[305]   *Historia crítica de España*, vol. VI (*Colección epigráfica*), pp. 152 and 153; volume XIX, p. 192.

[306]   Vid. Aureliano Fernández-Guerra's *Discurso leído ante la Academia de la Historia en la recepción de D. J. De la Rada y Delgado*. This work by my good friend Fernández-Guerra is truly admirable. Far from me the vain enterprise, worthy of censure, of attempting to extract it or summarise it. Let the reader read it in its entirety. He will esteem it one of the best works written thus far in this century in the Castilian language. I will add only that according to Aureliano's considered opinion, in the antiquities of Yecla there are *Chaldean, Phoenician, Greek and Egyptian elements, all outdone by the latter however, as proven by the statue of Isis, the Canopy, the Phoenix,* etc.

made up) given by one Assyrian by the name of Damis who supposedly had been Apolonius' companion: a sort of Sancho Panza to this knight-errant of Philosophy.

Apollonius, as Philostratus' portrays him, was almost the god Protheus himself, incarnate. He had the power of exorcism, resurrected the dead, evoked darkness, had *double sight* and the virtue of divination. He had journeyed far, to India, Egypt and Ethiopia and had consulted Brahmin and Gymnosophists alike, whose miracle-working powers, we are told, were almost as good as his. One can read here all about moving tripods, cups being filled all by themselves, the earth swelling like the waves of the sea, etc. etc.

Philostratus' book is full of monstrosities: satyrs, pigmies, and *empusas*. But that is not all we know of him. Apollonius was also a very pious man, chaste and sober, a man who rigorously practised Pythagorean abstinence. But one senses something of a revolutionary streak in him, probably the reason why Nero and Domitian were after him. He dodged them with his *arts*, apparently. Anyhow, in one of his restless wanderings he made it to Cádiz, but here Philostratus's story is as brief as it is full of tall tales. He says the people of Cádiz were Greeks, that they worshipped Death, Old Age, Art and Poverty. On the issue of climate, he got it right though: "as agreeable as that of Attica at the time of the mysteries". But can we judge his account credible when he says that the inhabitants of Hispola (probably Hispalis, Seville) had never seen scenic plays and that they thought an actor was the devil incarnate? Remember he is talking about Betis, a thoroughly Romanised region.

We are not sure that Apolonius managed to persuade many Spaniards to follow his theurgist science. He did hold long meetings with the Governor of Betis but the intent here was of a political nature, or so we infer from Philostratus' account. In any case, soon after these colloquia took place, the Vindex's revolution broke out. [307]

A good number of Hispano-Roman authors have written about the history of the occult sciences though never specifically about the Peninsula itself. Let's look at the Annaea family first. The philosopher Seneca treated of augurs in Book II of *Naturales Questiones* where he shows himself partial to stoic fatalism. As a poet, he describes the omens of witchcraft in *Medea,* one of his authentic tragedies. See, in Act IV, the invocation beginning with the words:

> vos precor, vulgus silentum, vosque ferales deos
> et chaos coecum atque opacam Ditis umbrosi domum.

But it is Hecate, *sidus noctium,* that the enchantress is really invoking here:
> pessimus inducta vultus: fronte non una minax.

---

[307] Vid. *Vida de Apolonio,* book 5, ed. Westerman, Paris, 1849, *Colección greco-latina*, Didot. See also the notes accompanying Chassang's French translation, Paris, 1862.

Seneca's enchantress "walks barefoot the hidden forests", brings rains, curbs the tides, makes the fainthearted Ursas bathe in the Ocean, the earth yield grain in the winter and flowers in the summer; she impels the waves of Phasis to flow back to their source and Istro to halt its waters. At Medea's mighty voice the clouds flee, the winds turn to tempests, the sun halts its course, and meek and docile stars descend from the heavens to obey her spells. The precious metal of Corinth is heard: the witch stabs her arm to accustom herself to blood, Hecate's carriage advances, and Medea beseeches her to empower her venemous concoctions that the nuptial tunic may char Creusa to her depths. [308]

Seneca makes excessive use of augurs, haruspices and magical resources in all of the tragedies that go by his name. In Act III of *Oedipus*, Creon describes at great length a necromancy act performed by diviner Tiresias in order to know Oedipus' Fates – a half-baked, thoroughly undigested and over-elaborate detailing of circumstances and adornments that goes on for one hundred and fifty verses.

Lucan suffers from this same ill though to a lesser extent, in the terrifying scene that closes Book VI of *Pharsalia.* From verse four hundred and twenty:

Sextus erat, Magno proles indigna parente...

On the eve of battle, Sextus Pompeii goes to consult a Thessalian sorceress called Erictho. Erictho can bring corpses back to life and make the dead respond to the questioning of the living. In a horrid grotto consecrated to funeral rituals, she arrays a person killed in a recent quarrel, fills his veins with new hot blood, makes a formidable brew made up of the froth of dogs, the inwards of a lynx, the hump of a foul hyena, the marrow of a stag stung by snakes, the eyes of a dragon, the flying serpent of Arabia, the *echenais* that keep ships motionless in mid-ocean, and the skin the horned-snake of Libya casts off in its lifetime, and the viper that is born of the Red Sea and guards the precious pearl-shells. And then, with a voice more potent than any she has hereto summoned, a voice that has something of the barking of a dog and the howling of a wolf, the hissing of a snake and the complaint of a night owl, of the bereaved roar (*planctus*) of waves dashing against rocks and the clamouring of thunder, she makes a frightening invocation calling up the Eumenides, Chaos, Stiglia, Persephone and the ancient ferryman of the fiery river. "I ask not" - she says – "for a soul that lurks in the depths of Tartarus and has long been accustomed to the darkness but for a soul that is just going down and leaving the light behind him; he still lingers at the entrance of the chasm that leads to gloomy Orcus":

...parete precanti
non in Tartareo latitantem poscimus antro
adsuetumque diu tenebris, modo luce fugata
descendentem animam primo pallentis hiatu

[308] Vid. *Medea*, act 4, p. 29, ed. Martín del Río. *(Syntagma tragediae latinae...Lutetiae Parisiorum, 1620).*

haeret adhuc Orci...

Suddenly a dim shadow appears: a ghost, the soul of the unburied corpse who is resisting coming back to life because, hapless wretch! Unjustly robbed of death's last gift – the inability to die a second time.

extremum...mortis mumus inique
eripitur, non posse mori.

Erichto is furious with the corpse for taking so long to decide. She lashes at him with fresh wounds, and threatens Tisiphone, Megauera and Pluto with letting light enter the infernal regions. Just then, the dead man's body quivers, his blood starts to boil: for an instant life battles with death. At last, the body rises, his mouth gaped wide and its eyes open, and to the sorcerer's interrogation he responds by predicting the disaster of Pompeii: a cause of pain in Eliseus for the Decii, Camillus, Curius and Scipio but an occasion for much rejoicing in hell for Catiline, Marius, Cethegos, Drussus and other tribunes, whose boldness knew no limit, and with such force characterised by the poet.

legibus inmodicos, ausosque ingentia Gracchos.

Having answered her questions, the dead man stood still in silence demanding to die at once and return to the kingdom of darkness, and Erictho, to indulge him, burns him alive: "Iam passa mori". [309] This is the *fantastical* in Pharsalia. There is no doubt about this: transit from life to death, so somberly described in most vivid colour by the Cordobese sage, fills one with terror.

So this is what the religion of the empire had come to: augurs and fears!

Columella, from Cádiz, wrote about rural life but not being a peasant himself (Leopardi tells us) he was spared from the everyday anxieties of country folk. In his elegant work, *De re rustica* (lib. I, ch. 8) he counsels rustics "not to give in to haruspices, witches (*sagas*) and other knaves out to swindle them with vane superstitions" who lead them to incur in profitless expenses, perhaps even crime. [310]

Finally, it is worth mentioning some of Martial's epigrams and the discourse that with the title *de Sepulchrum incantatum* we find among those attributed to Quintillian.

---

[309]   *M. Annei Lucano Pharsalia*, Lipsiae, Tauchnitz, 1834, pp. 128 and following.

[310]   'Haruspices, sagasque, quae utraque genera, vana superstitione rudes animos ad impensas et deinceps ad flagitia compellunt, ne admiserit' Edición of 1595, *ex H. Commelini Typographia.*

Acta from Sts. Lucianus and Martianus.
Superstitions anathematised at the Council of Elvira.
Theodosius' crusade against witchcraft.

Interesting but little known are the documents that refer to the martyrdom of Ss. Lucianus and Martianus, supposedly to have occurred in Vichy at the time of the persecution under Decius.

Both saints had been sorcerers and enchanters in their pagan days and used their perverted arts and loathsome potions to gain over the modesty of maidens and married women alike, [311] and to satisfy personal revenges. These two rascals fell in love with a God-fearing and modest Christian virgin - intact from impurity even in thought. In vain did they exhaust all means and resources procured by their diabolical learning: the virgin would not move. She kept them at bay through fasting, vigil and prayer. In vain did they try to win her over by calling on their gods (or devils), for they answered: "It was easy for us to come to your aid when all you sought was to crush infidels who knew not of God who is in heaven. But against this most chaste soul who keeps her virginity for Jesus we cannot prevail. He who died on the Cross for the salvation of all watches over her and afflicts us. There is nothing we can do for you here". Terrified, Lucianus and Martianus fell on their face as dead, and the moment they regained consciousness they resolved to abandon their wicked ways and the demons that had served them so ill: they lit a fire in the middle of the public square and threw all their books on necromancy into it following this with a public confession of their sins in church. And their life was thereafter a continual chain of austerities and penance. Proconsul Sabinus condemned them later to the flames". (The reader cannot fail to notice the similarity of this

---

[311] 'Nam et magis artibus maleficiis omnes coinquinabant adulteriis. Erant primi in subversione auctores, in magicis veneficiis subversores; ita ut omnes quaerentes voluptates suas perficere, vel quosdam nocere, ad eos concurrent... Famula quaedam erat Dei casta et fidelis, nuptias contemnes, virginitatem custodiens, forma speciosa, et anima tamen pulchrior; non aliud nisi Deum diligebat. Lucianus et Martianus hanc concupierunt, et cum non haberent quo genere cupidatis suae impudicitiam obtinerent, conversi non aliter se nisi magicis daemonicis artibus suis ostendissent, nihilque sibi prodesse viderent, conversi in furias, fremebant quod in nullo poterant praevalere. Illa vero serviens Deo, pernoctabat in vigiliis et oratione. At illi quandam magicam facientes, affligebant suos ut eis responderent. Et daemones eis responderunt: 'Quascumque animas non cognoscentes Deum qui est in coelo voluistis subvertere, invocantes nos, facillimum nobis fuit praestere. Sed quia ad hanc castissimam animam certamen nobis est, multa quidem fecimus, sed nihil potuimus perficere adversus eam. Haec vero virginitatem illibatam servat Jesu Christo, Domino suo et Deo omnium, qui crucifixus est pro salute omnium: ipse eam custodit, et nos affligit. Ideo nihil contra eam facere possumus, nec in aliquo superare...'Cum haec publice gererentur, stupore et timore percussi ceciderunt in faciem veluti mortui. Post paululum reversi ad se, facientes alia magica, a se daemones dimiserunt conquerebantur vero ad invicem dicentes, quoniam multum hic potest Jesus Christus crucifixus, qui omnium dominatur, et daemones et omnes artes nostras magicas et veneficia superat. Sic statim codices suos publice in media deferentes civitate igni tradiderunt'. España Sagrada, vol. XXVIII.

legend with that of St. Cyprian of Antioch and Justine, eternalised by Calderón in *El mágico prodigioso*). [312]

Fr. Flórez and Dr. Fuente accept the Vichy tradition that portrays Lucianus and Martianus as sons of that city. Fr. Villanueva in *Viaje Literario*, vol. 6, p. 113 rejects it (justly, in my opinion), basing his stand on the unanimous testimony of ancient martyrologies which place these saints' death in Nicomedia, or Africa. All that Vichy can allege in its favour is a *Flos Sanctorum* in a work in limousine paper from the fourteenth century, and a Pastoral from bishop Berenguer Zaguardia in 1326 - both fairly recent documents. True, the relics of these martyrs are preserved in the chapel of St. Saturninus in Vichy but this in itself does not mean they suffered martyrdom there.

In chapter I we saw that the Council of Elvira, in Canon VI, separated from communion, even at the hour of death, those who would cause the death of another by means of maleficent and idolatrous invocations. We have reason to believe that another pagan superstition was the lighting of candles in cemeteries at midday, prohibited in Canon XXXI, "that the souls of the saints may not be disturbed". And we have already given an account in chapter II of the Council of Saragossa's declarations and anathemas against the Priscillianists, their astrological beliefs and amulets, etc.

Universal belief in the power of astrologers and magicians was to bring tragic consequences at the time. In Valente's reign, the Chaldeans worked out a horoscope for who was to succeed him to the throne. The name they came up with began with the letters *Theo* and Valente, to frustrate the omen, gave a harsh and brutal death to his secretary Theodore and a Spaniard called Honorius Theodosius, then Governor of Africa. But, as it happened, Fate determined that it was to be one of Honorius' sons, also called Theodosius (and by History 'The Great') that was to be linked later to the empire via Gratian, Valente's nephew. And this Spanish Caesar, a passionate Christian and zealous foe of the vain and futile arts that had brought about his father's death, showed himself uncompromisingly severe with all occult lore and ritual. On 20th December 381 he forbade secretive and nocturnal sacrifices. [313] On 25th May 385 he condemned to the "final torment" all who engaged in performing sacrifices and the haruspices who foretold by means of studying the kidneys and other entrails of victims. [314] These prescripts carried with them a vigorous and subsequent war-plan against polytheism, by now reduced to a series of theurgic practices.

---

[312]   Calderón was inspired principally by the text of Simon Metaphrastes, translated from the Latin by Lipomanus. See an interesting study on the sources of *Mágico*, published by my good friend Morel Fatio at the beginning of his beautifully-presented critical edition of that comedy (Bonn, 1877). Needless to say, I condemn in the strongest possible terms all those anti-religious and anti-Spanish notions of his so prolific in the Prologue, even his appreciations on literary criticism.

[313]   *Cod. Theodosiano*, lib. XVI, tit. X, law VII.

[314]   *Cod. Theodosiano*, lib. XVI, tit. X, law IX.

The famed and honoured sophist Libanius protested in his *Oratio pro templis*, but to no avail. There came successively the prescripts of 27th February and 17th June 391, and later that of 8th November 392 (Law XII, tit. X, lib. XVI of *Cod. Theodosiano*) which prohibited sacrificing, immolation of victims, gift offerings, the lighting of candles around hearths, libations of wine to the all-powerful 'genie', burning incense to the *Penates* (household gods), and crowning altars with flowers; it declares guilty *laesae majestatis* the aruspice or whosoever endeavours to foresee the future by illicit means or malefice and attempts against the life, health or well-being of another person.[315]

It is through these laws that Theodosius came to be regarded as one of mankind's great benefactors. His desire to obliterate pagan cults was almost germane in his family. His niece Serena proved this when she, too, tore the necklace off a statue of Vesta. When Alaric's hordes were nearing the eternal city, she was violently and iniquitously slain by the Romans. The pagan Zosimus accuses this beautiful and distinguished Spanish lady, Stilicho's wife, of having administered a malefic potion to his son-in-law Honorius. [316]

The first Spanish Christians speak of magic in several places. Prudentius (lib. I, *Contra Simaccus*, V, CXXXVIII and following) attributes its origin to Mercurius:

> necnon thesalicae doctissimus ille Magiae
> traditur extintas sumptae moderamine virgae
> in lucem revocasse animas, cocythia lethi
> iura resignasse, sursum revocantibus umbris:
> at alias dammasse, neci, penitusque latenti
> inmersisse Chao...
> murmure nam magico tenues excire figuras
> atque sepulchrales scite in cantare favillas
> vita itidem spoliare alios, ars noxia novit.

Prudentius considers the son of Maya not a myth or a demon but a thaumaturge, another Apollonius. In the hymn that the Celtiberian poet dedicated to the martyrdom of St. Cyprian of Carthage (different from Cyprian of Antioch, immortalised centuries later in *El Mágico Prodigioso* by another Spanish sage [317]) the saint appears before his conversion as given to the illicit arts:

> unus erat juvenum doctissimus artibus sinistris
> fraude pudicitiam perfringere, nil sacrum putare
> saepe etiam magicum cantamen inire per sepulchra,
> quo geniale thori jus solveret, aestuante nupta. [318]

---

[315]   Vid. A. Maury, *Lid del Cristianismo con la magia*, in his book *La Magie et l'astrologie*, etc.

[316]   Vid. The curious book *Serena*, by Adolfo de Castro, Cadiz, 1869.

[317]   Don Pedro Calderón de la Barca

[318]   Ed. Arevalo, p. 1205.

Orosius, also, following on St. Augustine, imprecated magic and astrological superstitions.

Superstitions in Galicia at the time of the Swabian domination. Treatise *De corruptione rusticorum* by St. Martin of Braga.

We know how persistent village and country folk (for this reason called *pagani*) can be with their ancient and profane rites. In Galicia, to all these sterile observances – the first cause of idolatry - we must add also the Priscillianist plague and all its magical and astrological beliefs. It was to lessen these grave evils in the region that St. Martin of Braga wrote the book *De correctione rusticorum*. [319]

This brief treatise is divided in two parts. The first deals with principal tenets of Christian dogma. In the second, the saint earnestly reprimands Galicians for their idolatrous cults. And to be easily understood, this erudite and learned scholar chooses to address the peasants of Galicia in this way:

"Many of the many demons that had been thrown out of heaven now lord over the seas, the rivers, the fountains and the forests. They pretend they are gods and enjoy seeing themselves worshipped as such, which is precisely what silly people do when they sacrifice to them. In the sea you call up Neptune, in the rivers the *lamias*, in the fountains, nymphs, in the woods, Diana... and with their names you name the days of the week and so we have the day of Mars, the day of Mercury, of Jove, of Venus, of Saturn... this was precisely what the worst among the Greeks did..." "And what can one say about those other superstitions where you venerate moth and mice? All that hopeless idolatry - sacrifices of lobsters and mice and a thousand other tribulations that God sends us – all of this you have done, publicly and secretly, and are still doing today..." "You do not seem to grasp how very much these devils are deceiving you when you perform these rituals - these omens you are hoping to see fulfilled. As Solomon the Wise said: *divinationes et auguria vana sunt*... O disconsolate people, what is it that you are hoping to see - continually looking out for the flight of birds? What is it but devil's worship to light candles to stones, trees, fountains or *trivios*, to observe the kalendas, to throw an offering into the fire over the trunk of a tree? What is it that you think you are doing when you leave wine and bread out for a fountain to have? What is it but a cult to the devil himself for women to call upon Minerva when they are weaving... or to enchant herbs with curses, or to conjure up devils with incantations? ...You

---

[319] Vid. Volume 15, *Historia Sagrada*, p. 425.

abandon the Sign of the Cross you received at baptism and wait instead for signs from demons through magic spells and sneezing!" [320]

We see clearly here that invoking pagan deities was still popular in Galicia in the sixth century in all facets of people's life: sacrifices and offerings to sacred fountains, the Roman rite of the kalendas, cursing by means of herbs, the Celtic cult to stones and trees, the veneration of *trivios* (the favourite place of Hecate worshippers for incantations and witchcraft), augural art, and two new superstitions (among many more St. Martin does not expressly mention): divination by sneezing, and the ridiculous observance of mice and moths. The latter were held to be good omens if found at the beginning of the year and foretold of abundance in the house where these unpleasant guests happened to drop by: "Ut quasi sicut in introitu anni saturetur laetus ex omnibus, ita et illi in toto anno contigit". St. Martin also objects to beginning the year with the kalends of January and not April - undoubtedly because the former was linked to the Celtic feast of the winter solstice named in other lands the *Feast of Joel* when the trunk of a tree was thrown into the fire with various ceremonies, something St. Martin asks the members of his diocese to refrain from doing. The pagan names of the week were preserved in all of Spain, but not in Portugal, where ecclesiastical terminology is used - *prima feira, terza feira*, etc.; it would not be bold to attribute this fact to the influence exercised by the bishop of Braga and other Bragan Metropolitans who followed in his footsteps.

Magic arts and divination among the Visigoths.

The Council of Narbonne that was convened in 580 during Recared's reign, separates from the Church and establishes a fine of six ounces of gold for any Goth, Roman, Syrian, Greek or Jew who consults diviners, *caragios et sorticularios* – the proceeds from the fine were to be given to the poor. Servants

---

[320]   "Praeter haec autem multi daemones ex illis qui de coelo expulsi sunt, aut in mari, aut in fluminibus, aut in fontibus, aut in sylvis praesident, quod similiter homines ignorantes Dominum quasi Deos colunt et sacrificant illis: et in mari quidem Neptunum appellant, in fluminibus Lamias, in fontibus Nymphas, in sylvis Dianam... Nomina ipsa daemoniorum in singulos dies nominant, et appellant diem Martis et Mercurii et Jovis et Veneris et Saturnis, qui... fuerunt homines pessimi in gente graecorum...Jam quid de illo stultissimo errore cum dolore dicendum fas est, ut homo Christianus pro Deo mures et tineas veneratur... Ecce istas supestitiones vanas aut occulte aut palam facitis, nunquam cessatis ab istis, sacrificia vana de locusta, de mure et de multis aliis tribulationibus quas Deus iratus immittit. Non intelligitis aperte quia qui mentiuntur vobis daemones, in istis observationibus vestris quae vane tenetis et in auguriis quae attenditis... Nam sicut dicit Sapientissimus Salomon: 'Divinationes et auguria vana sunt'. Qua tamdiu infelices per avium daemonia suadant..., etc. Nam ad petras, ad arbores, ad fontes et per trivia cercelum incendere, quid est aliud nisi cultura vulcanelia, et Kalendarum observare, mensas ornare, et fundere in foco super truncum frugem, et vinum et panem in fontem mittere? Quid est aliud nisi cultura diaboli mulieres in tela sua Minervam nominare?...Quid est aliud nisi cultura diaboli incantare herbas a maleficis et invocare nomina daemoniorum incantando? Dimissistis signum crucis quod in baptismo accepistis et alia diaboli signa per abicellos et stornutos et per multa alia attenditis'.

and maids (*servi et ancillae*) were to be whipped in public. In the following canon (XV) the same Synod reproves the pagan custom of celebrating Thursday (*diem jovis*) and not working on that day, which was another pagan practice. Those guilty of this sin would do penance for a year, and in the case of servants or maids, were whipped. What was happening in the Narbonne region must have been happening with little difference throughout all of the Visigoth dominions.

St. Isidore's *Etymologies* (Book VIII, chapter IX) contains a long list of definitions on the magic arts though without directly associating them with Spain. He holds Zoroaster to have been the first *magus;* Democritus perfected this art - one that flourished much among Assyrians and Chaldeans, so Lucan tells us. In their wake came *aruspicina,* augurs, oracles and necromancy, vanities all born out of folklore or teaching about evil angels *(ex traditione angelorum malorum).* St. Isidore cites the case of Pharaoh's *magi* and the pithonese of Endor (not admitting there was a true evocation of Samuel's soul there but a certain ghost, *phantasticam illusionem,* produced by the devil's art). He speaks of the Homeric Circe, and cites the verse of Virgil,

'haec se carminibus promittit solvere mentes'

as well as an extract from Prudentius against Simmacus in which Mercury is charged with the invention of goety. St. Isidore then goes on to make the following classification on the occult arts - his eye, no doubt, on the aberrations of his time, but not ignoring classical teachings:

❖ *Magi* or *malefics* – they disturb the elements, perturb people's minds, and without poison but by force of omens alone, cause death. They also make use of blood and victims.

❖ *Necromancers* – they presume to resuscitate the dead and to interrogate them; they bring life back to corpses via a transfusion of blood mixed with water, because of the love devils have for blood.

❖ *Hydromancers* – these evoke shadows in water, images, or ghosts of devils and the dead. Varro says this genre of divination came from the Persians. To this same genre refers divination using the soil of the earth (*geomancy*), air (*aeromancy*) and fire (*pyromancy*).

❖ *Diviners* (*divini*) – so called because they feign to embody divinity (*pleni a Deo*).

❖ *Enchanters* – they use conjuring words and spells.

❖ *Harioli (Latin)* – those who pronounce loathsome invocations before the altars of idols, or make abominable sacrifices and wait for demons to respond.

❖ *Haruspices* – so called, *quasi horarum inspectores,* because they point to the day and time when things will happen. They also examine the entrails of victims.

❖ *Augurs* – also *auspices*: they are said to understand the song and flight of birds. These observations are called *auspicia, quasi avium auspicia,* and *auguria, quasi avium garria.*

❖ *Pythons* – from Pythio Apollo, inventor of divination.

❖ *Astrologers* –who foretell by means of the stars (*in astris augurantur*).

❖ *Genethliacs* – they look at the day of birth and subjugate the free destiny of man to the twelve signs of the zodiac. Ordinary folk call them *mathematicians*; in ancient times, *magi*. This science was permitted before the Gospel (says St. Isidorus, with the Gospel's Magi in mind).

❖ *Horoscopes* (sic) – those who speculate on the time of a man's birth.

❖ *Sortileges* – those who under the false appearance of religion fortune-tell by invoking saints or opening any book of Sacred Scripture. (Remnants of *sortes homericae* and *virgilianae*, so common in antiquity).

❖ *Salisatores* – those who announce prosperous or sad events by the observation of any protruding member of the body, or from the movement of the arteries.

To all of which we must add the magical ligatures used for certain illnesses, invocations, characters, etc. The wise prelate of Seville attributes the invention of augurs to the Phrygians, the art of *praestigiatores* to Mercury, and the *aruspicina* to the Etruscans who learnt it from a certain Tages. [321] All these arts St. Isidore considers to be offensive and abhorrent to Christians.

The didactic leaning of all I have said above, the lack of contemporary references, and the fact that practically all of it is based on Greek and Roman reminiscences (from our compatriot Lucan who is so widely read in Spain), does not allow us to view it as an historical document; it is, simply, an outline for future research. It is a fact, however, that many of these superstitions did exist and continued to exist more or less obscurely in Spanish and Visigothic customs – a fact shown by the repeated prohibitions enacted by the Toledo Councils and our own *Fuero-Juzgo* Laws.

We read in the Fourth Council of Toledo, canon XXIX (year 633) - the soul and heart of which was St. Isidore himself: "Should any bishop, presbyter or cleric consult magicians, haruspices, ariolos, augurs, sortileges, or anyone professing the illicit arts, let him be deposed of his dignity and condemned to perpetual penance in a monastery".

Toledo V, convened at the time of Chintilla (year 636) anathematises in canon IV those who, by illicit means, attempt to divine when the king will die so as to succeed him to the throne.

Contact with magic arts grew in parallel as the Visigoth Empire degenerated. Chidasvint and his son Recesvint tried to curb this growth with harsh prohibitions. Law numbers I, III and IV, of *Titulo* II, Book VI of *Fuero-Juzgo* speak of ariolos, haruspices and prophesiers who predict the death of kings; of magicians and enchanters - agents of thunder storms (*tempestarii* or *nuberos*); of ravagers of cornfields, bidders and ministers of the devil; of *pulsatores* or binders, ligatures exercised on men and animals: they killed, took away

---

[321]   *Praeclarissimum opus divi Isidori Hispalensis Episcopi quod ethimologiarum institulatur* (Paris, 1499), fols. 42, *vuelto* and 43. I have also consulted Arevalo's edition and a beautiful codex at the *Ambrosiana* in Milan, comprehensive only of the ten first books originally from the abbey of St. Columbano of Bovio.

speech (*obmutescere*) and could sterilise the fruits of the earth. Whoever was naïve enough to participate in such prevarication was thereby subjected to loss of property and perpetual servitude; the slave could be whipped, shaven, sold in foreign lands (probably Mauritania), physically punished in several ways (*diverso genere tormentorum*), publicly put to shame as an example (*ut alii corrigantur*), and imprisoned perpetually, that he may no longer be a danger to the living (*ne viventibus nocendi aditum habeant*). In addition, if he conspired against the well being of his neighbour with evil arts [322] he was subject to Talion's penalty on life or property.

All this is well known but we still read in places that Recesvint himself, who enacted some of these laws, "sacrificed to the devils", that is to say, was given to the magic arts, as Rodrigo Sánchez de Arévalo says in his *Historia hispánica*. "Fuit autem pessimus, nam sacrificabat demoniis"! I have no idea where this Castilian from Santángelo got that idea.

This cult to the devil and these magic arts in fact consititute that sacrilegious idolatry which was so widespread in Spain and Gaul, and against which the Third Council of Toledo protested. Disorder had reached its limits by the time of Ergivio's last sad days and the Twelfth Council of Toledo (in 681) had to condemn worshippers of idols, instructing priests and judges to extirpate this scandal. Excommunication and exile for the ignorant and lashes for the slaves were the penalties the Council imposed.

Law III, Titulo II, Book VI of *Fuero Juzgo*, enacted by Ergivius, shows well the depth of these wounds: there were judges who went to clairvoyants and haruspices precisely to find out about the truth of the crimes they were investigating; the law here called for a public punishment of fifty lashes (*quinquagenis verberibus*). [323] Imagine! A judicial system in the hands of diviners and sorcerers!

But the decadence went further. Canon I of the Sixteenth Council of Toledo again calls for the condemnation of those who worship idols, stones, fountains and trees; those who light fires, augurs and enchanters ("cultores idolarum, veneratores lapidum, accensores facularum, excolentes sacra fontium vel arborum, auguratores quoque seu praecantores"). Toledo XVII, in Canon V, prescribes the removal from office of a priest who "celebrates a Requiem Mass in order to cause the death of a person": an abominable superstition if ever there was one and truly the last delirium that a perverse will can play on a twisted mind. Canon XXI (Addenda) expels from the Church the cleric who is a magician or enchanter, or makes amulets called "phylacteria quae sunt magna obligamenta animarum".

---

[322]   All these elements on Visigoth superstitions were treated, in a manner that barely leaves room for emulation, by my learned teacher José A. de los Ríos, in volume I of his *Historia crítica de la literatura española*, and on articles on *Artes mágicas en el suelo ibérico*, included in *Revista de España*, 19 November 1870.

[323]   *One hundred lashes* says the Castilian translation.

Among the Goths, in addition to magic arts and other pagan customs, there remained also the *epitalamios,* defined by St. Isidore as 'wedding songs sang by students in praise of the bride and bridegroom' ("carmina nubentium quae cantantur a scholasticis in honorem sponsi et sponsae"); the *trenos* - a compulsory accompaniment to funerals ("similiter ut nunc", says the saint); theatre or amphitheatre "scenic plays" with their taste of pagan superstitions of old. St. Isidore, in Book XVIII, chapters XLI and LIX, exhorts Christians to abstain from them. Sisebutus, as far as we can deduce from his letters, reprimanded Eusebius, bishop of Barcelona, for consenting to profane performances in his diocese.

But of all these lethal elements, none was more disastrous than the Magic Arts for clouding a man's conscience, weakening his will, packing his mind with omens and terrors, and feeding him with concupiscence, ambitions and lust; in a word, there was nothing better than the magic arts for doing away with a man's awareness of his own human free will. I have no doubt that these superstitions accelerated the fall of the Visigoth empire. When a people's self-will weakens, it is not enough to guide them with a strong hand and firm understanding: these people are dead, or soon will be. Ultimately, none of the Visigoths was immune to this disease: neither the king, nor the clergy, nor the judges, nor the masses at large. [324]

Other superstitions and pagan abuses besides magic were to last among Spanish Christians. It is a pity that the book entitled *Cervus,* or *Kerbos,* has been lost. It was a book written by St. Pacianus of Barcelona about the custom practised in his diocese where people disguised themselves with animal hides, especially deer skins, during the January kalends and in this manner ran through the streets asking for *estrenas,* or handouts, and commit a thousand and one excesses and abominations! Some of these customs lived on, either as celebrations at the beginning of the year or in the *Carnestolendas,* or Carnivals.[325] With regard to the *estrenas,* who can ignore their Roman origin if only because of Tibullus's eulogy:

Martis romani festae venere Kalendae?

St. Pacianus notes that despite his pastoral exhortations the people of Barcelona did not stop celebrating the *Hennula Cervula,* or *Fiesta of the Deer* the following

---

[324]   Sr. Navarro Villoslada, in his charming novel entitled *Amaya or the Basques during the eighth century* published in *Ciencia Cristiana,* speaks of a secret society of Basque astrologers, sworn enemies of Christianity though very tolerant of any other religion. I accept this fact as the fiction of a novelist's imagination. In the sources I have consulted I can find no record of such a connection. Nor do I believe that astrology reached such a point among us that it becaume organised as a sacerdotal college or secret society, except in the Priscillianist case, of course. But Priscillianism did not penetrate the Basque country.

[325]   St Jerome speaks of this same writing in chapter CVI of *De viris illustribus,* and St. Paciano himself alludes to it at the beginning of his *Paraenesis.*

[On disguises with animal hides, see the curious work of Ernest William Hawkes *La fete 'des invités' des Esquimaux d'Alaska,* Otawa, Imprimerie du Gouvernment, 1915. (Editor, 1912).

year, but rather did so with the same hullabaloo and scandal as was customary. It is said that this custom, such as he describes it, lasted in areas of Southern France right up until the end of the last century.

www.ingramcontent.com/pod-product-compliance
Lightning Source LLC
Chambersburg PA
CBHW020848090426
42736CB00008B/286